10670144

A RESEARCH GUIDE TO HUMAN SEXUALITY

GARLAND REFERENCE LIBRARY
OF SOCIAL SCIENCE
VOL. 836

A RESEARCH GUIDE TO HUMAN SEXUALITY

Kara Ellynn Lichtenberg

Indiana University
Library
Northwest

Z
7164
.S42
L55
1994

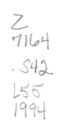

GARLAND PUBLISHING, Inc.
New York & London / 1994

Copyright © 1994 by Kara Ellynn Lichtenberg
All rights reserved

Library of Congress Cataloging-in-Publication Data

Lichtenberg, Kara Ellynn.
    A research guide to human sexuality / Kara Ellynn
Lichtenberg.
        p.   cm. — (Garland reference library of social
science ; vol. 836)
    Includes index.
    ISBN 0–8153–0867–1
    .1. Sex—Reference books.   2. Reference books—
Sex.   3. Sex—Library resources.   4. Sex—
Bibliography.   I. Title.   II. Series: Garland refer-
ence library of social science ; v. 836.
Z7164.S42L55   1994
[HQ21]
016.3067—dc20   93–37236
                                                          CIP

Printed on acid-free, 250-year-life paper
Manufactured in the United States of America

To Peter, without whom I would've never taken on this project, and
To David, without whom I would've never let it go.

Contents

viii   CONTENTS

Sign Language • Sexual Slang • Transvestites/Transsexuals • Women's
Sexual and Reproductive Health

_____ Part III Background Sources _____

AIDS • Abortion • Drugs and Sex • General Works • Homosexuality •
Marriage and Family • Pornography • Reproduction • Sex Anatomy •
Sex Education • Sex and Law • Sex and Religion • Sex Therapy •
Sexual Medicine • Women's Sexual and Reproductive Health

_____ Part IV Accessing Tools _____

Research Library Catalogs • Sex Library Catalogs (Kinsey Institute
Catalogs)

Abortion • Adolescent Sexuality and Pregnancy • Aging and Sexuality •
AIDS • Alcohol and Drugs • Bioethics • Bisexuality • Childbirth •
Circumcision/Female Genital Mutilation • Disability and Illness • Erotic
Art • Erotic Literature • Family Planning • Gender Dysphoria • General
Works (Kinsey Bibliographies, SIECUS Bibliographies) • History of

Sexuality • Homosexuality • Language • Men's Studies • Mothers and Mothering • Pedophilia • Pornography • Prostitution • Reproduction • Sadomasochism • Sex Customs • Sex in Cinema • Sex Education • Sex and the Law • Sex in Literature • Sex in Mass Media • Sex and Religion • Sex Researchers • Sexual Abuse (Child Abuse and Incest, Rape, Sexual Harassment) • Sexual Health and Medicine • Sexually Transmitted Diseases • Women's Issues

Sex Library Indexes • Alternative Publication's Indexes • Current Awareness Services • Magazines • Newspapers • Scholarly Literature Indexes • AIDS • Anthropology • Biology • Bioethics • Child and Adolescent Studies • Criminal Justice • Disability and Illness • Drug and Alcohol Abuse • Education • Family Planning • Gerontology • Humanities • Law • Literature • Marriage and Family Studies • Medicine and Allied Health • Mental Health • Multidisciplinary • Philosophy • Population Studies • Psychology • Public Affairs • Religious Studies • Sciences • Sexology • Social Sciences • Social Work • Women's Studies

Abortion • Adolescent Sexuality & Pregnancy • Aging • AIDS • Alternative Lifestyles • Bioethics • Birth Defects • Bisexuality • Breastfeeding • Childbirth • Conservative/Traditionalism • Contraception • Controversial Issues/Public Affairs • Disability and Sexuality • Erotica • Family Planning • Fertility and Infertility • Fetishes • Homosexuality (Periodical Directories, Newsmagazines, Lesbian, Resource Reviews, Scholarly and Professional) • Impotence • Language • Marriage and Family • Men's Magazines • Non-Monogamy • Nudism • Pedophilia • Population Studies • Pornography/Obscenity • Prostitution • Repro-

Part V Source Materials

Part VI Statistical and Survey Data

Abortion (Anti-Abortion, Pro Choice, RU-486) • Adolescent Sexuality (Gay Youth, Teen Pregnancy) • Adoption • Aging and Sex (Gay and Lesbian, Women) • AIDS (People with AIDS) • Alcohol and Drugs (Gay and Lesbian) • Alternative Lifestyles • Archives & Special Collections (Gay/ Lesbian Archives) • Bioethics • Bisexuality • Childbirth (Alternative Childbirth, Birth Psychology, Cesarean Births, Post Partum Depression, Professional Associations) • Circumcision • Conservative/ Traditionalists • Contraceptive Methods (Condoms, Contraceptive Devices, Contraceptive Drugs, Natural Family Planning, Sterilization) • Controversial Issues/Public Affairs • Cross Cultural Research • Disability and Illness (Social) • Erotica • Family Planning • Fertility and Infertility • Fetishes • Gays and Lesbians (Gay and Lesbian Studies) • Impotence • Lactation and Breastfeeding • Language • Marriage and Family (Gay and Lesbian) • Masturbation • Maternal and Child Health (Birth Defects, Infant Death and Illness) • Men • Menstruation/Menopause • Misc. • Non-Monogamy • Nudism • Pedophilia • Population Studies •

Pornography and Censorship (Federal Activities, Conservative Anti-Pornography, Feminist Anti-Pornography, Anti-Censorship) • Professional Associations • Prostitution (Archives, Prostitutes Organized) • Reproduction • Reproductive Health and Medicine • Reproductive Technologies (Support Groups) • Sadomasochism • Sex Addiction • Sex Crimes • Sex Education (Training) • Sex Information Services • Sex and the Law (Sexual Orientation) • Sex in the Media (Gay and Lesbian) • Sex and Religion (Gay and Lesbian) • Sex Research • Sex Therapy • "Sex Toys" • Sexual Abuse and Coercion (Child Abuse and Incest, Rape, Sex Offenders, Sexual Harassment) • Sexual Freedom • Sexually Transmitted Diseases • Transvestites/Transsexuals • Women's Sexual and Reproductive Health

PREFACE

To my knowledge, this is the first attempt to compile a comprehensive directory and research guide for those seeking information and materials on human sexuality and related topics, be they researchers, educators, clinicians, students, or the general public.

It describes nearly 1,000 print and electronic resources, discusses how to locate 13 types of experts, and fully describes the missions, services, and publications of over 400 organizations, businesses, institutions, and government agencies providing free or low-cost information to the public. Reflecting the multi-disciplinary and multi-professional nature of sex studies, it provides access to resources in anthropology, biology, education, counseling, law, theology, sociology, medicine, literature, psychology, public affairs, religious studies, social sciences, and women's studies, among others, and includes scholarly, professional, governmental, commercial, clinical, and popular sources. A wide diversity of viewpoints is represented in both the print and non-print listings, including descriptions of both the American Life League and the National Abortion Rights Action League, Feminists Fighting Pornography and Fans of X Rated Entertainment, the National Pro Family Coalition and the North American Swing Club Association.

Intending this to be a research guide and not simply a series of subject bibliographies, I've arranged the subject-classified listings into chapters by format (e.g. books, indexes, curricula, etc.). Each chapter contains brief introductory notes discussing the utility of that class of resource for sex research, and a shaded "How to Find" box containing detailed instructions on how to locate general and sex specific items of that type, as well as citations to specific print and non-print resources. This unique feature serves a number of purposes. First, unlike traditional bibliographies and directories which quickly become obsolete, it gives this guide enduring value, providing the user guidance in updating the information contained herein, and in locating new resources long after those described in this volume have become outdated. Second, it provides a means by which to identify materials falling outside the scope of the present volume (see "Listings" below). Finally, it provides an overview of general reference works and research techniques which can be applied to virtually any topic, in any field, making the book especially useful both to experienced researchers seeking an update on new resources, and students and the general public with little previous experience using research libraries.

LISTINGS

Most chapters include descriptive listings of specific resources: 14 special libraries, 96 general reference works, 10 thesauri, 15 subject dictionaries, 27 text books, 34 encyclopedias and handbooks, 7 library catalogs, 109 subject bibliographies, 66 indexes, 163 periodicals, 24 specialized bookdealers and publishers, 2 compendia of public opinion, 4 federal statistics agencies, 34 sexual behavior surveys, 4 compendia of measurement tools, and 300 organizations and institutions, among others. Additional titles are included in "How to Find" boxes throughout each chapter and within the entries themselves. Items falling in the following categories have not been listed by name or title:

- Those for which lists are easy to obtain and too numerous to list here (e.g. a printout of the 600+ sex education curricula held by SIECUS);

- Those which, by their very nature, would be outdated before publication (e.g. dates and sponsors for sex related conferences);

- Topic specific source materials such as book titles, journal articles, government documents, and dissertations, which are easily identified in subject searches of readily available catalogs and indexes and which, given the breadth of the sex field, would be impossible to cover in depth here;

- Those which are already listed in readily available directories (e.g. gay and lesbian organizations listed in the *Gay Yellow Pages*).

In each of these cases, the resources needed to identify and locate the materials in question are noted under "How to Find."

Subjects Included. All major subject areas addressed by introductory human sexuality texts are represented–see p.xxi for details–with materials on gender, sex roles, and interpersonal relationships excluded for the most part. The subjects covered in each chapter were to a large degree guided by the materials available. The techniques and resources delineated in the "How to Find" sections of each chapter, when combined with the Library of Congress subject headings listed in Appendix 1 (see p.422 for a list of subjects represented in the appendix), can be used to locate items on virtually any sex or reproduction related topic.

Selection Criteria. All print and electronic materials are in English and, with a few exceptions, published in the United States. Emphasis is on works published from 1982 to 1993; however, I've also included classics of the reference literature in sexuality, much of it published in the 1970's, as well as some forthcoming titles. With the exception of organizations' publications and a few periodicals, available for purchase only, all titles are readily available in U.S. research libraries, although some may need to be requested through interlibrary loan. As the libraries at SIECUS (see A5) and The Kinsey Institute (see A4) don't lend their holdings through interlibrary loan, I've excluded titles held in their libraries alone. All organizations, institutions, and businesses listed respond to phone or mail inquiries and are national in scope. Specific selection criteria vary for each type of resource, from an attempt to be comprehensive (with text books) to deliberately selective (with encyclopedias and handbooks); consult the scope notes under "Listings" in each chapter for details.

Annotations. Bibliographic citations do not reflect the items' complete publishing history: the current publishers of periodicals and indexes are cited, and for other items, the edition cited was the one I viewed. (See "Sources," p.467, for the specific resources consulted.) Except for text books and sexual behavior surveys, which are unannotated, all entries include strictly descriptive annotations focusing on the scope and content of each item, including sex subjects covered as indicated by controlled vocabulary, section headings, and index headings. Computer readable formats of print directories and indexes are noted when available. Except where specifically noted, I examined all print materials; descriptions of organizations and institutions were drawn from their publications and responses to a questionnaire. See under "Listings" in each chapter for additional notes on annotations.

Comments, suggestions, and information on new resources should be directed to the author c/o the National Sex Information Network: 3805 Bohemian Hwy, Box 902, Occidental, CA 95465.

• • • •

I am indebted to the following people, without whom this book would have never been completed: Robert Francoeur for providing early encouragement for this project and suggestions in finding a publisher; the reference librarians at New York University, the Library of Congress, and the New York Public Library, and Jim Shortridge at SIECUS, for invaluable assistance in locating the materials here described, and guidance in the use of some of the greatest research libraries in the world; the computer consultants at NYU and Word Perfect Customer Support, who worked valiantly to turn WordPerfect into a desk top publisher; and my editors, Phyllis Korper and Adrienne Makowski for their endless patience as weeks repeatedly stretched into months.

On a personal note, I am grateful to: Martha Harrison (and Lucy) for so graciously tolerating me strewing mounds of papers around the house for months at a time and for always having her I.D. handy; Peter Nappi for his editorial assistance (especially his bemused answers to my early morning grammatical queries), and for so exuberantly and lovingly giving me New York; David Shafer, my lover, partner, and soon-to-be husband, for taking care of everything these past few months; and my parents Sue and Ed Smith for their unwavering support, always.

User's Guide

BOOK ORGANIZATION

Material is organized by format into chapters (see the table of contents for details), which are grouped into sections as follows:

I.   *Research Assistance*. Print and institutional sources of research assistance and guidance. The specialized libraries listed in Chapter 1 should be one of the first resources consulted.

II.   *Terminology*. Sources for terms with which to search catalogs and databases, and subject dictionaries indicating how a word is used in a particular field. These resources are also useful in defining and refining research topics.

III.   *Background Sources*. Sources for introductory or background information on a subject.

IV.   *Accessing Tools*. Resources used to identify and locate primary materials on a particular subject (e.g. indexes for journal articles, library catalogs for book titles).

V.   *Source Materials*. Resources used to locate five classes of source documents: periodicals, books, dissertations, government documents, and conference proceedings. For resources used to locate particular books and journal articles, see "Accessing Tools."

VI.   *Statistical and Survey Data*. Sources of numerical and survey data.

VII.   *Tools*. This section is addressed primarily to researchers seeking data sets or measurement tools for use in primary research, and for educators seeking curricula for use in sex education courses (see also "Media Resources").

VIII. *Media Resources*. Resources used to locate educational audiovisuals for use in sex education; feature films and sexually explicit "sexvids" for use in primary research; and entertainment and public affairs television programming for use in research and educational settings.

IX. *Human Resources.* These two chapters discuss thirteen different types of experts and seven types of organizations and institutions, all of whom provide free or low cost information and services to the public. Chapter 30 concludes with descriptive listings of nearly 300 organizations, government agencies, businesses, and institutions.

CHAPTER ORGANIZATION

With a few exceptions, all chapters begin with a brief overview of the resource under discussion, followed by a shaded "How to Find" box, and concluding, in most cases, with descriptive listings of particular resources:

Overview: I have presented only a brief overview of the utility of each type of resource. For additional information, I recommend the introductory essay in Marda Woodbury's *Youth Information Resources* (Westport, CT: Greenwood, 1987).

"How to Find": Use the resources and techniques detailed in each "How to Find" section for the following:

- To identify materials falling outside the scope of this volume, due to their subject, publication dates, languages, etc. (e.g. non-English language materials and historical documents). See notes in Preface.

- To update the information found in this volume. Due to the long process of manuscript preparation and publishing, like all reference book, this one was out-of-date before it was even published; new books are published, others go out-of-print, addresses and phone numbers change, organizations go defunct. Most of the resources listed under "How to Find" are updated regularly–be sure to use the most recent edition.

- To find resources which, while not focusing exclusively on sexuality and therefore not listed in this volume, are excellent sources for information on specific sexual topics. For example, a folklore index identified using *Index and Abstract Directory*, cited under "How to Find" indexes, may be more useful to a researcher doing work on bawdy limericks than the more general humanities indexes listed in Chapter 12. As might a library specializing in oriental medicine, identified using *Directory of Specialized Libraries and Information*

Centers, cited under "How to Find" Libraries, be more useful to someone researching Chinese aphrodisiacs than those more general libraries described in Chapter 1.

The form subdivisions and subject headings noted in each "How to Find," are Library of Congress subject headings–see Chapter 3 for further information, and Appendix 1 for a list of relevant subject headings. For descriptions of the general reference works cited throughout the "How to Find" sections, and an indication of the sex subjects each covers, see the works main entry in Ch.2.

Listings: In all chapters with descriptive listings, the "Listings" section begins with scope notes delineating the selection criteria for the entries that follow (see also p.xvii) and any chapter specific notes regarding the annotations (see also p.xvii). All annotations are strictly descriptive; for critical reviews, consult the resources listed under "Book Reviews," p. 229, and for reviews of reference works, p.16. Note that some annotations include "Sex Subjects Covered" drawn from the title's thesaurus, index headings, and section headings. These are intended only to indicate the range of topics addressed by the work; consult the title itself, or its publisher, for further details.

The descriptive listings are arranged under the following subject headings, with materials covering a variety of sex related topics listed under "General Works." Organizations and publications whose primary mission is to advocate "traditional" family and sexual values are listed under the heading "Conservative/Traditionalists." All headings are not utilized in all chapters; consult the table of contents for those used in a particular chapter. Use the techniques discussed under "How to Find," along with the Library of Congress subject headings listed in Appendix 1, to locate materials on a specific topic.

AIDS	Alternative Lifestyles	Controversial Issues /
Abortion	Archives	Public Affairs
−Anti-Abortion	Bioethics	Cross Cultural Research
−Pro-Choice	Bisexuality	Disability and Illness
Adolescent Sexuality	Childbirth and	Erotic Art
−Teen Pregnancy	Postpartum	Erotic Literature
−Gay Youth	Circumcision	Family Planning
Adoption	Conservative /	Fertility and Infertility
Aging and Sex	Traditionalist	Fetishes
Alcohol and Drugs	Contraceptive Methods	Gays and Lesbians

History of Sexuality
Homosexuality
Impotence
Lactation / Breastfeeding
Language
Marriage and Family
Masturbation
Men's Issues
Menstruation and
  Menopause
Mothers
Non-Monogamy
Nudism
Pedophilia
Population Studies

Pornography and
  Censorship
Pregnancy
Professional
  Associations
Prostitution
Reproduction
Reproductive Health and
  Medicine
Reproductive
  Technologies
Sadomasochism
Sex Crimes
Sex Customs
Sex Education
Sex and the Law

Sex in Media
Sex and Religion
Sex Research
Sex Therapy
"Sex Toys"
Sexual Abuse
–Child Abuse and Incest
–Rape
–Sexual Harassment
Sexual Freedom
Sexually Transmitted
  Diseases
Transvestites and
  Transsexuals
Women's Sexual and
  Reproductive Health

CROSS REFERENCES

Cross references are copious as there is no subject index. In addition to cross references to specific entries, given wherever necessary, the "Listings" section of each chapter includes cross references to other relevant sections of the book. Whenever possible, cross references are to chapter numbers or entry numbers rather than page numbers. Entries are marked alphanumerically by chapter as follows (chapters without numbered entries are not included in the alphabetic sequence):

A Ch.1   Libraries
B Ch.2   Reference Works
C Ch.3   Thesauri
D Ch.4   Subject Dictionaries
E Ch.6   Text Books
F Ch.7   Encyclopedias
G Ch.8   Library Catalogs
H Ch.10 Subject Bibliographies
I Ch.11 Computer Data Bases
J Ch.12 Indexes and Abstracts
K Ch.14 Periodicals
L Ch.15 Books

M Ch.16 Dissertations
N Ch.17 Government Documents
P Ch.19 Public Opinion Polls
Q Ch.20 Statistics
R Ch.21 Sexual Behavior Surveys
S Ch.22 Records, Lists, etc.
T Ch.24 Measurement Tools
U Ch.25 Data Sets
V Ch.26 Educational Audiovisuals
W Ch.27 Entertainment Films/Videos
X Ch.30 Organizations & Institutions

INDEXES

Entries are classified by subject within each chapter; consult the table of contents for subject arrangement and page numbers. The Title Index includes titles of publications, audiovisuals, databases, etc. The Name Index, includes names of businesses, organizations, government agencies, institutions, etc.; it does not include author's names. There is no subject index. Entries are classified be subject within each chapter; see the table of contents for details.

OBTAINING MATERIALS

Most general reference works (directories, indexes, etc.) cannot be borrowed through interlibrary loan. If a title is unavailable or not of the most recent edition and your question is simple, contact the telephone reference services of a library which holds the work (try the nearest university library or the Library of Congress). Many reference titles are now available on compact disc or on-line via Internet or a commercial database vendor (see Chapter 11), as well as in print. To access, and for information on fee-based search services, see Chapter 11.

All books and most of the journal titles listed are cataloged in RLIN and/or OCLC and can be ordered through interlibrary loan. Books currently in print can be purchased directly from the publisher or ordered through a bookstore. Particular journal articles can be requested through interlibrary loan. Although the libraries of SIECUS, The Kinsey Institute, SIECCAN, and Planned Parenthood (see Chapter 1) don't loan their materials in this way, they will make copies of articles unavailable elsewhere within copyright limitations. Those periodicals not available in libraries can be purchased from the publisher–most will send sample issues on request.

When contacting a publisher or distributor for information about a product or publication, begin with the customer service department; however, for information beyond price and availability you will need to contact the relevant editorial office–customer service can provide referrals. Publishers' and distributors' phone numbers and addresses are listed in regularly updated directories available at the reference desks at all libraries. Have the title of the work and the publisher's name and location available when making an inquiry.

SECTION ONE
PRINT RESOURCES

Part I
Research Assistance

1

LIBRARIES

The information specialists in public and private libraries can provide general research assistance, as well as referrals to specific print and non-print resources held at their institutions or available elsewhere.

Research Libraries. Although research libraries have always collected sex related literature, in the past such materials were often segregated from the main collection, sometimes, as in the Library of Congress's Delta collection, to be literally kept in locked cages. Nowadays, a wide range of scholarly, professional, and popular materials addressing sex related topics are integrated into the collections of all libraries, although due to ongoing debates over what is appropriate to be collected by public institutions, budget limitations, and the likelihood that such materials will be destroyed, defaced, or stolen, it may still be necessary to consult a specialized library (see below). Explicitly erotic/pornographic works, when collected at all, are usually microfilmed or kept in special collections. (See F20 for a discussion of the treatment of sexually explicit materials in libraries over the past 25 years.) Public research libraries such as the Library of Congress (see A1) and the New York Public Library (see A2), are freely accessible to anyone over eighteen but materials from their collections can't usually be checked out. Universities and colleges often maintain separate research collections in medicine, law, business, art, theology, women's studies, or other specialized areas, in addition to their main collections. Although access

5

How to Find

• For works describing library collections, search library catalogs using the form subdivision *–Library resources* under names of countries, cities, etc., names of individual persons and corporate bodies, classes of persons or ethnic groups, and topical headings (e.g. *Free love–Library resources*); or search using *Libraries–Special collections* followed by the subject heading (e.g. *Libraries–Special collections–Erotica*).

• Consult library directories. Some are comprehensive, listing libraries in all subject areas: *American Library Directory* (see B60), *Directory of Specialized Libraries and Information Centers* (see B62), *Directory of Federal Libraries* (see B63). Others, such as *Alternative Lifestyles: A Guide to Research Collections on Intentional Communities, Nudism and Sexual Freedom* (see p.338), focus on a particular topic.

• The following associations provide library referrals and produce reference materials (see especially the American Library Association—contact their in-house library to identify particular titles, or request a catalog from the publishing department). For more information on the Association for Population/Family Planning Libraries and Information Centers, see X167:

> **American Association of Law Libraries**: 53 W. Jackson Blvd., Suite 940, Chicago, IL 60604. PH: (312)939-4764.

> **American Library Association**: 50 East Huron, Chicago, IL 60611. PH: (800)545-2433.

> **American Theological Libraries Associations**: 820 Church St., 3rd Fl., Evanston, IL 60201. PH: (708)869-7788.

> **Association For Population / Family Planning Libraries and Information Centers International**: c/o Population Council Library, One Dag Hammarskjold Plaza, New York, NY 10017. PH: (212)339-0532.

> **Medical Library Association**: 6 N. Michigan Ave, Suite 300, Chicago, IL 60602. PH: (312)419-9094.

> **Special Library Association**: 1700 18th St., NW, Washington, DC 20009. PH: (202)234-4700.

may officially be restricted to those affiliated with the university, public libraries will often provide free passes to the institution if it's the only one in the area holding a particular item (e.g. the New York Public issues access cards to the libraries at Columbia University, New York University, and others in the NYC area which are generally closed to the public). Items from virtually any library in the country can be obtained through your local library via interlibrary loan; search print or on-line library catalogs for relevant titles (see Ch.8). Consult a social science librarian for basic research assistance, as most general sex related materials are shelved in this section of the library. (See Ch.9 for details on the physical arrangement of sex related titles in libraries.)

Specialized Libraries. For more detailed information than is available at a general reference library or access to specialized materials, contact a library specializing in the particular subject area. Focusing on a single topic or set of closely related topics (e.g. homosexuality, maternal health), such libraries are maintained by government agencies, schools, businesses, organizations, and in some cases, individuals. Access to their collections vary—some are open to the general public, others only to qualified researchers, with others only accepting phone or mail queries. (See also "Archives," p.315 and "Information Clearinghouses," p.319.)

•   •   •   •

Listings: Under "Research Libraries" are described the two largest such institutions in the country. The telephone number noted for each is that of their telephone reference desk. To identify research libraries with special sex related collections, see "How to Find" Archives and Special Collections, p.316. Under "Specialized Libraries" are described the largest sex libraries in the U.S., plus one in Canada. All maintain multi-disciplinary collections covering a wide range of sexuality related topics and, with the exception of A3, provide services to the general public and/or qualified researchers. Libraries and information clearinghouses focusing on a single topic (e.g. Homosexual Information Center, Johnson Archives on Nudism, Human Lactation Center Library) are described in Ch.30; an "L" code under "Services" in the descriptive listings indicates the organization is a library, maintains a library collection, or provides similar information services. Archives of primary materials are described in Ch.30 under "Archives" (for general collections) and under relevant subject headings.

➤ RESEARCH LIBRARIES (*See also*: X204)

A1.   **Library of Congress**: Washington, DC 20541. PH: (202)707-5522.

Founded in 1800 as the reference library for the U.S. Congress, the Library is now the world's largest, serving not only members and committees of Congress and other branches of the U.S. Government, but through their National Reference Service, scholars, researchers, students, and libraries worldwide. With more than 20 million volumes, it holds comprehensive collections in all fields of knowledge and as it grants U.S. copyrights, receives many items not widely collected by other libraries, including publications of organizations, government agencies, small presses, text books, and privately published materials. In addition to print material, the Library has an extensive audio, video, and film collection.

In the 1920s and 1930s erotica and other sex related materials were segregated into what was known as the Delta Collection. Dispersed in 1964, half of the 3,000 titles remain in the Rare Book and Special Collections Division, with the rest shelved with the general collection. The Library currently collects a full spectrum of sex-related materials.

PREMARC (see G2) and LCMARC (see G1), the on-line catalogs of the collection, can be accessed via computer terminals in the main reference room or off-site through DIALOG or Internet (see Ch.11). LCMARC includes records for forthcoming titles submitted to the Library for copyright but not yet published. Materials not available elsewhere can be requested through interlibrary loan or photo-duplicated (within copyright restrictions)—send requests to the General Reading Room.

A2.   **New York Public Library**: 5th Ave. and 42nd St., New York, NY 10018. PH: (212)340-0849.

Founded in 1895, the New York Public Library System is comprised of the Research Libraries (consisting of the main library—with extensive holdings in all scholarly/professional areas except medicine and law—the Schomburg Center for Research in Black Culture, and the Performing Arts Research Center) and 81 branch libraries (the Mid-Manhattan Library being the largest). Titles added to the research collection since 1971 are cataloged on-line in *CATNYP: The Public Catalog of the Research Library of the N.Y. Public Library*, and are also included in RLIN (see G4). For older holdings, consult the print card catalog or the 800 v. *Directory/Catalog of the Research Library*. The branch library catalog is available on-line as *NYPL Branch Library Catalog* and records are also included in OCLC (see G3).

Unlike most libraries, the Research Library actively collects three types of "pornographic/erotic" books and magazines: (1) representative titles, in all languages, listed in national or trade bibliographies, with authors of merit and works of significant publishers or presses collected comprehensively; (2) privately printed works appearing in specialized booksellers catalogs under the headings *erotica, curiosa,* or *facetiae*; and (3) representative books and magazines sold at "adult" bookstores in the NYC area. Materials are microfilmed and cataloged in *CATNYP*, with representative samples placed in the Rare Books and Manuscripts collection.

▶ SPECIALIZED LIBRARIES *(See also*: notes under "Listing," p.7)

A3.   Institute for the Advanced Study of Human Sexuality—Library: 1523 Franklin St., San Francisco, CA 94109. PH: (415)928-1133.

The Institute maintains 11 specialty libraries holding over 60,000 books, 100,000 magazines and pamphlets, 10,000 videotapes (including videos of all lectures given at the Institute), 100,000 films, and over 500,000 photographs and slides. All aspects of sexuality are represented, including an extensive collection of sexually explicit materials. The collection is currently closed except to students, faculty, and alumni of the Institute but serious researchers may submit a written request for library access.

A4.   The Kinsey Institute for Research in Sex, Gender, and Reproduction—Library and Information Services: 313 Morrison Hall, Indiana University, Bloomington, IN 47405. PH: (812)855-7686. FAX: (812)855-8277. INTERNET: libknsy@ indiana.edu.

Information Services is the reference and referral department of the library of The Kinsey Institute for Research in Sex, Gender, and Reproduction (see X256), the premier sex and erotica research collection in the U.S. It provides extensive coverage of all aspects of human sexual behavior, gender dysphoria, and some aspects of reproduction. (Abortion and family planning are only marginally covered, but they do provide ready reference and referrals to other agencies and collections.) The Institute houses several collections: (1) the library, which includes a film/video collection;

(2) art, artifacts, and photography; and (3) archival. Together, these constantly expanding collections contain 80,000 volumes; 56 vertical file drawers containing newspaper clippings, newsletters, advertisements, catalogs, photocopies, and pamphlets; 209 reels of microfilm; 105 audio tapes and 108 phonograph records; 3500 objects and sexual ephemera; 70,000 still photos, 5000 slides, and 25,000 pieces of flat art; and 6500 films and videos (including medical, erotica, educational, and feature films—see p.296). (See *Alternative Lifestyles*, p.338, for a detailed description of the general collection.) They currently subscribe to over 100 journals and newsletters and their extensive periodical collection includes professional and scholarly journals, organizational newsletters, nudist magazines, homosexual titles, soft-core "men's" magazines, and hardcore pornographic magazines (see also p.200, p.203). Their historically and geographically representative erotica collection is one of the finest in the world, even though the Institute spends no public monies to acquire erotic materials and depends heavily on the gifts of donors who wish their materials to be housed securely, preserved, and made accessible for research by the scholarly community.(See F20 for a complete description of the erotica collection, and notes under "Erotica," p.355.)

Two print catalogs cover the monograph and periodical collection through 1975 (see G6, G7) and the current catalog is in the form of a computer database—see G5 for details. The art, literature, and film collections are cataloged separately (see p.296). Holdings are classified according to terms from *Sexual Nomenclature: A Thesaurus* (see C4). The library's collection was the source for *Sex Studies Index: 1980* (see H40); *Sex Research: Bibliographies from the Institute for Sex Research* (see H37); and *Sex Research: Early Literature from Statistics to Erotica* (see H43). Library staff also compile, maintain, and distribute hundreds of bibliographies on frequently requested topics (see H39), and can compile custom bibliographies using their own and national databases.

Staff provide research assistance and referrals primarily to researchers, scholars, and the media, although they will also field questions from the general public. Researchers with demonstrable needs to use the collection in person are welcomed, with out-of-state users and those engaged in commercial projects assessed a $50 quarterly users fee, which goes to help preserve the collection. An additional fee will be assessed when extraordinary demands are put on staff time. Although materials don't circulate, photocopies of items unavailable elsewhere can be purchased (within copyright restrictions).

A5. **Mary S. Calderone Library / Sex Information and Education Council of U.S. (SIECUS):** 130 West 42nd St., Suite 2500, New York, NY 10036. PH: (212)819-9770. FAX: (212)819-9776.

Founded in 1964, SIECUS (see X225) is committed to promoting sexual and reproductive rights and fighting sexual ignorance through sex education. To this end, the library develops, collects, and disseminates sex information to students, the media, clergy, professionals (especially therapists and educators), the general public, and others. Although the emphasis is on comprehensive sexuality education, the collection includes materials addressing a wide range of sex related topics, including parent/child communication, sexual development, aging, physical and mental disabilities, child sexual abuse, gay/lesbian sexuality, curricula evaluation and development, religion, legislation and policy development, HIV/AIDS education, and pregnancy, among others. Holdings include more than 5,000 volumes, 9,000 articles, 40 journals (including all the professional English-language sexuality periodicals), 100 newsletters, extensive vertical files, and a unique collection of over 600 sexuality and HIV/AIDS education curriculum (see Ch.23). All the books and journals are indexed in the SIECUS database according to *Sexual Nomenclature* (see C4), and searches are conducted for a fee of $7. plus $1. per page of citations (free for SIECUS members). SIECUS also has the capacity to search national databases (e.g. *MEDLINE, AgeLine,* the *Exceptional Child Education Resource Database,* and the *AIDS Information Network*) for additional fees. The library compiles and regularly updates annotated bibliographies (see H46) and distributes SIECUS publications (see X225). Free library use (by appointment) is included with SIECUS membership; a fee is assessed to non-members. Mail and phone queries are accepted.

A6. **Sex Information and Education Council of Canada (SIECCAN):** 850 Coxwell Ave., East York, Ontario M4C 541, Canada. PH: (416)466-5304.

Dedicated to "informing and educating the public and professionals about all aspects of human sexuality in order to support the positive integration of sexuality into people's lives." Holdings include over 1,000 books and 25 journal and newsletter titles. Emphasis is on subjects of interest to educators and therapists, with about a third of the collection addressing medical aspects of sexuality. Information services include personalized reading packets, referrals, and custom bibliographies. Publishes the *Canadian Journal of Human Sexuality* (formerly *SIECCAN Journal,* see

K130) and *SIECCAN Newsletter* (see K118). The library is open to the public and responds to requests from across Canada and the U.S.

—— PLANNED PARENTHOOD LIBRARIES (*See also*: L18, L19)

Planned Parenthood International and Planned Parenthood Federation of America (PPFA) and their affiliates form a worldwide network of resource centers and libraries, which although associated with family planning and reproductive health issues, collect information on a wide range of sex and reproductive related topics, including abortion, sex and family life education, sexual behavior, women's health issues, adolescent sexuality and teen pregnancy, sexually transmitted diseases, reproductive freedom, birth control and contraception, rape and sexual abuse, maternal and child health, international population control efforts, childbearing, pregnancy and parenting, and sterilization.

In addition to the two major research centers (see A7, A8), there are over 70 Planned Parenthood libraries around the country. A few of the larger ones are listed below (see A9-A14); obtain a full directory from the Education Department of PPFA in New York (see X223). All collect books, journals and newsletters, curriculum, pamphlets, and booklets, as well as slides, films, videotapes, and filmstrips. Their holdings are briefly described in *Directory of Special Libraries and Information Centers* (see B62), and all will provide audiovisual and publications catalogs on request.

A7.   Katherine Dexter McCormick Library / Planned Parenthood Federation of America (PPFA): 810 7th Ave., 11th Fl., New York, NY 10019. PH: (212)261-4639.

Under the auspices of the Education Department of PPFA (see X223), the McCormick Library is the leading resource center in the U.S. for information on issues relating to family planning and reproductive health. Its collection of over 4,000 volumes, 50,000 articles and clippings, 150 scholarly journals, and extensive vertical files, includes materials on the following topics: *Advocacy*—reproductive rights, socio-political aspects of family planning, politics of sexuality education, new right literature; *Birth Control*—history of contraceptives, contraceptive methods, use and current research, abortion, infertility, reproductive technology, Margaret Sanger and the birth control movement, legal aspects, religious and ethical views; *Family Planning*—programs in the U.S. and abroad, funding, clinic services, training of personnel; *Human Sexuality, Reproductive Health,* and

Sexuality Education—teenage sexuality, pregnancy and birth, sexual behavior and reproductive health, sexually transmitted diseases, training in reproductive health and sexuality/family life education, program evaluation methodologies, women's status and men's role in sexuality issues; and *Population*—statistics and population characteristics, changes and trends, theories and policies. The McCormick Library's catalog and the Education Department's Clearinghouse of Educational Resources are available in the on-line database *LINKLine* (see I6). Although their first priority is service to Planned Parenthood clients, staff, board members, and volunteers, library staff will also assist students, researchers, professionals, and the media by providing referrals, program and research consultation, photo-duplication of material unavailable elsewhere, and custom searches of *MEDLINE*, *LINKLine*, and all DIALOG and BRS databases. The library is open to the public by appointment only. Publications include: *Current Literature in Family Planning* (see K55, J31); *LINK Line* (see K58); *The Family Planning Library Manual* (see C9); *A Small Library in Family Planning* (see H44); and reference sheets, bibliographies, and position papers.

A8.   International Planned Parenthood Federation (Western Hemisphere Region)—Library: 902 Broadway, 10th Fl., New York, NY 10010. PH: (212)995-8800.

Maintains a 10,000 volume library. Subscribes to over 200 journals and other serials. Contact the library for more information.

A9.   Leslie Resource Center, Planned Parenthood of America, Chicago: 17 N. State St., Chicago, IL 60602. PH: (312)781-9550.

A10.   Maurice Ritz Resource Library and Bookstore, Planned Parenthood of Wisconsin: 302 N. Jackson St., Milwaukee, WI 53202. PH: (414)271-7930.

A11.   Phyllis Cooksey Resource Center, Planned Parenthood of Minnesota: 1965 Ford Parkway, St. Paul, MN 55116. PH: (612)698-2401.

A12.   Planned Parenthood of Arizona—Library: 5651 N. 7th St., Phoenix, AZ 85014. PH: (602)265-2495.

A13. **Planned Parenthood of Connecticut—Library**: 129 Whitney Ave., New Haven, CT 06510. PH: (203)865-5158.

A14. **Planned Parenthood of S.E. Pennsylvania Resource Center**: 1144 Locust St., Philadelphia, PA 19107. PH: (215)351-5590.

2

REFERENCE WORKS

Reference works—research guides, directories, bibliographies, source books, and the like—provide guidance to print and non-print resources, and individual, organizational, and institutional information sources. Some, such as the *Encyclopedia of Associations*, cover a full range of topics, containing listings of interest to "swingers," transvestites, and sex educators, as well as garlic lovers, toy train collectors, and Elvis fans. Others are more specialized, providing research assistance to those working within a particular discipline (e.g. *Social Science Reference Sources*) or studying a particular topic (e.g. the *Gay Yellow Pages*).

• • • •

Listings: Described below are the 96 general reference tools cited in the "How to Find" sections throughout this volume; sex specific items are described within each chapter. With the exception of a few non-print resources, all are standard reference works available in research libraries. Most are regularly updated or published on an ongoing basis. (For the specific editions consulted in compiling this volume, see p.467). Annotations focus on each item's utility for sex research (including sex subjects covered as indicated by controlled vocabulary and index headings) and do not fully describe its organization, contents, or usage—see *ARBA* (B78) or Sheehy's *Guide* (B81) for more complete descriptions. Computer

How to Find

• Search library catalogs using the Library of Congress subject heading *Reference books–* followed by a topical subject heading, or a topical heading followed by *–Reference books*. To locate a specific type of reference material, conduct a search using the topical subject heading followed by the form subdivision signifying the type of material sought (e.g. *–Encyclopedia, –Bibliography, –Abstracts*, etc.).

• Request catalogs from publishers specializing in reference books. R.R. Bowker, G.K. Hall, Gale Research, Garland Publishing, Oryx Press, Greenwood Press, Libraries Unlimited, McFarland & Co., and others, will send their catalogs free on request. *Literary Marketplace* (New Providence, NJ: R.R. Bowker) includes an index of publishers by specialty.

• For critical reviews of reference works, consult *American Reference Books Annuals* (see B78), which claims comprehensive coverage of English language reference books published in the U.S. *Reference Sources* (see B79) cites reviews appearing in over 260 sources.

• Consult a guide to the reference literature of the discipline in which your research is grounded (i.e. film studies, anthropology, women's studies, medicine, etc.). To identify, search library catalogs using the appropriate subject heading followed by the form subdivision *–Bibliography* or *–Research*; or use *Reference books* followed by the topical heading (e.g. *Reference Books–Medicine*). For tools published by the federal government, see *Government Reference Books: A Biennial Guide to U.S. Government Publications* (see B80). Sheehy's *Guide to Reference Books* (see B81) covers reference materials of all types, in all disciplines. For other general guides, search catalogs using the heading *Reference books–Bibliographies*.

• *Directories in Print* (see B33) describes thousands of directories to print and non-print materials (databases, videos, books, etc.), as well as organizational, institutional, and individual resources. See Ch.13.

• Many organizations and institutions (e.g. information clearinghouses, libraries, government agencies) produce resource guides, directories, bibliographies, or other reference materials. For selected titles, see under relevant subject headings in Ch.30.

readable formats are noted when available; see Ch.11 for information on accessing computer databases and contacting database vendors.

➤ AIDS (DISEASE)—RESOURCE GUIDES (*See also*: D1, F1, F17)

B1. Center for Women Policy Studies Staff. *The Guide to Resources on Women and AIDS*. 2nd ed. Women and AIDS Series. Washington: Center for Women Policy Studies, 1991. 450 p.

B2. Huber, Jeffrey T. *How to Find Information About AIDS*. 2nd ed. Haworth Medical Information Sources. New York: Haworth Press, 1992. 290 p.

Intended for both professionals and the general public, this directory lists AIDS related organizations, health departments, research institutes, grant funding sources, and federal agencies, as well as hotlines, databases, print resources, and audiovisuals.

B3. Malinowsky, H. Robert, and Gerald J. Perry. *AIDS Information Sourcebook*. Phoenix: Oryx Press. Annual.

The 1991 edition includes: (1) a directory of over 900 organizations and programs in the U.S. and Canada, indexed by state and by type (advocacy, client services, clinics, educational, fundraising, hospice, legal, support groups, religious, etc.); (2) a 1,194 item bibliography, covering all aspects of AIDS and safer sex, indexed by subject and format (articles, books, bibliographies, brochures, pamphlets, curriculum and educational programs, directories, films/video/audio recordings, periodicals, plays, posters, and on-line data bases); (3) a month by month chronology tracing the history of the AIDS epidemic from June 1981 to January 1991; and (4) statistical tables and a non-technical glossary of AIDS-related terms.

➤ ASSOCIATIONS (*See also*: Ch.30)

B4. *Encyclopedia of Associations*. Detroit: Gale Research, 1992. Annual.

Together, the twelve volumes of the *Encyclopedia of Associations* provide "detailed descriptions of more than 80,000 non-profit membership associations in all subjects and areas of interest at the international and national levels worldwide and at the regional, state and local levels in the U.S." (27th edition). Volume One, *National Organizations of the U.S.*, furnishes details on "more than 22,000 national and international non-profit trade and professional associations, social welfare and public affairs organizations, religious, sports and hobby groups, and other types of organizations that consist of voluntary members and that are headquartered in the U.S." (27th edition). Entries are arranged by subject, and provide complete contact information plus a description of activities, including date founded, number and description of members, publications, statistics collected, computerized services, convention schedules, speakers bureau, and more. Keyword and name index. SEX SUBJECTS COVERED: aging, AIDS, biomedical engineering, biotechnology, birth defects, censorship, child welfare, circumcision, conservative traditionalists, divorce, ethics, family law, family medicine, family planning, feminism, fertility, obstetrics and gynecology, gay/lesbian, human engineering, human life issues, impotence, marriage, multiple births, population, rape, reproductive rights, reproductive medicine, right to life, sex addiction, sexual abuse, sexual freedom, sexual health, STDs, sudden infant death syndrome, surrogate parenthood, and urology. COMPUTER READABLE FORMATS: on-line from DIALOG, and on compact disc.

➤ AUDIOVISUALS *(See also*: Ch.26, Ch.27)

B5.   ***Bowker's Complete Video Directory***. New Providence, NJ: R.R. Bowker. Annual.

In volume one of the 1992 edition, 35,000 entertainment and performance titles are classified by genre. In volume two, 52,000 educational and special interest videos (including documentaries, "how to's", sports, and titles for specialized audiences), are classified by subject. Most items are briefly described and the producer's and distributor's addresses are noted. SEX SUBJECTS COVERED: *Erotica* is one of the genres under which titles are classified in volume one. The subject index in volume two includes the headings AIDS, pregnancy and childbirth, child abuse, marriage, relationships, and sexuality (under which are described an eclectic range of titles—*The Art of Meeting Men, Rape: An Act of Hate, Before Stonewall: The Making of a Gay and Lesbian Community, Sex in the Soviet Union, How Not to Make a Baby, How to Strip for Your Lover*).

B6.   ***Education Film and Video Locator***. Consortium of College and University Media Centers. New York: R.R. Bowker. Annual.

The 4th edition cites 51,900 videos and films available for rent from the

46-member Consortium of College and University Media Centers. Each entry includes a brief description, an audience level indicator (kindergarten through college, general and special populations), and rental information. Lending policies of all libraries are detailed. Includes subject, title, and intended audience indexes. SEX SUBJECTS COVERED: reproduction, sex education, child abuse, homosexuality, human sexuality, marriage, childbirth, embryology, pregnancy, and venereal disease.

B7. *Film and Video Finders.* National Information Center for Educational Media. Albuquerque, NM: Access Innovations, 1987-. Quarterly.

Provides comprehensive coverage of educational films and videos intended for preschool through professional/graduate level audiences. The on-line version includes overhead transparencies, audio tapes, records, educational computer software, and compact discs, as well as films and videos. Brief descriptions are included when available. SEX SUBJECTS COVERED: AIDS, animal social and sexual behavior, birth control, abortion, gynecology and obstetrics, homosexuality, incest, population, rape, sex discrimination, sex roles, sexual education, sexual ethics, sexual hygiene, and social-sexual behavior. COMPUTER READABLE FORMATS: *AV On-line* (1964-), also known as the *National Information Center for Educational Media (NICEM) Database*, available from DIALOG.

B8. *Media Review Digest.* Ann Arbor, MI: Pierian Press. Annual.

A subject and title index to published reviews, evaluations, and descriptions of non-book educational and entertainment media, including films and videos, film strips, audio recordings, and slides. Each entry provides a brief description, intended audience, and rental and/or purchase information. SEX SUBJECTS COVERED: abortion, adultery in motion pictures, AIDS, AIDS in motion pictures, birth control, child molesting, childbirth, condoms, contraceptives, generative organs, impotence, labor (obstetrics), perinatal care, postnatal care, pregnancy, premenstrual syndrome, pro-choice movement, rape, sex, sex change, sex in motion pictures, sex instruction for children, youth, and teenagers, sexual disorders, sexual ethics, sexual intercourse, and STDs.

B9. **National Audiovisual Center**: 8700 Edgewood Drive, Capitol Heights, MD 20743. PH: (301)763-1896.

The central source for distribution of, and information about, audiovisual materials produced by or for the U.S. government, including video cassettes, films, and slide/sound programs. Most materials are available for purchase only. Request the catalog, *Selected Audiovisual Materials Produced by the U.S. Government.*

B10.   *National Library of Medicine Audiovisual Catalog.* Bethesda, MD: National Library of Medicine, 1983-. Quarterly.

"A cumulation of citations to audiovisual materials, and since 1988 to microcomputer software, cataloged by NLM or revised during the period given on the catalog." Arranged by subject using MeSH subject headings. SEX SUBJECTS COVERED: Covers a wide range of topics relating to reproduction, childbirth, pregnancy, sexual behavior, sexual deviation, sexual dysfunction, sex education, sexual health and medicine, and marital and sexual therapy. COMPUTER READABLE FORMATS: *AVLINE*, available on MEDLARS (see J45).

B11.   *The Video Source Book 1992.* Detroit: Gale Research. Annual.

The 13th edition describes over 76,500 videos available for rent, lease, loan, purchase, or duplication. All genres are included: Health/Science, How-to/Instruction, General Interest/Education, and Movies/Entertainment. Each entry includes a brief description, the producer and/or distributor, availability, and suggested use (e.g. home, institution, school). Subject, title, and genre indexes. SEX SUBJECTS COVERED: abortion, abortion clinic training, AIDS, birth control, breastfeeding, cesarean birth, child abuse, childbirth, geriatric sexuality, herpes, homosexuality, human reproduction, incest, marriage, massage, obstetrics, population, pornography (films about pornography and censorship, not erotica itself), pregnancy, puberty, sex roles, sexual child abuse, sexual education, sexuality, and STDs.

➤ BIBLIOGRAPHIES (*See also*: Ch.10)

B12.   *Bibliographic Index: a cumulative bibliography of bibliographies.* New York: H.W. Wilson, 1937-. Quarterly.

"A subject index of bibliographies published separately or appearing as parts of books, pamphlets or periodicals. Selection is made from bibliographies that have 50 or more citations." See footnote 1, p.156, for entry arrangement and subjects covered. COMPUTER READABLE FORMATS: on-line (1984-) from Wilsonline, updated twice weekly.

➤ BIOGRAPHY

B13. *Gale's Biography and Genealogy Master Index*. 2nd ed. 8 vols. Edited by Miranda C. Herbert and Barbara McNeil. Detroit: Gale Research, 1980. Annual supplements.

3,200,000 biographical sketches, from over 350 current and retrospective biographical sources, were cited in the 1980 volume, with millions more noted in the annual supplements. The on-line catalog includes over 8.25 million citations to biographical information on both contemporary and historical figures (e.g. Dr. Ruth, Alfred Kinsey, William Masters), appearing in more than 1,900 editions of over 680 biographical sources. COMPUTER READABLE FORMATS: on-line from DIALOG.

B14. *Marquis Who's Who Publications: Index to All Books*. Chicago: Marquis Who's Who, 1974-. Biennial.

A "guide to the information recorded in the current editions of ten Marquis Who's Who directories."

➤ BOOKS *(See also*: Ch.15)

B15. *Books in Series in the United States 1985-1989*. New Providence, NJ: R.R. Bowker, 1989. Irregular.

Cites "original, reprinted, in-print, and out-of-print books, published or distributed in the U.S., in popular, scholarly, and professional series." Indexed by series title, individual book title, and subject. Two older compilations cover the periods of 1876 to 1949 and 1950 to 1984.

B16. *Books in Print*. New Providence, NJ: R.R. Bowker. Annual.

The Subject Guide to Books in Print. New Providence, NJ: R.R. Bowker. Annual.

Forthcoming Books. New Providence, NJ: R.R. Bowker. Bi-monthly.

Books in Print (BIP) provides author and title access to "scholarly, popular, adult, juvenile, reprint, and all other types of books," currently in print in the United States. Entries include title, author, number of pages, price, and publisher (whose addresses and phone numbers are listed in a separate volume). *The Subject Guide* classifies BIP titles under more than 67,000 Library of Congress subject headings. Indexed by author, title, and subject, *Forthcoming Books* serves as a cumulative update to both titles, as well as announcing books scheduled to be published within the next five months. All three are available in all libraries and most bookstores. SEX SUBJECTS COVERED: most general sex books are classified under *sex*, *sex (biology)*, *sex (psychology)*, and *sex customs*. More specialized books are classified under detailed subject headings representing all aspects of human sexuality (e.g. *bestiality, fellatio, pregnancy, sex instruction for the mentally handicapped*, etc.). COMPUTER READABLE FORMATS: A single database, merging all three titles (plus citations from other Bowker bibliographies), is available on compact disc and on-line from DIALOG and BRS. It includes over 1.8 million citations to books currently in print, forthcoming, or declared out-of-print since July 1979, with over 7,000 new citations added monthly.

B17.   *Cumulative Book Index: A Word List of Books in the English Language*. New York: H.W. Wilson, 1898-. Monthly.

A cumulative bibliography of English-language books published worldwide since 1898. The following items are excluded: books with fewer than 50 pages, except for poetry, plays, bibliographies, juvenile literature and scholarly works; limited editions, self-published, or subsidy press publications; and other material of "local, fugitive, or ephemeral nature." Citations are arranged alphabetically by author, title, and Library of Congress subject headings. COMPUTER READABLE FORMATS: on-line (1982-) from Wilsonline, updated twice weekly; and on compact disc. Over 50,000 new records are added annually.

➤ BOOKDEALERS *(See also*: Ch.15)

B18.   *American Book Trade Directory*. New Providence, NJ: R.R. Bowker. Annual.

Includes geographically arranged lists of retailers, wholesalers, and antiquarian bookdealers in the U.S. and Canada, with a "Type of Store" index noting dealers with a subject specialty comprising at least 50% of their stock, including those specializing in alternative lifestyles, family studies, gay/lesbian studies, parenting, sexuality, and women's studies.

B19.   American Book Collector. *Directory of Specialized American Bookdealers*. Ossining, NY: Moretus Press. Annual.

Entries include address, phone number, business hours, and catalog availability. A specialization index notes dealers of erotica, sexology, and gay and lesbian literature.

—— OUT-OF-PRINT BOOKDEALERS

B20. Antiquarian Booksellers Association of America. *ABAA Membership Directory*. New York: Antiquarian Booksellers Association of America. Annual.

B21. Patterson, R.H. *Directory of American Book Specialists: Sources for Antiquarian and Out-of-Print Titles*. New York: Continental Publishing, 1972-. Annual.

B22. Robinson, Ruth E. *Buy Books Where—Sell Books Where: A Directory of Out of Print Booksellers and Their Author-Subject Specialties*. Morgantown, VA: Ruth E. Robinson. Annual.

A directory of over 2,000 active dealers and collectors of out-of-print books, including those specializing in erotica, homosexuality, sexual behavior, and sexual relations.

➤ BOOK REVIEWS *(See also*: Ch.15)

B23. *Book Review Digest*. New York: H.W. Wilson. 1905-. 10/year.

"Citations to and excerpts of reviews of current juvenile and adult fiction and non-fiction in the English language." Subject, author, and title index to book reviews appearing in approximately 100 periodicals (including library reviewing journals) published in the U.S., U.K., and Canada. Covers many fewer sources than the *Book Review Index* (see B24), but provides subject access and excerpts from reviews. COMPUTER READABLE FORMATS: on-line (1983-) from Wilsonline and Compuserve, updated twice weekly; and on compact disc.

B24. *Book Review Index*. Detroit: Gale Research, 1965-. Bimonthly.

Representing a wide range of popular, academic, and professional interests, BRI indexes by author and title reviews of books, periodicals, and books on tape appearing in more than 500 publications including reviewing journals such as *Choice, Booklist,* and *School Library Journal*; national publications of general interest; and scholarly and literary journals. COMPUTER READABLE FORMATS: on-line (1969-) from DIALOG.

➤ CONFERENCE / MEETING PROCEEDINGS (*See also*: Ch.18)

B25. *Bibliographic Guide To Conference Publications*. Boston: G.K. Hall. 1974-. Annual.

Indexes proceedings, reports, and summaries of conferences and meetings.

B26. *Index to Social Sciences and Humanities Proceedings*. Philadelphia: Institute for Scientific Information, 1979-. Quarterly.

Cites conference and meeting proceedings published collectively or as individual papers. Covers social science and humanities conferences worldwide. Access by title, conference name, and keywords.

B27. *Proceedings in Print*. Special Libraries Association: Arlington, MA. 1964-. Bimonthly.

An index to published conference proceedings in all disciplines and subject areas. Papers published individually are not included. Access by subject, publication title, and conference name but not by the titles of individual papers delivered at the conference.

➤ DATA BASES (*See also*: Ch.11)

B28. *Data Base Directory*. White Plains, NY: Knowledge Industry, in Cooperation with the American Society for Information Science. Annual.

Fully describes thousands of on-line and computer readable data bases, including producer, vendor, time coverage, type of database, materials included, and topics covered. Subject, producer, and vendor indexes.

B29. *Directory of Online Data Bases*. Santa Monica, CA: Cuadra/Gale. Quarterly.

Describes over 5000 databases available on-line to the public. Descriptions include type of database, subjects, provider, vendor, contents, language, time span covered, and updating frequency. Subject, provider, vendor, and title indexes. For compact discs, see Cuadra/Gale's *Directory of Portable Databases*.

B30.   Lesko, Matthew. *Federal Data Base Finder*. 3d ed. Kensington, MD: Information U.S.A., 1990. Biennial.

A directory of free and fee-based data bases maintained by the federal government, and accessible to the public either through commercial database vendors, or directly from the sponsoring agency. Arranged by agency, with a key word index. See also Lesko's *State Data and Database Finder* (Kensington, MD: Information U.S.A., 1989).

B31.   *On-line Database Search Service Directory*. 2nd ed. Edited by Doris Morris Maxfield. Detroit: Gale Research, 1987.

"A reference and referral guide to more than 1700 libraries, information firms and other sources providing computerized information retrieval and associated services using publicly available on-line databases." Entries include: fees, databases available, subject areas searched, search request procedures, and the databases searched most frequently (the more familiar a librarian is with a particular index, the faster, and therefore less expensive, the search will be).

B32.   St. George, Arthur, and Ron Larsen. *Internet-Accessible Library Catalogs and Databases*. College Park, MD: University of Maryland, 1992. Loose-leaf.

This directory is cataloged in RLIN and available through interlibrary loan. Consult an on-line directory for the most updated listings; see p.148.

➤ DIRECTORIES *(See also: Ch.13)*

B33.   *Directories in Print*. Detroit: Gale Research. Annual.

"An annotated guide to over 14,000 directories published worldwide, including: business and industrial directories; professional and scientific rosters; entertainment, recreation and cultural directories; directory databases and other non-profit products; and other lists and guides of all kinds" (9th edition). Includes directories to organizations, institutions, audiovisuals, and print materials, with items cited ranging from the 12 volume *Encyclopedia of Associations* to the list of impotence support groups found in the appendix of the consumer handbook, *Impotence: How to Overcome It*. Subject and title indexes. SEX SUBJECTS COVERED: all. COMPUTER READABLE FORMATS: data is included in the *Gale Publications Database*, available on-line from DIALOG.

➤ DISSERTATIONS (*See also*: Ch.16)

B34.   *Comprehensive Dissertations Index* (CDI). Ann Arbor, MI: UMI, 1861-. Monthly.

   Dissertation Abstracts International (DAI). Ann Arbor, MI: UMI. 1938-. Monthly.

CDI cites doctoral dissertations and masters theses from accredited universities in the U.S. and other institutions worldwide. Entries are classified first by discipline and then by author-chosen keyword, and are cross referenced to abstracts in *DAI*. Averaging 250 to 300 words in length, the author-written abstracts provide a detailed summary of the original work. COMPUTER READABLE FORMATS: available on compact disc in most research libraries, and as *Dissertation Abstracts On-line* (1891-) from BRS, DIALOG, and other vendors. The computer readable versions can be searched by title and abstract language, author, title, subject, degree granted, faculty advisor, institution, and date degree awarded.

➤ ENCYCLOPEDIAS (*See also*: Ch.7)

B35.   Ryan, Joe, ed. *First Step: The Master Index of Subject Encyclopedias*. Phoenix: Oryx Press, 1987.

Subject index to articles on nearly 40,000 topics, contained in 430 of the best English-language sources of background information, including subject encyclopedias, dictionaries, handbooks, comprehensive textbooks, yearbooks, annual reviews, and other standard sources. All articles cited are "authoritative, analytical and of some length [250 words or more] and accompanied by a bibliography." SEX SUBJECTS COVERED: *The Sex Atlas* (see F11) and the *Encyclopedia of Sex Behavior* (see F9) are the only two sex specific sources indexed, but many sex related articles are cited from other publications. Articles on abortion, for example, are cited from such diverse sources as *Constitutional Law Dictionary*, *Dictionary of Medical Ethics*, *International Encyclopedia of Psychiatry*, *Women's Encyclopedia of Myths and Secrets*, and the *Westminster Dictionary of Christian Ethics*.

➤ FACULTY (*See also*: Ch.29)

B36.   *Faculty Directory of Higher Education*. 12 vols. Detroit: Gale Research, 1988.

"A twelve-volume subject-classified directory providing names, addresses, and titles of courses taught for more than 600,000 teaching faculty at more than 3,100 U.S. colleges, universities, and community colleges and at 220 selected Canadian institutions." No updates are planned.

B37. *National Faculty Directory 1992.* Detroit: Gale Research. Annual.

"An alphabetical listing with addresses of approximately 606,000 members of teaching faculties at junior colleges, colleges and universities in the United States, and at selected Canadian institutions" (23rd edition). Only faculty with classroom teaching responsibilities are included. Entries include name, departmental affiliation, and institutional address.

➤ GOVERNMENT AGENCIES AND PERSONNEL (*See also*: Ch.29, Ch.30)

—— FEDERAL AGENCY DIRECTORIES

B38. Lesko, Matthew. *Lesko's Info Power.* Kensington, MD: Information U.S.A., 1990. Biannual.

Describes over 30,000 information sources at state and federal agencies, including details of their services and publications. Also includes telephone numbers of state information centers and a subject guide to the names and numbers of over 8,000 federal experts. A new edition is forthcoming in 1993. COMPUTER READABLE FORMATS: *Information U.S.A.* on-line from Compuserve, updated daily.

B39. Seager, Walter. *Federal Fast Finder: A Keyword Telephone Directory to the Federal Government.* Washington: Washington Researches Ltd. Biennial.

B40. *United States Government Manual.* Washington: Superintendent of Documents, GPO. Office of the Federal Register, National Archives and Records Administration. Annual.

The official handbook of the Federal Government. Covers the creation, organization, authority, activities, and chief officials of legislative, judicial, and executive departments and agencies, as well as quasi-official agencies, international organizations in which the U.S. participates, and federal boards, commissions and committees. Indexed by subject, agency, and personal name. For detailed administrative structure see B42 and B43.

B41. *Washington Information Directory*. Washington: Congressional Quarterly. Annual.

Describes both executive agencies and non-governmental organizations in the Washington, D.C. area (plus listings for regional agency information centers nationwide). Entries include director's name, contact information, and a brief description.

—— FEDERAL AGENCY STAFF DIRECTORIES

In addition to listing names and numbers of agency staff, federal staff directories detail the agency's organizational structure.

B42. *Federal Staff Directory*. Mt. Vernon, VA: Staff Directories Ltd. Semi-annual.

Names and phone numbers of the staff at offices, agencies, and departments of the executive branch of the U.S. government, as well as at quasi-official agencies and organizations, information centers, and libraries. Arranged by department, with a subject/keyword/name index.

B43. *Federal Yellow Book: Who's Who in Federal Departments and Agencies*. Washington: Monitor Publishing. Quarterly.

A federal staff directory arranged by department and agency. Unlike B42, it has no subject index, but is updated more frequently.

—— FEDERAL REFERRAL AGENCIES

B44. **Federal Information Centers**: P.O. Box 600, Cumberland, MD 21501. PH: (301)722-9098 (call information for local numbers).

The Federal Information Center program was established in 1966 as a one-stop source of assistance for callers with questions about the federal government's agencies, programs, and services. Staff at the seventy-two regional centers nationwide respond to inquiries—answering questions and/or providing referrals—using the most current government reference materials and directories. For a complete list of FIC addresses and phone numbers, write the Consumer Information Center, Pueblo, CO 81009.

B45. **National Health Information Center**: P.O. Box 1133, Washington, DC 20013-1133. PH: (800)336-4797.

An information and referral system developed to help professionals and the general public access health information. Center staff (1) provide referrals to federal and private health information sources from an on-line directory of more than 1,000 health-related organizations, including federal and state agencies, voluntary associations, self-help and support groups, trade associations, and professional societies; (2) distribute federal government publications; and (3) produce directories, resource guides, and bibliographies, including *Healthfinders*—a series of resource lists on current health concerns; *Health Information Resources in the Federal Government*—an annual directory of federal health agencies, information centers, and information clearinghouses which provide health related information, publications, and referrals; *Selected Federal Health Information Clearinghouse and Information Centers*; and *Toll-free Numbers for Health Information*. A complete publication list is available on request. The National Health Information Center library is open to the public by appointment. SEX RELATED SUBJECTS: all issues relating to sexual and reproductive health, including AIDS, abortion, birth defects, contraception, diseases and dysfunctions of reproductive organs, pregnancy, rape, incest and child abuse, infertility, maternal and child health, family planning, teenage pregnancy, STDs. COMPUTER READABLE FORMATS: the directory is available to the public as *DIRLINE*, see J45.

—— STATE AGENCY STAFF DIRECTORIES

B46. *State Executive Directory*. Washington, DC: Caroll Publishing. 3/year.

Arranged geographically with keyword index.

B47. *State Yellow Book*. New York: Monitor Publishing. Semiannual.

A directory of elected and administrative staff in county, regional, and multi-state agencies in all 50 states, the District of Columbia, and four U.S. territories. Arranged geographically.

▶ GOVERNMENT DOCUMENTS (*See also*: Ch.17; B85)

B48. *CIS/Federal Register Index*. Bethesda, MD: Congressional Information Service, 1984-. Weekly.

A comprehensive index to the daily *Federal Register of the U.S. Government*, each issue of which "consists of about 100 'documents'—rules, proposed rules, and notices—summarizing individual actions by the dozens of agencies to which Congress and the President have assigned responsibility for developing and implementing federal regulations," and provides public notice of actions, meetings, reports, and decisions in all areas of regulatory concern. The index can be accessed by general policy area, specific subject, responsible federal agency, authorized legislation, and by the affected industry, organization, individual, or geographic area. SEX SUBJECTS COVERED: abortion, AIDS, birth defects, contraceptives, family planning, maternity, midwives, obscenity and pornography, obstetrics and gynecology, pregnancy, reproductive diseases and disorders, reproductive genetics in vitro, sex crimes, sex discrimination, sex education, and sexually transmitted diseases, among others. For example: decency and moral contents requirements in AIDS education project grants; establishment of child pornographer producers identification system; presidential proclamation of Sanctity of Human Life Day; and prohibitions against false success claims by in vitro fertilization services.

B49. *CIS/Index and Abstracts to Publications of U.S. Congress (CIS/Index)*. Bethesda, MD: Congressional Information Service, 1970-. Monthly.

Comprehensive index, with abstracts, to all publications produced by committees and subcommittees of the U.S. Congress, including transcripts of committee hearings (with sub-records of witness testimony); analysis of federal legislation and activities; reports, articles, documents, and special publications (including Congressional Research Service reports, see B52); statistical publications; and non-Congressional publications inserted into congressional documents or presented at Congressional hearings. Cumulative indexes, each covering a particular type of material, index committee prints, committee hearings, serials sets, and reports and documents released from 1789 to 1969. SEX SUBJECTS COVERED: AIDS, abortion, contraceptives, family planning, gynecology and obstetrics, homosexuality, homosexual rights, obscenity and pornography, pregnancy, rape, sex education, sexual sterilization, STDs, sexual harassment, teen pregnancy. COMPUTER READABLE FORMATS: on-line (1789-) from DIALOG; and on compact disc.

B50. *Guide to U.S. Government Publications*. Edited by Donna Andriot. McLean, VA: Documents Index, 1990.

"An annotated guide to the important series and periodicals currently being published by the various U.S. government agencies as well as important reference publications issued within the various series." Arranged by departments and divisions, with a title and agency index.

B51. *Index to U.S. Government Periodicals*. Chicago: Infordata International, 1970-. Quarterly.

An index, with abstracts, to periodicals produced by more than 100 federal agencies. (For statistical publications see B85.) Subject, author, agency, and title indexes.

B52. *Major Studies and Issue Briefs of the Congressional Research Service 1916-1989 Cumulative Index*. Frederick, MD: University Publications of America (imprint of Congressional Information Service), 1989. Annual supplements.

Subject and title index to "significant" studies and issue briefs produced by the Congressional Research Service, the department of the Library of Congress which serves the research and reference needs of the U.S. Congress, its members, committees, and staff. Hundreds of accurate, objective, timely, non-partisan reports and issue briefs are cited. Collectively these reports include basic factual information, in-depth policy analysis and research, pro/con arguments, scientific, economic and legislative analysis, legal research, legislative histories, background analysis, and literature reviews. Less extensive issue briefs, intended to keep members of Congress informed on timely issues, are not indexed, but can be obtained through your Congressperson. SEX SUBJECTS COVERED: AIDS, contraceptives, family planning, gynecology and obstetrics, immigration law and homosexuality, homosexuality, obscenity and pornography, pregnancy, rape, sex discrimination, surrogate mother, teenage pregnancy. Sample titles: *Religious Teachings on Abortion from Major World Religions*; *Bibliography on Abortion Issues*; *Evolution of Judicial Studies on Censorship and Obscenity 1868-1974*; *Teenage Pregnancy Statistics*; *Supreme Court Abortion Rulings*; *Bibliography of Sexual Harassment in Employment 1987-1991*.

B53. *Monthly Catalog of U.S. Government Publications*. Washington: Government Printing Office, 1895-. Monthly.

Each issue lists approximately 14,000 titles published by the Government Printing Office (GPO) and currently available for purchase. Although comprehensive, it is not a complete record of all government publications.

Consult specialized indexes (e.g. B49) and individual agency catalogs for items published by other then the GPO. Arrangement is by SuDoc number, with access by keyword, Library of Congress subject headings, and title. To identify older materials consult: *Cumulative Subject Index to the Monthly Catalog of U.S. Government Publications 1895-1899* and *Cumulative Subject Index to the Monthly Catalog of U.S. Government Publications 1900-1971.* A list of depository libraries is included in each September's issue. COMPUTER READABLE FORMATS: *GPO Monthly Catalog* (1976-) available on-line from Wilsonline, BRS, and DIALOG; and on compact disc.

B54.   *Subject Bibliography Index.* Superintendent of Documents. Washington: Government Printing Office. Irregular updates.

An index to the over 200 free, regularly updated, subject bibliographies issued by the Government Printing Office (GPO). Each lists currently available GPO titles (books, periodicals, reports), as well as subscription services, federal clearinghouses and hotlines, and other non-print information sources. To order the free *Index,* call the GPO at (202)783-3238. (Note: bibliographies produced by government agencies are indexed in the *Monthly Catalog* [see B53].)

B55.   *U.S. Supreme Court Digest.* St. Paul, MN: West Publishing, 1969-. Annual.

Provides subject and case name access to Supreme Court decisions (e.g. cases regarding abortion, sodomy laws, obscenity/pornography, sexual orientation, etc.). See also D3 and F29.

➤ INDEXES *(See also: Ch.12)*

B56.   *Index and Abstract Directory: An International Guide to Services and Serials Coverage.* Birmingham, AL: EBSCO Publishing. Biennial.

Section I of the 1990 edition lists over 35,000 periodicals, and notes the indexes that cover them. Section II describes over 700 abstracting and indexing tools, and lists the periodicals they index. Entries are arranged alphabetically, with a subject/discipline index. COMPUTER READABLE FORMATS: available on compact disc.

B57. *Lathrop Report on Newspaper Indexes*. Wooster, OH: Norman Lathrop Enterprises, 1979-. Annual.

An illustrated guide to published and unpublished newspaper indexes in the United States and Canada.

B58. Miller, Anita Cheek. *Newspaper Indexes: A Location and Subject Guide for Researchers*. 3 vols. Metuchen, NJ: Scarecrow Press, 1977.

Directory of newspaper indexes available in libraries, newspapers, historical and genealogical societies, local papers, publishers, booksellers, and from "selected individuals."

➤ INFORMATION CLEARINGHOUSES (*See also*: Ch.30)

B59. *Clearinghouse Directory: A Guide to Information Clearinghouses and Their Resources, Services, and Publications*. Edited by Donna Batten. Detroit: Gale Research, 1991.

"One step guide to up-to-date and authoritative information on more than 600 major information clearinghouses—little known organizations that answer questions, make referrals, conduct computer searches, and provide information at little or no cost to the public." Includes both federal and private clearinghouses. SEX SUBJECTS COVERED: AIDS, bio-technology, child abuse, civil rights and liberties, disabled, education, ethics, family planning, geriatrics, health, homosexuality, law, obscenity, PMS, rape, religion, sexuality, sudden infant death syndrome, and teen pregnancy.

➤ LIBRARIES AND ARCHIVES (*See also*: Ch.1, Ch.30)

B60. *American Library Directory*. New Providence, NJ: R.R. Bowker. Annual.

Provides brief descriptions of public, academic, government, and special libraries, including library holdings and special collections, catalog availability, and the on-line or compact disc databases available for patron use or librarian conducted fee-based searches.

B61.   Ash, Lee, and William G. Miller. *Subject Collections: A Guide to Special Book Collections and Subject Emphasis as Reported by University, College, Public, and Special Libraries and Museums in the United States and Canada.* 6th ed. 2 vols. New York: R.R. Bowker, 1985.

B62.   *Directory of Special Libraries and Information Centers.* Detroit: Gale Research. Annual.

"A guide to more then 20,800 special libraries, research libraries, information centers, archives, and data centers maintained by government agencies, business, industry, newspapers, educational institutions, nonprofit organizations and societies in the fields of science and engineering, medicine, law, art, religion, the social sciences, and humanities" (16th edition). Entries include the following information: subjects represented; holdings (including special collections and subscriptions); services and publications; and catalogs and computerized information services. Subject index. SEX SUBJECTS COVERED: abortion, AIDS, birth control, birth defects, child abuse, family, homosexuality, infants—death, interpersonal relations, lesbianism, marriage, natural childbirth, obstetrics, parenting, rape, sex, sex change, sex crimes, sex instruction, and venereal disease.

B63.   Evinger, William R. *Directory of Federal Libraries.* 2nd ed. Phoenix: Oryx Press, 1992.

Describes 3,000 federal libraries, including presidential and national libraries, specialized libraries, and libraries in research centers, hospitals, and penal institutions.

➤ MANUFACTURERS *(See also:* Ch.30 under "Businesses")

B64.   *Brands and Their Companies.* Detroit: Gale Research. Annual.

Indicates the company which manufactures a particular brand name product. Includes manufacturers' addresses and phone numbers.

B65.   *Health Device Sourcebook 1991.* Plymouth Meeting, PA: ECRI. Annual.

Directory of medical device manufacturers, including name, address, phone and product line. Arranged by subject.

➤ MEASUREMENT TOOLS *(See also:* Ch.24)

B66. *Health and Psychosocial Instruments.* Pittsburgh: Behavioral Measurement Database Services, 1989-. Quarterly. Database.

Database available on-line from BRS, and on compact disc. Describes thousands of instruments with which to assess the health and behavior of infants, children, adolescents, adults, and the elderly. Entries include title, author, development date, subject, description, reliability and validity data, and full information on how to obtain each instrument. Subject access using the National Library of Medicine's *Medical Subject Headings* and the *Thesaurus of Psychological Index Terms.* Updated quarterly.

B67. *Mental Measurements Yearbook.* Highland Park, NJ: Mental Measurements Yearbook, 1941-. Monthly.

Cites commercially available educational, psychological, and vocational tests. Each entry contains a brief summary of the test, a bibliography of relevant published articles, validity and reliability data, intended population, critical review sources and, on occasion, an original test review. Provides name, test title, book title, and subject access. COMPUTER READABLE FORMATS: On-line (1972-) from BRS, updated monthly.

➤ PERIODICALS *(See also:* Ch.14; for gov't periodicals see B50, B51)

B68. *Gale Directory of Publications and Broadcast Media.* Detroit: Gale Research. Annual.

Formerly titled the *Ayer Directory of Publications.* "Annual guide to publications, broadcast stations including newspapers, magazines, journals, radio stations, television stations and cable systems" (125th edition). Bibliographic citations of 38,400 newspapers, magazines, journals published at least quarterly in the U.S. and Canada. Organized geographically and by subject. SEX SUBJECTS COVERED: "men's" magazines are the only titles listed under *Sex.* COMPUTER READABLE FORMATS: *Gale Publications Database,* available on-line from DIALOG.

B69. Katz, Bill, and Linda Sternberg. *Magazines for Libraries.* New Providence: NJ: R.R. Bowker. Annual.

Lengthy, critical descriptions of over 6,600 periodicals (including indexes and abstracts), which the "editors and consultants believe to be the best and most useful for the average elementary or secondary school, public, academic, or special library" (7th edition). Entries are arranged by subject. SEX SUBJECTS COVERED: sex related titles are classified under *Civil Liberties (bioethics, reproductive rights, right-to-life), Family and Marriage, Family Planning, Lesbian and Gay, Men, Population Studies, Singles, Women.* Use the subject index to locate sex related titles in other categories.

B70.   *Newsletters in Print.* Detroit: Gale Research. Annual.

"A descriptive guide to more then 11,000 subscription, membership, and free newsletters, bulletins, digests, updates and similar serial publications issued in the United States or Canada, and available in print or on-line" (6th edition). All titles are available to the public, and have national or broad regional focus. Subject, title, and keyword indexes. SEX SUBJECTS COVERED: AIDS, abortion, abortion—law and legislation, abortion—religious abstracts, adolescence, alternative life styles, birth control, birth defects, breastfeeding, contraception, childbirth, diseases (venereal), family, gynecology, homosexuality, homosexuality and media, homosexuality and religion, interpersonal relationships, lesbianism, marriage, mass media and society, men, obstetrics, obscenity, population control, pornography, rape, sex, sex—study and teaching, sudden infant death syndrome, urology, and women's health. COMPUTER READABLE FORMATS: *Gale Publications Database*, available on-line from DIALOG.

B71.   *Oxbridge Directory of Newsletters.* New York: Oxbridge Communications. Annual.

The 10th edition of this directory cites over 20,000 titles, and claims to be the most comprehensive guide available to U.S. and Canadian news-letters, although some of the titles (e.g. corporate newsletters) are unavailable to the general public. Entries provide bibliographic and subscription information but no descriptions. Indexed by publisher, title, and broad subject. SEX SUBJECTS COVERED: Sex related titles are classified under *Sex* (14 titles listed), *Women, Baby, Gay and Lesbian Literature,* and *Men's.*

B72.   *The Serials Directory: An International Reference Book.* Birmingham, AL: EBSCO. Annual.

The 6th edition cites over 142,000 international titles, including monographs, compact discs, newsletters, journals, magazines and other serials, classified by broad subject. Entries note where each item is indexed. SEX SUBJECTS COVERED: sex related periodicals are classified under the headings *Sexual Life, Birth Control, Family and Marriage, Gynecology and Obstetrics, Population Studies, Urology.* COMPUTER READABLE FORMATS: available on compact disc.

B73. **The Standard Periodical Directory.** New York: Oxbridge Communications. Annual.

The 15th edition briefly describes 75,000 U.S. and Canadian periodicals, including consumer magazines, scholarly journals, directories, government publications, house organs, newsletters, trade journals, transactions and proceedings of scientific societies, yearbooks, and association publications, among other types of serials. Classified by general subject headings. SEX SUBJECTS COVERED: sex related periodicals are classified under the headings *Family, Gay and Lesbian Literature, Health, Lifestyle, Medicine, Men's, Sex, Social Service and Welfare,* and *Women's.*

B74. **Ulrich's International Periodicals Directory.** New Providence, NJ: R.R. Bowker. Annual.

The 31st edition describes 126,000 international serials published at least triannually. Arranged by broad subject. SEX SUBJECTS COVERED: sex related periodicals are classified under the headings *Birth Control, Children and Youth, Homosexuality, Medical Science* (see especially under *Dermatology and Venereology* and *Obstetrics and Gynecology*), *Men's Health, Men's Interest, Population Studies,* and *Women's Health.* For sex education titles, see under *Physical Fitness and Hygiene.* COMPUTER READABLE FORMATS: available on-line from BRS and DIALOG as *Bowker's International Serials Database* (a.k.a *Ulrichs International Periodical Directory Database*), updated monthly. Data from *Irregular Serials and Annuals, Bowker's International Serials Database Update,* and *Sources of Serials,* is also included in the on-line database.

➤ PUBLIC OPINION POLLS (*See also*: Ch.19)

B75. **American Public Opinion Index.** Louisville, KY: Opinion Research Service 1981-. Annual.

Describes national, state, and local surveys and polls, conducted of scientifically drawn random samples of the general public or designated target groups. Includes polls conducted by over 200 sources. Entries note the polling date, sample size and characteristics, polling method, and the specific questions asked. Survey results are available on microfilm from Opinion Research Service, or directly from the pollster. A subject index provides access to the individual questions asked in each poll. SEX SUBJECTS COVERED: coverage varies depending on the polls conducted each year. The 10th edition included questions relating to birth control, morality, obscenity, population, pornography, pregnancy, sex, sex education, and spouse abuse.

B76.   *Gallup Poll Monthly*. Princeton, NJ: Gallup Poll, 1965-. Monthly.

Previously known as *Gallup Political Index*, *Gallup Opinion Index*, and *The Gallup Poll*. A monthly compilation of national Gallup polls of representative adult samples. Gallup Polls are also indexed in SRI (see B91). An annually updated cumulative index covers polls conducted since 1965. SEX SUBJECTS COVERED: The 1965-1991 cumulative index cites polls on abortion, birth control, body image, homosexuals (acceptance, adoption, legalization of relations), nudism, pornography, premarital sex, sex, sex freedom, sexual violence in media, and virginity.

B77.   Roper Opinion Locator Library / Roper Center for Public Opinion Research: P.O.Box 440, Storrs, CT 06268-0440. PH: (203)486-4440.

The library contains an extensive, constantly updated collection of polling data and public opinion surveys conducted by Yankelovich, Skelly and White Inc., Gallup, National Opinion Research Center, The Roper Organization, CBS/New York Times, ABC/Washington Post, NBC/Wall Street Journal, International Research Associates Group, U.S. Information Agency, and other commercial, academic and government agencies worldwide. Their on-line database, *Public Opinion On-line* (1960-), available from DIALOG, includes more than 140,000 questions and responses from public opinion surveys conducted throughout the U.S. since 1960, with selective coverage of polls conducted between 1940-1959. Updated daily, over 1000 new records are added each month. Entries include survey questions, results, sponsoring organizations (including addresses and phone numbers), subject categories, interview methods, number of respondents, survey population, and bibliographic citations to source documents. Contact the library for information on fee-based searches.

➤ REFERENCE BOOKS (*See also*: Ch.2)

B78. *American Reference Books Annuals (ARBA)*. Englewood, CO: Libraries Unlimited. 1969-. Annual.

Claims to provide comprehensive coverage of all English-language reference books published in the United States and Canada the previous year. Each volume contains lengthy, critical reviews (written by subject specialists), classified either by subject or by type (e.g. directories, thesauri, encyclopedias, etc.). Volume 22 includes the chapters "Sex Studies" and "Family, Marriage and Divorce." Each volume includes detailed subject, author, and title indexes, and cumulative indexes are compiled every five years.

B79. *Reference Sources*. Ann Arbor, MI: Pierian Press, 1970/72-. Annual.

Formerly titled *Reference Book Review Index*. Each volume cites approximately 4,500 reviews of 3,500 reference books published in over 260 periodicals. Entries include quotes from the reviews, in addition to full bibliographic citations.

B80. Schwarzkopf, Leroy C. *Government Reference Books: A Biennial Guide to U.S. Government Publications*. Englewood, CO: Libraries Unlimited. 1968-. Biennial.

Comprehensive guide to reference materials published by the U.S. Government in the preceding two years, including atlases, bibliographies, catalogs, compendiums, dictionaries, guides, handbooks, indexes, and other items. The 11th edition describes over 1,200 reference documents. Subject, author, and title index.

B81. Sheehy, Eugene P., ed. *Guide to Reference Books*. 10th ed. Chicago: American Library Association, 1986.
Guide to Reference Books Covering Materials from 1985-1990, Supplement to the 10th ed. Edited by Robert Balay. Chicago: American Library Association, 1992.

This classic guide to reference books, commonly known as "Sheehy's Guide," briefly describes library reference tools of all types, in all disciplines and subject areas. Entries are grouped by subject and type of material into broad categories: General Reference Works; Social and Behavioral Sciences; Humanities; History and Area Studies; Science,

Technology and Medicine. Title, subject, and format indexes provide detailed access. Updated between editions by the semi-annual feature, "Selected Reference Books," published in the January and July issues of *College and Research Libraries*.

➤ RESEARCH CENTERS *(See also:* Ch.30)

B82. *Government Research Directory.* Detroit: Gale Research. Annual.

The 7th edition describes over 3,700 research centers operated by or for the federal government. Arranged by agency, with a subject index.

B83. *Research Centers Directory.* Detroit: Gale Research. Annual.

The 17th edition claims to provide "the most comprehensive guide to North American university research centers and independent non-profit research organizations in all fields of endeavor," including behavioral and social sciences, biological, government and public affairs, technology, law, medical science, humanities, and religion. Entries include research activities and educational activities, services, publications, library services, and meetings. Subject/keyword and name index. SEX SUBJECTS COVERED: AIDS, abortion, adolescent parents, adolescent pregnancy, artificial insemination, bioethics, birth control, birth defects, breast feeding, censorship, child abuse, childbirth, child pornography, contraception, divorce, embryo transfer, fertilization in vitro, herpes, homosexuality, human fertility, human reproduction, infertility, lactation, love, marriage, marriage counseling, maternal and infant mortality, maternal and infant welfare, maternity care, men, obstetrics/gynecology, parenthood, pregnancy, population, pornography, premenstrual syndrome, prostitution, sex (biology), sex (psychology), sex instruction, sex role, sexual disorders, sexual harassment, sexual identity (psychology), sterilization (birth control), sudden infant death syndrome, surrogate parents, television and family, toxic shock syndrome, transvestism, urology, and venereal disease. COMPUTER READABLE FORMATS: on-line through DIALOG.

➤ SPECIAL EVENTS

B84. *Chase's Annual Events: Special Days, Weeks and Months.* Chicago: Contemporary Books. Annual.

Subject access to specially designated days, weeks, months, etc. (e.g. Birth

Defects Prevention Month, National Nude Days, Gay and Lesbian History Month, National Condom Week, National Family Sexuality Education Month, World AIDS Day, etc.).

➤ STATISTICS (*See also*: Ch.20)

B85. *American Statistical Index (ASI)*. Bethesda, MD: Congressional Information Service, 1974-. Monthly.

Comprehensive index, with abstracts, to statistical data published by the U.S. Federal Government, including executive, legislative, and judicial departments and agencies; research, administrative and regulatory agencies; and special Congressional and Presidential bodies. Describes statistical monographs and periodicals published annually, periodically, or biennially. Indexed by subject, agency name, report title, and agency report number. SEX SUBJECTS COVERED: AIDS, contraception and family planning, homosexuality, sex crimes, obscenity and pornography, sexual behavior (usually relating to social or health problems such as teenage pregnancy), and vital and health statistics. For example: "Enrollment in sex education by grade level and course content" (1991); "Women abstaining and never having had intercourse and using periodic abstention as birth control" (1990). COMPUTER READABLE FORMATS: on-line from DIALOG, updated monthly. *ASI*, *CRI* (see B91), and *ITS* (see B87), are combined on compact disc as *Statistical Masterfile*.

B86. Evinger, William R., ed. *Federal Statistical Specialists: The Official Directory of Names and Numbers*. Phoenix: Oryx Press. Annual.

B87. *Index to International Statistics*. Bethesda, MD: Congressional Information Service, 1983-. Monthly.

Statistics produced by United Nations agencies and commissions, and international and intergovernmental organizations. COMPUTER READABLE FORMATS: *Statistical Masterfile*, available on compact disc.

B88. *State and Local Statistics Sources 1990-1991: A Subject Guide to Statistical Data on States, Cities and Locales*. Edited by M. Balachandran and S. Balachandran. Detroit: Gale Research, 1990.

A subject index to statistical publications produced by state, local, and national agencies, university research centers, and commercial agencies.

B89.   *Statistics Sources*. Detroit: Gale Research. Annual.

"Best described as a finding guide to statistics," this is "a guide to current sources of factual, quantitative information on more than 20,000 highly specific subjects." The 15th edition includes over 95,000 citations to published and unpublished statistical data from over 2,000 sources. Includes a selected bibliography of key statistical sources (including major statistical compendia and on-line databases), federal statistical telephone contacts, and federal statistical data bases.

B90.   *Statistical Abstracts of the United States*. U.S. Bureau of the Census. Washington: GPO, 1879-. Annual.

An annual compendium of U.S. social, political, and economic statistics, "designed to serve as a convenient volume for statistical reference and as a guide to other statistical publications and sources." Most of the data is from government sources, although statistics from private groups, such as the Alan Guttmacher Institute, are also cited. Footnotes and a "Guide to Sources of Statistics" note further resources. SEX SUBJECTS COVERED: unmarried mothers, teenage mothers, cesarean births, legal abortions, contraceptive use, fertility rates, birth rates, and marriage rates by previous marital status and other factors.

B91.   *Statistical Reference Index (SRI)*. Bethesda, MD: Congressional Information Service, 1980-. Monthly.

Similar in format to *ASI* (see B85), SRI indexes statistical publications issued by major U.S. associations and institutions, business organizations, commercial publishers, independent and university affiliated research centers, academic groups, and state, local, and foreign government agencies. Entries include brief annotations. SEX SUBJECTS COVERED: AIDS, contraception, family planning, homosexuality, obscenity and pornography, prostitution, rape, sex discrimination, sex education, sexual behavior, sexual sterilization, sex crimes, sexually transmitted diseases, and teenage pregnancy. For example: "Video cassette adult films released, sales and renter characteristics," "Analysis of the sexual behavior and early pregnancy rates of children of black teenage mothers," "Prostitution: New York State crimes and arrests". Indexes statistics produced by the Alan Guttmacher Institute (see X253). COMPUTER READABLE FORMATS: *Statistical Masterfile* on compact disc.

➤ TELEVISION (*See also*: Ch.28)

B92.   Burrelle's Transcripts: P.O. Box 7, Livingston, NJ 07039. PH: (800)777-8398.

Provides transcripts of news and public affairs programming broadcast on CBS and NBC (e.g. *60 Minutes*, *48 Hours*, *Oprah*, *Geraldo*)—a complete list of transcribed shows is available on request. No index is available, but topical searches will be conducted on request.

B93.   *Index to the Annenberg Television Script Archives*. Edited by Sharon Black and Elizabeth Sue Moersh. Television Script Archives, Annenberg School of Communication, University of Pennsylvania. Phoenix: Oryx Press, 1990.

An index to the "television fiction" scripts—situation comedies, dramas, soap operas, made-for-TV movies, etc.—housed in the Annenberg School of Communication's Television Script Archives. In 1990, the archive held over 27,000 scripts, mostly of prime time programming broadcast since 1976 on ABC, CBS, NBC, and FOX. Over 1,500 new scripts are received each television season. The *Annenberg TSAR Database*, a continually updated on-line catalog of the collection, is available for free in-house use, and custom searches will be conducted for a fee. Each record indicates the major themes addressed in the script using terms from the *Thesaurus of Subject Headings for Television: A Vocabulary for Indexing Script Collections* (Phoenix: Oryx Press, 1990). SEX SUBJECTS COVERED: the thesaurus includes the subject headings AIDS, abortion, attitudes towards sex, birth control, cohabitation, extramarital relations, family planning, homosexuality, illegitimacy, incest, marriage—alternative forms (including open, homosexual, polygamous, etc.), pregnancy and childbirth, pornography/erotica, prostitution, romantic/sexual relations, sex education, sexual assault, sexual minorities (transvestites, transsexuals), sexual problems, and sexually transmitted diseases.

B94.   Journal Graphics: 1535 Grant St., Denver, CO 80203. PH: (800)825-5746.

Transcribes public affairs programming broadcast since 1968 on ABC, PBS, FOX and CNN (CBS programming was covered until 1991), including over 120 news, talk shows, news magazines, and public affairs programs (e.g. *ABC News Specials*, *A World of Ideas with Bill Moyers*, *Crossfire*, *Larry King Live*, *Donahue*, *Face to Face with Connie Chung*,

Frontline, Good Morning America, Nightline, Nova, Primetime Live, Sally Jessy Raphael)—a complete list of transcribed shows is available on request. Full text transcripts of programs can be purchased for $3.00-$8.00. Their subject classified *Transcript/Video Index*, published quarterly since 1990, includes a brief description of each broadcast. Two cumulative indexes cover programming aired between 1968-1986 and 1987-1989. Journal Graphics will perform free searches via phone by the show's name, broadcast date, topic addressed, or an individual's or organization's name. SEX SUBJECTS COVERED: in the 1990 index, 13,000 citations are classified under 233 topics, including abortion, adoption, adultery, AIDS, birth control, biotechnology, breast cancer, censorship, child abuse, childbirth, family, divorce, gays/lesbians, infertility, interpersonal relations, love/romance, marriage/couples, parenting, pharmaceutical, pregnancy, pornography, prostitution, rape, sex crimes, sex education, sexual abuse, sexuality, surrogate mothers. COMPUTER READABLE FORMATS: *Transcripts* on-line from Compuserve, updated daily.

B95. ***Television News Index and Abstracts***. Nashville: Vanderbilt University, Vanderbilt Television News Archive, 1968-. Monthly.

An index, with abstracts, to the Vanderbilt Television News Archive's videotape collection, tapes from which are available for rent or purchase. The archives currently hold over 20,000 evening news broadcasts televised since August 1968, and more than 5,000 additional hours of special reports and news related programming. Current newscasts are taped off the air daily. Custom tapes, can be compiled from various broadcasts. For more information contact the Archives: Vanderbilt University, 110 21st Ave., Suite 704, Nashville, TN 37203. PH: (615)322-2927.

➤ TEXT BOOKS (*See also*: Ch.6)

B96. ***El Hi Text Books in Print***. New York: R.R. Bowker. Annual.

Bibliographic citations to K-12 textbooks, professional teaching and development materials, and curriculum. Items are classified by discipline. SEX SUBJECTS COVERED: sex related materials are classified under the headings: *Health and Physical Education–Hygiene, Health and Physical Education–Sex Education, Home Economics–Marriage and Family, Home Economics–Child Care and Development,* and *Science–Biology and Physiology*. COMPUTER READABLE FORMATS: available as a file in *Books in Print* on-line and on compact disc (see B16).

Part II
Terminology

3

THESAURI

Thesauri, lists of authorized terms and subject headings (also known as *controlled vocabulary*), are employed when materials are cataloged or indexed to insure that items on similar subjects are consistently classified under the same heading. Their primary utility to the researcher is to identify terms with which to subject search on-line databases, print indexes, and library catalogs. Thesauri may also suggest research topics and assist in expanding or narrowing one's research focus. Generally, they identify major subject headings and their hierarchical subdivisions, refer users from unauthorized to authorized terms, and provide cross references to broader, narrower, and related concepts. Consult thesauri for proper punctuation (*Marriage–Annulment (Canon Law)* not *Marriage annulment in Canon law*), word order (*Drugs and sex* not *Sex and drugs*), spelling (*Transsexuals* not *Transexuals*), and word choice (*Group sex* not *Orgies*), all of which are especially important in computer assisted searches, as the computer will only call up items associated with the exact character configuration entered as a search term.

Unfortunately, in a cross disciplinary field such as sexuality, there is no single, standard set of classification terms used by all relevant indexing tools and libraries, although the Library of Congress subject headings are the most commonly used in the U.S. The *Cross-Reference Index: A Guide to Search Terms* (New York: R.R. Bowker, 1989) cross references selected subject headings from eight major sources: the *Library of*

HOW TO FIND

• Search library catalogs using the appropriate subject heading followed by the form subdivision *–Thesauri, –Abstracting and indexing,* or *–Terminology*; or use the form descriptor *Subject headings* followed by the subject.

• Consult *American Reference Books Annual* (see B78) for reviews of new titles. Interdisciplinary thesauri are described in the "Cataloguing and Classification" section of the "Library and Information Science" chapter of each annual volume; for other titles, arranged topically, consult the index.

• Contact people who use thesauri professionally—librarians, providers of on-line data bases, publishers of print indexes, and others engaged in information management in your subject area—to determine if existing thesauri have been updated or new titles developed.

• An index's introductory notes (see Ch.12) should specify the classification scheme used to organize materials in the publication and if a thesaurus is available.

• The full library cataloging record for any given work includes the subject heading(s) assigned it at cataloging. As authorized headings may have since been changed (e.g. from *Venereal disease* to *Sexually transmitted diseases*), use these records to identify terms with which to search for works published in a particular time period.

Congress Subject Headings, Sears List of Subject Headings, Readers Guide to Periodical Literature, New York Times Index, PAIS, Thesaurus of ERIC Descriptors, Thesaurus of Psychological Index Terms, and the *Subject Guide to IAC Databases.*

• • • •

Listings: Described below are three thesauri of Library of Congress subject headings and seven specialized thesauri. All were developed or revised since 1972, or are currently employed by a library, data base, or index. Non-sexually specific thesauri used exclusively by a particular index (e.g. *Thesaurus of Psychological Index Terms* and *Thesaurus of ERIC Descriptors*) are noted in the index's description in Ch.12.

➤ LIBRARY OF CONGRESS SUBJECT HEADINGS

C1. *Library of Congress Subject Headings*. 15th ed. 4 vols. Washington: Cataloging Distribution Service, Library of Congress, 1992. 5091 p.

Developed in 1898 for use in the Library of Congress, this constantly updated, alphabetical listing of subject headings and cross references covers all areas of knowledge, and is the subject classification system most frequently used by U.S. libraries. Codes indicate hierarchical relationships between terms (i.e. "BT" for *broad term*, "NT" for *narrow term*, "RT" for *related term*, and "SA" for *see also*), and cross references are provided from unused terms (marked "xx") to authorized headings. Subdivisions indicating types of material, classes of people, geographic location, time period, and other factors can be added to main headings to further refine searches. When an item could be classified under any of several closely related headings, as in a work on sexuality in fiction which might be classified under *Erotic books*, *Erotica*, *Erotic literature*, *Pornography*, *Sex in literature*, or *Literature, Immoral*, the subject heading(s) assigned the work are left to the judgement of the individual cataloger; for comprehensive coverage, check under all relevant terms. Appendix 1 contains an alphabetically arranged list of Library of Congress subject headings relating to sex, reproduction, intimate relationships, and related topics (see also C3). Since 1968, when the catalog of the Library of Congress went on-line, whenever a subject heading has been changed the new term has been automatically substituted for the old wherever it occurs in the catalog. The same is not true in most other libraries—each new edition of *Subject Headings* includes a list of obsolete headings.

C2.   Dickstein, Ruth, Victoria A. Mills, and Ellen J. Waite. ***Women in LC's Terms: A Thesaurus of Library of Congress Subject Headings***. Phoenix: Oryx Press, 1988. 221 p.

"A guide to the Library of Congress (LC) subject headings used for women and topics of relevance to women's lives." Includes: gender specific terms (e.g. *girls*, *motherhood*, *housewife*); terms representing aspects of women's lives or issues of interest to women (e.g. *love*, *marriage*, *equal pay for equal work*); sexual, medical and health terms that deal exclusively or primarily with women (e.g. *abortion, orgasm, oral contraception*) or which, while not women centered, are important to women (e.g. *vasectomy, condoms*); and terms representing groups of people that include women (e.g. *homosexuals, single people, single parents*). In Part I, authorized terms and cross references are arranged alphabetically, in Part II by broad subject area. Most terms relating to sexuality, pregnancy, birth control, and childbirth are grouped in the chapter "Health and Biological Sciences." Concludes with a detailed listing of LC call numbers relating to women.

C3.   Ellynn, Kara S. *Sex in Library of Congress Terms: A Thesaurus of Subject Headings Used to Locate Information About Sex, Reproduction, and Related Topics*. Palo Alto, CA: National Sex Information Network, 1993.

A comprehensive list of Library of Congress subject headings and cross references representing all aspects of human sexuality and reproduction. In Part I, terms are arranged by subject (see Appendix 1 for details); in Part II, alphabetically. We have included the alphabetically arranged portion in Appendix 1 and the complete thesaurus is available for purchase in a spiral bound format from the National Sex Information Network (see X230).

➤ SPECIALIZED THESAURI (*See also*: X217 for sex crimes)

C4.   Brooks, JoAnn, and Helen C. Hofer. *Sexual Nomenclature: A Thesaurus*. Boston: G.K. Hall, 1976. 403 p.

Developed for use in the library of the Institute of Sex Research (now known as the Kinsey Institute for Research in Sex, Gender, and Reproduction, see A4 and X256), this was intended to "represent the beginning of vocabulary standardization in the multi-disciplinary field" of sexuality studies. Containing over 2,000 terms representing all important concepts in the literature of the time, it is currently being updated in conjunction with the development of an on-line catalog of the library's holdings (see G5). The thesaurus not only facilitates access to the Institute's extensive collection, but may also suggest research topics (e.g. *amputees and sex behavior, Judaic attitudes on homosexuality, legal aspects of cross dressing, fantastic coital positions*). Custom bibliographies are available on any topic indicated (see H39).

C5. Capek, Mary Ellen S., ed. *A Women's Thesaurus: An Index of Language Used to Describe and Locate Information By and About Women*. New York: Harper & Row, 1987. 1052 p.

Over 5,000 terms for use when indexing or subject cataloging works related to women. Terms are classified into broad subject categories, with cross references to broader, narrower and related terms. A "use/do not use" listing refers readers to nonsexist terms (e.g. for *adultery* use *extramarital affairs*, for *falsies* use *padding*, for *gestation* use *pregnancy*, for *girl watching* use *street harassment*, for *frigidity* use *nonorgasmic women*). This is not a thesaurus of Library of Congress subject headings (see C2), making it especially useful for searching databases and indexes by document language and keywords.

C6. Michel, Dee A. *Gay Studies Thesaurus*. Los Angeles: Dee A. Michel, 1985.

1,215 descriptors for "indexing and accessing materials of relevance to gay culture, history, politics and psychology." Male oriented. Order from Dee A. Michel: 11070 Mississippi Ave., Los Angeles, CA 90025.

C7. Murdock, George P., et al. *Outline of Cultural Materials*. 5th ed. HRAF Manual Series. New Haven, CT: Human Relations Area Files Press, 1982. 273 p.

This handbook, which "presents a comprehensive subject classification pertaining to all aspects of human behavior and related phenomena," details the classification system used by the Human Relations Area Files Archives (see X96). Not intended exclusively or "even predominantly" for use by anthropologists, it serves all sciences concerned with a broad perspective on human behaviors, including sociology, psychology, cultural anthropology, human biology, geography, and population studies. Cultural and background information is classified under 79 major and 637 minor subdivisions, including those relating to abortion and infanticide, conception, childbirth, difficult and unusual birth, illegitimacy, marriage, menstruation, polygamy, postnatal care, pregnancy, reproduction, sex training, sex, sexuality, sexual stimulation, sexual intercourse, sex restriction, kinship regulations of sex, premarital sexual relations, extramarital sexual relations, homosexuals, sex and marital offenses, and organized vice. Scope notes specify in detail the subjects included under each heading (e.g. *recruiting of prostitution, theories of impregnation and paternity, sex taboos during lactation, reactions to curiosity of children about sex, occurrence of female orgasm, keeping of mistresses, artificial means of augmenting sexual sensation*).

C8.   Population Information Program. *A User's Guide to POPLINE Keywords*. 3d ed. Baltimore, MD: Population Information Program, Center for Communication Programs, Johns Hopkins University, 1991. 195 p.

Employed by the on-line database *POPLINE* (see J49), and the collections of most population libraries (see X167-X171), the terms in this thesaurus can be used to access information in the multi-disciplinary population and family planning fields, including materials on the anthropological, political, medical and socioeconomic aspects of abortion, contraception, child and maternal health, fertility, family planning, infertility, pregnancy and pregnancy prevention, reproductive technologies, sexual behavior, therapeutic techniques, and related concepts. Terms are cross referenced to those from the *Population Multilingual Thesaurus*, used internationally, and the National Library of Medicine's *Medical Subject Headings*. Order from X171.

C9.   Roberts, Gloria A. *The Family Planning Library Manual*. 4th ed. New York: Kathryn Dexter McCormick Library, Planned Parenthood Federation of America, 1982.

Part I discusses establishing a family planning library. Part II delineates the book and vertical file classification schemes used in Planned Parenthood's Katherine Dexter McCormick Library (see A7). Terms are grouped by subject: sexuality and sexual relations, the family, information/education/communication, religious and ethical views, population, family planning, government policies and programs, birth control, and Planned Parenthood Federation of America. Concludes with a glossary of family planning/population terms. Order from A7.

C10.   Speert, Kathryn H., and Samuel M. Wishik. *Fertility Modification Thesaurus; With Focus on Evaluation of Family Planning Programs*. New York: Division of Social and Administrative Sciences, International Institute for the Study of Human Reproduction, Columbia University, 1973. 186 p.

A thesaurus of terms used to classify documents describing the development, implementation, and evaluation of family planning programs worldwide. Representative terms include: *IUD life expectancy, family planning personnel, religion and family planning, repeat abortion seekers, post-conception birth control, contraceptive distribution, high fertility populations, multiple marriages, pregnancy outcomes, pregnancy history analysis, contraception termination rate, births averted.*

4

SUBJECT DICTIONARIES

Subject dictionaries, those focusing on a particular topic or discipline, provide detailed explanations of the meaning and usage of specialized terms and phrases not usually found in general dictionaries (including, in sexology, slang and "obscenities"), as well as common terms uniquely used within a particular field. Computer databases can now be searched using document language as well as controlled vocabulary (see Ch.3 THESAURI), making subject dictionaries important sources of search terms. Some titles are almost encyclopedic, with lengthy entries on prominent practitioners and researchers in the field, important reports and studies, landmark legal cases, medical procedures, theoretical paradigms, etc.

Glossaries are usually more brief than dictionaries and appended to the books or articles in which the terms defined appear; text books (see Ch.6) almost always include them. Dr. John Money's books often include extensive glossaries of sexological terms; see H93 for a complete bibliography of his writings. To locate glossaries of sex slang, see p.60.

• • • •

Listings: Described below are thirteen English-language dictionaries of sex related terminology, plus two of American Sign Language. Excluded are dictionaries intended for children or adolescents, those focusing on the

---

HOW TO FIND

• Search library catalogs using the appropriate subject headings followed by the form subdivision *–Glossaries, vocabularies, etc., –Dictionaries, –Terminology, –Terms and phrases, –Nomenclature, –Language,* or *–Slang.*

• For dictionaries currently in print, consult *Subject Guide to Books in Print* (see B16), where *–dictionaries* is used as a subdivision under many subject headings (e.g. *medicine–dictionaries, homosexuality–dictionaries*). For older titles, consult the resources listed under "How to Find" Books, p.228.

• See *American Reference Books Annual* (see B78) for reviews of new dictionaries.

---

etymology of sexual terminology, foreign language dictionaries and, with two exceptions, those published prior to 1982.

➤ AIDS *(See also*: B3)

D1.   Huber, Jeffrey T. *Dictionary of AIDS Related Terminology*. New York: Neal-Schuman Publishers, 1992. 175 p.

Provides definitions of approximately 1,100 words, names, and phrases relating to AIDS and HIV, including abbreviations and acronyms; historical terms such as *gay-related immune deficiency* and *HTLV III*; key names such as *Gallo* and *Sonnabend*; medical terminology such as *cryptosporidiosis* and *toxoplasmosis*; and AIDS-specific sources of information such as the *AIDS Knowledge Base, AIDSLINE*, and the *National AIDS Information Clearinghouse*. (Information provided by publisher.)

➤ GENERAL WORKS

D2.   Carrera, Michael A. *The Language of Sex: An A-to-Z Guide*. New York: Facts on File, 1992. 224 p.

A basic sex dictionary, written for the general public, comprised of hundreds of entries defining technical and commonplace terms relating to contemporary sexuality. Emphasis is on health and medical information with entries covering medical conditions and diseases, sexual practices, body organs and processes, sexually transmitted diseases, birth control procedures, "and much more." Includes a bibliography. (Information provided by publisher.)

D3.   Francoeur, Robert T., Timothy Perper, and Norman A. Scherzer, eds. *A Descriptive Dictionary and Atlas of Sexology*. Westport, CT: Greenwood Press, 1991. 733 p.

This dictionary is intended to provide a standard basis of communication among all professionals working in the multi-disciplinary, multi-professional field of "sexology," including "philosophers, religious thinkers, Marxists, biologists, anatomists, artists, politicians, economists, explorers, social workers, entomologists, historians, psychiatrists, psychologists, anthropologists, sociologists and poets," among others. Over 6,000 lengthy entries, some including bibliographies, cover sex related terms and phrases, individuals prominent in the field, and titles of important works. The following resources were consulted in compiling the work: other sexuality related dictionaries; dictionaries in the social sciences, medicine, biosciences, and women's studies; and glossaries of sexuality text books. Concludes with five appendices: a glossary of philias, paraphilias, phobias, and sexual anxieties; an index to the biographical sketches in the dictionary; decisions of the U.S. Supreme Court relating to sexual behavior; and an atlas of human sexuality.

D4.   Goldenson, Robert M., and Kenneth N. Ardenson. *The Language of Sex from A to Z*. New York: World Almanac, 1989. 314 p.

Defines over 5,000 sex related terms and phrases, including those drawn from anatomy, physiology, medicine, literature, folklore, anthropology, genetics, religion, sociology, law, and psychology; sexual slang and colloquial expressions; titles of well known reports (e.g. *Kinsey Report on Female Sexuality*); and notable contributors to the sexology field.

D5.   Richter, Alan. *The Language of Sexuality*. Jefferson, NC: McFarland & Co., 1987. 159 p.

An analysis of sexual language rather than strictly a dictionary (although a glossary is included). Discusses the meaning and derivation of slang and standard English words relating to sex, including the language of sex, sexual intercourse, female organs, male organs, caressing, masturbation, anal sex, orgasm, oral sex, anus and buttocks, prostitution, homosexuality, bisexuality, brothels, menstruation, pregnancy, lust, erection, and sex aids and objects. Concludes with a glossary and a bibliography of the dictionaries and other resources consulted.

► HOMOSEXUALITY *(See also:* F15)

D6.   Dynes, Wayne. *Homolexis: A Historical and Cultural Lexicon of Homosexuality.* New York: Scholarship Committee, Gay Academic Union, 1985. 177 p.

Treats 600 terms and expressions—both popular and scientific, current and historical—pertaining to homosexual behavior (primarily male). Includes a bibliography of international homosexuality dictionaries and glossaries.

D7.   Rodgers, Bruce. *The Queens' Vernacular: A Gay Lexicon.* San Francisco: Straight Arrow Books, 1972. 265 p.

An "admittedly random, passionately gathered and meticulously collated compendium of the current 'slanguage' of a very large group of people who are members (part- or full-time) of the homosexuality community." Each of the over 12,000 dictionary styled entries includes derivations, synonyms, examples of usage, and region and time period when spoken.

► SADOMASOCHISM

D8.   Murray, Thomas E. and Thomas R. Murrell. *Language of Sadomasochism: A Glossary and Linguistic Analysis.* Westport, CT: Greenwood Press, 1989. 197 p.

Begins with an overview of the history of sadomasochistic subcultures and the professional/scholarly study of them. Sadomasochism is defined as occurring "when two adults agree to allow it to occur within certain preset rules and boundaries, and can include both psychological and physical abuse, fetishes and fantasies, and role playing, any or all of which may or may not culminate in sexual orgasm." Following is an 800 item glossary of terms currently in use by sadomasochists (e.g. *electric zapper, enema discipline, dungeon, amputee fetish, dominatrix bitch, wax torture, cat-o-nine-tails, petticoat discipline, penis bondage, hoods, spanking glove*). Terms were drawn from personal ads, publications produced explicitly for members of the S/M subculture, and personal interviews. Each entry notes the part of speech, etymology, definition, and source for the term. How the language of sadomasochism relates to the subculture that uses it, and to English as a whole, is analyzed. Concludes with a bibliography of scholarly and popular works on sadomasochism, including a list of 148 S/M serials (e.g. *Slave of Lust, Dominatrix Domain, 7" Shoes and Boots, Enema Thrills, Flaming Bottoms, Shaved Bondage,* and *Dominated and Diapered*).

➤ SEX IN SIGN LANGUAGE

D9. Minkin, Marlyn, and Laurie Rosen-Ritt. *Signs for Sexuality: A Resource Manual for Deaf and Hard of Hearing Individuals, their Families, and Professionals.* 2nd ed. Seattle: Planned Parenthood of Seattle-King County, 1991.

Contains more than 600 photographs, illustrating 250 signs signifying sexuality related concepts and terms.

D10. Woodward, James. *Signs of Sexual Behavior: An Introduction to Some Sex-Related Vocabulary in American Sign Language.* Silver Spring, MD: TJ Publishers, 1979. 81 p.

Illustrates 131 American Sign Language signs used by the deaf to communicate sex related concepts. An introductory essay discusses language attitudes and sexual signs, problems of data collection and the implications for sociolinguistic and anthropologic research, and the use of sex related signs in education, medicine, and law. Signs described signify body parts (e.g."bouncing breasts," clitoris, anus, penis), sexual excitement (e.g. ejaculation, female lubrication, "horny"), masturbation, oral sex, intercourse and other sex related activities (e.g. rape, mate swapping, bestiality), individuals and relationships (e.g. virgin, gay, incest, promiscuous person), birth control, sexual health and functioning (e.g. vaginal discharge, hot flashes, tampons, impotence), and miscellaneous other concepts (e.g. foreplay, "thinking dirty thoughts," "hickey"). Concludes with a bibliography.

➤ SEXUAL SLANG (*See also*: D2-D5, D7, D8)

D11. Norris, Jim. *Smut: American Sex Slang: Over 4,500 Entries.* Los Olivos, CA: Olive Press Publications, 1993. Forthcoming.

Unable to view. Contact the publisher for information.

HOW TO FIND

• For glossaries of sexual slang and bibliographic references to slang dictionaries, see *Maledicta: The International Journal of Verbal Aggression* (K85; see also p.127 and X129). Among past entries: *Wet Dream* and *Ejaculate*; Coprolites and Urolites; Usage of 121 Dirty Words; Lexicography of *Cock*; Lesbian Language; Genital Pet Names; *Gay, Fairy, Camping; Smegma* in Dictionaries; Gay Ingroup Insults; Sexual Intercourse Euphemisms; Masturbation Terms via Computer; American Condom Names; Slang of Prostitutes; Poetic Copulation Euphemisms; Language of Pedophiles, Flagellators, Transvestites, and Necrophiliacs; Dictionary Definitions of Sodomy, Bestiality, Buggery, and Pederasty.

• Search library catalogs using the subject headings *Obscene words– Dictionaries, Sex–Slang–Dictionaries,* or *Scatology–Dictionaries.*

D12.   Richter, Alan. *Dictionary of Sexual Slang: Words, Phrases, and Idioms from ACDC to Zig-Zig*. New York: John Wiley & Sons, 1993. Forthcoming.

Gives full etymologies, descriptions, and explanations of over 4,000 "words, phrases and quips that at one time or another have had a sexual connotation in the English language," including those used in the U.S., Britain, Australia, South Africa, and Canada. Entries include how, where, and when the terms were used, with illustrative quotations from sources ranging from Shakespeare and William Blake to Robin Williams and Bette Midler. As this volume is forthcoming, the title is subject to change; contact the publisher for more information. (Information provided by publisher.)

➤ TRANSVESTITES / TRANSSEXUALS

The International Foundation for Gender Education (see X292) publishes "Definition of Terms Commonly Used in the TV/TS Community" compiled by Merissa Sherrill Lynn for IFGE's Educational Resources Committee (originally published in issue 51 of *TAPESTRY* [see K162], and now available in reprints).

➤ WOMEN'S SEXUAL AND REPRODUCTIVE HEALTH

D13. Ammer, Christine. *The New A to Z of Women's Health: A Concise Encyclopedia.* New York: Facts on File, 1989. 472 p.

Intended for the general public, this encyclopedic dictionary covers the "insights, lore and treatments of the feminist clinics," as well as medical terms (from obstetrics, gynecology, and general medicine) translated into basic English. An attempt was made to present all sides of controversial questions and issues. Hundreds of entries, ranging in length from a few sentences to several pages, discuss the workings of the endocrine system from puberty through menopause; preventing pregnancy, overcoming infertility, and all aspects of normal and abnormal pregnancy and birth; functioning and malfunctioning of sexually active women; diseases and disorders of the reproductive system (including diagnosis and treatment); and the effects of chronic disease on women's sexuality. Arrangement is alphabetical, with the following subject index: abortion (e.g. *septic abortion, vacuum aspiration*); adolescence (e.g. *precocious puberty, secondary sex characteristics*); birth control and sterilization (e.g. *hysterectomy, cervical mucous method*); breast disease (e.g. *mastectomy*); cancer; chronic disease and disability; diagnostic tests and procedures (e.g. *early pregnancy test, breast self exam*); drugs and medications (e.g. *morning after pills*); heredity and birth defects; hormones; infertility; menopause; menstruation; mental health; nutrition and diet; pregnancy and childbirth; sexuality; and sexually transmitted diseases.

D14. Hughes, Edward C. *Obstetric-Gynecology Terminology, with Section on Neonatology and Glossary of Congenital Anomalies.* American College of Obstetrics and Gynecology Committee on Terminology. Philadelphia: F.A. Davis Company, 1972. 731 p.

Technical medical dictionary covering the anatomy of female generative organs, disease and conditions of generative organs, benign and malignant neoplasty, selected gynecologic topics (including hormones, menopause, sterility, and infertility), and the physiology of reproduction, obstetrics, and neonatology. Each entry includes a one sentence to paragraph length definition. Concludes with a glossary of congenital anomalies.

D15. Kahn, Ada P., and Linda Hughey Holt, M.D. *The A-Z of Women's Sexuality.* New York: Facts on File, 1990. 272 p.

An encyclopedic dictionary intended for the general public. Over 2,000 brief, alphabetically arranged entries discuss terms relating to the function and dysfunction of the male and female reproductive system, the psychology of sex, sexually transmitted diseases, safe sex and AIDS, pregnancy and childbirth, reproductive technologies, gynecological tests, contraceptives, sexual positions, typical and atypical sexual behavior and activities, and sexual function and dysfunction. Concludes with an unannotated bibliography of articles and books.

Part III
Background Sources

5

LITERATURE REVIEWS

Literature reviews synthesize the most significant research and thinking on a subject into a concise summary of the current state of knowledge in the area, usually taking the form of a bibliographic essay identifying major contributors to the literature during a specific time period. They range from the brief "review of the literature" sections found in all scholarly articles, to review articles published in journals—sometimes in special thematic issues (e.g. the "Human Sexuality and the Family Physician" issue of the *Journal of Family Practice Research*), to books with titles such as *The History of Sex*, which provide a comprehensive survey of a given topic. The *Annual Review of Sex Research* (see K128) is the only review journal in the field. *CQ Researcher* (see K43), publishes review articles on a wide range of current affairs/public policy issues, including many sex related topics.

HOW TO FIND

• To identify articles with extensive "review of the literature" sections, see "How to Find" Concealed Bibliographies, p.98—the longer the bibliography the more thorough the review. To find review articles, search periodical indexes for titles combining key subject words with the phrases *literature review, progress in, advances in, review, annual review of, yearbook of,* etc. The on-line or compact disc versions of some indexes (*Psychological Abstracts* for example), allow searches to be limited to a particular type of document, including review articles.

• To find monograph overviews of a topic, consult bibliographies (see Ch.10), or use the techniques indicated under "How to Find" Books, p.228. *Studies in Human Sexuality* (see H38) describes over 500 titles published prior to 1987.

• Government documents often include reviews of controversial affairs/public policy issues. See especially: transcripts of congressional hearings (see B49), court testimony (see B55), and Congressional Research Service reports (see B52).

6

TEXT BOOKS

Introductory human sexuality courses are offered at most universities and colleges, usually through the sociology, psychology, health education, or physical education departments. Although specific subject emphasis and theoretical perspectives vary, texts for such courses typically address the following issues: theoretical perspectives on sexuality, research on sexuality, sexual anatomy and hormones, gender differentiation, gender identity and gender role, sexual behavior and the sexual response cycle, fantasy and arousal, sexual dysfunction and therapy, conception, abortion, pregnancy and birth, contraception, sexual development throughout the life cycle (i.e. childhood to old age), marriage and divorce, sexuality and illness/disability, sexual orientation, prostitution, erotica/pornography, sexually transmitted diseases, sexual assault and incest, and atypical sexual activity. Most include a lengthy bibliography and glossary. Many libraries don't collect textbooks, but they are available through interlibrary loan (mostly from the Library of Congress) or directly from the publisher, to whom they can be returned in saleable condition, if necessary, for a full refund. (See *Books in Print* [B16] for publisher's addresses and phone numbers.)

● ● ● ●

Listings: We have attempted a comprehensive listing of undergraduate,

HOW TO FIND

• Search library catalogs for text books by author and title. The Library of Congress subject heading *Textbooks* is used to classify books about textbooks, not individual textbook titles themselves. As a result, although the Library of Congress receives copies of most textbooks published in the U.S., they are difficult to identify as such.

• Consult *El Hi Text Books in Print* (see B96) for K-12 textbooks. *Books in Print* (see B16) in its on-line and compact disc versions includes a textbook database providing subject, title, and author access to books and non book educational materials for use through the first year of college. In the print version of *Subject Guide to Books in Print* (see B16), text books are intermixed with other formats; scan entries under the headings *sex, sex (biology), sex (psychology)*, and *sex instruction* for titles marked "text ed.," or which indicate an instructor's guide or study guide is available.

• Both the Kinsey Institute (see A4) and SIECUS (see A5) collect human sexuality text books, although neither has a comprehensive collection. SIECUS is planning a textbook review in October 1992.

• For information on forthcoming titles and/or new editions of older works, contact the customer service department of the publisher.

introductory human sexuality text books, published since 1987, and listed in *Books in Print* as of March 1992, with the addition of a few forthcoming titles. Any omissions are unintended. All are listed in RLIN and available for interlibrary loan.

E1.   Allgeier, Elizabeth R., and Albert R. *Sexual Interactions*. 3d ed. Lexington, MA: D.C. Heath, 1991. 816 p.

E2.   Bancroft, John. *Human Sexuality and its Problems*. 2nd ed. New York: Churchill Livingstone, 1989. 748 p.

E3.   Byer, Curtis D., and Louis W. Shainberg. *Dimensions of Human Sexuality*. 3d ed. Dubuque, IA: W.C. Brown Publishers, 1991. 656 p.

E4. Crooks, Robert, and Karla Baur. *Our Sexuality*. 5th ed. Redwood City, CA: Benjamin/Cummings Publishing, 1993. 762 p.

E5. Denney, Nancy. *Human Sexuality*. 2nd ed. St. Louis: Mosby, 1992. 760 p.

E6. Francoeur, Robert T., and Anna K. *Becoming a Sexual Person*. 2nd ed. New York: Macmillan, 1991. 675 p.

E7. Gordon, Sol, and Craig W. Snyder. *Personal Issues in Human Sexuality*. 2nd ed. Boston: Allyn and Bacon, 1989. 384 p.

E8. Greenberg, Jerrold S., et al. *Sexuality: Insights and Issues*. 2nd ed. Dubuque, IA: W.C. Brown Publishers, 1989. 629 p.

E9. Haas, Kurt. *Understanding Sexuality*. 3d ed. St. Louis: Mosby, 1993. 690 p.

E10. Hyde, Janet Shibley. *Understanding Human Sexuality*. 4th ed. New York: McGraw-Hill Publishing, 1990. 732 p.

E11. Katchadourian, Herant A. *Biological Aspects of Human Sexuality*. Rev. ed. Fort Worth, TX: Holt, Rinehart & Winston, 1990. 266 p.

E12. Kelly, Gary F. *Sexuality Today: The Human Perspective*. 3rd ed. Guilford, CT: Dushkin Publishing Group, 1992. 576 p.

E13. Kelley, Kathryn, and Donn Byrne. *Exploring Human Sexuality*. Englewood Cliffs, NJ: Prentice Hall, 1992. 608 p.

E14. King, Bruce M., Cameron J. Camp, and Ann M. Downey. *Human Sexuality Today*. Englewood Cliffs, NJ: Prentice Hall, 1991. 496 p.

E15. Luria, Zella, Susan Friedman, and Mitchel Rose. *Human Sexuality*. New York: John Wiley and Sons, 1987. 636 p.

E16. Masters, William H., Virginia E. Johnson, and Robert C. Kolodny. *Human Sexuality*. 4th ed. New York: Harper Collins, 1992. 748 p.

E17. McKinney, Kathleen, and Susan Sprecher. *Human Sexuality: The Societal and Interpersonal Context*. Norwood, NJ: Ablex Publishing Corp., 1989. 528 p.

E18.   Nass, Gilbert D., and Mary P. Fisher. *Sexuality Today*. Boston: Jones and Bartlett, 1988. 488 p.

E19.   Nass, Gilbert D., Roger W. Libby, and Mary P. Fisher. *Sexual Choices: An Introduction to Human Sexuality*. 2nd ed. Boston: Jones and Bartlett, 1987. 650 p.

E20.   Rathus, Spencer A., et al. *Human Sexuality in a World of Diversity*. Needham Heights, MA: Allyn and Bacon, 1993. Forthcoming.

E21.   Rice, Philip F. *Human Sexuality*. Dubuque, IA: W.C. Brown Publishing, 1989. 624 p.

E22.   Schultz, David A. *Human Sexuality*. 3rd ed. Englewood Cliffs, NJ: Prentice Hall, 1988. 480 p.

E23.   Spurgen, Cole, et al. *Contemporary Human Sexuality*. Dubuque, IA: Kendall/Hunt Publishing, 1987. 272 p.

E24.   Steen, Edwin B., and James H. Price. *Human Sex and Sexuality*. 2nd ed. New York: Dover Publications, 1988. 380 p.

E25.   Strong, Bryan, and Christine DeVault. *Understanding Our Sexuality*. 2nd ed. St. Paul, MN: West Publishing, 1988. 566 p.

E26.   Turner, Jeffrey S., and Laurna Rubinson. *Contemporary Human Sexuality*. Englewood Cliffs, NJ: Prentice Hall, 1993. Forthcoming.

E27.   Wade, Carole, and Sarah Cirese. *Human Sexuality*. 2nd ed. San Diego, CA: Harcourt Brace Jovanovich, 1991. 740 p.

7

ENCYCLOPEDIAS & HANDBOOKS

(*See also*: Ch.4 SUBJECT DICTIONARIES)

Encyclopedias, handbooks, sourcebooks, and other reference works are excellent starting points for research, providing concise background information on an array of topics, definitions of terms, preliminary bibliographies of key works, and in the case of handbooks, quick access to frequently used information. Intended for the general public, popular, encyclopedic like texts (e.g. *The Family Book About Sex*) and topical consumer reference books (e.g. *The Safe Pregnancy Book*) provide easily understood introductions to many topics, especially technical and medical subjects such as gynecology and reproductive technologies.

Much of the reference literature in sexuality is now quite dated. Consult recent text books (see Ch.6) for the most up-to-date, introductory coverage of sex topics, as they are often updated every few years.

• • • •

Listings: The following selection of encyclopedias, professional handbooks, sourcebooks, multi-authored works, and authoritative popular books is by no means a comprehensive bibliography of all such works, but rather is intended to indicate the range of available resources. To identify additional titles, use the techniques described in this chapter and under "How to Find" Books, p.228. Under "General Works" are described

How to Find

• Search library catalogs using the appropriate subject heading followed by the form subdivision *–Atlases, –Handbooks, manuals, etc., –Dictionaries,* or *–Encyclopedias.* For books on scientific, technical, or legal topics, written for the general reader, search public library catalogs using the topical subject heading followed by the form subdivision *–Popular works* (e.g. *Pregnancy–Popular works, Gynecology–Popular works*).

• Consult *American Reference Books Annual* for critical reviews of new encyclopedias and other reference books (see B78). For older titles, consult the *ARBA Guide to Subject Encyclopedias and Dictionaries* (Littleton, CO: Libraries Unlimited, 1986).

• Consult published bibliographies (see Ch.10), especially *Studies in Human Sexuality* (see H38) and others listed under "General Works" in Ch.10.

• Sexuality related articles are often included in subject encyclopedias focusing on a particular discipline (e.g. sociology), profession (e.g. medicine), interdisciplinary field (e.g. women's studies), or topic (e.g. adolescence). *First Step: The Master Index of Subject Encyclopedias* (see B35) indexes the contents of over 430 such titles.

• Non-encyclopedia, multi-authored compilations of articles (e.g. *Rape and Sexual Assault: A Research Handbook, Issues in Reproductive Technology I: An Anthology*) are not classified in library catalogs under a unique form subdivision. Scan the *Subject Guide to Books in Print* (see B16) for relevant sounding titles, or request publisher's catalogs—see especially those of Haworth Press, Garland Publishing, and Greenwood Press.

all titles classified under *Sex–Encyclopedias* in RLIN and published since 1973, along with a selection of general encyclopedic-like works, and a few forthcoming titles. In selecting topical works, we emphasized those published since 1987, when *Studies in Human Sexuality*—describing over 500 titles—was published (see H38).

➤ AIDS (*See also*: B1-B3)

F1. Watstein, Sarah Barbara, and Robert Anthony Laurich, eds. *AIDS and Women: A Sourcebook*. Phoenix: Oryx Press, 1991. 176 p.

Fourteen chapters address issues of women and AIDS. Includes lists of relevant organizations, sources for audiovisual resources, a glossary, and forty pages of statistical tables.

➤ ABORTION (*See also*: F34)

F2. Costa, Marie. *Abortion: A Reference Handbook*. Contemporary World Issues Series. Santa Barbara: ABC-CLIO, 1991. 300 p.

Seeks "to provide access to the available information, as well as the full spectrum of thought on abortion. It is not intended to promulgate any view, except the view that all voices should be heard and listened to. Historical and factual background is presented, along with resources for further exploration into the social, psychological, legal, medical, political, and moral aspects of abortion." Includes a chronology of abortion from the Roman Empire to the present; facts and statistics (including laws and policies worldwide, abortion techniques and complications, public opinion); a directory of organizations; and selected print and non-print resources (bibliographies, articles, books, periodicals, subscriber-based news services, computer databases, and films and videotapes).

F3. Muldoon, Maureen. *The Abortion Debate in the United States and Canada: A Source Book*. Garland Reference Library in Social Science, v.648. New York: Garland Publishing, 1991. 256 p.

Examines the social, legal, religious, ethical, and moral implications of abortion. Each section begins with an extensive overview of the subject, and concludes with an annotated bibliography. Amongst the information included are descriptions of the origin and activities of major advocacy groups, the official positions of major religious denominations, data from public opinion polls and demographic studies, and a chronology of key court decisions. (Information provided by publisher.)

F4.   Tietze, Christopher, and Stanley Henshow. *Induced Abortion: A World Review 1986*. 6th ed. A Population Council Fact Book. New York: Alan Guttmacher Institute, 1986. 143 p.

Provides an overview of international data on induced abortion from public health, demographic, and public policy perspectives. Contact the Guttmacher Institute (see X253) for updates.

➤ DRUGS AND SEX (*See also*: H18)

F5.   Lieberman, M. Laurence. *The Sexual Pharmacy: The Complete Guide to Drugs with Sexual Side Effects*. New York: New American Library, 1988. 320 p.

Covers the effects of over 200 prescription and over-the-counter drugs on sexuality, as reported in the pharmaceutical and medical literature. Although most adversely affect sex-related functioning, sexual desire, contraceptive effectiveness, the menstrual cycle, fertility, or rates of spontaneous abortion, the work also includes those with aphrodisiacal effects. Each entry includes the drug's brand name, drug category, mode of action, approved uses, unlabeled uses, general side effects, sexual side effects as described by the manufacturer, sexual side effects according to the medical literature, dosage, remedies for sex related effects, and reversal of sex related effects.

F6.   Stark, Raymond. *The Book of Aphrodisiacs*. New York: Stein and Day, 1981. 195 p.

The author, a naturopathic physician, "covers close to six hundred aphrodisiac and potency items [substances which heighten the sexual sense within 1-2 hours], sterility and spermatorrhea aids, abortifacients, contraceptives, aids to barrenness, emmenagogues, anaphrodisiacs (which help curb sexual desires), medication for menorrhagia, and some postparturients." Entries, arranged alphabetically by botanical name, include the substance's preparation, use, and sexual effects (positive and negative). Concludes with a glossary, a brief bibliography, and an international directory of firms from which herbs and some of the other substances can be purchased.

➤ GENERAL WORKS (*See also*: Ch.6; D3, D13, D15)

Frayser and Whitby's *Studies in Human Sexuality* (see H38), while not an encyclopedia, consists of lengthy, critical annotations of over 500 books, arranged according to a detailed conceptual scheme which encompasses all major topics in the area.

F7. Bullough, L. Vern, Bonnie Bullough, and Alice Stein, eds. *Human Sexuality: An Encyclopedia.* New York: Garland Publishing, 1993. Forthcoming. 1000 p.

According to the publisher's catalog, the *Encyclopedia* "summarizes the state of knowledge on all aspects of human sexual behavior. Organization is by topical subject matter with cross-references to other articles and a thorough index. Each article is followed by a bibliography of essential primary sources for researching subjects in depth." Articles are written by nearly 100 experts, including psychologists, psychiatrists, physicians, sociologists, anthropologists, physiologists, biologists, historians, nurses, therapists, educators, philosophers, clergy, language and literature specialists, lawyers, and other professionals. An extensive range of subjects is addressed, including abstinence, adolescent sexuality, AIDS, birth control and contraception, brothels, child abuse and sexual exploitation, Christianity and sex education in sex, ethical issues in sex, exogamy, flagellation, frottage, G spot and female pleasure, infant sexuality, Judaism and sexuality, laws and sex, love maps, misoscopia, Nazis, obscenity, papacy and sex, polyandry, quackery and sex, rape, sex reform movements, substance abuse and sex, telegony, unconventional sex, voyeurism, witchcraft, yoga, and zoophilia, among others. (Information provided by publisher.)

F8. Camphausen, Rufus C. *Encyclopedia of Erotic Wisdom: A Reference Guide to the Symbolism, Techniques, Rituals, Sacred Texts, Psychology, Anatomy and History of Sexuality.* Rochester, VT: Inner Traditions International, 1991. 256 p.

"Designed and prepared to provide easy, meaningful, and intelligent access to a variety of lesser known facts concerning eros and sexuality," including medical, psychological, historical, and anthropological esoterica, ranging from the ancient erotic rituals and beliefs of the East, to the up-to-date scientific knowledge of the West. The author has excluded topics he regards as "well known and often written about matters," such as Freudian theory, AIDS, hygiene, fetishes, and homosexuality. The alphabetically arranged entries range from a few paragraphs to several pages in length, and 15 appendixes serve as subject indexes: religious groups, sects and schools; woman as goddess, demoness and cultural heroine; man as god, demon and cultural hero; aphrodisiacs; festivals, rituals, and customs; ritual promiscuity and sacred prostitutes; erotic symbology in native art and language; techniques, exercises, and positions (including those concerned with retention of sperm); body, brains, and genitals; "fountain of love"—human biochemical/sexual fluids and secretions; erotic fields of energy; primary literature; sacred locations; sacred and/or erotic numbers and numerology. Concludes with a nine page unannotated bibliography of secondary sources.

F9.   Ellis, Albert, and Albert Abarbanel, eds. *The Encyclopedia of Sex Behavior*. 2nd ed. New York: Jason Aronson, 1973. 1072 p.

Designed "so that its coverage would be comprehensive, authoritative, inclusive of a wide ranging viewpoint, and truly international. In addition to its extensive and intensive treatment of the major aspects of the biology, physiology, and anatomy of sex, it also covers the major facets of the emotional, psychological, sociological, legal, anthropological, geographical, and historical aspects of sexuality, including the related fields of love, marriage and the family." Includes approximately 100 articles, each written by an expert in their field. Attitudes and terminology are dated in some cases, as in the chapter "Negro, Sex life of the African and American."

F10.   Geer, James H., and William T. O'Donohue, eds. *Theories of Human Sexuality*. New York: Plenum Press, 1987. 428 p.

"Represents an attempt to exhibit some of the diverse questions, methods of inquiry, and knowledge claims concerning human sexuality." Fourteen major scholarly approaches to the human sexuality field are presented, selected because they "seem to have the greatest impact on the field of human sexuality or because [they] have been, in recent times, areas of great activity and growth": philosophical, theological, historical, feminist, political, evolutionary, phenomenological, developmental, anthropological, sociological, sociocultural, psychoanalytic, learning, cognitive, sexual scripts, and physiological. Each article is written by a leading proponent of the approach and provides an overview of the theoretical perspective as it relates to sexuality, including its assumptions and the primary research issues it addresses. Each concludes with a bibliography.

F11. Haeberle, Erwin J. *The Sex Atlas*. New Popular Reference Edition. New York: Continuum, 1982. 538 p.

F12. Love, Brenda. *The Encyclopedia of Unusual Sex Practices*. Fort Lee, NJ: Barricade Books, 1992. 352 p.

Seven hundred entries and 150 illustrations provide non-judgmental coverage of the "norms of sexual activity and its extremes," including the full "panorama of off-beat human sexual experience" (e.g. computer sex, love potions, erotic balls, transvestism, fetishism, Yoni worship, and more). Longer essays and historical surveys cover important contemporary sex issues ranging from birth control to sexual harassment. An advisory board of 15 internationally prominent sexologists was assembled to help ensure the book's accuracy. (Information provided by publisher.)

F13. Reinisch, June M., and Ruth Beasley. *The Kinsey Institute New Report on Sex: What You Must Know to be Sexually Literate*. New York: St. Martin's Press, 1990. 560 p.

Part I reports the results of a 1989 national survey of sexual literacy conducted by the Kinsey Institute for Research in Sex, Gender, and Reproduction (see X256). Part II, arranged in a question/answer format, provides information on all aspects of sex and reproduction: sex and disease, surgery and drugs, sex in parenthood, contraception, personal sexual health, physiology and anatomy, sex health, body image, attraction, love and commitment, the sexual adult, sex with a partner, problems with sexual functioning, puberty, sex and disability, transsexuals, sex and aging, sexuality before birth, and infant and child sexuality. Although intended for a popular audience, it is authoritative, and bibliographic citations include scholarly as well as popular sources. Concludes with an extensive bibliography and a detailed subject index.

F14. Wolman, Benjamin B., and John Money, eds. *Handbook of Human Sexuality*. Englewood Cliffs, NJ: Prentice Hall, 1980. 365 p.

Nineteen chapters, each written by an expert in the field, are grouped into three major sections: (1) the developmental phase of human sexuality (prenatal, birth to two years, childhood, early adolescence, adolescence, marriage, and aging); (2) sex and society (sexuality from an anthropological perspective, sex and power, sex and the law, sex discrimination and pornography); and (3) sexual disorders and their treatment (gender identity and role disorders, psychoanalytic approach to sexual behavior, behavioral approaches to sexual behavior, the treatment methods of Masters and Johnson, the treatment methods of Helen S. Kaplan, and holistic approaches to sex therapy). Each chapter provides an overview of relevant theory and research, and includes a bibliography.

➤ HOMOSEXUALITY (*See also*: D6, D7)

HOW TO FIND

• Most issues of the *Journal of Homosexuality* are devoted to a particular theme (see K83) and include numerous articles on that topic, as well as literature reviews and lengthy bibliographies.

• Garland Publishing (publisher of the *Reference Series in Homosexuality*) and Haworth Press (publisher of the *Haworth Series in Gay and Lesbian Studies*, see L10) distribute free catalogs of their gay and lesbian titles.

F15. Dynes, Wayne R., ed. *Encyclopedia of Homosexuality*. 2 vols. New York: Garland Publishing, 1990. 1484 p.

Over 770 articles, by 84 experts, cover all aspects of male and female homosexuality and bisexuality. Coverage is cross cultural, ranges from pre-literate peoples to the present, and interdisciplinary, encompassing perspectives from literature, the arts, religion, science, law, philosophy, sociology, history, psychology, medicine, and more. Entries, ranging from less than a column to over 14 pages in length, are arranged alphabetically, with a detailed index providing access to over 5,000 subjects and personal names. Each article concludes with a bibliography.

F16. Dynes, Wayne R., and Stephen Donaldson, eds. *Studies in Homosexuality: A 13-Volume Anthology of Scholarly Articles*. 13 vols. New York: Garland Publishing, 1992-.

An anthology of more than 350 important scholarly articles on homosexuality, lesbianism, and general sexuality drawn from a wide range of academic disciplines. Spanning the 20th century, many are rare, out-of-print, or not widely circulated. Each thematic volume begins with an essay presenting the historical context of the topic, an overview of current research, and suggestions for future work in the area. Thirteen volumes are available: *Homosexuality in the Ancient World*; *Ethnographic Studies of Homosexuality*; *Homosexuality and Homosexuals in the Arts*; *History of Homosexuality in Europe and America*; *Homosexual Themes in Literary Studies*; *Homosexuality: Discrimination, Criminology, and the Law*; *Asian Homosexuality*; *Homosexuality and Medicine, Health, and Science*; *Homosexuality and Government, Politics, and Prisons*; *Lesbianism*; *Sociology of Homosexuality*; *Homosexuality and Psychology, Psychiatry, and Counseling*; *Homosexuality and Religion and Philosophy*; and *Sociology of Homosexuality*.

F17. Gough, Cal, and Ellen Greenblatt, eds. *Gay and Lesbian Library Service*. Jefferson, NC: McFarland & Co., 1990. 379 p.

Written primarily by and for librarians, this collection of essays discusses "a number of theoretical and practical issues involved in improving library services and library collections of special interest to gay and lesbian library users . . . While primarily intended for librarians, this book is also a reference tool for students and scholars who want to identify both print and non print materials which focus on gay and lesbian concerns." Most useful for the non-librarian are the many resource guides and bibliographic essays covering gay and lesbian nonfiction, bibliographies, films and videos, music, plays, famous people, children and young adult literature, book publishers, special collections of gay and lesbian materials, professional groups, AIDS bibliographies, and AIDS films and videos. Ellen Greenblatt's "AIDS Information in Libraries" discusses directories, organizations, books, periodicals, audiovisuals, computer databases and bulletin boards, and government documents relating to AIDS.

F18. McWhirter, David P., Stephanie A. Sanders, and June Machover Reinisch, eds. *Homosexuality/Heterosexuality: Concepts of Sexual Orientation*. The Kinsey Institute Series, v.2. New York: Oxford University Press, 1990. 456 p.

Twenty-two papers, by 29 authors, provide a multi-disciplinary overview of "(1) what has been learned from various research perspectives about the nature of sexual orientation and what factors shape or alter orientation; and (2) how different assumptions about the nature of sexual orientation may influence research findings." Papers are grouped by perspective into seven sections: historical/research, conceptual/theoretical, evolutionary, cultural/sociological, relational, identity development, and psycho-biological. Articles are based on papers presented at a Kinsey Institute Conference on Homosexuality held in 1986.

➤ MARRIAGE AND FAMILY

F19.   Di Canio, Margaret. *The Encyclopedia of Marriage, Divorce and the Family.* New York: Facts on File, 1989. 607 p.

More than 500 entries, ranging from a paragraph to several pages in length, cover all aspects of current marriage and family life in North America. Appendixes include organizational resources and a 32 page unannotated bibliography.

➤ PORNOGRAPHY

F20.   Cornog, Martha, ed. *Libraries, Erotica, Pornography.* Phoenix: Oryx Press, 1991. 336 p.

Intended as a multifaceted resource guide on sex in library collections, this book of essays traces the treatment of sexually explicit materials by libraries over the past 25 years. It is largely written by and for librarians and others having professional interest in "writings and other forms of publications that have to do with sexuality, in particular with represen-tations of an explicitly sexual nature, representations of sexual activity and representations that are either intended to create or that reputedly create sexual arousal in those that read or see them." Among the chapters included: "Words, Libraries and Meaning" (on differing definitions of erotica and pornography); "Providing Access to Materials on Sexuality" (on library classification of sex materials); "Erotica Research Collections"; "Homosexuality Research Collections"; and "Libraries and Pornography: Annotated Selective Bibliography."

F21.   Osanka, Franklin Mark, and Sara Lee Johnson. *Sourcebook on Pornography.* Lexington, MA: Lexington Books, 1989. 627 p.

A "reference work for lay and professional people who want to familiarize themselves with different positions and philosophies concerning pornography." Claiming to "provide a directory of all the contemporary issues concerning pornography," it consists of fourteen chapters: (1) Defining Pornography; (2) Images of Pornography; (3) The Nature of the Pornography Industry; (4) Pornography's Victims and Perpetrators;

(5) Scientific Research Studies on Pornography's Influence on Behavior; (6) The Morality Perspective; (7) The Feminist Perspective; (8) Private Enterprise Interests and the Civil Libertarian Perspective; (9) Obscenity Law: Its Prosecution and Defense; (10) The Civil Rights Anti Pornography Law; (11) Other Ways of Regulating Pornography Through Law; (12) Model Pornography Law; (13) The National Studies; and (14) Child Pornography. Concludes with a 95-page unannotated bibliography (see H69).

➤ REPRODUCTION *(See also*: D13, D15)

F22. Guttmacher, Alan. *Pregnancy, Birth and Family Planning: The Definitive Work*. Revised by Irwin H. Kaiser. New York: New American Library, 1986. 596 p.

Authoritative guide to conception, fetal development, pregnancy, labor and birth, family planning, infertility treatment, and abortion. Intended for the general public, it is written by a physician in non-technical language.

F23. Hatcher, Robert A., et al. *Contraceptive Technology 1990-1992: With Two Special Sections on AIDS and Condoms*. 15th ed. New York: Irvington Publishers, 1990. 621 p.

Written for the health professional, this biannual volume reports on the latest developments in contraceptive technology (e.g. new methods, estimates of contraceptive effectiveness), as well as practical, up-to-date, scientific information on family planning, reproductive health care, HIV/AIDS testing and counseling, abortion, sterilization, infertility, menstruation and menopause, human sexuality and sexual functioning, and adolescent pregnancy.

F24. Rothman, Babara Katz. *Encyclopedia of Childbearing: Critical Perspectives*. Phoenix: Oryx Press, 1992. 464 p.

Essays on all aspects of childbirth and related topics, written by leading authorities in various disciplines. (Unable to view.)

➤ SEX ANATOMY *(See also*: D3, D13-D15, F51)

F25. Dickinson, Robert L. *Atlas of Human Sex Anatomy*. Melbourne, FL: Krieger Publishing, 1970 (reprint of 1949 edition). 382 p.

➤ SEX EDUCATION (*See also*: H83)

SIECUS (see Z225) publishes numerous sex education related reports, fact sheets, and policy statements, including *Guidelines for Comprehensive Sexuality Education, K-12*, the first national consensus about what should be taught within a comprehensive sexuality program. Two comprehensive, nationwide surveys, *Unfinished Business: A SIECUS Assessment of State Sexuality Education Programs* and *Future Directions: HIV/AIDS Education in the Nation's Schools*, assess the content, scope, and approach of states' curricula and guidelines within this model framework. *Future Directions* assesses what is being taught and what should be taught to students about HIV/AIDS using an in-depth content analysis of 34 guidelines/curricula being used around the country. They also publish a free fact sheet, *The Far-Right and Fear-Based Abstinence-Only Programs*, listing the major Far-Right organizations opposing comprehensive sexuality education, including information about the leaders and major tactics of each, as well as information about their views on sexuality education. Other titles are available; contact the publications department for a free catalog (see A5).

F26.   Kirby, Douglas, et al. *Sexuality Education*. 5 vols. Developed at Mathtech Inc. Santa Cruz, CA: Network Publications, 1984.

According to RLIN cataloging records, this five volume "Encyclopedia of Sexuality Education" makes up a final report to the U.S. Department of Health and Human Service's Center for Health Promotion and Education. It consists of 5 volumes: v.1 *An Evaluation of Programs and Their Effects*; v.2 *A Guide to Developing and Implementing Programs*; v.3 *A Curriculum for Adolescents*; v.4 *A Curriculum for Parent/Child Programs*; v.5 *A Handbook for the Evaluation of Programs*; v.6 *An Annotated Guide to Resource Materials*. Available through interlibrary loan, or contact Network Publications (see L20) or ETR (see X219) for more details. Douglas Kirby has written numerous other review articles on sex education—search *Psychological Abstracts* (see J52) and *ERIC* (see J27) for titles.

➤ SEX AND THE LAW

SIECUS (see X225) compiles an annual "Report Card on the States' Sexual Rights in America." The 1992 report (see *SIECUS Reports* v.20, no.3; see K119) discusses and grades state laws relating to sex education, HIV/AIDS education, abortion, sexual orientation, sexual behavior, and obscenity. It includes a state-by-state analysis of legislation promoting and/or restricting sexual rights.

F27. Friedman, Scott E. *Sex Law: A Legal Sourcebook on Critical Sexual Issues for the Non-Lawyer.* Jefferson, NC: McFarland & Co., 1990. 175 p.

Intended to be an "understandable resource guide for lawyers and non-lawyers alike, through what has become a complicated maze of laws governing individual sexual rights and responsibilities in the United States." Surveys federal and state laws relating to AIDS; reproduction (including abortion, surrogate motherhood, artificial insemination, contraception, sterilization, and rights of unborn); wrongful transmission of sexual disease; sexual orientation discrimination (including gay rights, right to marry, homosexuality as fault in divorce, child custody, criminal laws affecting gays and lesbians, and employment discrimination); sex based employment discrimination; and sexual harassment.

F28. Gage, William E., ed. *Sex Code of California: A Compendium of Laws and Regulations.* 3rd ed. Sacramento: Planned Parenthood Affiliates of California, 1981. 222 p.

Although limited in scope to the California legal code, this volume is useful in elucidating areas of sexuality which are regulated by laws or other governmental regulations, including contraception, sterilization, artificial insemination, abortion, sex education, venereal disease, paramedical personnel, adultery, prostitution, obscenity, nudity, bigamy, abduction, seduction, incest, rape, child molestation, oral sex, anal sex, bestiality, sex offenders, marriage, dissolution, annulment, and illegitimacy. The legal definition of each concept is presented, and relevant laws and regulations are cited. Concludes with a bibliography and glossary. A new edition is planned for 1993.

F29. Leonard, Arthur S., ed. *Sexuality and the Law: An Encyclopedia of Major Legal Cases.* New York: Garland Publishing, 1993. Forthcoming. 600 p.

Written for the lay person, this handbook discusses the most significant U.S. court decisions relating to sexuality, sexual identity, and sexual behavior. Most are decisions of the United States Supreme Court or the highest appellate state courts, but intermediate appellate and trial court opinions are also included. The cases examined deal with criminal and civil laws regulating sexual and reproductive decision-making and conduct, discrimination on the basis of sexual orientation or lifestyle, pornography, and domestic relations. They explore such topics as gays as adoptive parents, bookstore sex, individuals' reproductive freedom, definitions of unnatural sexual conduct, state sterilization of criminals, public displays of sexuality, gays as security risks, and other topics. Entries explain scientific and legal terms, evaluate the importance of each case in developing a particular area of law, and cite references for further reading and research. (Information provided by publisher.)

➤ SEX AND RELIGION

F30.   Melton, J. Gordon. *The Churches Speak On: . . .* Institute for the Study of American Religions. Detroit: Gale Research, 1989-.

Each volume in this quarterly monograph series addresses a particular contemporary issue, bringing together relevant official pronouncements issued by North American religious bodies with 10,000 or more members, as well as by smaller religious groups and secular organizations known to have special interest in the topic. Past volumes have addressed *Abortion* (1989), *AIDS* (1989), *Pornography* (1990), *Homosexuality* (1990), and *Sex and Family Life* (1991), among other topics. In addition to the formal statements, which are reproduced in their entirety, each volume includes an historical overview of the topic, background notes on the issuing organization and the circumstances under which each statement was made, and a bibliography of sources for further reading. Documents are arranged by religious family: the Roman Catholic Church, Protestant and Eastern Orthodox Churches, Jewish groups, and secular organizations and other religious bodies. See also X249.

➤ SEX THERAPY *(See also: L21)*

F31.   Leiblum, Sandra R., and Raymond C. Rosen. *Principles and Practice of Sex Therapy: Update for the 1990's*. 2nd ed. New York: Guilford Press, 1989. 413 p.

A compilation of 14 essays, by 17 authors, discussing recent theories and research on the evaluation and treatment of sexual problems. Covers desire disorders, female sexual disorders, male sexual disorders, and therapeutic issues of special populations (lesbians, gay men and bisexuals, the sexually abused, the chronically ill, the aged, and those engaging in atypical sexual behavior). Each article concludes with a lengthy unannotated bibliography. (See also: L21.)

➤ SEXUAL MEDICINE *(See also: D13, D15)*

F32.   DeMoya, Armando, et al. *Sex and Health: A Practical Guide to Sexual Medicine.* New York: Stein and Day, 1982. 369 p.

"This book brings you practical information drawn from the new multi-disciplinary branch of health care called sexual medicine . . . [dealing] with how sexual activities can affect physical health and how medical conditions can influence sexual functioning." Entries reflect research in urology, gynecology, pharmacology, endocrinology, psychiatry, and other medical specialties. Ranging from a paragraph to several pages in length, the 170 alphabetically arranged entries cover sexual anatomy, physiology and functioning; sex related conditions, concerns, and procedures; the effects of medications on sexuality; the health consequences of particular sexual activities; sexually transmitted diseases; health risks of sex related products (e.g. penis and breast enlargers etc.); and other topics. As indication of the broad range of coverage, the following are among the topics addressed: yeast infections, foreplay, hymen, diaphragms, vibrators, exhibitionism, amniocentesis, breast sagging, vaginal stretching, incest, pubic hair removal, scabies, syphilis, and tubal sterilization.

F33.   Lief, Harold I. *Medical Aspects of Human Sexuality: 750 Questions Answered by 500 Authorities.* Baltimore: Williams and Wilkins, 1975. 330 p.

"Originally published as part of the 'Questions and Answers' section in *Medical Aspects of Human Sexuality* [see K155] during 1969-1974."

➤ WOMEN'S SEXUAL AND REPRODUCTIVE HEALTH *(See also: D13-D15)*

F34.   The Boston Women's Health Collective. *The New Our Bodies Ourselves: Updated and Expanded for the 90's.* New York: Simon and Schuster, 1992. 751 p.

An expanded and updated version of the book that has been called "the most important work to come out of the women's movement." Chapters include, among others, "Relationships and Sexuality" (relationships with men, lesbian relationships, sex), "Controlling our Fertility" (anatomy and physiology of sex and reproduction, birth control, sexually transmitted diseases, AIDS/HIV infection and women, abortion, new reproductive technologies), and "Childbearing" (pregnancy, childbirth, postpartum, infertility, pregnancy loss). It also covers a wide range of women's health issues (breast cancer, hysterectomy, etc.). Extensive resource sections in each chapter list relevant readings (books, periodicals, and articles, both technical and popular), audiovisual materials, and organizations. For information on topics of special relevance to older women, see *Ourselves Growing Older: Women Aging with Knowledge and Power* (New York: Simon and Schuster, 1989). See also X298.

Part IV
Accessing Tools

8

LIBRARY CATALOGS

Catalogs provide subject, author, and title access to the holdings of a particular library or consortium of libraries. In addition to bibliographic information (i.e. author, title, series title, publisher, and publication date), complete cataloging records usually note the following: the work's contents (e.g. language, illustrations, presence and length of bibliographies and indexes, the authors and titles of the individual articles in multi-author works); its physical characteristics (e.g. number of pages, binding type, size); publishing history; subject headings assigned the work when cataloged; and in the case of journals, where the title is indexed. As most library catalogs are now in the form of computer readable databases, one can obtain bibliographic access to library collections worldwide via nonprofit computer networks such as Internet, or by subscribing to commercial database vendors such as DIALOG (see Ch.11). To identify materials collected by an institution prior to the introduction of on-line cataloging, consult the library's old card catalogs (or reproductions of them published in book form).

To conduct the most comprehensive review of the monograph literature, search the Library of Congress's catalogs (see G1, G2), which serve as our National Bibliography, or an on-line system such as RLIN (see G4) or OCLC (see G3) which electronically merges the catalogs of many libraries into a single database. For terms to use when searching library catalogs, see Ch.3 THESAURI.

HOW TO FIND

• For older materials, consult print catalogs issued by the library or by a commercial publisher such as G.K. Hall, who has published the catalogs of over 400 institutions, including the Kinsey Institute (see G5, G6) and the Population Council Library (see X170). To locate the catalog of a particular library, search RLIN (G4) or OCLC (G3) using as a search term the name of the library followed by —*Library catalogs*; or consult Sheehy's *Guide to Reference Books* (see B81).

• On-line catalogs available through commercial database vendors are listed in the subject index of the *Directory of On-line Databases* under the heading "Library Holdings" (see B29). For those available through the Internet network, consult *Internet-Accessible Library Catalogs and Databases* (B32), *Dial In: An Annual Guide to Library Online Public Access Catalogs* (Westport, CT: Meckler), or one of the Internet users guides noted on p.148. The Dartmouth College Library, among others, maintains an on-line index to Internet accessible catalogs. To connect, telnet lib.dartmouth.edu; for information, send e-mail to public-admin@dartmouth.edu.

• Library directories note the availability of print and on-line catalogs for each of the collections described (see B60-B63).

Listings: Under "Research Library Catalogs" are described the catalogs of the Library of Congress (see G1, G2), and the two largest multi-library catalogs in the U.S. (see G3, G4). All are accessible on-line through commercial database vendors and are available for free use in some libraries. Under "Sex Library Catalogs" are described the catalogs of the Kinsey Institute, the premier sex research library in the U.S. For catalogs of other collections, contact the institutions described in Ch.30 under "Archives," p.338, "Gay and Lesbian Archives," p.339, or those which have an "L" (for library), or "DB" (for database) code noted under "Services."

► RESEARCH LIBRARY CATALOGS (*See also*: A2, J45; *Catalogue of the Library of the Surgeon General Office, United States Army*, p.121)

For older print catalogs, consult Sheehy's *Guide* (see B81).

G1. *LC MARC.* Washington: Library of Congress, 1968-. Database.

G2. *PREMARC.* Washington: Library of Congress. Database.

Since 1968, the catalog of the Library of Congress has been maintained as an on-line database known as *LCMARC*. It contains over 2.8 million citations, including records for books submitted for copyright but not yet published, and is updated continuously. The on-line database *PREMARC* contains 5.2 million citations to English-language books published prior to 1968 (prior to 1979 for other languages) but is not a complete retrospective catalog of the library's holdings; for older materials, consult the old card catalogs reproduced in book and microfiche form in most research libraries. *PREMARC* and *LCMARC* can both be searched by Library of Congress subject headings (see C1), keywords, title, author, call number, and ISBN or ISSN. Both databases are available for free use at the Library of Congress, and are accessible on-line through DIALOG (see I3) and Internet (see Ch.11). Library of Congress cataloging records are also included in both *OCLC* (see G3) and *RLIN* (see G4).

G3. *OCLC (On-line Computer Library Center).* Dublin, OH: On-line Computer Library Center, Inc. 1971-. Database.

Over 15,362 libraries in 46 countries participate in OCLC to some degree, with over 4,867 libraries contributing cataloging records. Although there is some overlap with RLIN (e.g. the Library of Congress and National Library of Medicine catalog in both), OCLC holds the records of many more institutions, including public libraries and small college libraries, as well as the National Libraries of Australia, Canada, China, and the United Kingdom. It contains over 26 million cataloging records for books, serials, manuscripts, audio records, audiovisual materials, maps, musical scores, and computer readable files. Continuously updated, over 25,000 new records are added each week. Developed as a cataloging tool, up until recently it has not been accessible to the general public. In 1992 OCLC introduced *First Search Catalog*, a menu driven system designed specifically for use by library patrons, which can be searched by subject, author, title, Library of Congress call number, ISSN and ISBN, and other fields.

G4. *RLIN (Research Library Information Network).* Mountain View: Research Libraries Group, 1972-. Database.

This on-line database contains the cataloging records of approximately 200 research libraries worldwide, including the Library of Congress, National

Library of Canada, British National Library, U.S. Government Printing Office, National Library of Medicine, and New York Public Library, as well as many university based libraries (e.g. New York University, University of California). It consists of a number of files, the two most useful to the sex researcher being Books (Bks), containing over 48 million records, and Series (Ser), containing over 3.5 million records to periodicals and monograph series. Other files cover films, maps, sound recording, musical scores, archives, manuscripts, photographs, engineering articles, and computer programs. Searches can be conducted using any combination of title, keywords, author, L.C. call number and subject headings, and ISBN/ISSN. Publication date and language limitations can be specified to further narrow searches. Library of Congress records are updated weekly, others are added continuously as member libraries catalog new materials. RLIN is available for free patron use in some research libraries and in others the librarians will conduct searches for specific items on request. While not accessible through DIALOG or other commercial vendors, Research Libraries Group will sell individuals blocks of 200 RLIN searches for $190. Other types of accounts are also available—contact RLG at (800)537-7546 for information.

➤ SEX LIBRARY CATALOGS (*See also*: A6)

The catalogs of specialized libraries often incorporate features more typical of indexes and directories than library catalogs—citing not only book and serial titles, but the titles of individual journal articles and book chapters, as well as audiovisuals, curriculum, educational programs, and human and institutional resources. The catalog of Planned Parenthood Federation of America's Katherine Dexter McCormick Library (see A7) is included in the on-line database *LINKLine* (see I6). The computer-readable catalog of SIECUS's Mary S. Calderone Library (see A5) is not accessible directly to patrons but library staff will conduct custom searches on request; a search fee is assessed to non-SIECUS members. To locate additional catalogs, see the notes under "Listings," p.90.

—— KINSEY INSTITUTE CATALOGS (*See also*: A4)

Two published catalogs cover the monograph and periodical collection of what was then known as the Institute for Sex Research, through November 1975 (see G6 and G7). The current catalog of the library of The Kinsey Institute for Research in Sex, Gender, and Reproduction is in machine-readable format (see G5). The erotic art and literature collections are cataloged separately, as are films and videos (see p.296). A *Bibliography of 18th c. Holdings* is available for $24.50 (see H39). For their 17th and 18th c. microfilm holdings, see H43.

G5. ***Kinsey Bibliographic Catalog.*** Bloomington, IN: Kinsey Institute for Research in Sex, Gender, and Reproduction. Database.

The library is in the process of converting its machine-readable records of materials received by the library since approximately 1976 to an interactive catalog using NOTIS software. The new database will be accessible internationally via the computer network Internet (see Ch.11). The existing database is not accessible outside the library, but staff will perform custom searches for a fee. Retrospective conversion of the older print catalogs is planned.

G6. Institute for Sex Research Library, Indiana University. *Catalog of the Social and Behavioral Sciences, Monograph Section of the Library of the Institute for Sex Research.* 2 vols. Boston: G.K. Hall, 1975.

G7. Institute for Sex Research Library, Indiana University. *Catalog of Periodical Literature in the Social and Behavioral Sciences Section of the Library of the Institute for Sex Research, Including Supplement to Monographs 1973-1975.* 4 vols. Boston: G.K. Hall, 1976.

G6 contains "historical materials relating to sex behavior, including histories of early sex education, marriage, abortion, contraception, women's rights, sex ethics, religion, sex laws, venereal disease and prostitution, as well as contemporary research in sex behavior and attitudes." It provides author, title, and subject access to 30,000 books cataloged by the library through 1973, by reproducing the 36,500 cataloging cards in use at the time. All languages and time periods are represented, though most titles are in Western languages and bear 19th and 20th century imprints. G7 reproduces 68,800 cataloging cards, providing author, subject, and title access to 14,000 articles (mostly from medical, psychiatric, psychological, sociological, and legal journals) cataloged in the library to November 1975, or identified in an interdisciplinary literature search conducted between October 1973 and November 1975. Records for 200 doctoral dissertations and 1000 monographs cataloged by the library from 1973 to 1975 are also included.

9

LIBRARY CLASSIFICATION SYSTEMS

Although utilizing shelf arrangement for book retrieval is secondary in efficiency to computer catalog searching (see Ch.8), browsing through library stacks can be useful in the early stages of research to stimulate thinking of possible research topics, to indicate how much material is available on any given topic, and to provide a quick overview of previous work in the area. Due to concerns about vandalism and theft, and/or space restrictions, some collections are not shelved in open stacks accessible directly to the public. In these cases, one may be able to simulate browsing the shelves utilizing the on-line catalog—ask the librarian.

Library classification schemes group items in a systemized manner so that books on similar topics are shelved together. As books are classified first by discipline and then by subject, items addressing the same broad subject may be shelved in different areas of the library depending on the disciplinary perspective from which they were written, making subject searching library catalogs the most reliable way of locating all relevant titles (e.g. books on prostitution are shelved in the law, sociology, psychology, and economics sections of the library, but all will be retrieved in a catalog search using *Prostitution* as a subject heading).

Most libraries in the U.S. catalog their collections according to either the Dewey Decimal Classification (DDC) system, used primarily by public and small college libraries, or the more detailed Library of Congress Classification (LCC) system, typically used by academic and research libraries (the National Library of Medicine and the New York Public Library, each with their own classification system, being two major exceptions). As these universal classification systems attempt to cover all areas of knowledge, they don't cover any in great detail, so specialized libraries often develop unique classification systems tailored to their particular collections (e.g. the *Population and Family Planning Classification* used by International Planned Parenthood Federation libraries). For further discussion of the classification of sex materials in libraries, see "Providing Access to Materials on Sexuality" in F20.

➤ DEWEY DECIMAL CLASSIFICATION

A numerical system in which three digit numbers are subdivided with decimal points into increasingly specific topics. The following are the major sex related classification codes, with most general works being classified under 306.7, "Issues pertaining to relations of the sexes." Consult *Dewey Classification and Relative Index* (Albany, NY: Forest Press, 1989) for further details.

155.3	Sex psychology	364.153	Sexual offenses
157.7	Sexual deviation	392.4	Marriage and sex customs
176	Ethics of sex and reproduction	612.6	Reproduction
306.7	Institutions pertaining to relations of the sexes	613.9	Family planning/sex hygiene
		616.69	Sexual disorders (Male)
306.8	Marriage and family	616.858.3	Sexual deviations
363.4	Problems and controversies related to public morals and customs	618.17	Sexual disorders (Female)

➤ LIBRARY OF CONGRESS CLASSIFICATION (*See also*: C1)

An alpha-numerical classification system combining letters, representing broad classes of knowledge (e.g. *BF* Psychology, *K* Law, *L* Education), with numbers representing more specific topics and subtopics. For a summary of the system, consult the *Library of Congress Classification Outline* (Washington, DC: Library of Congress, 1984); to obtain more detailed information, see the notes in Appendix 2. Codes representing sexuality topics are spread throughout the classification system, with most sexuality related nonfiction classified in the HQ's (Sociology) under the euphemistic heading "The Family. Marriage. Women." See Appendix 2 for a list of sex related classification codes.

10

SUBJECT BIBLIOGRAPHIES

Subject bibliographies provide an overview of past work in a particular area and a starting point from which to survey current literature. They may suggest aspects of the topic not previously considered, cite additional bibliographies and other reference works (as well as classic titles in the field), and if well annotated, steer one away from materials that will be of little use.

Computer readable data bases, accessible to the public either on-line or on disc, can be used to generate bibliographies on any topic in seconds (see Ch.11, Ch.12). Although this technology makes previously compiled bibliographies less important than they once were, it does not eliminate their utility entirely. They continue to provide access to materials not in data bases (especially important in historical research as the earliest systems came on-line in the 1960s), as well as guidance in designing effective on-line search strategies: suggesting terms with which to conduct subject searches, identifying key articles for use when searching citation indexes (such as J61), and indicating databases to search by the types of journals (e.g. education, psychology) or other materials (e.g. dissertations, government documents) cited. Three types are discussed below:

"Concealed" Bibliographies. The often extensive bibliographies included as footnotes, end notes, or bibliographies in all scholarly works, including books, journal articles, dissertations, and text books. Although

HOW TO FIND

"CONCEALED BIBLIOGRAPHIES"

• *Bibliographic Index: a cumulative bibliography of bibliographies* (see B12) cites bibliographies of 50 items or more appended to books or articles, but does not index works whose bibliographic citations are imbedded in footnotes or end notes.

• Citation indexes note the bibliographic citations included in a given journal article, eliminating the need to consult the article itself for this information. The computer readable versions of these indexes allow one to easily access not only the bibliography of a particular article, but the bibliographies of the works cited in that bibliography, their bibliographies, and so on (see J34, J56, and J61 for details).

• Library cataloging records usually note if a work includes a bibliography, and if it does, its length.

UNPUBLISHED BIBLIOGRAPHIES

• Obtain bibliographies, in the form of reading lists or syllabi, from college and university faculty (see Ch.29).

• Request catalogs from specialized bookstores and publishers (see Ch.15), as they are essentially bibliographies of recent titles.

• To locate organizations and institutions which compile and/or distribute bibliographies, see the directories cited in Ch.30. Each entry in the *Encyclopedia of Associations*, for example, notes bibliographies under "Publications," and databases for use in custom bibliographic searches, under "Computerized Services." The staff at organizations that don't formally distribute bibliographies may still be able to provide resource referrals.

FREESTANDING BIBLIOGRAPHIES *(See also:* "How to Find" Books, p.228)

• Search the *Subject Guide to Books in Print* (see B16) for monograph bibliographies which are currently in print. *–Bibliography* is used as a subheading under some subjects, for others, listings must be scanned for relevant titles.

• Search library catalogs using the appropriate subject heading followed by the form subdivision *–Bibliography.*

• For bibliographies published as journal articles, search periodical indexes (see Ch.12) for titles which combine key subject words with *bibliography* or *literature review* (e.g. "Gays, Lesbians, and the Media: A Selected Bibliography," in the *Journal of Homosexuality*).

• To identify bibliographies published by government agencies, consult the *Monthly Catalog of U.S. Government Publications* (see B53) and government document indexes (see Ch.17).

• Consult *Bibliographic Index: A Cumulative Bibliography of Bibliographies* (see B12).

• Request catalogs from publishers specializing in bibliographies and other reference books, especially those publishing ongoing book series limited to bibliographies (e.g. Greenwood's *Bibliography and Indexes in Sociology Series*), or regularly including them (e.g. Garland's *Reference Library of Social Science Series*). Both Garland and Greenwood are prolific publishers of specialized bibliographies, including many sex related titles, and will send free catalogs on request. See also the publishers noted under "How to Find" Reference Books, p.16.

• To find older bibliographies, look for "bibliography of bibliographies" sections in published bibliographies (see Ch.10); consult antiquarian bookdealers (see L11, L12); or consult older library catalogs (see notes under "How to Find" Books, p.228).

---

not annotated in the usual sense, cited items are typically discussed in the main body of the work.

Unpublished Bibliographies. Bibliographies compiled, distributed, and regularly updated by organizations of all types, especially information clearinghouses and specialized libraries. Some groups distribute only previously compiled bibliographies on frequently requested topics, while others use in house and/or commercial databases to create custom bibliographies on request. More current than published bibliographies, they also indicate, in the form of organizational staff, a source for further information and updates.

Freestanding Bibliographies. Bibliographies published as books or journal articles. With thousands of new titles published each month and typically a six to eighteen month time lag between manuscript completion and publication date, such bibliographies are outdated before they are even published. However, unlike continuously updated bibliographies such as library catalogs, indexes, and computer data bases, they are selective, usually annotated, and often include an introductory essay on the subject.

● ● ● ●

Listings: We have attempted comprehensive coverage of book length, sex related bibliographies, published in the United States since 1982 and cataloged in RLIN as of March 1992 (see footnote 1 for exceptions). We've also included a few recently published "concealed" bibliographies on topics that would not otherwise be addressed, and two sources for unpublished bibliographies. Older bibliographies are included selectively, being either classics of the sex literature or addressing topics not covered by more recent titles. With a few exceptions, medical and legal bibliographies are excluded, as are government documents, bibliographies published as journal articles, and titles with fewer than 100 citations. The time period covered by each bibliography is noted in brackets at the beginning of the annotation. Each of the titles described under "General Works" addresses a wide range of topics. Also listed under this heading

---

[1] One may come across citations in library catalogs or *Books in Print* for sexually related bibliographies published by ABBE Publishing Association of Washington, D.C. Those published after 1988 were titled with the subject followed by "*index of modern information*" (e.g. *Sex and Intercourse research: Index of Modern Information* [1991], *Sex and Orgasm Research: Index of Modern Information* [1991], *Sex and Transsexualism: Index of Modern Information* [1989]); those published prior to 1988, with the subject followed by a variation on "*medical subject analysis and research bibliography*" (e.g. *Sexual Deviation and Paraphilia: Medical Analysis Index with Research Bibliography* [1987], *Sex Disorders: Medical Subject Analysis and Research Bibliography* [1987]). Each includes an unannotated, alphabetical and title keyword listing of 150-400 citations. Neither selection criteria nor compilation methods are indicated, nor are any topical overviews provided. We were unable to contact ABBE, and although some titles are available through interlibrary loan we have not described them in this volume.

are the unpublished bibliographies available from the Kinsey Institute and SIECUS, both of which compile and distribute regularly updated bibliographies on frequently requested topics, and create custom bibliographies on request (see H39 and H46). Other organizations and institutions which compile or distribute bibliographies are indicated by a "B" code under "Services" in the descriptive listings beginning on p.321.

▶ ABORTION *(See also*: Bioethics; Women's Issues; X7)

H1. Clements, Bonnie L. *Abortion and Family Planning Bibliography*. Troy, NY: Whitston Publishing, 1970-. Annual.

[SCOPE: annual since 1970] A comprehensive, unannotated bibliography of the worldwide English-language literature on abortion, family planning, and related topics. To compile each edition of this annual, a multidisciplinary selection of indexes are searched (55 for the 1989-1990 edition), and citations to all relevant books, monographs, pamphlets, dissertations, and periodical articles are classified by subject. The following subjects were covered in the 1989-1990 edition: abortifacient agents, abortion, abruptio placentae, artificial insemination, birth control, contraception, contraceptive agents, contraceptive devices, contraceptives, family planning, FDA, fertility, fertility agents, fetal tissue research, fetal tissue transplants, hysterectomy, infertility, in-vitro fertilization, National Institutes of Health, Planned Parenthood, pro-choice movement, pro-life movement, right-to-life movement, safe sex, sex education, sexuality, STDs, sterility, sterilization, surrogate mothers, vasectomy, and the World Health Organization. Topics peripheral to abortion (e.g. birth control, sterilization, family planning, fertility) were covered by Whitston's *Population Bibliography* until 1988, when the two titles merged.

H2. Dollen, Charles. *Abortion in Context: A Select Bibliography*. Metuchen, NJ: Scarecrow Press, 1970. 150 p.

[SCOPE: mostly 1967-1969, with some older materials] Unannotated bibliography focusing on the cultural and philosophical aspects of abortion and the social context within which these themes are often studied, including the sexual revolution, birth control pills, anti-abortion movements, and marriage and family. Cites English-language books and articles from magazines, newspapers, and journals (including both religious and academic titles). Arrangement is alphabetical, with subject and title indexes.

H3.   Dove, Charles P. *Abortion, an Historical Perspective: Selected References, 1973-1988.* Washington: Congressional Research Service, Library of Congress, 1988. 53 p.

H4.   Fitzsimmons, Richard, and Joan P. Diana, eds. *Pro Choice-Pro Life: An Annotated Selected Bibliography.* Bibliography and Indexes in Sociology Series, no.20. Westport, CT: Greenwood Press, 1991. 288 p.

[SCOPE: January 1972 to December 1989] Provides "access to literature published in the United States on the 'pro choice/pro life' issue, interrelating abortion, birth control, contraception, and family planning." Describes 1,660 articles, monographs, and non-print items covering the ethical, legal, moral, religious, social, and medical aspects of abortion in the United States in the period directly preceding the Supreme Court *Roe v. Wade* decision of January 22, 1973 and directly following their *Webster v. Reproductive Health Services* decision of July 3, 1989. Items reflect the positions of Pro Choice, Pro Life, and Right to Life movements. Arrangement is alphabetical, with a subject index.

H5.   Muldoon, Maureen. *Abortion: An Annotated Indexed Bibliography.* Studies in Women and Religion, v.3. New York: E. Mellen Press, 1980. 150 p.

H6.   Winter, Eugenia B. *Psychological and Medical Aspects of Induced Abortion: A Selective Annotated Bibliography 1970-1986.* Westport, CT: Greenwood Press, 1988. 162 p.

[SCOPE: 1970 to 1986] Covers elective, voluntary abortion—"the interruption of pregnancy before viability at the request of the woman but not for reasons of impaired maternal health or fetal disease." Describes 500 English-language books, journal articles (ranging from popular magazines to medical texts), and audio/visuals, all of which are "classics in the field or representative of the kinds of writings being published on the subject." Entries are arranged by subject: general texts, abortion clinics, abortion decisions, abortion techniques, counseling, morbidity and mortality, effects on subsequent pregnancy, psychological effects, and psychosocial aspects. Author, title, and subject indexes.

➤ ADOLESCENT SEXUALITY AND PREGNANCY *(See also*: H46, H82, H83, H89)

H7. Center for Early Adolescence. *Early Adolescent Sexuality: Resources for Professionals, Parents, and Young Adolescence.* Carborro, NC: Center for Early Adolescence, 1989. 60 p.

A fully annotated bibliography of approximately 300 books (fiction and nonfiction), videos, journals, curriculum, pamphlets, and organizations addressing issues relating to adolescent sexuality, AIDS, decision making, homosexuality, menstruation, parent/teen communications, puberty, and pregnancy prevention. See also X7.

H8. Creighton-Zollar, Ann. *Adolescent Pregnancy and Parenthood: An Annotated Guide.* Reference Books on Family Issues, v.16. Garland Reference Library of Social Sciences, v.523. New York: Garland Publishing, 1990. 244 p.

[SCOPE: mostly 1970 to 1990] Briefly describes the research studies held in the Data Archives of Adolescent Pregnancy Prevention (see U1), as well as 700 English-language journal articles, book chapters, and books selected from the social and psychological literature. Entries are arranged by broad subject: fertility behavior, reviews of the literature, adolescent sexuality, contraception, sex education, risk factors, pregnancy resolution, social consequences, medical and physiological consequences, adolescent fathers, services, and laws. No cross references or subject index.

H9. Education Department, Planned Parenthood Federation of America. *Adolescent Sexuality: Special Subjects Bibliography.* New York: Planned Parenthood Federation of America. 1987-. Annual.

[SCOPE: annual since 1987] An annotated bibliography of all books and articles about adolescent sexuality and pregnancy cataloged in Planned Parenthood Federation of America's Katherine Dexter McCormick Library (see A7) the previous year. Each issue averages about 30 pages.

➤ AGING AND SEXUALITY *(See also*: H26, H28, H43)

H10. Gemme, Robert, and Jean-Marc Samson, eds. *Gerosex*. Montreal: Robert Gemme, 1988.

[SCOPE: 1944 to 1988] "This is the most extensive bibliography of books and articles on sexuality and aging to have yet been published. It contains listings of French and English articles from hundreds of American, Canadian, French and Australian journals, and includes monographs and dissertations. Rudimentary knowledge of French makes the book easier to use, but it will be helpful for those who read only English. The book is updated periodically by the editors." (Unable to view. Description from SIECUS bibliography, *Sexuality in Middle and Later Life,* see H43.) To order, contact Robert Gemme, Department of Sexology, University of Quebec at Montreal, Case postale 8888, Montreal, H3C 3P8, Canada.

H11.   Wharton, George F. III. *Sexuality and Aging: An Annotated Bibliography.* Metuchen, NJ: Scarecrow Press, 1981. 251 p.

[SCOPE: mostly 1960s to 1970s, plus important older works] Describes 1,106 popular and professional books, book chapters, dissertations, and journal articles on sex and aging, with biological, medical, psychological, sociological, nursing, and mental health perspectives represented. Entries are arranged by topic: general reference works (including 167 bibliographies and resource lists), social and psychological aspects of sex and aging, sexuality and the aging female and male, sexual counseling, sexuality in nursing homes, homosexuality, fertility and reproduction, sexual problems with aging, chemical influences on sexuality and aging, the climacteric and estrogen therapy, sexuality and health, marriage and family, and sex roles. Titles that are "foreign, very dated, hard to obtain, out of print, or of little professional value" are cited under "Unclassified." Author and title indexes.

➤ AIDS *(See also:* B1-B3, H46, H106, J12; *AIDS: A Bibliography of Bibliographies* in F17)

Consult *Books in Print* (see B16) for the most current AIDS bibliographies. A number of regularly updated titles focus on particular aspects of the disease (e.g. the *AIDS Legal Bibliography* published by the Tarlton Law Library, University of Texas, Austin).

H12.   Anderson, John R., Jody L. Kerby, and Christine P. Landry, eds. *AIDS: Abstracts of the Psychological and Behavioral Literature 1983-1991.* 3d ed. Bibliographies in Psychology, no.6. Washington: American Psychology Association, 1991. 312 p.

H13. Clements, Bonnie L. *AIDS Bibliography*. Troy, NY: Whitston Publishing, 1981-. Annual.

[SCOPE: annual since 1981] To compile each annual edition of this comprehensive, unannotated bibliography of the worldwide AIDS literature, a multi-disciplinary selection of indexes, bibliographies, and catalogs are searched for AIDS and HIV related citations, which are then classified by subject into a single volume. Over 35 such sources were searched for the 1989 edition, and it includes citations to gay and lesbian literature, alternative press publications, scholarly and medical literature, and popular magazines and books.

H14. Levine, Paula L., John G. Bruhn, and Norma H. Turner. *The Psycho-social Aspects of AIDS: An Annotated Bibliography*. Contemporary Issues in Health, v.1. New York: Garland Publishing, 1990. 562 p.

[SCOPE: through 1988] Selective bibliography of sociological, educational, and psychological literature on the psychosocial aspects of AIDS. Entries are arranged by subject: history and overview of the epidemic, epidemiological aspects of HIV infection and AIDS, AIDS and society, education and prevention, caring for the AIDS patient, coping with AIDS, and AIDS information and resources. Includes a glossary. Author and title indexes.

▶ ALCOHOL AND DRUGS (*See also*: X42-X44)

H15. Abel, Ernest L. *Drugs and Sex: A Bibliography*. Westport, CT: Greenwood Press, 1983. 129 p.

Contains 1,432 unannotated citations to English-language periodical articles and monographs which address the medical and psychological effects of psychoactive drugs on sex drive, arousal, behavior, functioning, and reproductive and sexual physiology. An introductory essay defines terms, discusses each of the drugs covered (including how they work on the body), and summarizes the findings of the cited research. Entries are classified by type of drug, with a subject index: alcohol, amphetamines, antidepressants, antipsychotics, barbiturates, benzodiazepines, caffeine, cocaine, LSD, marijuana, methaqualone, narcotics, nitrites, phencyclidine (PCP), and tobacco. A final section cites 37 literature reviews. Abel has also compiled *Alcohol and Reproduction: A Bibliography* (1982), *Narcotics and Reproduction: A Bibliography* (1983), *Smoking and*

Reproduction: A Bibliography (1982), and *New Literature on Fetal Alcohol Effects: A Bibliography 1983-1988* (1990), among other titles.

H16.   Berg, Steven L., Dana Finnegan, and Emily McNally. ***NALGAP Annotated Bibliography: Resources on Alcoholism, Substance Abuse and Lesbian/Gay Men.*** Fort Wayne, IN: National Association Lesbian/Gay Alcohol Professionals, 1987. 259 p.

Nine hundred and eleven citations to resources on homosexuality and chemical dependency. Part I contains a comprehensive, briefly annotated bibliography of "everything that has been published and written concerning chemical addiction in the lesbian and gay community," including books, articles, brochures, pamphlets, conference papers, dissertations, theses, manuscripts, and unpublished papers available from NALGAP. Parts II and III contain, respectively, selected bibliographies of the "best and most available books" on lesbian and gay issues (100 items) and alcoholism and substance abuse (111 items). Arrangement is alphabetical, with author, subject, and title indexes. Updates are available from NALGAP (see X46).

H17.   O'Farrell, Timothy J., and Carolyn A. Weyand, with Diane Logan. ***Alcohol and Sexuality: An Annotated Bibliography on Alcohol Use, Alcoholism, and Human Sexual Behavior.*** Phoenix: Oryx Press, 1983. 131 p.

[SCOPE: 1900 to 1982] A "comprehensive reference resource . . . for those involved in research, education, or treatment in the sexuality and alcoholism field." Contains 542 annotated citations to English-language books and journal articles on the effects of alcohol on sexual behaviors and attitudes, with emphasis on medical and psychological literature. Entries are arranged by subject: effects of alcohol use and abuse on sexual functions (including sexual behavior and sex hormones); nature and treatment of sexual problems among alcoholics (including sexual adjustment problems, sex therapy, and sex education); social problems and cultural issues relating to alcohol and sexuality (including sexual deviance and crime, venereal disease, homosexuality, cross cultural/historical reports, alcohol and sexuality in media); and literature reviews and commentary articles. Excludes materials on sex roles, sex differences, and reproduction. Appendixes list sources of sex information, sources of alcohol information, and journals relating to sexuality and alcohol.

H18. Schuster, Carlotta L. *Alcohol and Sexuality*. Sexual Medicine Series, no.7. New York: Praeger Publishing, 1988. 122 p.

A review of the medical, scientific, and psychological literature on the effects of alcohol—and to a lesser degree, marijuana, amphetamines, cocaine, opiates, and sedatives—on sexual response in male and female social drinkers and alcoholics. Each chapter concludes with an unannotated bibliography.

➤ BIOETHICS

H19. *Bibliography of Bioethics*. Center for Bioethics, Georgetown University, Washington, DC. Detroit: Gale Research, 1975-. Annual.

[SCOPE: annual since 1975] Comprehensive, cross-disciplinary coverage of English-language materials addressing bioethical topics. Citations, classified by subject using terms from the *Bioethics Thesaurus*, include journals, newspaper articles, monographs, book chapters, court decisions, bills, and audiovisual materials. Subjects covered vary from year to year, but the following subjects are among those included in every volume: abortion, AIDS, artificial insemination, contraception, embryo transfer, embryos, fetuses, host (surrogate) mothers, human experimentation (including on embryos and fetuses), in-vitro fertilization, involuntary sterilization, personhood, reproduction, reproductive technology, sterilization, prenatal diagnoses, selective abortion, transsexuality, and venereal disease. See also J16, X61.

➤ BISEXUALITY (*See also*: Homosexuality)

H20. Steir, Charles, and Thomas Geller. "A Bibliography on Bisexuality." In *Bisexuality: A Reader and Sourcebook*, edited by Thomas Geller, 150-176. Ojai, CA: Times Change Press, 1990. 186 p.

[SCOPE: 1940s to 1990, with most published since 1960] With 400 unannotated citations to books and journal articles, the authors claim this is "the most exhaustive bibliography on bisexuality and related issues (such as androgyny) to date." Arrangement is alphabetical by author, with no subject access. Articles from gay/lesbian publications, pornographic and erotic publications, and newspapers are excluded. A "Bisexual Catalog" contains a bi-lexicon, a directory of bisexual special interest groups, a directory of lesbian and gay phone lines, a bibliography of periodicals on bisexuality, and a filmography of plays and films with bisexual themes or characters. The bibliography was originally published in *The Journal of Homosexuality* (v.11, nos.1/2), with additional citations added to bring it up-to-date. Contact the author for updates at 3875 Waldo Ave., Bronx, NY 10463.

▶ CHILDBIRTH (*See also*: H79, H107, H109, L16)

H21.   Diulio, Rosemary Cline. *Childbirth: An Annotated Bibliography and Guide*. New York: Garland Publishing, 1986. 203 p.

Intending to "assist expectant parents in selecting books they would like to consult, read at length, or purchase," Diulio critically reviews 174 recently published or recently revised titles. Subjects covered include attachment and bonding, baby/child care and development, babysitters, breast feeding, career and motherhood, cesarean birth, childbirth methods, childbirth options, childbirth resources and references, child rearing, circumcision, crying and sleep problems, legal and technological aspects of conception, emergency birth, emotional and spiritual aspects of pregnancy and birth, psychological aspects of pregnancy and birth, exercise, for fathers, for grandparents, high risk pregnancy, home birth, infant health care, infant massage, infertility, labor and birth, names, nurse-midwifery, prenatal nutrition, infant/child nutrition, postpartum adjustment, pregnancy and childbirth, pregnancy loss, premature birth, references and resource guides, second child, sibling preparation, single parents, toys and games for babies, twins, and women's health issues. Entries are arranged alphabetically, with subject and title indexes.

H22.   Kruckman, Laurence, and Chris Asmann-Finch. *Postpartum Depression: A Research Guide and International Bibliography*. New York: Garland Publishing, 1986. 162 p.

A lengthy introductory essay provides an overview of postpartum depression, including definitions, the influence of biological and social variables, incidence, and the larger social contexts in which it occurs (e.g. the family). Following is an alphabetical listing of "recent and important articles from all disciplines," including sociology, history, psychology, medicine, biology, biochemistry, and anthropology. The most current and/or widely cited items are selectively annotated. Subject and geographic/culture indexes.

➤ CIRCUMCISION / FEMALE GENITAL MUTILATION (*See also*: H64, H109)

H23.   Romberg, Rosemary. *Circumcision: The Painful Dilemma.* South Hadley, MA: Bergin and Garvey, 1985. 454 p.

Written by an author "strongly opposing infant circumcision," this volume discusses the history of circumcision, modern procedures, rationales given for the surgery and the anti-circumcision response to them, and practical aspects of the choice for non-circumcision. A 490 item unannotated bibliography follows the main text.

H24.   Sanderson, Lilian Passmore. *Female Genital Mutilation, Excision and Infibulation: A Bibliography.* London: The Anti-Slavery Society for the Protection of Human Rights, 1986. 72 p.

[SCOPE: 1940s to early 1980s] An unannotated bibliography of books and articles (mostly British), "intended for those working for the eradication of [female genital mutilation] and for students and others seeking greater knowledge and understanding of these customs and of the social pressures associated with them, in the hope that the accumulated knowledge and work of the past will enlighten and assist the activities of social reformers of the present." Entries are classified into three sections: anthropological/ sociological aspects (travelers tales, academic, and popular studies); medical aspects (the medical consequences of ritual mutilation, female genital surgery in the West); and philanthropic and journalistic approaches (arranged chronologically from 1940—when abolition campaigns began in Sudan—to 1979, and covering international philanthropic work, African woman reformers, and international press coverage). No indexes.

➤ DISABILITY AND ILLNESS (*See also*: D9, D10, H10, H11, H46)

H25.   National Information Center for Special Education Materials. *NICSEM Mini-Index to Special Education Materials: Family Life and Sex Education.* Los Angeles: National Information Center for Educational Media, University of Southern California, 1980. 51 p.

[SCOPE: to 1980] "Designed to assist professionals and parents in locating materials useful in teaching handicapped students about sex and family living." Cites both professional and learner use materials (including audiovisuals and pamphlets) on sex education, premarital counseling, marriage, family planning, and child care.

H26. Sha'ked, Ami. *Human Sexuality in Physical and Mental Illnesses and Disabilities: An Annotated Bibliography.* Bloomington, IN: Indiana University Press, 1978. 303 p.

[SCOPE: 1940 to 1977] Annotated citations to the English-language medical, sociological, psychological, and educational literature (including journal articles, books, monographs, and other published material), relating to sexuality and a wide range of physical and mental disabilities, medical conditions, and illnesses. Entries are arranged by illness or disability type: cardiovascular disease, diabetes and other endocrine disorders, renal failure, cancer, obesity, urological illness, gynecologic diseases, neurological disorders, spinal cord injury, brain injury, epilepsy, Parkinson's disease, cerebral palsy, multiple sclerosis, arthritis, low back syndrome, blindness, deafness, alcoholism, drug addiction, psychiatric illness, mental retardation and learning disabilities, and miscellaneous other medical conditions. Additional chapters cover general works on medical sexology, sex and disability, sex and the aged, sex education with the disabled, and a media review.

H27. Sobsey, Dick, Sharmaine Gray, and Don Wells, et al. *Disability, Sexuality and Abuse: An Annotated Bibliography.* Baltimore: Paul H. Brookes Publishing, 1991. 208 p.

Twelve hundred annotated citations to French, German, Italian, Dutch, and English-language research studies, position papers, program descriptions, clinical reports, and media accounts on the sexual abuse of persons with disabilities. Covers sex education, sexual abuse, sexual assault and exploitation, physical and psychological abuse, and developmental disabilities. A wide range of disciplines and perspectives are represented. Entries are arranged alphabetically, with subject and author indexes.

H28. Veterans Administration Hospital, Cleveland, Ohio. *Sex and the Handicapped: A Selected Bibliography 1927-1975.* Washington: Government Printing Office, 1975. 55 p.

[SCOPE: 1927 to 1975] Unannotated bibliography of medical literature relating to sexuality and a wide range of illnesses and disabilities (i.e. multiple sclerosis, urogenital diseases, neurological diseases, mental disorders, amputations, burns, spinal cord injuries, and cystic fibrosis, among many others). No introductory notes.

➤ EROTIC ART

H29. Burt, Eugene C. *Erotic Art: An Annotated Bibliography with Essays*. Boston: G.K. Hall, 1989.

[SCOPE: 1800s to 1988] Briefly describes 2,500 items that have "significantly contributed to an understanding of the history of erotic art," i.e. "art that primarily addresses some aspect(s) of the human sexual experience." Includes books, anthology chapters, periodical articles (from both academic journals and magazines such as *Penthouse*, *Playgirl*, and *Hustler*), dissertations, conference proceedings, and unpublished manuscripts. Entries are arranged by subject: (1) general surveys (erotic art surveys, nudes, fetishes, homo-erotic art, literature, sex devices, iconography and symbolism); (2) general background (sex customs and history, sex and religion, phallicism, erotic art and psychology, pornography and censorship); (3) erotic art worldwide (in the Ancient World, Asia, Africa, Oceania, Native Americas, and Latin America); (4) erotic art in the Western world to the end of the 19th c. (organized by period and by artist), and in the modern world (organized by individual artists and subject: background, art surveys, surrealism, graphics, bookplates, women's art movement, pinups, postcards, comics, kitsch, interior decorating, photography, and cinema). Each chapter begins with a bibliographic essay providing an overview of the literature in the area.

H30. Webbs, Peter. *The Erotic Arts*. Boston: NY Graphic Society, 1975. 514 p.

Includes a 28-page annotated bibliography divided into three sections: General Art (Prehistoric and Primitive, The Oriental World, Western World), Literature (Erotic, Pornography and Related Topics), and the Performing Arts.

➤ EROTIC LITERATURE (*See also*: Pornography; H29, H30, H71, J38)

H31. Deakin, Terence J. *Catalogi Librorum Eroticorum: A Critical Bibliography of Erotic Bibliographies and Book-Catalogues*. London: Cecil & Amelia Woolf, 1964. 28 p.

Describes 78 bibliographies and private catalogs of erotic literature, most citing titles published before or during the 19th c.

HOW TO FIND

• 42 English-language records are included in RLIN (see G4) under the subject heading *Erotic literature–Bibliography.* Many were privately printed and most were compiled prior to 1970. All are available through interlibrary loan. H71 discusses a number of erotic literature bibliographies.

• Consult the catalogs of out-of-print/antiquarian bookdealers specializing in sex and erotica (see L11, L12). In addition to citing older bibliographies, they are in themselves bibliographies of older works (although annotations focus on the condition of each book rather than its contents). Dealers not specializing in erotica may list selected titles in their catalogs under *erotica, curiosa,* or *facetiae.*

• Consult library catalogs. The N.Y. Public Library collects and microfilms a representative selection of contemporary erotic paperbacks, and catalogs them under the heading *erotic literature* (see A2). The Kinsey Institute Library (see A4) has an extensive collection of both classic and contemporary erotic literature. H71 describes the Kinsey collection, as well as a number of other erotica collections.

H32.   Kearney, Patrick J. *The Private Case: An Annotated Bibliography of the Private Case Erotica Collection of the British (Museum) Library.* Introduction by G. Legman. London: J. Landesmans, 1981. 354 p.

➤ FAMILY PLANNING (*See also*: H1, H107)

H33.   Moore, Gloria, and Ronald Moore. *Margaret Sanger and the Birth Control Movement: A Bibliography 1911-1984.* Metuchen, NJ: Scarecrow Press, 1986. 230 p.

[SCOPE: 1911 to 1984] Thirteen hundred annotated citations to books and articles by or about Sanger, or reflecting on her work or influence. Titles published from 1911 to 1967 (the year of Sanger's death) are arranged chronologically by year; those from 1967 to 1984, alphabetically by format (obituaries, major biographies, and reviews). Appendixes list major congressional bills favoring birth control introduced between 1930 and

1936, pro-birth control hearings held in the U.S. Congress between 1931 and 1934, and Margaret Sanger archives and special collections. Subject, author, and "titles by Sanger" indexes.

H34. Strettncr, Allison G., and Anita P. Cowan. *Health Aspects of Family Planning: A Guide to Resources in the United States.* New York: Human Sciences Press, 1982. 247 p.

[SCOPE: 1970s, but some items have since been updated] A selective bibliography of professional and patient education materials intended for those working in reproductive health care. The following subjects are covered: fertility attitudes, family planning, contraceptive research and methods, abortion, infertility, family planning services for adolescents, male involvement in family planning, family planning for mentally and physically handicapped, family planning training manuals, programs and program evaluation, rural family planning, law and public policy, and the history of birth control movements. Section I, arranged by subject, describes primary resources: selected journal review articles, conference and symposium proceedings, handbooks, textbooks and monographs, and other professional and patient education materials. Section II, arranged by format, describes secondary sources: bibliographies and catalogs, periodicals, indexes and abstracting services, directories, thesauri, dictionary and glossary, sources for patient educational materials, producers of print and audiovisual patient educational materials, private organizations, and U.S. government agencies.

➤ GENDER DYSPHORIA

H35. Denny, Dallas. *Gender Dysphoria: A Bibliography.* New York: Garland Publishing, n.d. Forthcoming.

A comprehensive bibliography covering all aspects of gender dysphoria, currently being compiled by the executive director of the American Educational Gender Information Service (AEGIS). A 25-page abridged version, *AEGIS Abbreviated Bibliography of Gender Dysphoria*, is currently available from AEGIS (see X290).

H36. Sullivan, Louis. *Information for the Female to Male Crossdressers and Transsexuals.* 3d ed. Seattle: Ingersoll Gender Center, 1990. 123 p.

Includes a thirty page bibliography.

► GENERAL WORKS (*See also*: F7, F13, G5, G6, J57, J58, M2; *Index Catalogue of the Library of the Surgeon General's Office, U.S. Army*, p.121)

Each of the bibliographies described below covers a wide spectrum of sexuality related topics. The *Subject Guide to Books in Print* (see B16) and *Cumulative Book Index* (see B17), both contain subject classified, unannotated listings of books on all topics.

H37.   Brewer, Joan Scherer, and Rod W. Wright. *Sex Research: Bibliographies from the Institute for Sex Research*. Phoenix: Oryx Press, 1978. 226 p.

[SCOPE: to 1978] A selection of the unannotated bibliographies most frequently requested from the Institute for Sex Research (now known as the Kinsey Institute for Research in Sex, Gender, and Reproduction). The over 4,000 books and articles cited "represent basic works, other bibliographies, and literature reviews," with emphasis on current, readily available, English-language materials, including journal articles, periodical titles, books and book chapters, conference papers, dissertations, cassette tapes, films, and organizational resources. All aspects of sexuality are represented, including sex behavior, sex variation, sexual response and physiology, sex counseling, sex and gender, sex education, sex and society, legal aspects of sexual behavior, eroticism, and sex research, among others. An introductory essay covers historical research sources. Author and subject index. See H39 for updates.

H38.   Frayser, Suzanne G., and Thomas J. Whitby. *Studies in Human Sexuality: A Selected Guide*. Littleton, CO: Libraries Unlimited, 1987. 550 p.

[SCOPE: most published between 1970 and 1987, plus older classics] With 631 lengthy, informative abstracts, arranged according to a detailed conceptual scheme, this is the most comprehensive overview to date of the contemporary monograph literature in the broad field of human sexuality. Included are "popular, technical and scholarly works from a variety of fields, including anthropology, biology, history, law, literature and the arts, medicine, politics, psychology, psychiatry, and sociology as well as available, albeit sparse, reference materials." In selecting titles for inclusion, the authors claim to have sought out the basic writings of pioneers in sexology (e.g. Sigmund Freud, Havelock Ellis, and Alfred Kinsey); the works of the leading figures currently working in the field; books which have had either an important societal impact, or which reflect the major areas and issues of concern today; and books that are informative, well written, well researched, and aesthetically appealing. A variety of perspectives are represented—conservative and liberal, feminist and traditional, secular and religious, scholarly and popular. Includes encyclopedias and dictionaries, terminology, nomenclature, thesauri, handbooks and manuals, sourcebooks and directories, guides and self help books, textbooks, autobiographies, biographies, histories of sex, readers, collections and conference proceedings, surveys and statistical works, research, theoretical overviews and philosophies, and topical works in all subject areas. Codes indicate each book's intended audience: professional (PR), intelligent layperson (IL), popular (PO), young adult (YA), and children (CH). The contents are indicated below, with the number in parentheses indicating the number of books classified in each category. (Due to space constraints, we have classified entries slightly differently then they are arranged in *Studies*.)

REFERENCE WORKS: Encyclopedias and Dictionaries (6); Terminology, Thesauri (3); Handbooks and Manuals (5); Sourcebooks, Directories (6)

THEORETICAL OVERVIEWS. PHILOSOPHY (13)

ORIGINS. EVOLUTION (9)

HISTORICAL WORKS: History of Sex (11); Autobiographies (12); Biographies (11)

READERS. COLLECTIONS (11)

SURVEYS AND STATISTICS (26)

RESEARCH: Background (4); Methodology, Ethics (2)

SEX EDUCATION (7): Textbooks (9); Classic Guides to Love and Sex (7); Contemporary Sex Manuals (13); Materials for Children (5); Materials for Youth (8)

DEVELOPMENTAL ASPECTS: Overview, Sex Differences (10); Life Cycle Stages (8)

ANATOMY. PHYSIOLOGY (9): Sexual Development (2); Sexual Response Cycle (4); Reproductive Cycle (4); Menstruation and Menopause (4); Pregnancy (3); Birth Control (7); Abortion (3); Birth (2); Lactation and Breastfeeding (1); STDs (8); Circumcision, Clitoridectomy (5); Disabilities, Handicaps (4)

PARTNER CHOICE: Attraction, Beauty, Dress (4); Male/Female Relationships (2); Dating, Courtship (2); Associated Feelings—Love (11), Pleasure (2), Jealousy (1); Marital (7); Pre-, Extra-, and Post-marital (8); Homosexual, Lesbian (23); Group (1); Celibate (1)

SEXUAL BEHAVIOR: Fantasy (3); Touching (3); Massage (2); Masturbation (2); Kissing (10), Oragenitalism (3); Genital Intercourse (1), Anal Intercourse (1); Orgasm (7); Sex Aids/Sex Toys (7)

SEXUAL DISORDERS: Psychosexual Disorders (1); Paraphilias (5); Gender Disorders, Transsexualism (8); Psychosexual Dysfunctions (9); Incest (8); Rape (5); Child Sexual Abuse (4)

GENDER ROLES (13): Masculinity/Femininity (5); Male/Female Relationships (6)

SEX IN SOCIAL INSTITUTIONS: Law and Law Enforcement; (5) Politics, Sexism, Feminism (11); Religion, Sexual Ethics (10); Economy, Workplace, Sexual Harassment (4); Marriage and Family (8); Prostitution (19); Sexual politics (1)
CULTURAL EXPRESSIONS: Erotic Arts, Communication (2); Literature (7); Art (22); Photography (16); Media (9); Advertising (4); Pornography, Obscenity, Censorship (16); Quotations, Jokes, Limericks (6); Body Language; Nudism (4)
CROSS-CULTURAL AND AREA STUDIES (11): Ethnographic Studies (7); Asia and Africa (6); Europe (6); Insular Pacific (4); Near East/Middle East (3); North America (3); Latin America (1)
BIBLIOGRAPHIES: Aging (1); Alcohol and Drugs (2); Cinema (1); Birth Control and Contraception (1); Disability (1); Homosexuality (5); Incest (1); Men's Studies (1); Prostitution (1); Rape (2); Sex Education (5); Sex Roles (2); Sexual Abuse (3); Sexuality (4); Women's Studies (3)

H39.   Kinsey Institute Bibliographies: see A4 for address and phone number.

Bibliographies compiled to 1978 by what was then known as the Kinsey Institute for Sex Research were collected in *Sex Research: Bibliographies from the Institute for Sex Research* (see H37). The Information Service of The Kinsey Institute for Research in Sex, Gender, and Reproduction, as it is now known, maintains more than 450 prepared bibliographies and will compile custom bibliographies on request. The following are only a selection of available titles—a complete list is available for $2. The compilation date is noted in parentheses and updates are available on request. A *Bibliography of 18th Century Holdings* is available for $24.50. The bibliographies listed below range in price from $1.00 to $27.00; a free order form, indicating the prices of each, is available on request. See also the Institute's print and computer readable library catalogs (see p.92), as they are essentially unannotated bibliographies.

ATTRACTION/COMMUNICATION
Body Language (12/92)
Flirting (2/83)
Kissing (4/86)
Partner Preference (7/83)
Pheromones (12/92)
Sensory Stimuli (11/87)

COMMERCIAL SEX
Brothels (1/87)
Electronic Sex (4/92)
Prostitution, Early Works-1899
Prostitution, 1900-1959 (2/86)

Prostitution, 1960-1985 (2/86)
Prostitution, 1986-1992 (9/92)

DISABILITY, ILLNESS, AND SURGERY
Alzheimer's Disease (2/92)
Cancer and Sex Behavior (7/86)
Developmentally Disabled & Sexuality (3/92)
Diabetes and Sex Behavior (8/86)
Diseases and Sex Behavior (12/81)
Heart Disease & Sex Behavior (8/86)
Hysterectomy (12/92)
Mental Illness and Sexuality (1/88)

Multiple Sclerosis and Sexuality (3/92)
Physically Disabled (5/88)
Prostate (4/92)

SEXUAL ENHANCEMENTS, DRUGS, AND ALCOHOL
Alcohol and Sex Behavior (5/92)
Aphrodisiacs (12/91)
Drugs and Sex Behavior (9/80)
Nicotine and Sex Behavior (7/86)
Sex Aids (2/84)
Substance Abuse & Lesbians (4/92)
Tantric & Taoist Sex Traditions (9/92)
Tatoos (9/92)

GENDER ISSUES
Dating: Gender Differences (9/92)
Prenatal Determination of Sex (11/85)
Sex Differences (3/92)
Transsexualism (11/83; 6/92)

HOMOSEXUALITY AND BISEXUALITY
Bisexuality (6/92)
Deafness and Homosexuality (2/92)
Homophobia (6/92)
Homosexuality and African-Americans (5/92)
Homosexuality and Youth (5/92)
Homosexuality Etiology (6/88; 12/92)
Homosexuality Twin Studies (4/92)

MARRIAGE/FAMILY/COHABITATION
Children and Adult Nudity (12/91)
Divorce (9/87)
Family Bed (12/87)
Homosexual-Heterosexual Marriages (2/87)
Homosexual Marriage (6/91)
Homosexuals as Parents (11/91)
Intimacy in Long-Term Relationships (6/92)
Marital Sex Behavior (3/87)
Marital Sex Problems (3/87)
Marriage Customs and Laws (11/86)

SEXUAL DYSFUNCTIONS
Erectile Dysfunction (1/91)
Hypersexuality (5/82; 9/91)
Inhibited/Low Sexual Desire (12/92)
Premature Ejaculation (8/87)

PSYCHOSEXUAL DEVELOPMENT
Prenatal Exposure to DES (10/92)
Testosterone: Male Sexual Behavior and Development (8/92)

REPRODUCTION & CONTRACEPTION
Artificial Insemination (4/88)
Condoms (3/92)
Contraception and Sexual Behavior (5/88)
Contraception, Attitudes on (6/88)
Intrauterine Devices (6/88)
Pregnancy and Sex Behavior (4/92)

SEX AND SOCIETY
Abortion, Attitudes on (12/87)
Advertising, Sex in (6/87)
Censorship in Art/Literature (11/87)
Censorship in Cinema (2/88)
Obscenity, Legal Aspects (2/88)

SEX BEHAVIOR
Aging & Sex Behavior (2/88; 10/92)
Anal Sex (12/88)
Sex Fantasy (3/92)
Coital Frequency (12/87)
Coital Techniques (1/88)
Cross-Gender Friendship (12/92)
Extramarital Sex Behavior (5/88)
Group Sex/Swinging (12/92)
Masturbation (5/87; 12/92)
Oral-Genital Sex Behavior (10/92)
Prison Sex Behavior (10/81)
Virginity (6/86)

SEX COUNSELING
Counseling, Heterosexual (11/91)
Counseling, Homosexual (12/91)

Ethical/Legal Aspects of Sex Research
    and Counseling (6/84)
Nude Therapy (4/92)
Surrogate Sex Partners (6/88)
Therapist/Patient Relationship (TBA)

SEX VARIATIONS/PARAPHILIAS
Autoerotic Asphyxiation (10/91)
Coprophilia (1/92)
Fetishism (5/87)
Pedophilia (10/91)
Sadomasochism (3/81; 2/92 Update)
Transvestism (1/92)
Voyeurism (9/88)

SEXUAL AGGRESSION/SEX OFFENSES
Acquaintance Rape (2/92)
Child Sexual Abuse (12/92)
Incest (12/92)
Obscene Phone Calls (1/92)

Rape (7/80)
Sex Offenders (6/84; 5/92)
Sex Offenders: Recidivism (5/91)
Sex Offenders: Treatment (6/92)
Sexual Harassment (2/92)
Romance in the Workplace (2/92)

SEXUAL PHYSIOLOGY
Breasts (6/88)
Female Ejaculation/G-Spot (1/92)
Sexual Response Physiology, ♀ (9/91)
Sexual Response Physiology, ♂ (9/87)

SEXUALLY TRANSMITTED DISEASES
AIDS: Sexual Transmission (TBA)
AIDS: Youth (11/92)
Herpes Genitalis (6/87)
STDs and Sex Behavior (1/88)
STDs, General (5/88)

H40.   Kinsey Institute for Sex Research, Indiana University Staff. *Sex Studies Index 1980*. Boston: G.K. Hall, 1982. 219 p.

Intended to be an annual, this was the only volume of this index ever published. Divided into general works, biology, psychology, religion, attitudes, deviation, disorders, education, literature, techniques, reproduction, ethics and social sexual problems. Classic texts are annotated.

H41.   Mair, George. *The Sex-Book Digest: A Peek Between the Covers of 113 of the Most Erotic, Exotic, and Edifying Sex Books*. New York: Quill, 1982. 309 p.

[SCOPE: 1966 to 1981] Reviews 113 popular books written about sex between 1966 and 1981.

H42.   Mason, Mervyn L. *Human Sexuality: A Bibliography and Critical Evaluation of Recent Texts*. Westport, CT: Greenwood Press, 1983. 207 p.

[SCOPE: mostly 1970 to 1983, with some earlier classics] Critically evaluates 180 books on female sexuality, the history of sexuality, male sexuality, philosophy and sex, sex education, sex research, sex therapy and counseling, and sexual minorities (including homosexuals, bisexuals, the disabled, and those engaging in alternative lifestyles). Emphasis is on works intended for professionals and students. Selection criteria included availability, excellence in its category, popularity with professionals, professional's knowledge of the book, and the book's scientific-sexological approach to the subject. Each annotation includes a brief summary and critique of the book's strengths and deficiencies, including evaluation of factual coverage, objectivity, attention to historical or cross-cultural comparisons, use of visual aids, assumptive biases, sexist presumptions, omission of sexual minorities, and other factors.

H43. Research Publications Inc. *Sex Research—Early Literature from Statistics to Erotica: Guide to the Microfilm Collection.* Woodbridge, CT: Research Publications, Inc., 1983. 130 p.

[SCOPE: 1700 to 1860] Author, title, and subject index to 943 18th c. and 19th c. works from the Kinsey Institute microfilm collection. Not limited to English-language titles, the items "span subject categories as diverse as medicine, biology, anthropology, law, the classics, art, erotic literature, and others. [Included are] social histories, guidebooks to cities, dictionaries, art books, and romances, as well as books on incest, homosexuality, divorce, rape, venereal disease and reproduction." Items are grouped under 31 topics, into 4 main sections: sexual behavior and attitudes, sex law and medicine, sex and literature, and sex and humanities. Although unannotated, as was customary at the time, many of the titles are long and descriptive, e.g. *The cases of polygamy, concubinage, adultery, divorce seriously and lernedly discussed. Being a compleat collection of all the remarkable tryals and tracts which have been written on those important subjects* (1731) and *Prostitution, considered in its moral, social and sanitary aspects; in London and other large cities: with proposals for the mitigation and prevention of its attendent evils* (1857).

H44. Roberts, Gloria A. *A Small Library in Family Planning.* 4th ed. New York: Planned Parenthood Federation of America, 1988. 40 p.

[SCOPE: mostly mid 1980s] A "handy reference for anyone seeking an authoritative introduction to population and family planning information, as a world, a family, or an individual concern," this 40 page booklet contains very brief descriptions of 224 recent books selected for their suitability for the small family planning library. The following topics are covered: birth control methods, sterilization, abortion, infertility and the childless couple, religious and ethical aspects, genetics, human reproduction, andrology, gynecology and obstetrics, women's health, women's movement, birth control movement, human sexuality, human sexuality and the handicapped, sexual abuse, STDs, sexuality education (for children, teens, young adults, parents), teenagers, parenting, professional education, population, population education, national fertility studies, reference, reproductive health, and reproductive rights.

H45.   Seruya, Flora C., Susan Losher, and Albert Ellis. *Sex and Sex Education: A Bibliography*. New York: R.R. Bowker, 1972. 266 p.

[SCOPE: to 1972] An unannotated bibliography intended for "anyone confronted with the teaching and learning of sex, be they parent, educator, or adult who wishes self instruction, or a professional who is seeking information or materials for recommended reading." Cites an estimated 2,000 English-language, scholarly, professional, and popular books, including both then current research, and significant older works in sexology. All aspects of sexuality are covered, with emphasis on psychological and social science perspectives. Entries are arranged by subject: reference works (bibliographies, dictionaries, encyclopedias, etc.); biology; family life (divorce, free love unions, marriage); psychology of love and sex; sex and religion; sex attitudes, customs and behavior (adults, incest, masturbation, oragenital, phallicism, sex customs, sexual behavior); sex deviation (homosexuality and lesbianism, sadism and masochism, general); sex diseases and disorders (frigidity, impotence, sterilization, venereal disease); sex education; sex in literature (censorship, sex in literature and the arts); sex, love, courtship and marriage; lovemaking techniques; reproduction (artificial insemination, birth control, cause and determination of sex, reproduction); sexual ethics; and social-sexual problems (abortion, illegitimacy, prostitution, sex offenses and offenders). Author, title, and subject indexes

H46.   **SIECUS Bibliographies**: see A5 for address and phone number.

The bibliographies compiled, distributed, and regularly updated by SIECUS are directed primarily towards educators and the general public. Up to 8 pages in length, each contains brief annotations to books, pamphlets, curricula, leader resources, audiovisual materials, journals, databases, and organizations. New titles are first published in *SIECUS*

Reports (see K49) and then sold individually as reprints. AIDS related bibliographies are free, others are $2.50 each. The following titles are currently available:

Child Sexual Abuse Education, Prevention, and Treatment (1990)
Children, Adolescents and HIV/AIDS Education (1991)
Current Books on Sexuality (1993)–for the general public
Current Religious Perspectives on Sexuality (1991)
Current Resources for HIV/AIDS Education (1992)
Gay Male and Lesbian Sexuality and Issues (1991)
Growing Up (1991)–books for children and adolescents
HIV/AIDS (1992)
Safer Sex and HIV/AIDS Education (1991)
Sexuality and the Developmentally Disabled (1992)
Sexuality Education Resources for Religious Denominations (1992)
Sexuality and Family Life Education: Curricula and Leader Resources (1993)
Sexuality in Middle and Later Life (1993)
Sexuality Periodicals for Professionals (1991)
Talking With Your Child About Sex and Other Important Issues (1993)

▶ HISTORY OF SEXUALITY (*See also*: H37, H54)

For those seeking primary materials for historical research, see "How to Find" older books, p.228. The *Catalogue of the Library of the Surgeon General's Office, United States Army: With an Alphabetical Index of Subject* (Washington, DC: Government Printing Office), first published in 1872, cites materials on many sex related topics (e.g. nymphomania, sex and sexual instinct, sodomy, pederasty) published in the 18th and early 19th century. It is available at the New York Library of Medicine (see X52), National Library of Medicine (see X204), and other libraries. See also, the catalogs of antiquarian bookdealers (see L11, L12).

H47. Salisbury, Joyce E. *Medieval Sexuality: A Research Guide*. Garland Medieval Bibliographies, v.5. New York: Garland Publishing, 1990. 210 p.

Eight hundred and fifteen annotated citations to works in English, Spanish, French, Portuguese, Italian, and German that discuss sexual practices and attitudes in Western and Northern Europe from the 2nd c. to the middle of the 15th c. Subjects covered include intercourse, fornication, adultery, homosexuality, prostitution, bestiality, medical gynecology, transvestism, and sex in satanism and witchcraft. Items are grouped into primary sources (history, law, literature, religion, medicine, philosophy, and science) and secondary sources (books and articles), with author/editor, subject, and century indexes. Each section begins with introductory notes on the nature of the sources cited.

➤ HOMOSEXUALITY *(See also*: H46, F17, K77, M1, X132)

HOW TO FIND

• The *Journal of Homosexuality* (see K83) frequently contains bibliographic articles, see H90 for example.

• The Information Clearinghouse of the American Library Association's Gay and Lesbian Task Force (see X53), collects bibliographies on topics of interest to gay and lesbian readers, and provides bibliographic assistance to those seeking information on gay/lesbian related issues.

• Many bookstores specializing in gay/lesbian titles distribute catalogs that are essentially briefly annotated bibliographies. Seven such dealers are described in Ch.15 (see L3-L9). See especially, the 11 bibliographies compiled by Glad Day Bookshop (see L5), and the catalog of LAMBDA Rising Bookstore (see L6).

H48.   Bullough, Vern L., W. Dorr Legg, Barrett W. Elcano, and James Kepner. *An Annotated Bibliography of Homosexuality*. 2 vols. New York: Garland Publishing, 1976. 436 p.

[SCOPE: to 1976] Intended to provide students with a comprehensive approach to the study of homosexuality, with the aim of bringing together representative entries from a multi-disciplinary point of view." Includes an essay on the state of the literature, a brief history of the homophile movement from 1948 to 1960, and 12,794 citations to French, English, and German-language periodicals and books drawn from the literature of religious studies, medicine and other sciences, social and behavioral sciences, and the humanities. Citations, which despite the title are unannotated, are classified by format and broad subject. In volume I: bibliographies, general studies, behavioral sciences (anthropology, history, psychology, sociology), education and children, medicine and biology, psychiatry, law and its enforcement, court cases, military, and religion and ethics. In volume II: biography and autobiography, studies in literature and the arts, fiction (movies, short stories, drama), poetry, homophile movement periodicals, and transvestites and transsexuals.

H49.   Dynes, Wayne R. "A Bibliography of Bibliographies of Homosexuality." *Cabirion and Gay Books Bulletin*, no.10 (1984): 16-22.

Describes 180 bibliographies in all major languages.

H50.   _____. *Homosexuality: A Research Guide*. New York: Garland Publishing, 1987. 853 p.

[SCOPE: Ancient Greece to 1986, with emphasis on 19th and 20th c. imprints] Contains 4,858 annotated citations to books, journal and newspaper articles, and pamphlets published worldwide. Fiction, poetry, and drama are excluded, but bibliographies of them are listed under "Literary Studies." Entries are grouped into the following chapters: reference materials, women's studies, history and area studies, anthropology, travel, humanities, philosophy and religion, language, lifestyles, economics, education, politics, military, sociology, social work, psychology, psychiatry, families, boundary crossings, law and law enforcement, violence, medical, and biology. Within each chapter, entries are further classified by topic (e.g. twin studies, prisons, animal homosexuality, children of lesbians and gay men, bathhouses and beaches, humor and camp, bisexuality, graffiti, lesbian mothers, blackmail, gay ghettos, transsexuality, DSM controversy, effeminacy, and Freudian theory, to name only a few). Subjects already well covered in the literature are cited selectively, lesser studied topics, more comprehensively. A full range of perspectives are represented, although H53 and H63 cite more anti-homosexual literature. See also F15.

H51A.   Fletcher, Lynne Y., and Adrien Saks. *Lavender Lists: New Lists for Gay and Lesbian Readers*. Boston: Alyson Publishing, 1990. 240 p.

H51.   Garber, Linda. *Lesbian sources: A Bibliography of Periodical Articles, 1970-1990*. Garland Gay and Lesbian Studies, v.9. New York: Garland Publishing, 1992. 730 p.

[SCOPE: 1970 to 1990] Cites over 3,500 lesbian studies articles published in periodicals worldwide. Entries are classified under over 100 categories, including traditional topics in the humanities and social sciences, as well as lesbian and feminist political issues pertaining to race, class, disability, nationality, homophobia, popular culture, and more. (Unable to review.)

H52.   Greenberg, Al. *1990 Gay/Lesbian Periodicals Index*. Charlotte, NC: Integrity Indexing, 1992. 9 microfilms.

[SCOPE: 1990] An index to all issues of 29 gay and lesbian periodicals published in 1990. A geographically balanced selection of major metropolitan newspapers are included, as well as representative lesbian and gay male titles. Contact Integrity Indexing for updates: 2012 Queens Rd. W., Apt. 1, Charlotte, NC 28207. PH: (704)335-9936.

H53.   Horner, Tom. *Homosexuality and the Judeo-Christian Tradition: An Annotated Bibliography*. ATLA Bibliography Series, no.5. Metuchen, NJ: Scarecrow Press, 1981. 131 p.

[SCOPE: mostly 1970s] Contains 459 annotated citations to modern works "that illuminate the subject of homosexuality in the Jewish and Christian traditions," including commentary on biblical references to homosexuality and religious anti-homosexual literature. Entries are arranged by format (i.e. books, articles and essays, pamphlets, and bibliographies), with subject and author indexes. Appendixes list principal biblical references to homosexuality and periodicals of gay religious organizations.

H54.   Katz, Jonathan Ned. *Gay American History: Lesbians and Gay Men in the U.S.A.* Rev. ed. New York: Meridian, 1992. 704 p.

[SCOPE: 1500s to 1991] Explores the history of American lesbians and gay men by reprinting and analyzing rare and hard to find primary documents. Organized into six chapters: "Trouble 1566-1966," "Treatment 1884-1974," "Passing Women 1782-1920," "Native Americans/Gay Americans 1528-1976," "Resistance 1859-1972," and "Love 1779-1932." Two bibliographies conclude the work: "Notes and Bibliographies," and "Major Texts for the Study of U.S. Lesbian and Gay History."

H55.   Legman, G. *Toward a Bibliography of Homosexuality (1500-1941)*. New York: New York Academy of Medicine. Unpublished.

[SCOPE: 1500 to 1941] Six drawers of cataloging cards, representing over

6,000 titles, held at the N.Y. Academy of Medicine (see X52).

H56. MacCowan, Lyndal, and Margaret Cruikshank. "Bibliography: Books on Lesbianism." In *Lesbian Studies: Past and Future*, edited by Margaret Cruikshank, 237-273. Old Westbury, NY: Feminist Press, 1982.

H57. Maggione, Dolores. *Lesbianism: An Annotated Bibliography and Guide to the Literature 1976-1986.* Metuchen, NJ: Scarecrow Press, 1988. 150 p.

[SCOPE: 1976 to 1986] "It is the hope of improving service offered by social workers to the lesbian that this researcher has undertaken this bibliography and guide to the literature." Describes 350 items selected from the literature of social work, sociology, psychology, law, contemporary women's literature, and feminist social analysis. Lesbian fiction is excluded, as are works whose perspective on lesbianism is negative, contains erroneous information, or which only generalizes findings to include lesbians. Entries are arranged into five chapters, each beginning with introductory notes and concluding with a list of relevant organizations: "Individual Lesbians," "Minorities Within a Minority," "Lesbian Families," "Oppression," and "Special Health Issues." A final chapter notes lesbian bookstores and publishers. A second edition, covering the literature from 1976-1991, is forthcoming in 1992.

H58. Parker, William. *Homosexuality: A Selective Bibliography of Over 3000 Items.* Metuchen, NJ: Scarecrow Press, 1971. 323 p.

_____. *Homosexuality Bibliography: Supplement 1970-1975.* Metuchen, NJ: Scarecrow Press, 1977. 337 p.

_____. *Homosexuality Bibliography: Supplement 1976-1982.* Metuchen, NJ: Scarecrow Press, 1985. 395 p.

[SCOPE: 1940s to 1982] The 1971 edition claims to cover "all the significant writings on homosexuality which have appeared in English through 1969"; together, the three volumes cite over 10,000 English-language works. In each edition, entries are arranged by type of publication, with a subject index: books, pamphlets, theses and disser-tations; articles in books, newspapers, popular magazines, and journals (including legal, religious, medical, scientific, and other specialized titles); court cases involving consenting adults; articles in homophile publications;

literary works (anthologies, novels, plays, short stories, poetry); and movies, television programs, audiovisuals, and records with homosexual themes. Items the author regards as the "most significant or influential writings on the subject" are so marked, but citations are otherwise unannotated. The appendix in each volume notes state laws applicable to consensual adult homosexuals as of 1970, 1976, and 1982 respectively.

H59.   Potter, Claire. *Lesbian Periodicals Index*. Tallahassee, FL: Naiad Press, 1986. 413 p.

[SCOPE: 1947 to 1986] A comprehensive author and subject index to the contents of 42 lesbian periodicals, all of which had ceased publication by 1986. The periodicals covered represent the diversity of lesbian life, including its political, racial, class, and cultural differences. Citations are arranged into four sections: (1) author/subject index to articles; (2) lesbian writings; (3) book reviews; and (4) visual arts (cartoons, drawings, photography, art). Concludes with a directory of 35 archives with lesbian periodicals holdings.

H60.   Ridinger, Robert B. Marks *The Homosexual and Society: An Annotated Bibliography*. Bibliographies and Indexes in Sociology, no.18. Westport, CT: Greenwood Press, 1990. 444 p.

[SCOPE: mostly mid 1960s to 1987] Focuses on seven areas where a coherent form of homophobia has had significant impact: adoption and foster care, child custody, the military establishment, employment discrimination, censorship, religion, and police attitudes and actions. Contains 1,583 annotated citations to articles from gay periodicals (e.g. *The Advocate, The Ladder, The Mattachine Review*), the literature of the legal profession, and popular periodicals and monographs.

H61.   Roberts, J.R. *Black Lesbians: An Annotated Bibliography*. Tallahassee, FL: Naiad Press, 1981. 93 p.

H62.   Sullivan, Gerard. "A Bibliographic Guide to Government Hearings and Reports, Legislative Action, and Speeches Made in the House and Senate of the United States Congress on the Subject of Homosexuality." *Journal of Homosexuality*. 10 (1/2): 135-189 (1984).

[SCOPE: 1920-1984] "This bibliography is a research aid for those interested in studying the relationship between the U.S. Federal

Government and civil rights for gay people." No mention of homosexuality was found in government documents prior to 1920, with the subject appearing sporadically in documents published from 1920 to 1975, and regularly since then. The chronologically arranged entries include details on how to locate each document. Includes a list of the indexes and other resources utilized in compiling the bibliography.

H63.   Weinberg, Martin S., and Alan P. Bell, eds. *Homosexuality: An Annotated Bibliography*. New York: Harper & Row, 1972. 550 p.

[SCOPE: 1940 to 1968] Contains 1,265 annotated citations to psychiatric, medical and social science literature relating to homosexuality, including anti-homosexual materials. Covers etiology and treatment; social and demographic aspects; homosexuality in history, non-Western societies, and special settings; societal attitudes towards homosexuality; homosexuality and law; and bibliographies and dictionaries. Excludes biography and autobiography, literary works, and newspaper and magazine articles. Author and subject indexes.

➤ LANGUAGE *(See also:* "Sexual Slang" p.59)

For information on sexual language, including both standard English and slang, consult Reinhold Aman of the International Maledicta Society (see X129). An expert on "maledicta" (i.e. "bad words"), he publishes the quarterly newsletter *Maledicta Monitor* and the annual journal *Maledicta: The International Journal of Verbal Aggression* (see K85); both always include bibliographies. (See especially, the 273 item bibliography in v.9 of *Maledicta* and the article on maledicta research methods in v.2.)

➤ MEN'S STUDIES

H64.   August, Eugene R. *Men's Studies: A Selected and Annotated Interdisciplinary Bibliography*. Littleton, CO: Librarians Unlimited, 1985. 215 p.

Believes that "neither fad nor backlash, men's studies are the logical complement to women's studies and a necessary component of any balanced gender related scholarship." Describes 519 books representing all aspects of male life, including male health, vasectomy, rape, male rape, boy prostitution, incest, domestic violence, male victimization and sexual exploitation in prisons, male physiology and biology, research studies on male sexuality, impotence, sexual dysfunction, sex advice and sexual health, homosexuality, transsexuality, transvestites, and homophobia. Entries are arranged by broad subject, but there is no detailed subject index and relevant materials are classified under both sex and non sex related subject headings (e.g. *Scoring: A Sexual Memoir* is listed under "Autobiography," *Phallic Worship* under "Masculinity").

➤ MOTHERS AND MOTHERING

H65.   Dixon, Penelope A. ***Mothers and Mothering: An Annotated Feminist Bibliography***. Women's History and Culture Series, v.3. New York: Garland Publishing, 1991. 232 p.

[SCOPE: 1970 to 1990, plus older classic works] A selective compilation of the most important feminist scholarship on motherhood. Grounded in sociology, psychology, history, and the arts, cited works address mothering in general, single mothers, working mothers, the relationships between mothers and daughters and mothers and sons, mother's role in the family, children, the impact of feminism, and psychoanalytic studies.

➤ PEDOPHILIA

H66.   Brongersma, Edward. ***Loving Boys: A Multidisciplinary Study of Sexual Relations Between Adult and Minor Males***. 2 vols. Elmhurst, NY: Global Academic Publishers, 1986-1990.

Scholarly study, written by a self-acknowledged pedophile, of male adult/male youth love and sexual bonding. Claims to examine virtually all the extant literature that has been written in English about this phenomena, as well as most of the material that has appeared in other Western European languages. Includes lengthy bibliographies of primary and secondary source materials. (Information provided by publisher.)

➤ PORNOGRAPHY (*See also*: Erotic Art; Erotic Literature; H84)

H67.   Byerly, Greg, and Rick Rubin. ***Pornography, The Conflict Over Sexually Explicit Materials in the U.S.: An Annotated Bibliography***. New York: Garland Publishing, 1980. 152 p.

[SCOPE: 1960 to 1980 for monographs and dissertation; 1970 to 1980 for journal articles] Selective, annotated bibliography of English-language works "primarily concerned with the creation, availability, dissemination, and effects of sexually explicit materials in the United States." Excludes works on art censorship, historical works, literary criticism of pornographic works, pornographic titles themselves, and works which primarily discuss contemporary sex behavior, attitudes, or mores. The 444 annotated citations—encompassing psychological, sociological, religious, philosophical, legal, and popular perspectives—are organized by format: books and dissertations, psychological articles, sociological articles, philosophical and religious articles, popular press articles, government documents, and legal articles. Author and subject indexes.

H68.   Nordquist, Joan. *Pornography and Censorship*. Contemporary Social Issues Series, no.7. Santa Cruz, CA: Reference and Research Services, 1987. 50 p.

Unable to review; see footnote 2 for more details.

H69.   Osanka, Franklin Mark, and Sara Lee Johann. "Bibliography." In *Sourcebook on Pornography*, 523-617. New York: Guilford Press, 1989.

Claims to be the "world's leading bibliography on issues concerning pornography." The unannotated citations are arranged according to the chapter headings in the *Sourcebook* (see F21), and are "limited to those types of materials that reasonable people and researchers would consider valuable to explore." No further scope notes are given.

H70.   Sellen, Betty-Carol, and Patricia A. Young. *Feminists, Pornography and the Law: An Annotated Bibliography of Conflict 1970-1986*. Hamden, CT: Library Professional Publications, 1987. 204 p.

[SCOPE: 1970-1986] Prepared to "help people form a thoughtful, active

---

² Each volume in this quarterly bibliography series presents a full spectrum of social and political viewpoints on a current "critical issue." Each contains approximately 500 citations to books, journal articles (from academic, scholarly and general readership titles), government publications, and pamphlets, as well as a resource section listing relevant organizations, activist groups, and reference publications. Although emphasis is on titles published in the last 5 years, all authoritative works are cited.

response to the complicated issues of equality for women, sexual freedom, and the preservation of free speech." A lengthy, introductory essay discusses conflicts over freedom of speech vs. restrictions on sexually explicit materials. The bibliography that follows cites scholarly and popular books, magazine and newspaper articles, unpublished reports, non-print materials, and relevant organizations. All viewpoints in the feminist anti-pornography debate are represented, including women's points of view on pornography and what it means in our culture, pornography as evidence of men's oppression against women, and critiques of the feminist anti-pornography movement. Works on the correlates between pornography and violence are excluded. The appendix lists publications which frequently contain references to feminist anti-pornography movements and contains a chronology/index of newspaper references. Author, title, and subject indexes. F20 also includes a brief unannotated bibliography on feminism and pornography.

H71.   Slade, Joseph W. "Pornography." In *Handbook of American Popular Culture*, edited by Thomas M. Inge, 957-1010. 2nd ed. Rev. and enl. New York: Greenwood Press, 1989.

This essay provides a historical outline of pornography and a review of research resources in the area, including reference books, and history and criticism titles. All forms of pornography and erotica are covered, including literature, art, photography, cinema, videos, magazines, and others. Concludes with an extensive bibliography.

▶ PROSTITUTION *(See also*: H84, H109; for male prostitution see H50)

H72.   Bullough, Vern, Barrett Elcano, Margaret Deacon, and Bonnie Bullough. *A Bibliography of Prostitution*. New York: Garland Publishing, 1977. 419 p.

[SCOPE: 1600 to 1976; literature references back to ancient Greece] In compiling this comprehensive international bibliography, the authors "tried to be all encompassing, gathering together scholarly, popular, and professional books, articles, and government documents by people who *said* that they were writing about prostitution and this can and does include almost any aspect of extramarital sexual activity," including mistresses, concubines, streetwalkers, call girls, brothels, gigolos, and both professional and amateur prostitutes. The 6,494 unannotated citations are classified into 19 categories: general works, anthropology, area studies, bibliography, biography and autobiography, business, fiction, guides and descriptive histories, history, juveniles, legal and police regulations, literature, males, medicine and public health, organizations, societies and publications, psychiatry, psychology, religion and morality, sociology, and war. Author index only. The cited materials form the backbone of a major research collection on prostitution housed in the Special Collections Department of California State University at Northridge's Oviatt Library (see X50).

H73.   Bullough, Vern L., Lilli Sentz, and Dorothy Tao, eds. *Prostitution: A Guide to Sources 1960-1990*. Garland Reference Library of Social Science, v.670. New York: Garland Publishing, 1992. 300 p.

[SCOPE: 1960 to 1990] Updates *A Bibliography of Prostitution* (see H72), with emphasis on material published since 1970. Covers both primary and secondary materials, including books, articles, and dissertations.

H74.   Delacoste, Frederique, and Priscilla Alexander. *Sex Works: Writings by Women in the Sex Industry*. Pittsburgh, PA: Cleis Press, 1987. 349 p.

A collection of essays by present and former sex workers. Concludes with a 127 item annotated bibliography of books and articles on prostitution. Entries are grouped into nine sections: the voice of the prostitute; global history of prostitution from the Ancient to Modern Era; modern history of prostitution in Western Europe and the U.S.; prostitution in non-Western countries; prostitution and the law in the U.S.; studies; psychology, sociology and criminology; feminist analysis of prostitution; the pornography debates; and prostitution in fiction.

H75.   Kantha, Sachi Sri. *Prostitutes in Medical Literature: An Annotated Bibliography*. Bibliography and Indexes in Medical Studies, no.6. Westport, CT: Greenwood Press, 1991. 288 p.

[SCOPE: 1900 to 1990, with emphasis on titles published between 1946 and 1990] A 1,440 item, selective bibliography of the international scientific literature on prostitution, including journal articles, research abstracts from international conferences, books and book chapters, doctoral dissertations, and reports from federal agencies and other institutions. Entries are arranged as follows: general and historical works (including bibliographies, autobiographies, and encyclopedia articles);

anthropology and sociology; sexuality of prostitutes and clients; psychology and mental health (of prostitutes, pimps, and madams); public health; sexually transmitted diseases; male, child and adolescent prostitution; and legislation and jurisprudence. Despite the title, items are only selectively annotated. Subject and author indexes.

▶ REPRODUCTION *(See also*: Bioetics; H15, H21, H34, H107, H109, L16)

HOW TO FIND

• The Science and Technology Division of the Library of Congress (see A1) compiles and distributes *LC Science Tracer Bulletins*, an informal series of reference guides to scientific topics (e.g. infertility, new reproductive technologies).

H76.   Abel, Ernest L. *Viruses and Reproduction: A Bibliography*. Westport, CT: Greenwood Press, 1988.

Abel has published a number of sex and reproduction related bibliographies, including *Lead and Reproduction* (1984), as well as titles addressing the effects of various drugs on reproduction (see H15). Each begins with a lengthy introductory essay summarizing the general findings of the cited literature, followed by alphabetically arranged citations and a subject index.

H77.   Holmes, Helen Bequaert. *Issues in Reproductive Technology I: An Anthology*. New York: Garland Publishing, 1992. 500 p.

An anthology of articles addressing issues relating to new technologies in reproductive medicine; each concludes with a bibliography. Articles are grouped into five sections: abortion, contraception, surrogate motherhood, cryopreservation of gametes and embryos, and psychosocial issues raised by in-vitro fertilization. Each section begins with an overview essay, followed by critical articles by professionals in philosophy, political science, sociology, medicine, biology, and women's health. Each article elucidates problems created by the technologies; the views of advocates, practitioners, and detractors; and related ethical and social issues.

H78. Nordquist, Joan. *Reproductive Rights: A Bibliography*. Social Issues Series, no.9. Santa Cruz, CA: Reference and Research Services, 1988. 68 p.

[SCOPE: mostly 1984 to 1988] Current literature on reproductive rights, including abortion (for minors, pro-choice and pro-life movements), fetal rights (forced caesareans, prenatal injury, wrongful life), paternal rights, reproductive techniques (in-vitro fertilization, surrogate parenting, artificial insemination), and sterilization and reproductive rights (mentally disabled, sterilization abuse). Political, sociological, legal, philosophical, scientific, and feminist perspectives are represented. Arranged by format (books, articles) and subject, with bibliographies and organizations listed separately. See also footnote 2, p.129.

H79. Paige, Karen E., et al. *Female Reproductive Cycle: An Annotated Bibliography*. Boston: G.K. Hall, 1985. 599 p.

[SCOPE: 1965 to 1982] "This [1,120 item] annotated bibliography is a multidisciplinary guide to the research literature on six major events in the female reproductive cycle: menarche, the menstrual cycle, pregnancy, birth, postpartum, and menopause." Emphasis is on English-language psychological, psychoanalytic, and sociological research, with biomedical research included when it focuses on "issues with important psychological or social implications or when its controversies have dominated the literature on a given reproductive event." Cross cultural research exploring controversial research questions is included, but research on tribal cultures and third world nations is not. Literature reviews, research studies, theoretical discussion, and "well-documented editorials" from academic and professional journals are cited. Entries are arranged by subject, with an author index: menarche (age at menarche, psychoanalytic studies, social-psychological studies, adolescent menstruation); menstruation (cycle physiology, variability and length, cycle synchrony and pheromones); duration and amount of menstrual flow; psychodynamic view of menstruation; menstruation and sexuality; premenstrual/menstrual syndromes; social opinion and cultural beliefs about menstruation; pregnancy (pregnancy beliefs and practices, and psychological, social, and psychosocial experiences); medical models of birth (controversial obstetrical practices, maternity care, correlates to morbidity and mortality, sociomedicine); and alternative models of childbirth (social and anthropological approaches, social-psychological correlates to birth experience, and the natural childbirth movement).

➤ SADOMASOCHISM (*See*: D8)

➤ SEX CUSTOMS (*See also*: F8, H47; General Works)

H80.   Frayser, Suzanne G. *Varieties of Sexual Experience: An Anthropological Perspective on Human Sexuality*. New Haven, CT: Human Relations Area Files Press, 1985. 546 p.

Includes an extensive ethnographic bibliography on sex and reproduction in 62 societies. Resources in history, sexology, biology, sociology, anthropology, and psychology are cited.

H81.   Goodland, Roger. *A Bibliography of Sex Rites and Customs: An Annotated Record of Books, Articles and Illustrations in All Languages*. Boston: Longwood Press, 1977. Originally published 1931. 752 p.

[SCOPE: 1700s to 1930] Intended to be of use to "anthropologists and others desirous of information concerning the sexual ideas and customs of savage and civilized peoples." Unannotated, but as was typical at the time, titles are lengthy and descriptive. Citations are arranged alphabetically, with subject and geographic indexes.

➤ SEX IN CINEMA (*See*: Ch.27—especially W1; H85)

➤ SEX EDUCATION (*See also*: H46, V2)

H82.   Campbell, Patricia J. *Sex Guides: Books and Films about Sexuality for Young Adults*. New York: Garland Publishing, 1986. 374 p.

[SCOPE: 1892 to 1985] Critically reviewing over 400 historic and contemporary sex education guides for adolescents, this claims to be "the definitive guide to sex guides, a resource that will give background and understanding and specific title suggestions to librarians, teachers, parents, youth advocates, and young adults themselves." Part I, arranged chronologically, traces the historical development of such guides by examining virtually all titles published in the U.S. between 1892 and 1979. (Most of this material was previously published as *Sex Education Books for Young Adults 1892-1979*.) Part II analyzes contemporary sex education materials, including teen sex guides (both general and specialized titles on pregnancy, abortion, sexually transmitted diseases, and homosexuality), films, young adult fiction, and religious "abstinence" guides. Items are discussed at length in the text, and a bibliography concludes each chapter. The appendix lists fiction and non-fiction titles recommended for junior high and high school libraries, and young adult sections of public library. Subject and title indexes.

H83. Cassell, Carol, and Pamela M. Wilson, eds. *Sexuality Education: A Resource Book*. Garland Reference Library of Social Sciences, v.416. New York: Garland Publishing, 1989. 446 p.

A book of practical essays describing the planning and implementation of sexuality education in the family, school, and community. Each of the three sections concludes with an annotated bibliography of resources: curricula, books and periodicals for professionals, audiovisuals, and books for adults, parents, children, and adolescents. Additional resource lists are scattered throughout the book, among them: Annotated Bibliography on Sexuality Education in Film, Resources on Child Sexual Abuse Prevention, Resources on Homosexuality, Annotated Bibliography of Sexuality Education in the Schools, Youth Organizations, Resources Available from Youth Organizations, Religion and Sex, Annotated Bibliography on Sexuality Education in the Community, and Resources on Sexuality and Disability.

➤ SEX AND THE LAW (*See also*: F29, H60, H62, H67, H70)

Although not specializing exclusively in sex related topics, the annual directory *Law Books and Serials in Print* (New Providence, NJ: R.R. Bowker) indexes law books by author, title, and subject (e.g. abortion, birth control, censorship, artificial insemination, homosexuality, marriage law, sex crimes, prostitution, child molestation, sex in business, etc.).

H84. De Coste, F.C., K.M. Munro, and Lillian MacPherson. *Feminist Legal Literature: A Selective Annotated Bibliography*. Garland Reference Library of Social Sciences, v.671. New York: Garland Publishing, 1991. 499 p.

[SCOPE: 1980 to 1990] Contains over 1,400 evaluative annotations to materials of interest to feminists, written from feminist perspectives, and of relevance to law. Cites English and French-language articles and book review essays published in legal periodicals, the alternative press, social science journals, and the international human rights literature. Entries are arranged by subject, including abortion, reproduction, lesbianism, marriage and divorce, pornography, prostitution, rape, sexuality, and sexual harassment. Author, periodical title, and subject indexes.

▶ SEX IN LITERATURE (*See also*: Erotic Art; Erotic Literature; Pornography; F8, F17, G6, G7)

H85.   Garber, Eric, and Lyn Paleo. *Uranian Worlds: A Reader's Guide to Alternative Sexuality in Science Fiction, Fantasy and Horror*. 2nd ed. A Reference Publication in Science Fiction. Boston: G.K. Hall, 1990. 325 p.

[SCOPE: 200AD to 1989] "Annotated bibliography of variant sexuality in science fiction, fantasy and horror literature and film from 200 AD through 1989." The focus is on homosexuality, particularly works that treat male homosexuality, bisexuality, and lesbianism with "intelligence, validation, and verisimilitude," but forms of sex that are neither heterosexual or homosexual are also included (e.g. androgyny, "three sexed aliens," transsexuality, hermaphroditism, and vampirism). Entries, arranged alphabetically by author, include a brief plot summary, biographical notes, and an indication of the type of sex portrayed. The appendix notes selected fan organizations and films and videos.

H86.   Grier, Barbara. *The Lesbian in Literature*. 3d ed. Tallahassee, FL: Naiad Press, 1981. 168 p.

[SCOPE: 1880s to 1979] An estimated 3,000 citations to biography and autobiography, novels, short stories, short novels, poetry, drama, and fictionalized biography, concerned with lesbianism or having lesbian characters. Cheap paperbacks of the 1950s and 1960s were included in the first edition (1967) but excluded in the second and third. The third edition includes non-fiction published since 1967, which are "accurate in their presentation and deserving of inclusion in this reference tool." Asterisks indicate the title's overall quality, and codes indicate main or minor lesbian characters, latent or repressed lesbianism, and whether the book is "trashy," but otherwise items are unannotated. Arranged alphabetically by author, with no subject index.

H87.   Rubinstein, Frankie. *A Dictionary of Shakespeare's Sexual Puns and their Significance*. 2nd ed. Houndmills, Basingstoke, Hampshire: Macmillan, 1989. 372 p.

Analyzes the meaning and significance of bawdy/erotic double entendres and puns in Shakespeare's plays and poems. Seeks to "identify the hundreds upon hundreds of still unannotated puns and to indicate their enrichment of the plays . . . [Covers] the erotic practices of heterosexuals and homosexuals (including lesbians), perverts, castrates, and the impotent." Entries are arranged alphabetically. Includes an unannotated bibliography of primary and reference works.

H88. Young, Ian. *The Male Homosexual in Literature: A Bibliography.* 2nd ed. Metuchen, NJ: Scarecrow Press, 1982.

Alphabetical listing, by author, of 4,282 English-language works of fiction, drama, film scripts, poetry, and autobiography, concerned with male homosexuality or having male homosexual characters. Does not include "pulp fiction," works appearing in periodicals, biography, or non-fiction other than autobiography. Works considered of primary importance are marked with an asterisk and codes indicate format, but otherwise items are unannotated. Concludes with five essays: the history of the gay novel, homosexuals in drama, gay literature and censorship, male love poetry, and gay publishing. Title index and index of gay anthologies.

➤ SEX IN MASS MEDIA (*See also*: Sex in Cinema)

H89. Alali, A. Odasuo. *Mass Media Sex and Adolescent Values: An Annotated Bibliography and Directory of Organizations.* Jefferson, NC: McFarland & Co., 1991. 138 p.

Selective coverage of "the current research findings, discussions, articles, and analyses of mass media products and their impact, or lack of it, on adolescents' sexual attitudes, values, and behavior." Contains 227 annotated and 65 unannotated citations to popular magazine and newsletter articles, as well as the scholarly literature of mass media and film studies, psychology, education, and the social sciences. Entries are grouped into four chapters, with author, title, and subject indexes: "Sex Role Portrayals" (media sex role stereotyping); "Sexual Curricula and Media Use" (analysis of the "relationship between the frequency of sex in the media, adolescent media use, and adolescent social learning and sexual development"); "Adolescent Attitudes and Values" (analysis of how sexuality in media influences adolescents), "Contraception, Pregnancy and Health Issues" (studies of adolescent knowledge, attitudes, and behavior regarding contraception, pregnancy, and STDs and how these are influenced by both entertainment media and media educational campaigns). Describes 57 research centers, self help groups and other organizations providing relevant services in the United States.

H90.   Fejes, F. **"Gays, Lesbians, and the Media: A Selected Bibliography."** *Journal of Homosexuality.* 21 (1/2): 261-277 (1992).

➤ SEX AND RELIGION *(See also:* F8, F30, H43)

H91.   Brewer, Joan Scherer. *Sex and the Modern Jewish Woman: An Annotated Bibliography.* Essays by Lynn Davidman and Evelyn Avery. Fresh Meadows, NY: Biblio Press, 1986. 125 p.

[SCOPE: 1960 to 1985; 1920 to 1985, for fiction] Begins with two lengthy essays: "Sex and the Modern Jewish Woman: An Overview," discussing traditional Jewish attitudes towards women and sex, the interpretation of this tradition by contemporary professionals and laypersons, and the sexual attitudes and practices of modern American Jews; and "Sex and the Jewish Woman in 20th c. Fiction," surveying Jewish fiction dealing with male/female relations published between 1920 and 1985. A bibliography of books and journal articles follows, covering issues relating to the meaning of sexuality within Jewish traditions and the sexual patterns of contemporary American Jews, with emphasis on attitudes and behavior of and towards Jewish-American women. Items were selected from the literature of religious and Judaic studies, feminism, sociology, mental health, literature, and psychology, and are arranged by subject: stereotypes of Jewish women's sexuality, Halakhic views of women and sexuality, niddah and mikveh, contraception and reproduction, orthodoxy and sexuality, homosexuality, non-marital sexual behavior, premarital, marital and extramarital sexuality, sexual dysfunction, aging and sexuality, and adolescents and sexuality. Additional sources for information, materials, and research data are noted in the appendix, which also includes a supplementary unannotated bibliography. Author index.

➤ SEX RESEARCHERS *(See also:* F10, F18)

H92.   Steakley, James D. *The Writings of Dr. Magnus Hirschfeld: A Bibliography.* Canadian Gay Archives Publications Series, No.11. Toronto: Canadian Gay Archives, 1985. 53 p.

Dr. Magnus Hirschfeld (1868-1935) was the most prominent and

> ## HOW TO FIND
>
> • Most contemporary sex researchers are affiliated with universities. Their curricula vita, which should be available from their department office, will include a bibliography of their work (see "How to Find" Faculty, p.309). For others, consult a biographical index for articles that may include bibliographies (see B13-B14); or search library catalogs using the name followed by –*Bibliography* or –*Biography*.

outspoken advocate for homosexual emancipation in Germany in the years prior to the Third Reich, and helped found the world's first gay rights organization. This unannotated bibliography cites, in chronological order, German and English-language translations of all his monographs, booklets, articles, prefaces, and reviews, authored or coauthored by Hirschfeld, as well as his doctoral dissertation, published letters, speeches, reports, poems, film texts, court depositions, and interviews. For more information contact the Magnus Hirschfeld Society (Magnus-Hirschfeld-Gesellschaft, Grossbeerenstrasse 13a, 1 Berlin 61, West Germany), which has as its primary goal the reestablishment of Hirschfeld's Institute for Sexology in Berlin—the original of which was raided by Nazis in 1933, who seized or destroyed its entire collection of books, documents, and photographs.

H93.   John Money. *Venuses, Penuses: Sexology, Sexosophy, and Exigency Theory*. Buffalo, NY: Prometheus Books, 1986. 659 p.

A collection of 48 of Money's papers, written between 1948 and 1985, including an extensive bibliography of his work. Volume 4, no.2 of the *Journal of Psychology and Human Sexuality*, a special issue tribute to Dr. Money on the occasion of his 70th birthday, includes a complete bibliography of his work, indexed by subject, year, and publication type.

➤ SEXUAL ABUSE

—— CHILD ABUSE AND INCEST (*See also*: X273; p.406)

H94.   De Young, Mary. *Incest: An Annotated Bibliography*. Jefferson, NC: McFarland & Co., 1985. 161 p.

[SCOPE: mid 1960s to 1985] Contains 410 annotated citations to journal articles and books (both professional and popular) covering all aspects of incest—"some kind of sexual activity between individuals who are in some fashion related to each other." Items are grouped into 11 chapters, each beginning with introductory notes: definitions of incest; father-daughter and father-son incest, and the effects of paternal incest on victims; sibling, maternal, and other types of incest (e.g. grandparents, aunts/uncles); systems intervention (e.g. medical, legal, counseling); treatment of incest offenders, victims and families; statistical studies; and books and literature reviews. Author and subject indexes.

H95. De Young, Mary. *Child Molestation: An Annotated Bibliography*. Jefferson, NC: McFarland & Co., 1987. 176 p.

[SCOPE: early 1960s to 1987] Journal articles and books on child molestation—"the exposure of a prepubescent child to sexual stimulation inappropriate for the child's age, psychological development, and psychosexual maturity, by a person at least 10 years older, who may either be unfamiliar to, or acquainted with the child, but who is *not* related to the child by blood or legal means." The 557 annotated citations—drawn from the social and behavioral sciences, medical, legal, and educational literature—are arranged by subject: historical studies, clinical descriptions of child molesters (motivation, cognition, emotions, and family background), homosexual child molestation, effects of molestation on children, treatment of offenders, treatment of victims, legal issues, child pornography and sex rings, abuse prevention, and pedophile groups. Additional sections cover literature reviews, books, and statistical studies.

H96. Rubin, Rick, and Greg Byerly. *Incest: The Last Taboo: An Annotated Bibliography*. Garland Reference Library of Social Science, v.143. New York: Garland Publishing, 1983. 169 p.

[SCOPE: emphasizes works published between 1973 and 1983, plus significant works from the 1960s] A 419 item "selected annotated bibliography on incest encompassing psychological, sociological, medical, anthropological, scientific, legal, popular and literary perspectives." Entries are limited to English-language books and journal articles concerned with incest in contemporary American society; works on child abuse, child pornography, and Oedipal and Electra complexes are excluded, as are historical works and fiction. Arrangement is by format: monographs and dissertations; psychology, sociology, anthropology, and legal articles; medical and scientific literature; popular presses; incest themed literature;

and audiovisuals. Subject index.

H97.   Schlesinger, Benjamin. *Sexual Abuse of Children in the 1980s: Ten Essays and an Annotated Bibliography*. 2nd ed. Buffalo, NY: University of Toronto Press, 1986. 201 p.

[SCOPE: 1980 to 1985] Reprints ten brief essays on various aspects of child sexual abuse, followed by a 301 item selective bibliography of English-language articles, books, booklets, and reports on the topic. Entries are arranged by format (bibliographies, newsletters, reviews of literature, surveys, research studies, handbooks, article and book overviews, and children's literature) and subject (including, among others, adolescents, father/daughter incest, mothers of victims, incidence, sex offenders, sibling incest, sexual abuse of the mentally retarded, mother/son incest, incest and alcoholism, prevention and treatment of abuse, and grandparent incest). Sources for audiovisuals are noted in the appendix. The first edition, *Sexual Abuse of Children: A Resource Guide and Annotated Bibliography* (1982), contains 180 annotated citations covering the literature through 1980.

—— RAPE

H98.   Barnes, Dorothy L. *Rape: A Bibliography, 1965-1975*. Troy, NY: Whitston Publishing, 1977. 154 p.

_____. **Rape Bibliography for 1976-1988**. Troy, NY: Whitston Publishing, 1991. 325 p.

[SCOPE: 1965 to 1988] Comprehensive, unannotated bibliographies of books and articles addressing rape from a range of perspectives, including medical, psychological, legal, feminist, and sociological. To compile the first volume (we were unable to view the 1991 edition) the author searched 31 indexes, catalogs, and bibliographies covering popular, scholarly, professional, alternative press, and clinical literature in all disciplines. Books were listed alphabetically by author; journal articles under 126 subject headings (e.g. hitchhikers, castration, gang rape, etc.).

H99.   Chappell, Duncan, and Faith Fogarty. *Forcible Rape: A Literature Review and Annotated Bibliography*. Washington, DC: Government Printing Office, 1978. 84 p.

[SCOPE: 1969 to 1978] Annotated bibliography of 152 English-language books and articles (mostly scholarly plus a few popular items). Items are arranged into six sections: sociocultural and descriptive features of rape, rape victimization, rape offenders, investigation of rape, legal issues and legislative reform, and rape in foreign countries. Author index.

H100. Kemmer, Elizabeth Jane. *Rape and Rape-Related Issues: An Annotated Bibliography.* Garland Reference Library of Social Science, v.39. New York: Garland Publishing, 1977. 174 p.

H101. Nordquist, Joan. *Domestic Violence, Spouse Abuse/Marital Rape.* Contemporary Social Issues Series, no.4. Santa Cruz, CA: Reference and Research Services, 1986. 64 p.

[SCOPE: 1981 to 1986, plus important older works] Part I covers all aspects of domestic violence and spouse abuse; Part II, marital rape. The unannotated citations are arranged by subject and format (books and book chapters, articles in periodicals, and handbooks, guides, and pamphlets). Includes both descriptive and theoretical works, selected from the English-language literature of law, psychology, political and social sciences, activist organization and government publications, and the popular press. A range of political and social viewpoints are represented. Part III cites bibliographies, resource lists and directories, organizations, and periodical titles. Emphasis is on literature published in the last five years, with particularly important work cited regardless of publication date. No indexes. See also footnote 2, p.129.

H102. _____. *Rape: A Bibliography.* Contemporary Social Issues Series, no.19. Santa Cruz, CA: Reference and Research Service, 1990. 72 p.

[SCOPE: 1985 to 1990, plus important older works] Unannotated citations to books, pamphlets, documents, and periodical articles selected from the English-language literature of psychology, women's studies, the social sciences, and law. Entries are arranged by format, under the following subjects: types of rape and occurrence (general, marital, date/acquaintance, male rape), psychological impact, treatment and services for survivors, attitudes about rape, race and class issues, rapists, pornography and rape, prevention, and legal aspects. Bibliographies, directories, statistical sources, and organizations are listed separately. Emphasis is on literature published in the last five years, with particularly important work cited regardless of publication date. See also footnote 2, p.129.

H103. Picquet, Cheryn D., and Reba A. Best, eds. *Post-Traumatic Stress Disorders, Rape Trauma, Delayed Stress, and Related Conditions: A Bibliography and Directory of Veterans Outreach.* Jefferson, NC: McFarland & Co., 1986. 208 p.

H104. Wilson, Carolyn F. *Violence Against Women: An Annotated Bibliography.* Boston: G.K. Hall, 1981. 111 p.

[SCOPE: 1975 to August 1980, plus earlier classics] Contains 213 fully annotated citations to readily available newsletters, journal articles, popular magazines, and monographs, including both general works and those addressing battered women, rape, sexual abuse of children (with emphasis on father/daughter incest), and pornography. Each topical section begins with a 3-6 page introductory essay, written from a feminist perspective, covering the subject's historical background, research and theory in the area, and policy implications. Social science, legal, law enforcement, historical, medical, psychological, and legislative/criminal law perspectives are represented. Author, title, and subject indexes.

— SEXUAL HARASSMENT

H105. McCaghy, Dawn M. *Sexual Harassment: A Guide to Resources.* Women's Studies Publications. Boston: G.K. Hall, 1985. 181 p.

[SCOPE: 1974 to 1984] Describes 299 books, book chapters, organizational and advocacy publications, government reports, dissertations, periodical articles, and audiovisuals addressing issues of sexual harassment—"any sexual attention on the job which makes a woman uncomfortable, affects her ability to do her work, or interferes with her employment opportunities. It includes: degrading attitudes, looks, touches, jokes, innuendo, gestures, and direct propositions." Items were selected from the literature of the social sciences, women's studies, alternative press, business, law, education, and popular press. Entries are arranged into five chapters, each beginning with an overview of the literature in the area: general works (bibliographies, overviews, surveys, research, feminist perspectives), academic settings, legal and personal coping strategies, legal perspectives, and management responses. Author/title and subject indexes.

➤ SEXUAL HEALTH AND MEDICINE

The National Library of Medicine publishes *Current Bibliographies in*

Medicine (previously titled *Literature Search Series* and *Specialized Bibliography Series*), a bibliographic series which frequently includes sexual health and reproduction related titles (e.g. no. 88-1 *Pregnancy in the Older Woman: Jan. 1983 through Dec. 1987*). Search the *Monthly Catalog of U.S. Government Publications* (see B53) for relevant titles, all of which are available in government depository libraries.

▶ SEXUALLY TRANSMITTED DISEASES *(See also*: AIDS; H46)

H106.   Margolis, Stephen. *Sexually Transmitted Diseases: An Annotated Selective Bibliography*. Garland Reference Library of Social Science, v.290. New York: Garland Publishing, 1985. 162 p.

[SCOPE: 1980 to 1985, plus selected older references] Intended for both professionals and the general public, this 257 item selective bibliography cites both medical/epidemiological literature and popular news magazine articles relating to 27 sexually transmitted diseases and syndromes, and the 23 microorganisms that cause them. Covers laboratory analysis, clinical and basic research, behavioral research, field epidemiology, professional training and client education, and disease management. Entries are arranged into four sections: resources (standards and objectives, statistics, history); medical and epidemiological information; patient behavior, compliance, and education, and health professional training; and diseases and syndromes (AIDS, chancroid, chlamydia infections, gonococcal infections, hepatitis, herpes, simplex virus infections, homosexuality and STDs, minor STDs, nongonococcal urethritis, pelvic inflammatory disease, children and rape victims, syphilis, therapy and adverse reactions, vaginitis, and warts). Includes a glossary and subject index.

▶ WOMEN'S ISSUES *(See also*: F34, H84, H91; *A-Z of Women's Sexuality* [see D15] includes a 5,000 item unannotated bibliography)

H107.   Ballou, Patricia K. *Women: A Bibliography of Bibliographies*. 2nd ed. Boston: G.K. Hall, 1986. 268 p.

[SCOPE: 1960s to 1985] Describes 906 bibliographies (in the form of monographs, journal articles, and government publications) on topics pertaining especially to women, including the following (parenthetical numbers indicate the number of bibliographies in each category): fertility and contraception (5), abortion (6), menstruation (5), pregnancy and childbirth (8), lesbians (20), incest (2), pornography (2), prostitution (1), rape (12), sexual harassment (6), sexuality (3), teenage pregnancy and sexuality (10). Author, title and subject index.

H108. Sahli, Nancy Ann. *Women and Sexuality in America: A Bibliography*. Boston: G.K. Hall, 1984. 404 p.

[SCOPE: Late 19th c. to 1984] Contains 1,684 citations to English-language materials "directly relating to the definition and behavior of women as sexual beings" in 19th and 20th century America. Includes journal articles (unannotated), and books and pamphlets (critically annotated), selected from the professional literature in medicine, psychology, history, sociology, and women's studies. Does not include popular publications, biography, literary works, or highly technical or scientifically complex materials. Entries are grouped as follows, with author, subject, and title indexes: bibliography, surveys and other studies of behavior and attitudes, prescriptive literature before and after 1920, historical interpretation, social/political analysis and theory, legal and ethical perspectives, psychoanalysis, medical and scientific writing before and after 1920, transsexuals and others with gender identity problems, women prisoners and girl delinquents, disabled women, sexual dysfunction and related problems, older women, lesbianism, sexual behavior and prescriptions for children and adolescents, masturbation, and nymphomania. Each chapter begins with a brief overview of the topic.

H109. Stineman, Esther F., with the assistance of Catherine Loeb. *Women's Studies: A Recommended Core Bibliography*. Littleton, CO: Libraries Unlimited, 1979. 672 p.

Loeb, Catherine, Esther F. Stineman, et al. *Women's Studies: A Recommended Core Bibliography, 1980-1985*. Littleton, CO: Libraries Unlimited, 1987. 538 p.

[SCOPE: to 1987] Interdisciplinary, annotated bibliographies of books and periodicals covering the full range of women oriented topics, including rape, pregnancy and childbearing, sexual assault, genital mutilation, sexuality, reproduction, heterosexuality, and lesbianism. The 1,763 annotated citations in the 1970 edition, and the 1,211 entries in the 1987 edition, are classified by discipline (e.g. education, history, law, literature), and by format (e.g. autobiography, reference, periodicals), with author, title and subject indexes.

11

ELECTRONIC DATA BASES

(See also: Ch.12 INDEXES & ABSTRACTS)

The following is a very brief discussion of accessing electronic databases. The field of electronic information retrieval is constantly changing—consult a librarian for the most recent publications on locating, selecting, and accessing databases, and constructing effective searches.

There are four broad categories of databases available on compact disc (CD) or on-line: (1) bibliographic databases (e.g. periodical indexes, library catalogs), some including abstracts as well as bibliographic citations; (2) databases citing non-print materials (e.g. audiovisuals); (3) directories of human or institutional resources; and (4) databases containing the full text of a document rather than just a citation or abstract. Interactive computer systems, such as computer bulletin boards or the forums on *HSX* (see I5), allow two way communication, and are briefly discussed under "Computer Forum Users," p.312.

Most libraries have at least a few bibliographic data bases available on compact disc for free patron use (the NY Public Library, for example, has over 50). Although some on-line databases, such as library catalogs, are accessible through free, non-commercial computer networks such as BITNET (an international network connecting over 2,000 universities and research centers) and Internet (an international network connecting over

HOW TO FIND

• Consult a directory: *Directory of Online Data Bases* (B29), *Data Base Directory* (B28), *Federal Data Base Finder* (B30), and *CD-Roms in Print* (Westport, CT: Meckler). Databases maintained by organizations and accessible only to in-house personnel are not listed in these directories, even though many will perform custom search on request for little or no charge. The *Encyclopedia of Associations* lists available databases and on-line services under "Telecommunication Services," in each entry.

• Order catalogs from data base vendors I1-I4. The *DIALOG Database Catalog* describes 425 databases, the *BRS Database Catalog*, 150. *Compuserve from A-Z* fully describes Compuserve's services and products and is available in bookstores and libraries.

• For detailed information on accessing and using Internet, consult one of the many available users guides, such as *Internet: Getting Started* (Englewood Cliffs, NJ: PTR Prentice Hall, 1993)—search library catalogs for titles using the heading *Internet (Computer network)*. The *Whole Internet: A User's Guide and Catalog* (Sebastopol, CA: O'Reilly and Associates, 1992) includes a detailed subject index to resources available on the network. Be cautioned, however, that as Internet is user driven what is available is constantly changing—on-line directories, such as ARCHIE, provide the most up-to-date information. Universities may provide menu driven access to selected Internet databases and catalogs through their university wide computer systems; contact a reference librarian for assistance.

10 million users), accessing most databases requires both a computer with modem and a subscription to the vendor handling the product. (The "producer" creates and maintains the database; the "vendor" provides a means by which it can be accessed by the public.) Most databases of interest to sex researchers are available through one of the following vendors:

I1.   **BRS Information Technology**: 1200 Rt.7, Latham, NY 12110. PH: (800)345-4277.

I2.   **Compuserve**: 5000 Arlington Center Blvd., Columbus, OH 43220. PH: (800)848-8199.

I3.   **DIALOG Information Service**: 3460 Hillview Ave., Palo Alto, CA 94304. PH: (800)334-2564.

I4.   **Wilsonline**: 950 University Ave., Bronx, NY 10452. PH: (212)588-8400.

Subscriptions to these vendors can be quite expensive and may not be justified for the occasional user. Many libraries offer fee-based on-line search services to their patrons, as do a growing number of private organizations. *On-line Database Search Service Directory* (see B31), indexes such services by the databases to which they have access. The *Directory of Special Libraries* (see B62) notes the on-line systems to which each library subscribes, and details search request procedures and fees. In addition, some providers will conduct fee-based or free searches on request, allowing one to bypass the vendor altogether.

● ● ● ●

Listings: Directory and bibliographic databases are described in Ch.2, Ch.8, and Ch.12. When available, computer readable versions of print indexes and directories are noted in that items entry. Organizations maintaining databases are indicated by a "DB" code, under "Services," in the descriptive listings beginning on p.321.

I5.   **Human Sexuality (HSX)**. Shady, New York: Clinical Communications Inc., 1983-.
An interactive, on-line computer system, which seeks to provide "a helpful, authoritative source of sex-related information and advice," and to create "a compassionate community, where members feel comfortable sharing their feelings, experiences and relationships." They claim that "through Human Sexuality your computer provides you with a direct line to foremost authorities in sexual medicine. Our Consulting Editors and other specialists offer you knowledge and guidance on virtually any sex-related concern." Files include: (1) *Human Sexuality and Information Advisory Service*: an electronic magazine providing full text of over 2,000 articles, written for a general audience, by experts in the fields of gynecology, sex therapy, psychiatry, pharmacology, endocrinology,

urology, and others, including prominent professors, researchers, and practitioners; (2) *Answering Your Questions*: brief expert replies to reader's inquiries; (3) *On-Line Transcripts*: conversation with experts on sexual dysfunction; (4) *Personals and Letters*; (5) *Human Sexuality Support Groups and Forums*: over 30 interactive forums designed for ongoing dialogue between users (see "Computer Forum Users," p.312); and (6) *Interactive Programs*: interactive computer assisted sex instruction. Files are accessible only by subscription to Compuserve (see I2). For more information about the database, contact Clinical Communications: 132 Hutchin Hill, Shady NY 12409. PH: (914)679-2217.

I6. *LINKLine* (Library and Information Network). New York: Planned Parenthood Federation of America. Database.

A listing of curricula, programs, pamphlets, audiovisuals, and other materials for use in sexuality and reproductive education. Cites over 20,000 books, journal articles, brochures, posters, programs, curricula, videos and papers on all aspects of sexuality and reproductive health cataloged or reviewed by the Katherine Dexter McCormick Library (see A7) or by the Education Department's Federation Clearinghouse of Educational Resources. It consists of five data bases: *Audiovisual Data Base*—ratings and reviews of audiovisuals; *Clearinghouse Data Base*—pamphlets, brochures, newsletters, curricula, conference announcements, conference meetings, training manuals; *Program Data Base*—descriptions of programs in schools and communities; *Library Catalog*—bibliographic citations to books and research articles held in the library; and *Sexperts Database*—referrals to trainers and speakers. Input is drawn from 125 journals, as well as publisher's and distributor's catalogs, book reviews, acquisition lists, curricula, and newsletters. It is available for free use at the McCormick Library and many affiliated libraries (see p.12), and staff will conduct fee-based searches in response to mail or phone queries. For more information, contact the McCormick Library (see A7) or the education department (see X223). SEX SUBJECTS COVERED: all subjects, especially those relating to family planning, reproduction and reproductive health, and adolescent sexuality, including men and family planning, STDs, abortion, disability and sexuality, substance abuse and reproductive health, birth control, child sexual abuse prevention, parent-child communication about sex, infertility, school sexuality education, AIDS, peer education/teen theaters, menopause, teen pregnancy and parenting, non-English educational materials, religious family life education.

12

INDEXES & ABSTRACTS

Indexes provide access to materials published in a particular field of knowledge or in a particular format. All provide sufficient bibliographic information and subject access to allow quick identification of relevant items, and some include abstracts summarizing the facts, ideas, or opinions presented in the cited works. Many indexes are now available in computer readable formats, either on compact disc—available for free use in libraries—or on-line through a database vendor such as DIALOG or BRS (see Ch.11). As they allow complex searches linking two or more concepts and specifying search limitations by publication date, language, and other factors, these technologies expand user access beyond the simple author, title, and subject access provided by most print indexes. Use the on-line version of an index when the most current information is sought (many are updated weekly or even daily) or if the print version is unavailable (indexes can't be borrowed through interlibrary loan).

Research and writing on sexuality related issues is conducted by professionals working within a wide variety of academic disciplines and professions, and published in a correspondingly diverse range of journals. As there are no comprehensive, interdisciplinary "sexuality studies" or "sexology" indexes currently available, conducting a comprehensive literature review on a sexuality related topic will necessitate employing a number of indexing tools.

HOW TO FIND

• Search library catalogs using the appropriate subject heading for the topic, discipline, or type of material sought, followed by the form subdivision –*Abstracts*, or –*Indexes* (e.g. *Anthropology–Abstracts*, *Periodicals–Indexes*).

• Consult *Index and Abstract Directory: An International Guide to Services and Serials Coverage* (see B56) or a periodical directory (see B69, B72-B74), especially *Magazines for Libraries* (see B69), which includes lengthy descriptions of over 243 of the most important titles. For newspapers, see *Newspaper Indexes: A Location and Subject Guide for Researchers* (B58) or the *Lathrop Report on Newspaper Indexes* (B57). For computer readable databases, see B28, B29.

• Consult *American Reference Books Annual* (see B78) for reviews of new indexes. Those with interdisciplinary coverage are described in the chapter "Library Service"; more specialized titles, under the relevant topic.

• To identify articles appearing in a particular journal or magazine, ask the publisher if a cumulative index is available or if they offer subject searches of any in-house database.

• To identify the indexes covering a particular journal, check the front pages of the journal itself, where they are often listed, or contact the publisher directly—periodical directories list their addresses and phone numbers.

• Indexes maintained by organizations and institutions are noted in the directories cited in Ch.30 and described in Ch.2. (*Encyclopedia of Associations*, for example, notes available databases under "Computer Services" in each entry). Some are accessible to the public via commercial database vendors (see Ch.11). The providers of others may conduct free or fee-based searches on request.

• • • •

Listings: Described below are 66 print and computer readable indexes and abstracts which either specialize in sexuality related topics or frequently cite sex related literature. Most are periodical indexes, although some index other types of materials as well. Indexes to dissertations (see B34), bibliographies (see B12), government documents (see B48-B54), books (B15-B17), statistics (see B85, B87, B91), audiovisuals (see B5-B11), and measurement tools (see B66) are described in Ch.2. With the exception of a few specialized sexology titles, all are readily available in research libraries. Current publishers and titles are cited; if the title was changed in the past but the original numbering system continued, the publication date indicated is that of the first issue of the original title (see Sheehy's *Guide* B81, for complete publishing history). In addition to bibliographic information, annotations include sex subjects covered (as indicated by controlled vocabulary and subject index headings), the types of materials indexed, and the index's availability in a computer readable format. All of the computer databases described are accessible to the public on compact disc or on-line through commercial database vendors (see Ch.11). Organizations and institutions maintaining databases are indicated by a "DB" code under "Services" in the descriptive listings beginning on p.321. Non-serial, single volume indexes (e.g. *Lesbian Periodicals Index*) and annual bibliographies (e.g. Whitston's *AIDS Bibliography*) are described in Ch.10.

> SEX LIBRARY INDEXES

Sex library catalogs serve as both a record of the book and journal titles cataloged by a library, and an index of the journal articles and book chapters those titles contain. See "Sex Library Catalogs," Ch.8.

> ALTERNATIVE PUBLICATIONS INDEXES

J1. *Alternative Press Index: An Index to Alternative and Radical Publications.* Baltimore: Alternative Press Center, 1969-. Quarterly.

Subject index to over 200 English-language "alternative and radical publications," including gay/lesbian (e.g. *The Advocate* [see K68], *Gay Community News* [see K69], *Lesbian Contradictions* [see K73]), feminist, Native American, environmental, animal rights, Marxist, etc.; radical right wing titles are not covered. SEX SUBJECTS COVERED: The only widely available index covering a significant number of gay/lesbian titles. Subjects covered vary from issue to issue, but usually include the following: AIDS, AIDS demonstrations, AIDS education, abortion, androgyny, anti-abortion movements, bisexuality, celibacy, children and sex, gay/lesbian, heterosexuality, intergenerational sex, masturbation, monogamy, orgasm, pro-choice movements, prostitution, rape, safe sex, sex law, sex offenders, sexual assault, sexual ethics, sexuality, and sodomy laws.

J2. *The Left Index.* Santa Cruz, CA: Reference and Research Services, 1982-. Quarterly.

Author and subject index to professional and scholarly periodicals written from "Marxist, radical or left perspectives."

► CURRENT AWARENESS SERVICES *(See also:* K64, K131)

J3. *Current Contents:* . . . Philadelphia: Institute for Scientific Information, 1961-. Weekly.

Reproduces the complete table of contents of the latest issues of over 6,500 of the "world's most important journals," as well as those of relevant multi-authored books. Seven sections are presently published, including *Current Contents: Arts and Humanities, Current Contents: Social and Behavioral Sciences, Current Contents: Life Sciences,* and *Current Contents: Clinical Practice.* Use them to locate articles not yet indexed elsewhere and to identify features which are not usually indexed at all (e.g. calendars, audiovisual reviews, employment opportunities). Title and author indexes. COMPUTER READABLE FORMATS: *Current Contents Search* (covering the most recent 3-4 weeks of all seven sections) available on-line from BRS and DIALOG, updated weekly.

J4. *Newsearch.* Foster City, CA: Information Access. Current citations only. Database.

A computer readable database, with no print equivalent, available on microfiche, compact disc, and on-line from BRS, DIALOG, and other vendors. Indexes the complete contents of a wide range of magazines, journals, and newspapers published in the past 2-6 weeks. Over 2,000 new records are added daily and citations are transferred monthly to one of five cumulative databases: *Magazine Index* (see J7); *National Newspaper Index* (see J9); *Academic Index* (see J47); *Legal Resources Index* (for law journal and legal newspapers); and *Trade and Industry Index* (for trade and industry journals).

J5. *Newspaper and Periodical Abstracts.* Louisville, KY: UMI/Data Courier. 1988-. Daily. Database.

A computer readable database, with no print equivalent, providing comprehensive indexing, with abstracts, to more than 25 major national, regional, and international newspapers, and over 450 general interest, professional, and scholarly periodicals. Updated daily within 48 hours of publication. Available on-line from DIALOG, and on compact disc.

➤ MAGAZINES

J6. *ACCESS: The Supplementary Index of Periodicals.* Edited by John Gordon Burke and Ned Kehde. Evanston, IL: John Gordon Burke Publisher. 1975-. 3/year.

ACCESS indexes magazines not presently covered by the *Readers Guide to Periodicals Literature* (see J8). 120 titles are currently covered, including general and special interest magazines, regional and city publications, and professional library science magazines; titles added to *Readers Guide* are dropped by *ACCESS*. Consists of two parts: an author index covering periodical articles, fiction, and poetry; and a subject index providing access to nonfiction articles and reviews of books, theater, art, films, etc. SEX SUBJECTS COVERED: Indexes *Playboy* and *Penthouse*.

J7. *Magazine Index.* Foster City, CA: Information Access. 1959-. Monthly. Database.

Available on compact disc in many libraries as part of the InfoTrac system and on-line (1959-) from BRS, DIALOG, and others. Indexes the complete contents of more than 550 U.S. and Canadian magazines, including feature articles, news, letters to the editor, editorials, book and film reviews, columns, fiction, and poetry. Provides subject, title, name, and author access. Records are added daily to *NewSearch* (see J4), and transferred to this database monthly.

J8. *Reader's Guide to Periodical Literature.* New York: H.W. Wilson, 1901-. Bi-weekly.

Cumulative index to over 400 English language general interest and news periodicals published in the U.S. (e.g. *Time, Newsweek, U.S. News and World Report, Vanity Fair, Sports Illustrated, Science,* etc.). Indexed items include articles of at least one column, book reviews, selected letters to the editor, editorials, short stories and poetry, and other features. Citations are unannotated, and are alphabetically arranged by subject and author. See footnote 1 for additional details. SEX SUBJECTS COVERED: all topics; see footnote 1. COMPUTER READABLE FORMATS: on-line (1983-) from BRS and Wilsonline; and on compact disc.

➤ NEWSPAPERS

J9.   *National Newspaper Index*. Foster City, CA: Information Access Company, 1970-. Monthly. Database.

Available on microfilm or on compact disc in many libraries, and on-line (1970-) from BRS and DIALOG. Title and author index to articles, news reports, columns, editorials, letters to the editor, obituaries, cartoons, illustrations, and reviews (e.g. film, theater, book, restaurant) published in *The Christian Science Monitor*, *New York Times*, *Los Angeles Times*, *Wall Street Journal*, and *Washington Post*. Records are added daily to *NewSearch* (see J4) and transferred to this database monthly. There are no abstracts, although titles may be enhanced with descriptive words.

J10.   *New York Times Index*. New York: New York Times, 1913-. Semi-monthly.

Provides subject, name, and geographic access to articles, reviews of all

---

[1] H.W. Wilson publishes a number of readily available indexes. Each indexes the most prominent journals in its field, selected for their reference value and the need to insure that no important area of the field is overlooked. Arrangement is similar in all Wilson indexes; bibliographic citations are alphabetically classified by author and subject, with extensive cross references. Subject headings are derived from the literature, reference works, the various Wilson databases, and Library of Congress subject headings. They vary by index, but all titles include many sexuality and reproduction related subject headings, such as celibacy, change of sex, child molesting, homosexuality, incest, lesbians, masturbation, pedophilia, safe sex, sex and law, sex and religion, sex crimes, sex education, sex hormones, sex in television, sex oriented businesses, sexual desire, sexual disorder, sexual deviation, sexual ethics, sexual fantasy, sexually transmitted disease, and sexual behavior in general, and sexual behavior of particular groups (eg. priests–sexual behavior, astronauts–sexual behavior). Most Wilson indexes are available in print, on compact disc, and on-line through Wilsonline (see I4) and other vendors.

types, obituaries, editorials, columns, and other features appearing in the "newspaper of record." Lengthy, descriptive abstracts are provided for "significant news, editorial matter and special features." For other items, only the title, subject matter, and date of appearance are noted.

➤ SCHOLARLY LITERATURE INDEXES

The interdisciplinary indexes, J39, J47, J52, J61, J62, and J63, each cover a wide range of sexuality related subjects and should be consulted when researching all but the most specialized topics.

➤ AIDS *(See also*: J24)

HOW TO FIND

• There are many AIDS related indexes and on-line databases available. To identify additional resources, consult directories B1-B3; request the *Directory of AIDS Related Databases and Bulletin Boards* from the National AIDS Information Clearinghouse (see X35); or search the *AIDS Research Database* on AIDSQuest (see J11).

J11.   *AIDSQuest On-line*. Atlanta: CDC AIDS Weekly, 1988-. Weekly. Database.

Updated weekly, this on-line database provides international coverage of AIDS and HIV infection. It consists of ten files: (1) *AIDS Meeting Database*—a calendar of meetings and conferences; (2) *AIDS Periodical Information Database*—full text of over 8,000 English-language articles and book reviews published since 1985 (for more comprehensive coverage of AIDS related literature, see *AIDSLINE*, J45); (3) *AIDS Research Databases*—descriptions of computer readable and on-line AIDS databases; (4) *Database of AIDS Information and Support Services*—telephone numbers of organizations worldwide; (5) *Database of AIDS Specific Periodicals*—titles and publishers of over 250 AIDS specific periodicals worldwide; (6) *Database of Antiviral and Immunomodulatory Therapies for AIDS*—development of AIDS research and treatment since 1985; (7) *CDC AIDS Weekly*—full text (see K14); (8) *CDC AIDS Surveillance Reports*—full text (see K15), including demographic statistics on AIDS by state and city; (9) *CDC MMWR AIDS Data*—full text of AIDS related articles from *Morbidity and Mortality Weekly Report* (see K156); and (10) *CDC's Understanding AIDS*—full text of the brochure *Understanding AIDS*, produced by the CDC in 1988.

J12.   *AIDS Bibliography*. National Library of Medicine. Washington, DC:. Government Printing Office, 1988-. Monthly.

A print record of journal articles, monographs, conference proceedings, and audiovisuals, catalogued in the on-line database *AIDSLINE* (see H45). Entries are classified by author and subject using terms from the National Library of Medicine's thesaurus, *Medical Subject Headings* (known as MeSH). Items cited address pre-clinical, clinical, epidemiological, diagnostic, and preventative issues. New AIDS/HIV related serial titles are cited in the June and December issues. For older items, see the seventeen AIDS bibliographies published in the National Library of Medicine's now defunct *Search Service Series* between 1983 and 1987. COMPUTER READABLE FORMATS: *AIDSLINE* (see J45).

J13.   *AIDS Literature and News Review*. Frederick, MD: University Publishing Group, 1987. Monthly.

Contains abstracts to articles on all aspects of AIDS, published in over 500 medical, public policy, law, education, psychology, and social science publications.

➤ ANTHROPOLOGY

See also, *Anthropological Literature, Abstracts in Anthropology*, and *International Bibliography of Social & Cultural Anthropology*.

J14.   *Human Relations Area Files Index*. New Haven, CT: Human Relations Area Files Archives, 1988.

A subject index on microfiche to the Human Relations Area Files Archives (see X96 for a full description of the collection). SEX SUBJECTS COVERED: cross cultural coverage of all aspects of sexuality, marriage and family, reproduction, sex crimes, and sexual abuse, including: sexuality, sexual stimulation, sexual relations, sexual practices, premarital sex, extramarital sex, sex restrictions, homosexuality, celibacy, reasons for marriage, types of marriage, arranged marriage, irregular marriage, polygamous families, rape and sex crimes, puberty rites, and sex training.

For more details, see the *Outline of Cultural Materials* (C7). COMPUTER READABLE FORMATS: a portion of the archives is available on compact disc and custom searches of the collection can be requested.

➤ BIOLOGY

J15. *Biological Abstracts*. Philadelphia: Biological Sciences Information Services (BIOSIS), 1926-. Semi-monthly.

Index, with abstracts, to the worldwide periodical literature in the life sciences, including both biological and biomedical journals. For abstracts of research reports, review articles, U.S. patents, books, and conference proceedings, consult *Biological Abstracts/RRM*. (Philadelphia: BIOSIS, 1962-. Monthly.) COMPUTER READABLE FORMATS: *BIOSIS Previews* (1969-) combines both titles, and is available on-line from DIALOG (updated weekly), and BRS (updated monthly).

➤ BIOETHICS

J16. *BIOETHICSLINE*. Washington: National Reference Center for Bioethics, Kennedy Institute of Ethics, Georgetown University, 1973-. Bimonthly. Database.

An on-line index to the worldwide English-language literature relating to the ethical and public policy aspects of medicine, health care, and biomedical and behavioral research. Provides coverage of relevant literature in the health sciences, law, public policy, religion, philosophy, social sciences, and popular press, with over 90 periodicals, 30 indexes, and 13 on-line data bases monitored. Books, audiovisual materials, unpublished documents, journal articles, government documents (e.g. laws, regulations, court decisions), newsletters, and newspapers are classified by author, title, and subject using terms from *Bioethics Thesaurus*. The database is publicly accessible via *MEDLARS* (see J45), or contact the National Reference Center for Bioethics Literature (1-800-MED-ETHX) for custom search services. See also X61. SEX SUBJECTS COVERED: sexuality, contraception, abortion (moral, religious, legal, and social aspects), population, reproductive technologies (including artificial insemination and surrogacy, cryobanking, in vitro fertilization and embryo transfer, sex selection), HIV and AIDS, human experimentation and genetics, and other topics.

➤ CHILD AND ADOLESCENT STUDIES

J17. *Adolescent Mental Health Abstracts*. New York: Center for Adolescent Mental Health, Columbia University, School of Social Work, 1983-1988. Quarterly. Ceased.

Ceased publication in 1988. Abstracted articles from over 350 journals "pertaining to research, theory, policy and service delivery in adolescent mental health." Subject access. SEX SUBJECTS COVERED: sexuality and pregnancy were primary subject headings.

J18. *Child Abuse and Neglect Database*. Washington: National Center on Child Abuse and Neglect, Clearinghouse on Child Abuse and Neglect Information. 1967-. Biennial. Database.

An on-line database (available from DIALOG), with no print equivalent, of English language materials of interest to those working in the field of child abuse and neglect, including social workers, sociologists, educators, mental health professionals, criminologists, and legal researchers. Focus is on materials relating to the definition, identification, prevention, and treatment of child abuse. Consists of five files: (1) descriptions of research projects; (2) descriptions of service programs; (3) bibliographic references; (4) excerpts from state laws and legal references; (5) audiovisual descriptions. See also X273. SEX SUBJECTS COVERED: include incest, sexual abuse, child pornography and prostitution, treatment of sex offenders and victims.

J19. *Child Development Abstracts and Bibliography*. Society for Research in Child Development. Chicago: University of Chicago Press. 1927-. 3/year.

Contains abstracts of professional journal articles and books relating to the physical and psychological growth and development of children and adolescents. Subject and keyword access. SEX SUBJECTS COVERED: subjects vary, but usually include AIDS (e.g. "Children's Conceptions of AIDS"), sexual abuse, sexual behavior, and teen pregnancy.

➤ CRIMINAL JUSTICE

J20. *Criminal Justice Abstracts*. National Council on Crime and Delinquency. Monsey, NY: Willow Tree Press. 1968-. Quarterly.

Contains abstracts of current books, newspapers, magazine and journal articles, dissertations, and reports drawn from the worldwide criminal justice and criminology literature. Author, geographic, and subject access. Most issues contain a literature review or bibliography synthesizing research on a subject of current importance. SEX SUBJECTS COVERED: AIDS, child sexual abuse, incest, pedophilia, rape, sex offenders, sex offenses, and sexual assault. COMPUTER READABLE FORMATS: on-line (1968-) from West Publishing Company, and on compact disc.

J21. *CJPI: Criminal Justice Periodical Index*. Ann Arbor, MI: Indexing Service, UMI, 1975-. 3/year.

Indexes over 100 U.S., British, and Canadian journals and newsletters in corrections, criminal law, criminology, drug abuse, family law, juvenile justice, police studies, prison administration, rehabilitation, and security systems. Author and subject access using terms from the *CJPI Thesaurus*. SEX SUBJECTS COVERED: AIDS, abortion, adultery, child abuse and neglect, homosexuals, obscenity (law), prostitution, pornography, rape, and sex crimes. COMPUTER READABLE FORMATS: on-line (1975-) from DIALOG.

J22. *National Criminal Justice Reference Service Database*. Rockville, MD: National Criminal Justice Reference Service, National Institute of Justice. 1972-. Monthly. On-line.

Represents the holdings of the National Criminal Justice Reference Service, an international information clearinghouse covering all aspects of crime prevention, corrections, criminology, and prosecution (see X217). Includes over 110,000 abstracts to books, government documents, research reports, periodical articles, program reports, government documents, dissertations, and audiovisual materials. Subject access using terms from the *National Criminal Justice Thesaurus*. SEX SUBJECTS COVERED: see X217. COMPUTER READABLE FORMATS: on-line from DIALOG.

➤ DISABILITY AND ILLNESS (*See*: X101-X103)

➤ DRUG AND ALCOHOL ABUSE (*See also*: X42-X44)

J23. *Drug Information and Alcohol Use and Abuse*. Minneapolis: Drug Information Services, 1968-. Database.

An on-line database, with no print equivalent, covering the psychological, sociological, educational, and biomedical aspects of alcohol and drug use.

Indexes English-language journals, books, unpublished papers, pamphlets, and audiovisual materials. See X43 for access information.

➤ EDUCATION

J24. *Combined Health Information Database.* Bethesda, MD: U.S. National Institute of Health. 1979-. Quarterly. Database.

An on-line database, intended for both professionals and the general public, of health education and health promotion materials. Consists of 14 files (all of which are available from BRS), three of which contain sex related materials: (1) *AIDS Education Materials Database* (1984-)— contains abstracts of over 5,000 published and unpublished educational items, including pamphlets, curriculum, audiovisual materials, comic books, journal articles, and books. Produced by the National AIDS Information Clearinghouse (see X35); (2) *AIDS School Health Education Database* (1987-)—complete text and/or abstracts of educational materials, journal articles, books, pamphlets, and program descriptions related to AIDS education for children and youth. Produced by C.D.C Prevention and Health Promotion; and (3) *Health Education Database* (1977-)— contains abstracts of curriculum materials, journal articles, conference proceedings, descriptions of programs, and other materials on the methods, research, and practice of health education and promotion, including items relating to sexually transmitted disease education, sexual abuse prevention, sex education, teenage pregnancy prevention, and family planning. Produced by C.D.C. Prevention and Health Promotion.

J25. *Current Index to Journals in Education* (**CIJE**). Phoenix: Oryx Press, 1969-. Monthly.

Produced under the auspices of the U.S. Department of Education's Educational Resource Information Centers network, known as ERIC. Provides comprehensive indexing, with abstracts, to over 800 education periodicals, as well as select coverage of educational articles from other periodicals. Author, title, and subject access using terms from the *Thesaurus of ERIC Descriptors*. SEX SUBJECTS COVERED: all topics, including sex education, treatment of sex offenders, programs for victims of sex crimes, adolescent and child sexuality, STD prevention programs, teen pregnancy. COMPUTER READABLE FORMATS: *ERIC* (see J27).

J26. *Education Index*. New York: H.W. Wilson, 1929-. 10/year.

Indexes 400 English-language education periodicals as well as selected yearbooks and monographs. Entries are arranged alphabetically by subject and author. See footnote 1, p.156, for additional details. SEX SUBJECTS COVERED: sexual behavior and attitudes (primarily of adolescents and college students); sex attitudes–tests and scales (*–tests and scales* can be used as a subdivision under any topic; AIDS (disease) education, family life education, sex education, sexual abuse prevention education, and sexually transmitted disease education. Includes critiques, methods (e.g. curriculum for all age levels), theory, and practice. COMPUTER READABLE FORMATS: on-line (1983-) from BRS and Wilsonline, updated twice weekly; and on compact disc.

J27. *ERIC*. Rockville, MD: U.S. Dept. of Education, Educational Resources Information Center. 1966-. Databases.

The U.S. Department of Education maintains a network of Educational Resource Information Centers throughout the country which collect and index educational materials for inclusion in the ERIC database. (Each clearinghouse also produces and disseminates reference materials in its area of focus). Corresponding to two print indexes—*CIJE* (see J25) covering journal articles, and *RIE* (see J30) covering other items—ERIC contains more than 700,000 abstracts and is updated monthly. It is available on compact disc in many libraries and on-line from DIALOG, BRS, and other vendors. For more information contact ACCESS ERIC: 1600 Research Blvd., Rockville, MD 20850. PH.(800)USE-ERIC.

J28. *Exceptional Child Education Resources* (**ECER**). Council for Exceptional Children. Reston, VA: Council for Exceptional Children. 1969-. Quarterly.

Contains abstracts of resources on the education and development of "exceptional" people of all ages, including gifted and talented, those with physical, mental, emotional, or learning disabilities, and the culturally different. Includes books, journal articles (200 titles scanned), research reports, curriculum and other teaching materials, dissertations, ERIC documents, and other print and non-print resources. About half of ECER documents are also cited in ERIC. Author, title, and subject access. SEX SUBJECTS COVERED: include sexual abuse of the disabled, sex and disability, and sex education. COMPUTER READABLE FORMATS: *ECER Database* (1966-) on-line from BRS and DIALOG, updated monthly.

Custom searches are available from the Council.

J29. *Physical Education Index.* Cape Girardeau, MO: Ben Oak Publishing, 1978-. Quarterly.

Indexes over 175 English-language periodicals in dance, health, physical education, physical therapy, recreation, sports, and sports medicine. Subject access. SEX SUBJECTS COVERED: AIDS education and prevention, adolescent sexual behavior and pregnancy, family life education, homosexuality (e.g. "Combatting homophobia in sports and physical education"), menopause, menstruation, pregnancy, public health, sex education, sexual health, toxic shock syndrome, and venereal diseases, among others.

J30. *Resources in Education (RIE).* U.S. Dept. of Education, ERIC. Washington: U.S. Department of Health, Education, and Welfare. 1966-. Monthly.

A product of the U.S. Department of Education's ERIC system (see J27). Abstracts books, technical reports, indexes, tests, questionnaires, meeting proceedings, speeches, unpublished manuscripts and documents, and policy papers by local, state, and federal agencies. Access by author, format, and subject using terms from the *Thesaurus of ERIC Descriptors.* Updated monthly, with over 15,000 items added annually. SEX SUBJECTS COVERED: includes sex related curriculum and measurement tools. COMPUTER READABLE FORMATS: *ERIC* (see J27).

➤ FAMILY PLANNING

J31. *Current Literature in Family Planning.* New York: Education Department, Planned Parenthood Federation of America, 1966-. Monthly.

An annotated list of books and journal articles relating to family planning in the U.S., recently cataloged by Planned Parenthood Federation of America's Katherine Dexter McCormick Library (see A7). Reprints of cited articles are available for $1.00; an order form is included in each issue. SEX SUBJECTS COVERED: items are classified under more than 100 sex, reproduction, and family planning topics; see C9 and A7 for details. COMPUTER READABLE FORMATS: see LINKLine (G8).

➤ GERONTOLOGY

J32. *Abstracts in Social Gerontology: Current Literature on Aging.* National Council on Aging. Newbury Park, CA: Sage Publications, 1957-. Quarterly.

Titled *Current Literature on Aging* until 1989. Indexes English-language periodical articles, books, government documents, legislation, research studies, and fugitive documents related to aging. Each issue contains approximately 250 abstracts of "important recent literature" classified by subject, plus an additional 250 bibliographic citations arranged alphabetically. Keyword and author access. SEX SUBJECTS COVERED: sexuality, singlehood, couples, family relations, and homosexual relations are primary subject headings; other sex subjects are listed in the index.

J33. *AgeLine.* Washington: National Gerontology Resource Center, 1978-. Bimonthly. Database.

Also known as *AARP Data Base.* Intended for researchers, older persons and their families, and service providers, this on-line database provides bibliographic coverage of the literature on aging, social gerontology, and geriatrics, with emphasis on the study of aging in social, psychological, health-related, public policy, and economic contexts. Updated bimonthly, it includes abstracts to English-language journal articles, books, book chapters, reports, government documents, conference papers, and dissertations. Subject access using terms from the *Thesaurus of Aging Terminology.* Available from BRS and DIALOG, or the National Gerontology Resource Center will perform custom searches (see X28).

➤ HUMANITIES

J34. *Arts and Humanities Citation Index.* Philadelphia: Institute for Scientific Information, 1976-. Biannual.

A citation index covering the international periodical literature in the arts and humanities, including art, dance, film, folklore, history, humanities, language and linguistics, literature, music, philosophy, radio, religion, television, and theater. It fully indexes over 1,300 leading arts and humanities journals, plus relevant material from an additional 5,000 social and natural science journals. See J61 for details of arrangement and use. COMPUTER READABLE FORMATS: *Arts and Humanities Search* (1980-) on-line from DIALOG.

J35. *Humanities Index.* New York: H.W. Wilson, 1974-. Quarterly. The "leading cumulative index to English language periodicals in the humanities," this index currently covers over 345 periodicals in theology, religion, performing arts, language and literature, philosophy, history, folklore, classical studies, and archeology. Citations are arranged alphabetically by subject and author. See also footnote 1, p.156. SEX SUBJECTS COVERED: Sex (religious aspects), sex in the bible, homosexuality and religion; pornography, erotic literature, and pornographic films; sex and history, humor, law, and politics; sex attitudes and customs; birth control–moral and religious aspects; sexual behavior of authors, musicians, philosophers, actors, politicians; sex symbolism in art, literature, and motion pictures; the treatment of sex in literature, motion pictures, art, music, television, theater, and the performing arts, including the treatment of adultery, androgyny, celibacy, chastity, generative organs, homosexuality, impotence, incest, lesbians, love, masturbation, pedophilia, rape, sadism, sadomasochism, seduction, sex role, sexual fantasy, and sexual deviation. COMPUTER READABLE FORMATS: on-line (1984-) from Wilsonline, updated twice weekly; and on compact disc.

▶ LAW (*See also*: J20-J22)

J36. *Index to Legal Periodicals.* American Association of Law Libraries. New York: H.W. Wilson, 1908-. Monthly.

Indexes English-language legal periodicals worldwide, which "regularly publish legal articles of high quality and permanent reference value." Arranged alphabetically by subject and author. Subject headings, drawn from the legal vernacular, are listed in each annual cumulative volume. See also footnote 1, p.156. SEX SUBJECTS COVERED: abortion, adultery, AIDS, artificial insemination, bigamy, birth control, censorship, genetic engineering, in-vitro fertilization, obscenity, prostitution, rape, reproductive technology, sex crimes, sexual harassment, surrogate motherhood, transsexuality, wrongful birth, wrongful life, and wrongful pregnancy. COMPUTER READABLE FORMATS: on-line (1981-) from Wilsonline and other vendors, updated twice weekly; and on compact disc.

J37. *Index to Periodical Articles Related to Law.* Dobbs Ferry, NY: Glanville Publishers, 1958-. Quarterly.

Cites English-language articles of "research value" to law but which aren't published in law journals (with the exception of new periodicals not yet indexed elsewhere). Among the 239 titles scanned are a wide range of social and behavioral sciences journals, popular magazines, and trade publications (e.g. *Journal of American Medical Association, Psychology Today, Rolling Stone, American Journal of Sociology,* and *Billboard*). Author/title and subject access. A *Thirty Year Cumulation 1958-1988,* is available. SEX SUBJECTS COVERED: indexes law related articles from *Playgirl, Playboy,* and the gay newsmagazine, *The Advocate* (see K68). Subject headings include: abortion, AIDS, bioethics, censorship, child abuse, incest, obscenity, pornography, privacy rights, rape, reproduction, sexual harassment, and sex offenders.

➤ LITERATURE

J38. *MLA: International Bibliography of Books and Articles in the Modern Languages and Literature.* New York: Modern Language Association of America. 1921-. Annual.

"A classified listing and subject index for books and articles published [in all languages] on modern languages, literature, folklore and linguistics." Entries include monographs, articles in multi-author works, collections, conference proceedings, and reference works, including dictionaries, bibliographies, research guides, and encyclopedias. Author, title and subject access. SEX SUBJECTS COVERED: erotic literature, poetry, folksongs, ballads, and folk literature; pornography; sexual metaphors, sexual allusions, sexual imagery, and sexual symbolism; the treatment of sex in literature, poetry, drama, novels, and folklore, including the treatment of abortion, bestiality, chastity, erotic love, eroticism, incest, marriage, pedophilia, prostitution, sadism, sexual desire, sexual initiation, sexual intercourse, sexual relations, sexuality, virginity, and voyeurism. COMPUTER READABLE FORMATS: on-line from DIALOG (1963-) and Wilsonline (1981-), updated 10x/year; and on compact disc.

➤ MARRIAGE AND FAMILY STUDIES

J39. *Family Resource Database of the Family Resource and Research Center.* Minneapolis: National Council on Family Relations, 1970-. Monthly. Database.

An on-line database covering the interdisciplinary family studies field. Consists of three files: (1) *Inventory of Marriage and Family On-line* (corresponds to J40)—abstracts of English-language books, journals and newsletters (over 1500 scanned), dissertations, government publications, conference proceedings, instructional materials, audiovisuals, and audio/video catalogs from the worldwide literature of education, psychology, sociology, health sciences, anthropology, economics, theology, law, home economics, and social work. Access by author, subject, title, document language, and type of material; (2) *Human Resources Bank*—a multi-professional, multi-disciplinary directory of family experts worldwide willing to be contacted by the general public, including psychologists, counselors and therapists, educators, researchers, and health professionals; and (3) *Idea Bank*—current works-in-progress, planned work, and ideas which have not yet been formalized, at the international, national, regional, state, and local levels. All three files are available on-line from DIALOG, BRS, and other vendors; or contact the National Council on Family Relations directly for custom searches (see X131). SEX SUBJECTS COVERED: provides comprehensive coverage of all aspects of marriage and family. Items are classified under over 200 topics in 11 major subject areas, including "Issues related to reproduction," "Sexual attitudes and behaviors," "Trends and change in marriage and family," "Family relationships and dynamics," and "Mate selection, marriage and divorce." Specific topics covered include: premarital, marital, and extramarital sexual behavior, abortion, birth control, bisexuality, child sexual abuse, childlessness/fecundity, family planning, fertility rates, homosexuality and the family, illegitimacy, incest, intimacy, interpersonal relationships, lesbianism, marriage counseling, marital enrichment, menopause, population studies, pregnancy, childbirth and postpartum, prostitution, rape/sexual victimization, singles (lifestyle), teen pregnancy, transsexuals, sex education, sex selection, sex therapy, sexual behavior, sexual dysfunction, STDs, and unmarried mothers.

J40.   *Inventory of Marriage and Family Literature*. Minneapolis: National Council on Family Relations, 1964-. Annual.

Continues the *International Bibliography of Research in Marriage and Family* (1900-1964). A comprehensive, interdisciplinary index to marriage and family related literature, drawn from family studies, social and behavioral sciences, humanities, health sciences, and other fields. Over 500 professional and scholarly journals are regularly scanned. Abstracts are included in the on-line database, *Family Resources Database* (see J39). SEX SUBJECTS COVERED: see J39 for details. COMPUTER READABLE FORMATS: *Inventory of Marriage and Family Online* (see J39).

J41. *Sage Family Studies Abstracts.* Newbury Park, CA: Sage Publications, 1979-. 3/year.

Contains abstracts of major articles, reports, government documents, pamphlets, theses and dissertations, books, and other materials relating to the family and interpersonal relationships, with emphasis on those addressing theoretical, research, and public policy issues. Author and subject access. SEX SUBJECTS COVERED: subject headings include: sexual attitudes and behavior; sexual deviance; sex problems and treatment; homosexuality and homosexuals; pregnancy and childbirth; fertility, birth control and abortion; singlehood, mate selection and marriage; adolescent pregnancy, childbearing and parenthood; issues in marital relations; trends in marriage and family; domestic abuse and violence; personal and relational problems; child abuse, neglect and intervention; and incest. Other sex subjects are represented in the index.

➤ MEDICINE AND ALLIED HEALTH (*See also*: for older indexes, see the titles described in Sheehy's *Guide*, B81)

J42. *Cumulative Index to Nursing and Allied Health Literature.* Glendale, CA: Glendale Adventist Medical, 1955-. Bimonthly.

Titled *Cumulative Index to Nursing Literature* from 1955 to 1976. Claims comprehensive coverage of English-language nursing journals worldwide (over 500 titles are currently indexed), as well as coverage of the primary journals in more than a dozen allied health fields. Books, dissertations, conference proceedings, and standards of professional practice are also cited. Subject access. SEX SUBJECTS COVERED: AIDS, contraception, contraceptive devices, pregnancy, sex education, sexual dysfunction, sexual counseling, sexual abuse, sexuality, sexually transmitted diseases, sexuality and disability, sexuality in health and illness, and reproductive health, among other subjects. COMPUTER READABLE FORMATS: *Nursing and Allied Health Databases* (1983-) available on-line from BRS and DIALOG, updated monthly; and on compact disc.

J43. *Excerpta Medica; the international medical abstracting service.* Amsterdam: Elseiver Science Publishing, 1947-. Frequency varies.

Abstracts articles from over 4,000 medical and biomedical journals worldwide, representing the entire field of human medicine and related disciplines. Abstracts are grouped by subject into 54 separately published sections, each with its own subject and author index. Sex related sections include: *Sect. 7 Pediatrics and Pediatric Surgery* (1947-); *Sect. 10 Obstetrics and Gynecology* (1948-); *Sect. 13 Dermatology and Venereology* (1947-), including articles on sexually transmitted diseases; *Sect. 17 Public Health, Social Medicine and Hygiene* (1955-) which includes a section on "Sexual and Social Behavior"; *Sect. 28 Urology and Nephrology* (1967-) including impotence, male sterility; *Sect. 32 Psychiatry* (1948-); and *Sect. 54 AIDS* (1989-). COMPUTER READABLE FORMATS: *EMBASE* (1974-), on-line from BRS and DIALOG, includes abstracts from all 54 sections, plus an additional 100,000 records annually not included in the print versions. Updated weekly.

J44.   *Index Medicus*. U.S. National Library of Medicine. Washington, DC: U.S. Government Printing Office, 1960-. Monthly.

Comprehensive index, with abstracts, to the worldwide literature in the basic biomedical sciences and clinical medicine—over 3,000 English and foreign language journals are covered. Since 1967, a topically arranged bibliography of survey articles, bibliographies, and literature reviews has been included in each issue. Author, title, and subject access using terms from the National Library of Medicine's thesaurus, *Medical Subject Headings* (known as MeSH). SEX SUBJECTS COVERED: all topics, including sexual and reproductive health and medicine, sexual dysfunction, sexually transmitted diseases, sex therapy, paraphilias, sex in disability and illness. COMPUTER READABLE FORMATS: *MedLine* (see J45) available on-line from BRS, DIALOG, and MEDLARS.

J45.   *MEDLARS (Medical Literature Analysis and Retrieval System)*. Bethesda, MD: National Library of Medicine, MEDLARS Management Section.

An on-line catalog of the holdings of the National Library of Medicine (NLM), the world's largest medical library (see X204). Forty-four databases, containing over 13 million records, are available through MEDLARS, with those listed below being the most useful for sex related research (see also POPLINE, J49, and BIOETHICSLINE, J16). For a complete list of available databases, access information, or other research assistance, contact the National Library of Medicine, MEDLARS Management Section, Bethesda, MD 20894. PH: (800)638-8480.

MEDLINE (1966-)—the on-line equivalent to the print indexes, *Index Medicus* (see J44), *International Nursing Index*, and *Index to Dental*

Literature. Covers over 3,600 journals representing the worldwide biomedical literature. Over 6.6 million research, clinical practice, administration, and policy articles are cited, with an additional 30,000 new records added monthly. Approximately 70% of entries include English-language abstracts. Author, title, and subject access using terms from NLM's thesaurus, *Medical Subject Headings* (MeSH). Available from BRS and DIALOG, in addition to MEDLARS.

CATLINE (1400-)—approximately 675,000 cataloging records representing virtually all book titles held in the NLM. Updated weekly.

AVLINE (1975-)—cites both government and commercially produced audiovisual materials and computer software cataloged by NLM, including motion pictures, videocassette, slide/cassette and filmstrip/cassette programs, and computer software. Purchase, rental, and loan procurement information is noted. Updated weekly. Corresponds to the *National Library of Medicine Audiovisual Catalog* (see B10), published quarterly.

AIDSLINE (1980-)—cites AIDS related literature, including journal articles, government reports, letters, technical reports, conference proceedings, monographs, special publications, and audiovisuals. Corresponds to *AIDS Bibliography* (see J12).

SERLINE—cataloging records for approximately 74,000 serial titles held by NLM.

DIRLINE—A directory of over 11,000 organizational sources of health and biomedical information, including federal, state and local government agencies, information centers, professional societies, voluntary associations, support groups, academic and research institutions, and research facilities. Accessible by organization name and subject. Updated quarterly. Federal Information Centers (see B44) provide referrals from this directory by phone.

➤ MENTAL HEALTH *(See also:* Psychology)

J46. *Mental Health Abstracts.* Alexandria, VA: IFI/Plenum Data. 1969-. Monthly. Database.

On-line database, with no print equivalent, containing abstracts of the worldwide mental health literature, including books, journals (over 1,200 titles scanned), dissertations, research reports, and conference proceedings, as well as audiovisuals and other non-print materials. Emphasis is on literature addressing the behavioral, social, and biomedical aspects of mental health and "normal behavior," and the treatment, diagnosis, prevention, and causes of mental illness. Available from DIALOG.

➤ MULTI-DISCIPLINARY *(See also:* J52, J56, J59, J61, J62)

J47.   *Academic Index.* Foster City, CA: Information Access, 1976-.
Monthly. Database.

A computer readable data base, with no print equivalent, covering 950
scholarly and general interest journals in anthropology, sociology,
psychology, area studies, art, education, general science, geography,
history, literature, and politics. Emphasis is on those titles most useful for
undergraduate level research. In addition to articles, it indexes news
reports, reviews, editorials, letters to the editor, obituaries, and other
features often excluded by other indexes. Records are added daily to
NewSearch (see J4) and transferred to this database monthly. Available
on-line from BRS and DIALOG, and on compact disc.

➤ PHILOSOPHY *(See also:* J34, J35)

**J48.   *The Philosophers Index: An International Index to
Philosophical Periodicals and Books.*** Bowling Green, OH:
Philosophy Documentation Center, Bowling Green State
University, 1967-. Quarterly.

Abstracts articles from over 350 philosophy journals (including all major
titles in English, French, German, Spanish, and Italian), as well as books
and monographs. Author and subject access. COMPUTER READABLE
FORMATS: on-line from DIALOG.

➤ POPULATION STUDIES *(See also:* Family Planning)

J49.   *POPLINE* (POPulation information on-line). Baltimore, MD:
Population Information Program, Center for Communication
Programs, Johns Hopkins University, 1970-. Monthly. Database.

Produced by the Population Information Program at Johns Hopkins
University, with the assistance of the Population Index at Princeton
University. On-line database containing abstracts to the worldwide
bio-medical and social science literature on family planning and
population. Cites books and book chapters, technical reports, journal and
newspaper articles, laws, court decisions, conference proceedings, theses
and dissertations, training manuals, government documents, international

agency publications, and unpublished documents. Author, title, keyword, and subject access using terms from *A Users Guide To POPLINE Keywords* (see C8). Available on-line from MEDLARS (see J45), and on compact disc. The Population Information Program will conduct custom searches for a fee (see X171). SEX SUBJECTS COVERED: human fertility, family planning technology, family planning programs, fertility, AIDS and other sexually transmitted diseases, maternity and child health, sexual behavior as it relates to fertility and fertility control, sexually transmitted disease prevention, contraceptive methods, maternal and child health care, statistics, among other topics (see C8 for additional details).

J50. *Population Index*. Princeton, NJ: Office of Population Research, Princeton University, 1935-. Quarterly.

Abstracts the worldwide literature in population and family planning, including books, monographs, and periodicals. Abstracts are classified by subject (see below), or by format (surveys, professional meetings and conference proceedings, bibliographies, directories, new periodicals, statistical publications, and machine readable data bases). "Bibliographic, state-of-the-art, review type essays" are often included. Author, geographic and subject access. SEX SUBJECTS COVERED: general fertility, differential fertility, sterility and other pathologies, general fertility control and contraceptive use, clinical aspects and use effectiveness studies, evaluation of programs, attitudes toward fertility and fertility control, induced abortion, factors other than contraception affecting fertility, fertility outside marriage, marriage and divorce, prenatal and perinatal mortality. COMPUTER READABLE FORMATS: *POPLine* (see J49).

➤ PSYCHOLOGY

J51. *Chicago Psychoanalytic Literature Index*. Chicago: Institute for Psychoanalysis, 1920-1989 (?). Quarterly.

Provides subject and author access to the English language literature in psychoanalysis, psychosomatic medicine, and related fields, including books, annuals, reviews, symposia proceedings, and professional journal articles. The 1987-1988 cumulative volume contains no scope notes or users guide. A three volume cumulative index covers the literature from 1920 to 1970. SEX SUBJECTS COVERED: include abortion, bestiality, birth trauma, bisexuality, castration anxiety, childbirth psychosis, Electra complex, homosexuality, incest, masturbation, masochism, Oedipal complex, pedophilia, penis envy, sadism, sex and sexuality, sex crimes and sexual psychopathy, transvestism, and transsexualism.

J52. *Psychological Abstracts.* Washington: American Psychological Association, 1927-. Monthly.

Abstracts journal articles, books, research reviews, conference reports, technical reports, monographs, and dissertations from the worldwide literature of psychology and other behavioral sciences, as well as related disciplines such as psychiatry, sociology, anthropology, education, pharmacology, physiology, and linguistics. Author and subject access using terms from the *Thesaurus of Psychological Index Terms.* For books and book chapters, consult *PsycBooks: Books and Chapters in Psychology* (Washington: American Psychological Association, 1989-). SEX SUBJECTS COVERED: all subjects. COMPUTER READABLE FORMATS: *Psych Literature* on compact disc, and *Psych Info* (1967-) available on-line from BRS and DIALOG; both are updated monthly. Since 1980, the computer readable databases have included more records than the print version.

➤ PUBLIC AFFAIRS

J53. *PAIS International in Print.* New York: Public Affairs Information Service, 1915-. Monthly.

New title formed by the 1991 merger of *PAIS Bulletin* and *PAIS Foreign Language Index.* Covers "all subjects that bear on contemporary public issues and the making and evaluating of public policy, irrespective of source or traditional disciplinary boundaries." Abstracts books, periodical articles (1,600 journals are currently scanned), government documents, pamphlets, microfiche, and public and private agency reports, from the worldwide literature of the "academic social sciences such as economics, political science, public administration, international law and relations, the environment and demography; professional publications in fields such as business, finance, law, education, and social work; and reports and commentary on public affairs from the serious general press." Emphasis is on factual and statistical information. Author and subject access using terms from *PAIS Subject Headings.* A *Cumulative Subject Index to the PAIS Annual Bulletins 1915-1974* (Arlington, VA: Carrolton Press, 1978) is also available. SEX SUBJECTS COVERED: abortion, AIDS, adoption, artificial insemination, bioethics, birth control, censorship, change of sex, discrimination against homosexuals, fertility, gay liberation movement, gay rights, homosexuality, incest, obscenity, privacy, pornography, pro-life movement, pro-choice movement, prostitution, rape, right of life movement, sex and law, sex and religion, sex crimes, sex education, sex in advertising, sex in literature, sex in mass media, sex in movies, sex oriented businesses, surrogate parenting, sexual ethics, homosexuals, lesbians, sexual behavior, and STDs. "Sexual behavior" is used as a subheading under particular groups, i.e. "prisoners–sexual behavior." COMPUTER READABLE FORMATS: *PAIS International On-line* available from BRS and DIALOG; and on compact disc. Corresponds to three print indexes: *PAIS Bulletin* (1976-1990), *PAIS International* (1991), and *PAIS Foreign Language Index* (1972-1990). Call (800)288-7247 for assistance.

➤ RELIGIOUS STUDIES

J54. *Catholic Periodical and Literature Index*. Haverford, PA: Catholic Library Association, 1930-. Bimonthly.

International index to Catholic periodicals, Papal documents and commentaries, books by Catholics, and Catholic interest books by non-Catholics. Includes popular, devotional, and scholarly materials. Papal documents and books are briefly annotated. Author, title, and subject access. SEX SUBJECTS COVERED: "Provides a broad Christian approach to currently significant topics," including AIDS, abortion, abortion clinics, artificial insemination, birth control (i.e. Papal teaching, moral and ethical aspects), chastity, homosexuality and Christianity, natural family planning, sex education and youth, sex in marriage, sex and religion, sexual ethics, sexual behavior, sexual deviation, and surrogate motherhood.

J55. *Religion Index One: Periodicals*. Evanston, IL: American Theological Association, 1949-. Semiannual.

Continues *Index to Religious Periodicals Literature*. Indexes "those articles in the field of religion—particularly religion and religious scholarship in the West—which are germane to research in, and serve to document that field." Author/editor, scripture, and subject access using terms from the *ATLA Religion Index: Thesaurus*. SEX SUBJECTS COVERED: abortion, adultery, AIDS, artificial insemination, bioethics, birth (in religion, folklore), birth control, celibacy, homosexuality–Biblical teachings, masturbation, Pro-Choice movement, Pro-Life movement, religious prostitution, sex (in religion, folklore), sex (theology), sex and religion, sex in the Bible, sexual ethics, sodomy, surrogate mothers, and tantrism. COMPUTER READABLE FORMATS: *Religion Index* on-line from BRS, DIALOG, and Wilsonline, updated monthly. Corresponds to several print indexes: *Religion Index One: Periodicals* (1949-1959, 1975-); *Religion Index Two: Festschriften* (1960-1969); *Religion Index Two: Multi-Author Works* (1970-); *Research in Ministry* (1981-date); and *Index to Book Reviews in Religion* (1986-).

➤ SCIENCES

J56.   *Science Citation Index*. Philadelphia, PA: Institute for Scientific Information, 1961-. Bimonthly.

"An international, interdisciplinary index to the literature of science" including life, physical, behavioral, and earth sciences such as public health, medicine, psychology, and biology. Cites published symposium proceedings, monographs, and journal articles (with over 3,500 titles currently covered). Follows the same format and indexing approach as *Social Science Citation Index* (see J61 for details). COMPUTER READABLE FORMATS: *SciSearch* (1974-) on-line from DIALOG.

➤ SEXOLOGY (*See also*: Sex Library Indexes, p.153; J39, K64, K131)

J57.   *Bibliosex*. Edited by Robert Gemme and Jean Marc Samson. Montreal, Canada: Département de sexologie, Université du Québec à Montréal, n.d.

Comprehensive index to sex related articles from over 450 French and English-language journals in the humanities, social sciences, and clinical sciences. The vast majority of citations are in English, but as subject headings and scope notes are in French, rudimentary knowledge of the language will facilitate use, although it is not essential. SEX SUBJECTS COVERED: all sexual topics. Order from: Bibliosex a/s Professeur Robert Gemme, Département de sexologie, Université du Québec à Montréal, Case postale 8888, succursale "A", Montréal, Québec, Canada, H3C 3P8.

➤ SOCIAL SCIENCES

J59.   *Applied Social Sciences Index and Abstracts (ASSIA)*. London: Library Association Publishing, 1987-. Bimonthly.

Abstracts articles from the worldwide literature in the applied social sciences (e.g. special education, anthropology, demography, social welfare), with the aim of meeting the "informational needs of all those who seek to serve people, be this in the social services, prison services, youth work, economics, politics, employment, race relations, etc." Covers more than 500 English-language journals worldwide, including the core sociology journals and selected medical, psychological, psychiatric, regional planning, and general interest titles. Subject, author, and title access. Coverage overlaps with *SSCI* (J61) and *Social Science Index* (J62), but they don't include abstracts. COMPUTER READABLE FORMATS: on-line (1987-) from Data Star, updated bimonthly.

J60. *Social Planning, Policy and Development Abstracts*. San Diego: Sociological Abstracts, 1979-. Semi-annual.

Formerly *Social Welfare, Social Planning/Policy and Social Development*. Abstracts practical rather than theoretical periodical articles and published conference proceedings, with emphasis on the application of sociology and other social sciences to social problems. Author and subject access. COMPUTER READABLE FORMATS: *SO-PODA*, a file in the on-line version of *Sociological Abstracts* (see J63).

J61. *Social Sciences Citation Index (SSCI)*. Philadelphia: Institute for Scientific Information, 1972- (1966). 3/year.

An international, multidisciplinary index to the literature of the social, behavioral, and related sciences, providing comprehensive coverage of 1,400 social science journals and selective coverage of over 3,300 natural, physical, and biomedical science journals. Citation indexes are unique in that they allow one to (1) search for articles which cite a particular reference known to have relevance to the topic in their bibliography, and (2) to identify and cross reference works cited in a particular article without having to see the article itself. They are based on the premise that such articles address related issues, employ similar methodological, theoretical, or philosophical approaches, or are otherwise related. (A list of the types of questions citation indexes are especially suited to answer appears in the introductory notes of each issue.) The index has three sections: (1) *Permutation Subject Index*—a subject index to current articles by key title words in various combinations; (2) *Source Index*—a list of current articles by author; and (3) *Citation Index*—an index by author to the books and articles cited in the bibliographies of the articles cited in section 2. See also notes under "How to Find" Concealed Bibliographies, p.98. COMPUTER READABLE FORMATS: *Social SciSearch* (1972-) on-line from DIALOG and BRS, updated weekly; and on compact disc.

J62.   *Social Sciences Index*. New York: H.W. Wilson, 1974-. Quarterly.

Author and subject index to over 342 key English-language periodicals in the fields of anthropology, community health and medicine, economics, geography, international relations, law, criminology and police science, political science, psychology, psychiatry, public administration, sociology, social work and public welfare, and gerontology. Arranged alphabetically by subject and author. See footnote 1, p.156, for additional details. SEX SUBJECTS COVERED: all topics. COMPUTER READABLE FORMATS: available on-line (1983) from BRS and Wilsonline, updated twice weekly; and on compact disc.

J63.   *Sociological Abstracts*. San Diego: Sociological Abstracts, 1952/53-. Bimonthly.

Abstracts the worldwide periodical literature in sociology, plus selective coverage of anthropology, economics, education, medicine, development, communication, philosophy, statistics, political science, and the humanities. Articles are classified under 33 broad subject headings, each further subdivided so as to represent all major areas of sociological study. Author, title and subject access using terms from the *Thesaurus of Sociological Indexing Terms*. SEX SUBJECTS COVERED: all. Primary subject headings include: sociology of sexual behavior, birth control (i.e. abortion, contraception, fertility, childbearing), and family and socialization. COMPUTER READABLE FORMATS: on-line (1963-) from DIALOG and BRS, updated 7x/ year; and on compact disc.

> ➤ SOCIAL WORK

J64.   *Social Work Research and Abstracts*. Silver Springs, MD: National Association of Social Workers, 1965-. Quarterly.

Contains original clinical and theoretical research articles, and abstracts of English-language journal articles, dissertations, and books in social work and related fields. Author and subject access. Consult *Users Guide to Social Work Abstracts* for research assistance. COMPUTER READABLE FORMAT: *Social Work Abstracts Database* (1977-) on-line from BRS, updated quarterly.

➤ WOMEN'S STUDIES

J65.   *Women's Studies Abstracts*. Rush, NY: Rush Publishing Co., 1972-. Quarterly.

Contains abstracts of women related articles published in a wide range of academic, professional, and feminist periodicals. Subject and keyword access. Often includes bibliographic review essays. SEX SUBJECTS COVERED: primary subject headings include abortion; family planning; sexuality; violence against women; and pregnancy, fertility, childbirth and neonate. Other topics are included in the subject index.

J66.   *Women's Studies Index*. Boston: G.K. Hall, 1989-. Annual.

Cites articles from over 86 scholarly and popular periodicals ranging "from professional to artistic, academic to popular" (e.g. *Glamour, Family Circle, Working Mother, Vogue, Journal of Feminist Studies in Religion, Gender and Society, Journal of Women and Aging, Lesbian Ethics*, and *Minerva: Quarterly Report on Women and the Military*). Author and subject access.

13

DIRECTORIES

Directories provide access to print and non-print materials as well as individuals, organizations, and institutions. There are a number of types:

Membership Directories. Directories compiled by organizations to facilitate contacting their members or others with similar interests, such as membership directories, mailing lists, or more informal in house directories, accessible only through staff referrals (e.g. a staff member's rolodex).

Topical Directories. Directories focusing on a particular topic compiled by organizations or associations as a service to their clients (e.g. Planned Parenthood's *Directory of Hormonal Contraceptives*) and either sold separately or published in the groups newsletter or journal; or trade titles published by commercial publishers. The latter range from those focusing on a very specific subject (e.g. Scarecrow Press's *TAPP Sources: A National Directory of Teenage Pregnancy Prevention*) to more comprehensive titles (e.g. Gale Research's *The Women's Information Directory*).

Concealed Directories. Directories included in the text or appendixes of self help/consumer information books (e.g. the directory of penile implant manufacturers in *Impotence: How to Overcome It*) or professional handbooks.

HOW TO FIND

• Search library catalogs using the name of a country or city, class of people, type of organization or institution, topical heading, or type of material followed by the form subdivision –*Directories*.

• Consult *Directories in Print* (see B33), a directory of all types of directories.

Library Reference Books. Comprehensive, multi-volume library reference books (often available in computer-readable formats) covering a particular type of print material (e.g. *Books in Series*), non-print resource (e.g. *Data Base Directory*), or institution, organization, or class of individual (e.g. *Research Centers Directory, Encyclopedia of Associations, National Faculty Directory*). See also "Concealed Bibliographies," p.98.

Directories are described throughout this volume. Comprehensive directories of print and non-print resources are noted in Ch.1 through Ch.28, and described in Ch.2. Comprehensive directories to individual and institutional resources are cited in Ch.1, Ch.29, and Ch.30, and described in Ch.2. For membership directories, see "How to Find" Professionals in the Field, p.311. Topical directories are described in "How to Find" listings throughout the book, or when published by an organization, under their entry. A "D" code under "Services" in the descriptive listings beginning on p.321 indicates the group produces or distributes a directory, even though its title may not be noted.

Part V
Source Materials

14

PERIODICALS

Periodicals—newsletters and bulletins, popular magazines and newspapers, scholarly and professional journals, and yearbooks and annuals—provide the most current information in print on all subjects, as well as information on topics too specialized for book-length treatment.

Use the resources described in this chapter to identify periodicals which focus on a particular topic. (To access individual articles published in periodicals, see Ch.12 INDEXES.) As indexes are often published months behind the journals they cover, scanning titles directly is often the only way to access the most current research in a field, as well as those portions of periodicals not generally indexed, such as conference schedules, grant announcements, employment opportunities, letters to the editor, advertisements, and news items. Subscription lists of specialized journals may be purchased to facilitate contacting particular audiences for commercial or research purposes (e.g. the *Journal of Reproductive Medicine* for gynecologists, *Journal of Sex and Marital Therapy* for sex therapists, *Journal of Nurse-Midwifery* for midwives).

Newsletters. Issued by associations, information clearinghouses, government agencies, individuals, and commercial enterprises, newsletters provide up-to-date news and information on very specific topics, usually in a concise, relatively inexpensive format. They usually contain up-dates of organizational activities, calendars of upcoming events, brief articles,

How to Find

• Search library catalogs using *Sex oriented periodicals* as a search term, or the appropriate subject heading followed by the form subdivision *–Periodicals*, or *–Newsletters*. The on-line catalog RLIN (see G4), includes a series file citing periodicals, books in series, newsletters, newspapers, etc.—search this file by subject alone.

• Consult periodical directories (see the entry numbers indicated for sex subjects covered). *The Standard Periodicals Directory* (see B73), *Ulrich's International Periodical Directory* (see B74), *The Serials Directory: An International Reference Book* (see B72), *Magazines for Libraries* (see B69), and *Gale Directory of Publications and Broadcast Media* (see B68) all contain bibliographic information on a wide range of periodicals, although none are comprehensive. For newsletters, see *The Oxbridge Directory of Newsletters* (B71) and *Newsletters in Print* (B70). Entries in such directories typically include price, circulation, editor, publisher, frequency, a brief description (more lengthy in B69), and in the case of B72, where the title is indexed. B74 notes cessations and title changes. To find topical or disciplinary periodical directories (e.g. *The International Directory of Homosexual Periodicals* or the *Authors Guide to Social Work Journals*), search library catalogs using the appropriate subject headings followed by the form subdivision *–Periodicals–Directories* or *–Periodicals–Catalogs*.

• Request the periodical holdings list from a library, information clearinghouse, or archive specializing in your area of interest (see Ch.1, Ch.30). The Kinsey Institute library has the most comprehensive collection of historical sex related periodicals in the U.S. (see A4). For other collections, see under "Gay and Lesbian Archives," p.339, and under other relevant subject headings in Ch.30. The periodical holdings of 36 collections are described in *Alternative Lifestyles: A Guide to Research Collections on Intentional Communities, Nudism and Sexual Freedom* (see p.338). To locate other published descriptions of periodical collections, search library catalogs using the term *Libraries–Special collections* followed by *–Sex oriented periodicals* or other topical headings (e.g. *Libraries–Special collections–Homosexuality–Periodicals*).

• For the titles of newsletters, magazines, or journals published by organizations and institutions, consult the directories cited in Ch.30.

• Consult directories of specialized publishers (e.g. *Erotic Writer's and Collector's Market*, p.355)—see "How to Find" Publishers, p.229. Use the *Encyclopedia of Associations* (see B4) to identify press associations whose members specialize in publishing books and periodicals in a particular area (e.g. the Gay and Lesbian Press Association); most publish membership directories.

• Consult the bibliographies of relevant books and articles (see "How to Find" Concealed Bibliographies, p.98) for the journal titles in which cited articles were published.

• Indexes generally cover the key periodicals in their discipline (see Ch.12). Consult the index itself for a list of titles covered, or contact the customer service department of the publisher.

announcements of research and employment opportunities, resource reviews, directories of related organizations, and classified advertising.

Popular Magazines and Newspapers. While not usually reliable as a primary research source, popular periodicals are an excellent source for the following: information and analysis of current events and trends, controversial social and political issues, and public policy; simplified explanations of highly technical concepts; names and affiliations of experts in the area; opinions and editorials; and the results of new studies and polls, which are often reported in the popular media long before they appear in scholarly indexes.

Scholarly and Professional Journals. Journals, written by and for professionals and scholars, contain research and clinical reports; theoretical essays; articles on current trends and issues, often providing several points of view in one volume; letters to the editor and other devices which allow for two-way debate and discussion; books and audiovisual reviews; conference announcements, continuing education programs, and employment opportunities; and advertisements for new publications and products.

● ● ● ●

Listings: 163 journals, magazines, and newsletters are described below. We have attempted comprehensive coverage of sex related titles published in the U.S., and selective coverage of titles in related areas which frequently address sex related issues. With a few exceptions, medical and legal journals are excluded. Few newsletters are described as they change titles, format, frequency, and publisher often; those annotated below are well established, in an area not covered by a journal, and contain more than just organizational news. Additional newsletters are noted in the description of the issuing organization in Ch.30. Each entry includes bibliographic information (indicating current publisher only), a brief description, and when applicable, where the title is indexed (index codes refer to the entry numbers in Ch.12). Indexing information may not be complete; contact the publisher for the most up-to-date information. Many specialized libraries do not circulate their periodical holdings through interlibrary loan, but will provide photocopies of articles unavailable elsewhere. Organizations publishing newsletters, journals, or magazines are indicated by a "P" (for publications) code in the descriptive listings beginning on p.321.

➤ ABORTION *(See also:* Conservative; Family Planning; K56)

K1.   *Abortion Research Notes.* Bethesda, MD: Transnational Family Research Institute, 1972-. 3/year.

Newsletter concerned with the psychosocial aspects of fertility behavior and the contraception/abortion relationship; legal, social and psychological aspects of abortion; international abortion trends and legislation; and abortion services and techniques. Contains research analysis and citations to journal articles and books. See also X113. INDEXED: J31.

K2.   *C.D.C. Abortion Surveillance Report.* Atlanta: U.S. Centers for Disease Control, 1969-. Quarterly.

Comprehensive government report containing articles and statistical data on abortion, including number and demographics of women having undergone the procedure, average weeks of gestation, number of previous abortions, abortion related morbidity and mortality, and types of procedures performed. All data is correlated by age, race, marital status, and previous births. INDEXED: J31.

K3. *National Right to Life News*. Washington: National Right to Life Committee Inc., 1973-. Semi-monthly.

Tabloid examining medical, ethical, social, and public policy aspects of abortion and other "life" issues from a pro-life perspective. Includes letters to the editor, interviews, book reviews, editorials, and research notes. Annual cumulative index. See also X7.

K4. *Reproductive Rights Update*. New York: American Civil Liberties Union, Reproductive Freedom Project. Bi-weekly.

Reports on current issues relating to reproductive freedom including legislative actions and court cases concerned with reproductive rights. The ACLU also publishes *Reproductive Freedom* annually, a national compendium of reproductive rights cases. See also X12.

▶ ADOLESCENT SEXUALITY AND PREGNANCY (*See also:* Family Planning)

K5. *Adolescent and Pediatric Gynecology*. North American Society for Pediatric and Adolescent Gynecology. New York: Springer-Verlag Journals, 1988-. Quarterly.

Journal containing case reports, clinical and basic science research papers, and review articles on adolescent and pediatric gynecology, obstetrics, pediatrics, endocrinology, and psychiatry.

K6. *Adolescent Pregnancy Prevention Clearinghouse Reports*. Washington: Children's Defense Fund, 1985-. Bimonthly.

Each issue of this newsletter focuses on a specific aspect of teen pregnancy in the U.S., including pregnancy prevention strategies. See also X22. INDEXED: J31.

K7. *Common Focus: An Exchange of Information About Early Adolescents*. Carrboro, NC: University of North Carolina, Center for Early Adolescence, 1978-1989 (v.9, no.1). Ceased.

Newsletter containing resource reviews (e.g. books, curriculum, and films), conference announcements, and program and research reports of interest to those working with 10-15 year old youths. Often addressed sex related topics. Ceased publication in 1989. See also X17. INDEXED: J31.

K8.   *Journal of Early Adolescence*. Newbury Park, CA: Sage
           Publications, 1981. Quarterly.

Goal is "to increase our understanding of individuals, age 10 to 14 years,"
including aspects of adolescent sexuality and sexual socialization. Includes
major theoretical papers, current research reports, and resource reviews (of
professional books, and juvenile books and films). INDEXED: J17, J19, J26,
J27, J31, J52, J62, J63.

K9.   *OPTIONS*. Washington: Center for Population Options, 1980-.
           Quarterly.

Newsletter of the Center for Population Options (see X18), which seeks
to improve adolescent decision making through sex education, prevent
teen pregnancy, HIV and other STDs, and improve adolescent access to
family planning through community and school based clinics. Contains
notices of publications, letters to the editor, research news, meetings and
conference reports, and book reviews.

➤ AGING *(See also: SAGE News* [X31], for gay and lesbian issues; *Hot Flash*
[X32], for women's issues)

K10.   *Sex Over Forty*. Chapel Hill, NC: DKT International, 1982-.
            Monthly.

"A practical authoritative newsletter directed to the sexual concerns of the
mature adult." Each eight page issue contains information and brief
research reports on sexuality and aging, and responses to readers queries.

➤ AIDS *(See also*: Sexually Transmitted Diseases)

The following is only a brief selection of the hundreds of AIDS/HIV
journals and newsletters currently being published, many of which focus
on very specific aspects of the AIDS crisis (e.g. *AIDS Litigation Reporter*,
AIDS Treatment News, *People with AIDS Update*).

K11.   *AIDS Education and Prevention: An Interdisciplinary Journal*.
            International Society of AIDS Education. New York: Guilford,
            1989-. Quarterly.

Interdisciplinary, international journal on the development, implementation, and evaluation of AIDS education and prevention programs, and
related public health, psychosocial, ethical, and public policy issues.

HOW TO FIND

• *AIDSQuest* (see J11) includes a database describing over 250 AIDS and HIV related journals worldwide. *AIDS Bibliography* (see J12) cites new serial titles in each June and December issue. The *AIDS Information Hotline* (see X35) will provide referrals. See also directories B1-B3.

Contains scientific research articles, program reports, critiques of educational programs and strategies, and resource reviews. INDEXED: J11, J12, J13, J43, J44, J45, J52.

K12. *AIDS and Public Policy Journal.* Frederick, MD: University Publishing Group. 1986-. Quarterly.

An "international journal addressing the social, political, ethical, and legal issues that arise in public health and health policy, especially as they relate to acquired immunodeficiency syndrome (AIDS). [Publishes] work arising from a variety of disciplines and intellectual perspectives, including medicine, law, philosophy, business, and the social sciences." Original articles, case studies, commentaries, book reviews. INDEXED: J11, J12, J13, J16, J45, J53, J63.

K13. *AIDS Scan: Current Literature in Perspective.* Chicago: Yearbook Medical Publishing, 1989-. Quarterly.

Publishes condensations of articles from the worldwide AIDS literature, along with expert commentary.

K14. *C.D.C. AIDS Weekly.* Centers for Disease Control. Atlanta: Charles W. Henderson Publisher, 1985-. Weekly.

Comprehensive, international coverage of the prevention, detection and treatment of AIDS and HIV infection. Each issue contains four features: *News Reports*—informative briefs, from sources worldwide, on new developments in health care, clinical trials, and patient care and support; *Periodical Reports*—reviews and information from journals and newsletters worldwide; *Research Reports*—information about grants and research worldwide; *Meetings Report*—calendar of conferences, seminars, symposia, and meetings worldwide. Also includes book reviews and statistical data. Available on-line as a file on AIDSQuest (see J11), and from DIALOG, Compuserve and other vendors. INDEXED: J11, J12, J13

K15. *HIV/AIDS Surveillance.* Atlanta: Division of HIV/AIDS, National Center for Infectious Diseases, Centers for Disease Control, 1982-. Quarterly.

(Frequency has varied since 1982 from weekly, to monthly, to quarterly as of October 1992.) Statistical information on AIDS and HIV infection, including weekly updates of the number of AIDS cases and deaths reported to the C.D.C. Single copies are available free from the National AIDS Information Clearinghouse (see X35). For full text on-line, see J11.

▶ ALTERNATIVE LIFESTYLES *(See also:* Non-Monogamy, Nudism)

K16. *Lifestyles: Family and Economic Issues.* New York: Human Sciences Press, 1978-1992. Quarterly.

Titled *Alternative Lifestyles* from 1978 to 1984. From 1978 to 1991, *Lifestyles* published articles on "changing patterns in marriage, family, and intimacy," often including articles on sexually alternative lifestyles. The title changed to *Journal of Family and Economic Issues* in 1992, and it no longer addresses such issues. INDEXED: J3, J64, J26, J28, J41, J52, J61.

▶ BIOETHICS

K17. *Bioethics.* Cambridge, MA: Basil Blackwell Ltd., 1987-. Quarterly.

Journal containing "rigorously argued articles discussing ethical issues raised by medicine and biological sciences," related commentary, and book reviews. INDEXED: J16, J31, J48.

K18. *Ethics and Medics.* Pope John XXIII Medical/Moral Research and Education Center. Braintree, MA: Pope John XXIII Center, 1976-. Monthly.

Four page newsletter containing brief articles, written from a Catholic perspective, on a range of health and life sciences issues, including abortion, AIDS, amniocentesis, artificial insemination, birth defects, contraception, ectopic pregnancy, embryo/fetus, natural family planning, GIFT, gender reassignment surgery, hermaphroditism, herpes, heterosexuality, homosexuality, in-vitro fertilization, infertility treatment, marriage, masturbation, pedophilia, semen collection/testing, post abortion syndrome, sex, and transsexuality. See also X250.

K19. *Hastings Center Report.* Briarcliff Manor, NY: Hastings Center, 1971-. Bimonthly.

Journal examining ethical and legal issues in medicine, life sciences, and the professions. Contains articles, book reviews, literature abstracts, a calendar, conference announcements, current news, and legal items. INDEXED: J3, J15, J31, J44, J53, J55, J61, J62.

K20. *Kennedy Institute of Ethics Journal.* Kennedy Institute of Bioethics, Georgetown University. Baltimore: Johns Hopkins University Press, 1991. Quarterly.

A scholarly forum for diverse views on the major issues in bioethics. "Features opinions and analysis by top thinkers in medical ethics, law, medicine, philosophy, and theology." Each issue includes a report on bioethics activities at the federal level, and an overview and annotated bibliography of a specific bioethical topic. See also X61.

➤ BIRTH DEFECTS

K21. *Birth Defects: Abstracts of Selected Articles.* White Plains, NY: March of Dimes Birth Defects Foundation, 1964-. Monthly.

Abstracts selected articles relating to birth defects from over 3,200 periodicals worldwide. Order from the Professional Services Department of the March of Dimes (see X137).

➤ BISEXUALITY

K22. *Anything that Moves: Beyond the Myths of Bisexuality.* San Francisco: Bay Area Bisexual Network. 1991-. Quarterly.

64 page national magazine offering a "multi-cultural, multi-sexual, multi-gendered, and multi-bi identity perspective through its editorials, feature articles and essays, letters, fiction and poetry, arts and culture, reviews, advice column, science fiction and news. ATM also addresses health issues . . . and features an up-to-date and comprehensive bi group and resource listing." Order from X62.

K23.   *Bisexuality: News, Views and Network / A North American Journal of Bisexuality*. Long Beach, CA: Gibbin Publications, 1988-. Quarterly.

National newsletter containing articles and a resource directory. Order from P.O. Box 20917 Long Beach, CA 90801-3917. PH: (213)597-2799.

➤ BREASTFEEDING

K24.   *Breastfeeding Abstracts*. Franklin Park, IL: La Leche League International, 1981-. Quarterly.

Contains abstracts of the professional literature on the medical aspects of breastfeeding. See also X128.

K25.   *Journal of Human Lactation*. International Lactation Consultants Association. New York: Human Sciences Press, 1984-. Quarterly.

Contains research and clinical reports, commentary, and film and book reviews relating to lactation and breastfeeding. See also X127. INDEXED: J42, J44.

K26.   *New Beginnings*. Franklin Park, IL: La Leche League International, 1958-. Bimonthly.

Written for the general public, this 32 page newsletter contains medical and scientific information pertaining to breastfeeding, and related issues of childbirth, nutrition, and child care. Book reviews. Order from X128.

➤ CHILDBIRTH *(See also*: for cesarean childbirth see *C/Sec Newsletter*, X228)

K27.   *Birth: Issues in Perinatal Care and Education*. Cambridge, MA: Blackwell Scientific Publishing Inc., 1973-. Quarterly.

Formerly, *Birth and Family Journal*. Covers issues in childbirth education, perinatal care, and perinatal technology including obstetric practices, parent education, contraception, abortion, childbirth, breastfeeding, and family life. Articles are directed towards childbearing families, childbirth educators, midwives, physicians, and those who evaluate childbearing care (e.g. public health officials, epidemiologist). INDEXED: J3, J42, J44, J52, J61.

K28. *Birth Psychology Bulletin.* New York: Association of Birth Psychology, 1979-. Semi-annual.

Publishes clinical, theoretical, and empirical articles focusing on the correlation between prenatal, birth, and neonatal experiences, and later psychological development. See also X71. INDEXED: J27, J52.

K29. *International Journal of Childbirth Education.* Minneapolis: International Childbirth Education Association, 1986-. Quarterly.

Directed towards childbirth educators, expectant parents, and midwives. Contains review articles with lengthy bibliographies, booklists of titles available from the ICEA Bookstore (see L18), and organizational news. See also X70. INDEXED: J42.

K30. *Journal of Nurse-Midwifery.* American College of Nurse Midwives. New York: Elsevier Science Publishing, 1955-. Bimonthly.

"Promotes the writing and publication of timely, relevant, and provocative literature on and for nurse-midwives which is consistent with the philosophy, objectives, policies and positions of the American College of Nurse Midwives." Includes both clinical and research articles. See also X78. INDEXED: J3, J42, J43, J44, J59, J61.

K31. *Midwifery.* New York: Churchill Livingstone, 1986-. Quarterly.

Journal. Unable to review.

K32. *Midwifery Today and Childbirth Education: A Journal of Childbirth Education, Midwifery, and Birth.* Eugene, OR: Midwifery Today, 1987-. Quarterly.

Magazine of "education and encouragement" for midwives, birth practitioners, and childbirth educators. Contains full length articles and professional columns on all aspects of midwife attended births, prepared childbirth instruction, and women's reproductive health; abstracts of articles published elsewhere; and books and media reviews.

K33. *NAPSAC News.* Marble Hill, MO: International Association of Parents and Professionals for Safe Alternatives in Childbirth, 1976-. Quarterly.

Newsletter addressing issues of nutrition, pregnancy, midwifery, obstetrics, pediatrics, birth (especially home births), breastfeeding, parenting, medical politics, legal issues of alternative childbearing, and health rights and legislation. Includes articles, editorials, and a calendar of upcoming events in the birth reform movement. See also X69.

K34. ***Pre- and Peri-Natal Psychology Journal.*** New York: Human Science Press. 1986-. Quarterly.

Publishes articles exploring the psychological dimensions of embryology, pregnancy, childbirth, and mother/child relationships. INDEXED: J19, J52.

➤ CONSERVATIVE / TRADITIONALISTS *(See also:* K18)

K35. ***All About Issues.*** Stafford, VA: American Life League. 1979-. 9/year.

Magazine covering family and life issues from a pro-life, "traditional family values" perspective. See also X2.

K36. ***Human Life Issues.*** Steubenville, OH: Human Life Center, 1975-. Quarterly.

Previously, *Love, Life, Death Issues.* 16 page newsletter with information and analysis of pro-life issues, natural family planning, and "traditional" marriage, family, and sexual values. See also X87.

K37. ***Human Life Review.*** New York: Human Life Foundation, 1975-. Quarterly.

Publishes original articles, reprints, and columns on abortion and other "life issues," and traditional sexual values. INDEXED: J31, J53.

K38. ***International Review.*** Steubenville, OH: Human Life Center, 1977-. Quarterly.

Formerly *International Review of Natural Family Planning,* journal containing articles and book reviews. The 1991 annual index includes the following subject headings: abortion, abstinence, Catholic Church teachings on sexuality and life issues, natural family planning, conjugal love, family life, contraception, in-vitro fertilization, marital love, ovulation methods, reproductive technology, sex education, teen pregnancy, sexuality, contraception, sterilization. Order from X87. INDEXED: J31, J54.

► CONTRACEPTION (*See also*: Family Planning; K156)

K39. *Advances in Contraception*. Society for the Advancement of Contraception. Hingham, MA: Kluwer Academic Publishing Group, 1985-. Quarterly.

Journal. Unable to review. INDEXED: J3, J15, J17, J43, J44.

K40. *Advances in Contraceptive Delivery Systems*. World Federation of Contraception-Health. Kiawah Island, SC: Reproductive Health Center, 1980-. Quarterly.

Formerly titled *Contraceptive Delivery System*, journal covering human sexuality, male contraception, oral contraceptives, I.U.D. controversies, and public policy and ethical aspects of contraception. INDEXED: J3, J15, J43, J56.

K41. *Contraception: An International Journal*. Stoneham, MA: Butterworth-Heinemann Ltd., 1970-. Monthly.

Publishes technical reports on experimental and clinical aspects of contraception from biochemistry, chemistry, physiology, endocrinology, biology, medical sciences, and demography perspectives. INDEXED: J3, J15, J31, J43, J44, J50.

K42. *Contraceptive Technology Update*. Atlanta: American Health Consultant, 1980-. Monthly.

"A monthly newsletter for health professionals" containing brief, non-technical reports on new developments in contraception and related issues. Also includes *STD Quarterly* and *Women's Health Quarterly*. INDEXED: J31.

► CONTROVERSIAL ISSUES / PUBLIC AFFAIRS

K43. *CQ Researcher*. Washington: Congressional Quarterly, 1923-. Weekly.

Formerly *Editorial Research Reports*. "Each [issue] provides background on a current topic of widespread interest. Designed as a starting place for research, the reports define the issue and include a chronology and extensive bibliographies," as well as background, the current situation, outlook for the future, and quotes from opposing experts. Sex subjects addressed have included teenagers and abortion, "Do Americans still love marriage?", sexual harassment, fetal tissue research, the obscenity debates, and AIDS. INDEXED: J47, J53.

K44. *Human Sexuality.* Annual Editions Series. Guilford, CT: Dushkin Publishing, 1975-. Annual.

Formerly *Readings in Human Sexuality* and *Focus: Human Sexuality.* Newspapers and magazine articles on current sexual topics.

K45. *Human Sexuality Annual.* Opposing Viewpoints Sources Series. St. Paul, MN: Greenhaven Press, 1985-. Annual. Quadrennial, with annual supplements.

Titles in the opposing viewpoints series include abortion, AIDS, teenage sexuality, biomedical ethics, and sexual values. Each includes articles, bibliographies, and lists of relevant organizations.

K46. *Sexuality.* Edited by Eleanor C. Goldstein. Social Issues Resources Series. Boca Raton, FL: Social Issues Resources Series, 1978-. Quinquennial, with annual supplements.

Each quadrennial volume contains 100 newspaper and magazine articles, with annual supplements of 20 articles each.

➤ DISABILITY AND SEXUALITY

K47. *C.S.D. (Coalition on Sexuality and Disability) Newsletter.* New York: Coalition on Sexuality and Disability, 1978-. Quarterly.

8 page newsletter. See also X97.

K48. *National Information Center for Children and Youth with Handicaps, News Digest.* Washington: National Information Center for Children and Youth with Handicaps, 1985-. 3/year.

Each issue focuses on a specific topic, often sex related. See also X102.

K49. *Newsletter of National Task Force on Sexuality and Disability.* Ann Arbor, MI: Michigan University Hospital Dept.of Physical Medicine, n.d. Annual.

Unable to review. For more information contact: Nathan D. Zasler, M.D., 11654 Rutgers Drive, Richmond, VA 73233. See also X100.

K50. *Peoplenet.* Levittown, NY: Robert Mauro, 1987-. 3/year.

Newsletter containing articles on dating, friendship, and sexuality for disabled persons. To order: P.O. Box 897, Levittown, NY 11756. PH: (516)579-4043.

K51. *Sexuality and Disability.* New York: Human Science Press, 1978-. Quarterly.

Journal addressing the psychological and medical aspects of sexuality in rehabilitation settings; the sexual expression of people with physical or mental disabilities, illnesses, or other disabling conditions; and special programs in sex education and counseling for people with disabilities. Contains clinical practice reports, case studies, research and survey data, "state of the art" papers, guidelines for clinical practice, and consumer articles. INDEXED: J15, J39, J42, J43, J52, J63, J61.

▶ EROTICA *(See also:* "Men's" Magazines; for lesbian erotica see K71, K75)

In 1989, Slade (see H71) estimated there to be approximately 170 hard core heterosexual magazines, an equal number of heterosexual soft core magazines (more if you include such mainstream titles as *Playboy*), 48 hard core homosexual titles, two dozen soft core gay titles, and another 24 lesbian titles, readily available in the U.S. Such erotic periodicals range from erotic literary magazines such as *Yellow Silk*, available in libraries, to pictorials focusing on conventional heterosexual and homosexual intercourse and oragenital activities, to fetish pictorials with titles such as *Anal Blondes*, *Enema Thrills*, and *Lactating Lesbians*, available only in specialty bookstores.

K52. *Adam Film World.* Los Angeles: Knight Publishing, 1966-. Quarterly.

Consumer guide to adult films and videos. Available on newsstands in urban areas, and by subscription.

K53. *Libido: The Journal of Sex and Sensibility.* Chicago: Libido, 1988-. Quarterly.

Erotic literary magazine. Includes book reviews, articles, photographs, sexual trivia, and humor, as well as erotic stories. To order: Box 146721, Chicago, IL 60614. PH: (312)281-0805.

HOW TO FIND

• Comprehensive periodical directories list erotic titles under *Men's,*
Erotica, and *Sex* (see B68-B74). Consult directories K65-K67 for gay/
lesbian oriented titles. *Erotic Writer's and Collector's Market* (see
p.355) includes a list of publishers and titles.

• Identify hard core erotic/pornographic magazine titles by scanning
the collections in "adult" bookstores—either general, gay/lesbian, or
specialized (where titles are generally arranged by fetish specialty).

• Consult archives and libraries. Search library catalogs for print
descriptions of special collections, using the search terms *Libraries–*
Special collections–Pornography or *Libraries–Special collections–*
Erotica. The New York Public Library microfilms representative titles
purchased from Times Square sex shops (see A2). The collection of
the Kinsey Institute Library (see A4, especially the notes on p.10)
includes over 15,000 individual issues of over 1,300 titles published
since the 1920s, including nudist magazines of the 1950s, popular
mens magazines such as *Playboy*, and heterosexual and homosexual
hard core erotica and fetish magazines (see also under "Fetishes").
The Institute for the Advanced Study of Human Sexuality's extensive
collection of erotic magazines is currently closed to the public (see
A3). For gay and lesbian erotica, see X53-X60. The erotica holdings
of other archives are fully described in *Alternative Lifestyles* (see
p.338).

K54. *Yellow Silk: Journal of Erotic Arts*. Albany, CA: Very Graphics,
1981-. Quarterly.

Erotic literary magazine with the motto "all persuasions, no brutality."
Primarily heterosexual in orientation, includes poetry, erotic art, short
stories, and essays on erotic literature and art. INDEXED: J1.

➤ FAMILY PLANNING (*See also*: Abortion; Conservative; Contraception)

K55. *Current Literature in Family Planning*. New York: Planned
Parenthood Federation of America, 1966-. Monthly.

"Classified annotated list of books and articles in the field of family planning, received in the Library of Planned Parenthood Federation of America." See also A7. INDEXED: J31.

K56. *Family Planning Perspectives.* New York: Alan Guttmacher Institute, 1969-. Bimonthly.

Journal publishing practical and scholarly research articles, research updates, statistical reports, and other features on subjects of interest to professionals in the fields of family planning, population studies, and maternal and child health. Frequently addresses the following topics: adolescent sexuality, pregnancy and parenthood; reproductive decision making; birth control methods, fertility, and abortion; sex education; sexually transmitted diseases; and reproduction and reproductive health. Emphasis is on the United States and other developed countries. INDEXED: Cumulative Index of v.1-20 (1969-1988) available from Guttmacher Institute (see X253); J3, J15, J17, J39, J40, J41, J42, J43, J44, J50, J64, J52, J53, J60, J63, J65.

K57. *International Family Planning Perspectives.* New York: Alan Guttmacher Institute, 1975-. Quarterly.

A journal—intended for professionals in the field of fertility, family planning, maternal and child health, and population policy—containing articles on population research and programs in the developing world. Topics addressed include: contraceptive practices and research, pregnancy termination, reproduction, sexually transmitted diseases, child spacing, etc. See also X253. INDEXED: J31, J43, J49, J50, J53, J65.

K58. *LINKLine.* New York: Planned Parenthood Federation of America, 1983-. Bimonthly.

Bimonthly newsletter of PPFA (see X111). Contains announcements of professional conferences, workshops and training programs; news items; and reviews of audiovisuals, instructional materials, curricula, books, pamphlets, brochures, training manuals, and programs. See also A7.

K59. *Open File: A News Digest of the International Planned Parenthood Federation.* London: International Planned Parenthood Federation, 1952-. Monthly.

Newsletter containing brief research reports, news and current events (including developments in law, public policy, and medicine); meetings and conference announcements worldwide; and resource reviews (reports, books, information packages, information services, videos, meetings, and training courses). See also A8.

K60. *Population Reports.* Baltimore: Center for Communication Programs, Population Information Program, Johns Hopkins University, 1973-. 5/year.

Provides a comprehensive, up-to-date overview of the entire field of family planning, including family planning methods and programs, contraceptive technologies, and health concerns such as AIDS and maternal and child health. Five issues are published annually from 11 ongoing series, each providing a comprehensive, thoroughly referenced guide to a specific topic in the area: oral contraception, I.U.D., female sterilization, male sterilization, laws and policy, pregnancy termination, barrier methods, periodic abstinence, family planning programs, injectables and implants, issues in world health, and special topics. See also X171. INDEXED: J49, J50, annual cumulative index.

K61. *Studies in Family Planning.* New York: Population Council, 1963-. Bimonthly.

Journal "concerned with all aspects of fertility regulation and family planning, particularly in developing countries." Topics covered include contraception technology, the social context of reproductive behavior, and policies and programs affecting fertility. Most articles include extensive statistical data. See also X170. INDEXED: J3, J15, J17, J42, J43, J44, J50, J53, J59, J61, J63, J60, J65. Cumulative Index (1979-1990).

➤ FERTILITY AND INFERTILITY *(See also:* Reproductive Technologies)

A number of highly technical medical journals focusing on fertility and sterility are listed in periodical directories (see B68-B74).

K62. *Fertility and Sterility: The Official Journal of the American Fertility Society.* Birmingham, AL: American Fertility Society, 1950-. Monthly.

Medical journal intended for gynecologists, endocrinologists, urologists, and andrologists, containing technical articles and case reports on fertility and infertility, sterility, assisted reproductive technologies, and the

physiology of reproduction. Book reviews, calendar. See also X114.
INDEXED: J15, J31, J43, J44, J61.

➤ FETISHES   (*See also*: Erotica; K99, K112)

HOW TO FIND

(*See also*: "How to Find" Erotica, p.200)

• The Kinsey Institute Library (see A4, especially notes on p.10) maintains a large collection of fetish/paraphilia magazines, including both current and historical publications. Titles represent body part fetishes (e.g. feet, hair), inanimate fetishes (e.g. rubber), physical activities (e.g. coprophilia), and bondage and S/M.

K63.   *Fetish Times*. Van Nuys, CA: B&D Co., 1974-. Monthly.
Magazine covering all fetish subjects from bondage to foot worship. Contains classified letters, reviews of magazines and videos, pictorials, news items, and advertisements for special interest groups.

➤ HOMOSEXUALITY   (*See also*: Sex and the Law; K150)

There are hundreds of community based periodicals focusing on gay, lesbian, and bisexual issues (e.g. *Ache: A Journal for Lesbians of African Descent*; *Sports Pride: National Gay and Lesbian Sports Magazine*). Only a few are described below; see "How to Find" to locate additional titles.

HOW TO FIND

• Consult periodical directories (see B68-B74 and K64-K67). *Magazines for Libraries* (see B69) fully describes 87 gay/lesbian titles the editors consider the "best and most useful" for the average library.

• Request periodical holdings lists from lesbian and gay archives, libraries, and special collections (see X53-X60).

• The Gay and Lesbian Press Association (see X244) compiles an annual directory of publishers (see K65).

The *Alternative Press Index* (see J1) is the only periodical index currently covering significant numbers of non-scholarly gay and lesbian titles (although see the forthcoming title, K64). The Broomfield St. Educational Foundation of the Gay Community News Library (62 Berkeley St., Boston, MA 02116-6215. PH: 617/426-4469) will conduct on-line searches of the index for a fee.

—— PERIODICAL DIRECTORIES

K64.   *Contents at a Glance: Gay and Lesbian Studies*. Palo Alto, CA: National Sex Information Network. 1994-. Forthcoming.

Reproduces the tables of contents of current gay and lesbian interest journals, magazines, and newspapers. For more information, contact the National Sex Information Network (see X230).

K65.   *Gay and Lesbian Media Directory Worldwide*. Universal City, CA: Gay and Lesbian Press Association. Annual.

K66.   Malinowsky, H. Robert. *International Directory of Gay and Lesbian Periodicals*. Phoenix: Oryx Press, 1987. 226 p.

Describes 1,924 titles, including newsletters, newspapers, journals, magazines, and other publications. Title and subject indexes.

K67.   Miller, Alan V. *Our Own Voices: A Directory of Lesbian and Gay Periodicals 1890-1990*. Toronto: Canadian Gay Archives, 1991. 704 p.

Bibliographic citations to over 7,200 titles, published in over 30 countries between 1890 and 1990. Includes annual guides, directories, and serials of all types, many of which are no longer in print but are available in archives. Titles on transsexualism, transvestism, bisexuality, and AIDS are also cited. Geographic and chronology indexes only.

—— GAY / LESBIAN NEWSMAGAZINES

K68.   *The Advocate*. Los Angeles: Liberation Publishers, 1967-. Biweekly.

National news and culture magazine with emphasis on the gay male. Contains national and international news articles, in depth commentary and analysis, advertisements, and book and media reviews. INDEXED: J1; *Index to The Advocate, the National Gay News Magazine 1967-1982* (Los

Angeles, CA: Liberation Publications, 1987).

K69. *Gay Community News: The National Lesbian and Gay Weekly*. Boston: Broomfield St. Educational Foundation, 1973-. Weekly. "Dedicated to providing coverage of events and news in the gay and lesbian liberation movement." Contains news, reports, commentary, and reviews. INDEXED: J1.

K70. *Out/Look: National Lesbian and Gay Quarterly*. San Francisco: Out/Look Foundation, 1988-. Quarterly.

Provides a national forum for all elements of the lesbian, gay and bisexual community. INDEXED: J1.

—— LESBIAN (*See also*: H59; *Words to the Wise*, p.239)

The following is only a selection of titles in which sex related articles appear. To identify additional titles, see K65-K67, p.203, or contact X59.

K71. *Bad Attitudes: A Lesbian Sex Magazine*. Cambridge, MA: Bad Attitude Inc., 1984-. Bimonthly.

Contains erotica, editorials, and feature articles on the political aspects of the "lesbian sex movement."

K72. *Lesbian Connection*. Helen Diner Memorial Women's Center. East Lansing, MI: Ambitious Amazons, 1974-. Bimonthly.

National "bulletin board" for the lesbian community, including listings of conferences, festivals, publications, and organizations. Forum for news by, for, and about lesbians. To order: P.O. Box 811, East Lansing, MI 48823.

K73. *Lesbian Contradictions: A Journal of Irreverent Feminism*. San Francisco: LesCon, 1982-. Quarterly.

"A newspaper designed to cover topics debated and discussed within lesbian communities. It features testimony, commentary, and responses to social and political issues as they impact lesbian lives" (p.687 in B69).

K74. *Lesbian Ethics*. Albuquerque, NM: L.E. Publications, 1984-. 2x/yr.

Each 125 page issue of this radical lesbian journal contains 5-8 articles focusing on how lesbians interact with each other. Sex related issues (e.g.

sadomasochism, butch/femme relationships) are often addressed.

K75. *On Our Backs: Entertainment for the Adventurous Lesbian.* San Francisco: Blush Entertainment, 1984-. Bimonthly.

Publishes lesbian erotica (stories, poetry, art work, and photographs), columns, and articles addressing issues of lesbian sex (e.g. lesbian safe sex, butch-femme relationships, sadomasochism). Order from L13.

—— RESOURCE REVIEWS (*See also*: K64, X53)

K76. *GLTF Newsletter.* Chicago: Gay and Lesbian Task Force, American Library Association, 1988-. Quarterly.

Newsletter with information on new publications and resources. See also X53.

K77. *LAMBDA Book Report: A Review of Contemporary Gay and Lesbian Literature.* Washington: Lambda Rising Inc., 1987-. Monthly.

Published by the Lambda Rising Bookstores (see L7). The only national publication dedicated to reviewing gay and lesbian interest publications, it claims comprehensive coverage of all new titles published in the U.S. "Not restricted to any one viewpoint regarding gay and lesbian issues," it seeks to review books representing as wide a spectrum of gay and lesbian perspectives as possible. INDEXED: J1, B24.

K78. *Lesbian Herstory Archives Newsletter.* New York: Lesbian Herstory Education Foundation, 1975-. Irregular.

Provides updates on the Archive's collection, including announcements and reviews of new acquisitions, bibliographies, and brief historical accounts. See also X59.

K79. *L.G.S.N. (Lesbian and Gay Studies Newsletter).* Rocky Mount, NC: Gay and Lesbian Caucus for the Modern Languages, 1973-. 3/year.

K80. *Matrices: Lesbian Feminist Resource Network.* Minneapolis: Women's Studies Department, University of Minnesota, n.d. Quarterly.

Contains book and film reviews, dissertation abstracts, directories of lesbian periodicals and archives, descriptions of new books, and other features.

— SCHOLARLY AND PROFESSIONAL

K81. *Journal of Gay and Lesbian Psychotherapy.* New York: Haworth Press, 1988-. Quarterly.

Articles relating to the use of psychotherapy with gay, lesbian and bisexual clients in the fields of psychiatry, social work, and psychology, as well as subspecialties such as drug and alcohol counseling, family and couples therapy, adolescent treatment, group therapy, and bereavement counseling. It does not support any philosophy which "degrades or engenders self-hatred or despair among gay and lesbian people." INDEXED: J1, J46, J52, J64, J39, J41.

K82. *Journal of Gay and Lesbian Social Services: Issues in Practice, Policy, and Research.* New York: Haworth Press, 1993-. Quarterly.

"Aims to promote the well being of homosexuals and bisexuals in contemporary society through disseminating information on innovative approaches to the design, evaluation, and delivery of social services to lesbian and gay [individuals, couples, families and communities]." Information provided by publisher. INDEXED: J64.

K83. *Journal of Homosexuality.* San Francisco State University Center for Research and Education in Sex. New York: Haworth Press, 1974-. Quarterly.

"Devoted to scholarly research on homosexuality, including sexual practices and gender roles, and their cultural, historical, interpersonal, and modern social contexts . . . Also explores political, social, and moral implications of research on human sexuality." Contains research articles (theoretical, empirical, and historical), book reviews, and annotated bibliographies. Thematic issues are published by Haworth Press as monographs (see L3). Past issues have included *Homosexuality and the Law*; *Nature and Causes of Homosexuality*; *Bisexualities: Theory and Research*; *Lesbians Over 60 Speak for Themselves*; *Homosexuality and Religion*; among other titles—contact the publisher for a complete list. INDEXED: J3, J43, J52, J39, J41, J46, J53, J61, J64, J63, J65.

➤ IMPOTENCE

K84. *Impotence Worldwide.* Maryville, TN: Impotence Institute International, 1985-. Quarterly.

Directed towards both urologists and the general public. Contains information on the treatment and cure of chronic male impotence, including research news, book reviews, and columns. See X123.

➤ LANGUAGE *(See also:* X129)

K85. *Maledicta: The International Journal of Verbal Aggression.* Santa Rosa, CA: Maledicta Press Publications, 1977-. Annual.

"Neither boringly academic nor vulgar, [each 320 page volume] contains scholarly and popular, witty and serious, long and short, important and ephemeral, essays and glossaries about "bad" words [past and present] in English and in many foreign languages." Areas of interest include the origin, etymology, meaning, usage, and influence of jokes, graffiti, slang, nicknames, proverbs, verbal abuse, insults, curses, blasphemies, sexual slurs and stereotypes, "vulgar," "profane," or "obscene" language (including that for sexual and excretory body parts and activities), slang and jargon of all subgroups, and offensive gestures. Emphasis is on sexual words, but all subjects are represented. Also includes research announcements, bibliographies of new publications, and conference announcements. Maledicta Press also publishes the *Maledicta Monitor*, a quarterly newsletter containing conference announcements and resource updates. See also p.60, p.126. INDEXED: J38, J63.

➤ MARRIAGE AND FAMILY *(See also:* K139, K140, K142)

K86. *American Journal of Family Therapy.* New York: Brunner/ Mazel, 1972-. Quarterly.

Publishes scholarly articles on the latest techniques in family therapy, theory on normal and dysfunctional family relationships, and research on sexuality and intimacy, the effects of traditional and alternative family styles, community approaches to family intervention, and other topics. Regular departments include "Family Measurement Techniques," "Family Law Issues," "Continuing Education and Training," "Book and Media Reviews," "Journal Files," and "International Dept." INDEXED: J25, J39, J41, J52, J60, J61, J63.

K87. *Australian Journal of Marriage and Family.* Concord, New S.Wales, Australia: Australian Journal of Marriage and Family, 1980-. Quarterly.

Formerly *Australian Journal of Sex, Marriage, and Family.* Professional journal for those working with sexual, marital and family issues, including academics, researchers, administrators, educators, and clinicians in the helping professions. Publishes scholarly and clinical research reports and articles, book reviews, and abstracts of significant recent publications. Includes the *Newsletter of Australian Association of Marriage and Family Counselors.* INDEXED: J39, J41, J52, J53. To order: P.O.Box 143, Concord NSW. 2137 Australia.

K88. *Family Relations: Journal of Applied Family and Child Studies.* Minneapolis: National Council of Family Relations, 1952-. Quarterly.

Scholarly journal "directed towards practitioners serving the family field through education, counseling and community service." Emphasizes the implications and application of research and theory to family life education, counseling, the development of community programs, and public policy. Contains articles, program evaluations, and literature and resource reviews. See also X131. INDEXED: J17, J25, J31, J32, J39, J52, J61-J64.

K89. *Journal of Family Issues.* National Council of Family Relations. Newbury Park, CA: Sage Publications, 1980-. Quarterly.

Articles and commentary devoted to "contemporary social issues and social problems related to marriage and family life, and to theoretical and professional issues of current interest to those who work with and study families." Publishes two general issues and two thematic issues per year (e.g. *Adolescent Sexuality, Pregnancy and Childbearing*). See also X131. INDEXED: J19, J20, J31, J37, J39, J50, J41, J52, J60, J61, J63, J64.

K90. *Journal of Marital and Family Therapy.* Washington: American Association of Marriage and Family Therapy, 1975-. Quarterly.

Formerly *Journal of Marriage and Family Counseling.* Seeks "to advance the professional understanding of marital and family behavior and to improve the psychotherapeutic treatment of marital and family disharmony." Articles cover research, theory, clinical practice, and training in marital and family therapy. INDEXED: J43, J25, J52, J61, J63, J64.

K91. *Journal of Marriage and the Family.* Minneapolis: National Council of Family Relations, 1938-. Quarterly.

Professional journal publishing original theoretical articles, research interpretations, and critical discussions on subjects relating to marriage and family life. See also X131. INDEXED: J3, J15, J17, J25, J28, J31, J39, J40, J41, J43, J50, J52, J61, J62, J64.

➤ "MEN's" MAGAZINES *(See also*: Erotica)

Playboy and other popular "men's" magazines, such as *Penthouse*, are especially good sources for film and book reviews, articles relating to sexual freedom and sex and law, and contemporary sexual behavior.

HOW TO FIND

• Popular magazines with high sexuality content (e.g. *Playboy* and *Penthouse*), as well as more explicit titles, are listed in periodical directories under "Men's" or "Sex" (see B68-B74).

K92. *Forum: The International Journal of Human Relations.* New York: Forum International Ltd., 1976-. Monthly.

Continued by *Penthouse Forum.* Contains articles written by sexologists and therapists, columns, readers' letters.

K93. *Playboy: Entertainment for Men.* Chicago: Playboy Enterprises. 1953-. Monthly.

In addition to its centerfolds, *Playboy* includes feature articles, reviews, news, and editorials. The November issue contains a review of sex in films the previous year. INDEXED: J6, J7.

➤ NON-MONOGAMY

K94. *Emerge Playcouple.* Anaheim, CA: North American Swing Club Association, 1971-. Bimonthly.

"Written for those unique couples who have romance and adventure in their hearts and seek excitement and freedom in their social and intimate life and erotic relationships" through "swinging." Contains an events calendar, articles, reviews, and news of swinging tours. See also X155.

K95. *Floodtide.* Mill Valley, CA: Intinet, 1992-. Quarterly.

Newsletter of Intinet (see X154), a resource center on "ethical non-exclusive relationships." Contains news, resource reviews, and a directory.

K96. *Loving More: A Group Marriage Journal and Network.* Captain Hook, HI: Paradise Educational Partnership, 1984-. Quarterly.

Newsletter on group marriage and other forms of committed, adult multiple relationships. Includes articles and personal accounts on the dynamics and psychology of multiple relationships, personals advertising, an events calendar, book reviews, and a resource directory. See also X156.

K97. *NASCA Inside Report: For Those Who Want More Than Just One Bite.* Anaheim, CA: North American Swing Club Association, 1980-. Bimonthly.

For adults involved or interested in swinging and other forms of social recreation. Contains articles, commentary, organizational and member's news, an events calendar, a directory of affiliated clubs, and new publication announcements. See also X155.

➤ NUDISM

HOW TO FIND

• The Kinsey Institute archives (see A4) include an extensive collection of nudist magazines and newsletters dating back to the 1950s. See also the archives listed under "Nudism" in Ch.30. *Alternative Lifestyles* (see p.338) fully describes their periodical holdings.

K98. *Journal of the Senses.* Topanga, CA: Elysium Institute, n.d. Quarterly.

Magazine produced by the Elysium Institute, a nudist organization. It is designed to "broaden public recognition of the naturalness and rightness of the human body and its functions; to eliminate the attitude of guilt and shame toward natural processes of life." Contains book reviews, articles, news of legal action, calendar of events, publication reviews and announcements. See also X159.

➤ PEDOPHILIA

K99.   *NAMBLA Bulletin*. New York: North American Man/Boy Love Association, 1979-. 10/year.

Journal of the North American Man/Boy Love Association (see X165), an organization supporting intergenerational sexual relationships. Contains articles on issues relating to age of consent, youth rights, and the legal and criminal justice aspects of such relationships. INDEXED: J1.

K100.   *PADIKA: The Journal of Paedophilia*. Amsterdam: Stichting Paidika Foundation, 1987-. Quarterly.

Intended for researchers as well as pedophiles and pederasts, this scholarly journal focuses on issues relating to homosexual pedophilia, especially the study of pedophilia within the humanities, history, and social sciences. Emphasis is on the positive aspects of consensual intergenerational sexual relations. "Articles speak to the social and political conditions of pedophiles, gays, lesbians, and other sex radicals. *Padika* raises issues crucial to the mature consideration of pornography, censorship, consent, abuse and incest" (from p. 888 in B69).

➤ POPULATION STUDIES *(See also*: Family Planning)

HOW TO FIND

• Most periodical directories cite population studies journals under "Population Studies," "Demographics," or "Family Planning" (see B68-B74). *Ulrichs* (see B74), for example, cites 18 pages of titles under the heading "Population Studies."

• Request the periodical holdings list from a population studies library (see X168-X172).

K101. *Social Biology.* Port Angeles, WA: Society for the Study of Social Biology, 1954-. Biannual.

Publishes scientific articles in demography, genetics, psychology, medicine, sociology, anthropology, and other cross disciplinary fields, which further "discussion, advancement and dissemination of knowledge about biological and socio-cultural forces which affect the structure and composition of human populations," e.g. sex selection, infant mortality, abortion, infertility, natural disasters, and contraceptive technologies. See also X198. INDEXED: J15, J31, J43, J44, J50, J52, J60, J61, J63, J65.

➤ PORNOGRAPHY / OBSCENITY (*See also*: Sex and Law; K150)

K102. *Backlash Times.* New York: Feminists Fighting Pornography, 1983-. Semi-annual.

Each issue of this newsletter contains over 50 news briefs, culled from the press and media, on pornography, sexual abuse of women, prostitution, sexual slavery, sexism in mass media, and sex in advertising. Chronicles legislation, legal cases, statistics, and surveys. See also X180.

K103. *Censorship News.* New York: National Coalition Against Censorship, 1975-. Quarterly.

Newsletter for those concerned with protecting First Amendment rights. Promotes free speech, expression, and inquiry in all areas, including those relating to sexual behavior and sexual expression. See also X182.

K104. *Obscenity Law Bulletin.* New York: National Obscenity Law Center, 1977-. Monthly.

Newsletter containing current information, articles, and commentary on current obscenity cases nationwide. See also X176.

K105. *Women Against Pornography—Newsreport.* New York: Women Against Pornography, 1979-. Quarterly.

Newsletter containing articles on the international feminist anti-pornography movement, an events calendar, legislative reviews and research updates, and reports of sexual violence and sex role stereotyping in art, books, films, and advertisements. See also X181.

➤ PROSTITUTION

K106. *Whorezine*. San Francisco, CA: Vic St. Blaise, n.d. Monthly.

Contains an events calendar, news of local political issues, and articles on prostitution. The publisher maintains an article clipping service. To order: 2300 Market St., Suite 19, San Francisco, CA 94114.

➤ REPRODUCTION

K107. *Biology of Reproduction*. Champaign, IL: Society for the Study of Reproduction, 1969-. Monthly.

Medical journal. See also X198. INDEXED: J3, J15, J43, J44.

K108. *Research in Reproduction*. London: International Planned Parenthood Federation, 1969-. Quarterly.

Summarizes advances in reproductive physiology and provides details on current events relevant to the field. Intended for research workers, doctors, teachers, students, and general readers, it is available free on request. INDEXED: J15, J31.

➤ REPRODUCTIVE TECHNOLOGIES

K109. *Issues in Reproduction and Genetic Engineering: Journal of International Feminist Analysis*. Elmsford, NY: Pergamon Press, 1988-. 3x/year.

Formerly *Reproductive and Genetic Engineering*. Feminist, multi-disciplinary, international analysis of new reproductive technologies and their impact on women. Seeks to recognize the use and abuse of women as central to the development of reproductive technologies and to highlight the relevance of these technologies to the social and political conditions of women. INDEXED: J65.

K110. *Journal of Assisted Reproduction and Genetics*. New York: Plenum Press, 1984-. Bimonthly.

Formerly *Journal of in Vitro Fertilization and Embryo Transfer*.

K111. *Reproductive Technology Update*. Atlanta: American Health Consultants, 1989-. Monthly.

➤ SADOMASOCHISM *(See also: First Link* [see X117])

K112. *The Eulenspiegel Society Newsletter.* New York: The Eulen-spiegal Society, n.d. Quarterly.

Newsletter of the Eulenspiegel Society (see X211). Publishes articles and fiction on dominant/submissive and sadomasochistic relationships. Also includes classified and commercial advertisements, publication announcements and reviews, a calendar of events, and a directory of organizations.

➤ SEX EDUCATION

K113. *Contemporary Sexuality.* Chicago: American Association of Sex Educators, Counselors and Therapists, n.d. Monthly.

Newsletter of AASECT (see X183). Contains brief articles, a column on sexuality and the law, a calendar of upcoming conferences and workshops, reviews of new resources, and listings of education and training opportunities.

K114. *Family Life Educator.* ETR Associates. Santa Cruz, CA: Network Publications, 1982-. Quarterly.

Journal directed toward the family life and sexuality educator, containing up-to-date information and thinking on the moral, physical, psychological, and social dimensions of family life and sexuality education, teaching activities and tools (e.g. lesson plans, materials, and procedures), resource reviews (of books, curricula, and videos), and abstracts of recent journal articles. See also X219. INDEXED: J31.

K115. *Journal of Sex Education and Therapy.* American Association of Sex Educators, Counselors and Therapists. New York: Guilford Publications, 1975-. Quarterly.

"Publishes research on correlates of sexual knowledge, and research that evaluates interventions for providing sex education and therapy." Includes articles on therapeutic and educational techniques, and reviews of books, curriculum, and audiovisuals. See also X183. INDEXED: J31, J63, J64.

K116. *Sexology: Educational Facts for Adults.* v.1-43. New York: Sexology Publications, 1933-1980?

Publisher and title have varied. No longer being published, this title is of historical interest and is available on microfilm through interlibrary loan.

K117.   *Sexuality Today*. New York: Atcom Inc, 1969-1991. Weekly.

A newsletter for professionals working in human sexuality. The title changed in 1991 to *Behavior Today*, and now only occasionally contains sex related items. INDEXED: J31.

K118.   *SIECCAN Newsletter*. Sex Information and Education Council of Canada. Toronto: SIECCAN, 1966-. Quarterly.

Contains organizational news, book and video reviews, practical teaching and counseling ideas, media reports, and commentary. See also A6.

K119.   *SIECUS Report*. Sex Information and Education Council of the United States. New York: SIECUS, 1972-. Bimonthly.

Journal/newsletter emphasizing topics relevant to sex and HIV/AIDS education, but containing articles on all topics in the human sexuality field, as well as reviews of contemporary books, curriculum, and audiovisual materials; bibliographies and resources lists; articles and commentary by experts in the field; advocacy updates and news items; and a conference/seminar calendar. See also A5, X189. INDEXED: J26.

➤ SEX AND THE LAW *(See also:* K150)

K120.   *Journal of Sexual Liberty*. San Francisco: Committee to Preserve Our Sexual and Civil Liberties, 1985-. Monthly.

Reprints newspaper articles and news reports on recent happenings in the areas of sex and civil liberties. For topics covered, see X233.

K121.   *Lambda Update*. New York: Lambda Legal Defense and Education Inc., 1973-. Quarterly.

Reports on litigation to counter discrimination against gay men and lesbians. Includes articles on the legal and educational issues surrounding gay and lesbian rights, docket updates, and reports on the status of current legal cases. For topics covered, see X238.

K122.   *Sexual Law Reporter*. Princeton, NJ: National Committee for Sexual Civil Liberties, n.d. Quarterly.

Contact X235 for details.

K123. *State Reproductive Health Monitor.* New York: Alan Guttmacher Institute, 1990-. Quarterly.

Addresses the legal aspects of abortion, birth control, reproductive technologies, human reproduction, and sexuality. See also X253.

K124. *Reporter on Human Reproduction and the Law.* Boston: Legal-Medical Studies Inc., 1972-. Bimonthly.

Loose-leaf publication providing regular updates of legal, medical, ethical, and social developments in abortion, artificial insemination, surrogate motherhood, conception control, eugenics, medical malpractice, the family, and reproduction. Includes legal perspectives and court decisions.

➤ SEX IN MEDIA (*See also*: Pornography)

K125. *GLAAD Bulletin.* New York: GLAAD, nd. Bimonthly.

Pubication of Gays and Lesbians Against Defamation (see X243), a media watchdog organization. Reports on representations of gays and lesbians in the media (print, broadcast, and visual arts), including both positive and homophobic depictions. Also publishes the quarterly *GLAAD Newsletter*.

➤ SEX IN RELIGION (*See also*: K35-K38)

K126. *Conscience: A Newsjournal of Prochoice Catholic Opinion.* Washington, DC: Catholics for a Free Choice, 1979-. Bimonthly.

Each 24 page issue examines ethical questions relating to abortion, human reproduction, and sexuality, including news of legislative and court actions, and relevant activities and developments in the Catholic Church and medical science. Seeks to change the attitudes of the Catholic Church towards abortion and birth control. See also X246.

➤ SEX RESEARCH

K127. *Annals of Sex Research.* Toronto: Juniper Press, 1988-. Quarterly. (Contact SIECCAN [A6] for information)

K128. *Annual Review of Sex Research.* Mt.Vernon, IA: Society for the Scientific Study of Sex, 1990-. Annual.

Intended for educators, clinicians, and researchers, each volume contains

10-12 authoritative review articles highlighting and synthesizing current controversies, and important theoretical and research advances in the field of human sexuality. See also X189.

K129. *Archives of Sexual Behavior.* International Academy of Sex Research. New York: Plenum Publishing, 1971-. Bimonthly.

Journal dedicated to the "publication of information that will enhance understanding of human sexual behavior." All sexual topics are covered, including normal sexual behavior, physiological aspects of sexual functioning and dysfunctioning, psychopathology and sex, cross cultural studies, sex and aging, and transsexualism and gender dysphoria. Articles are written by researchers in many academic disciplines, including psychology, psychiatry, biology, criminology, endocrinology, and sociology. Includes conference/meeting announcements. INDEXED: J3, J15, J20, J43, J44, J51, J52, J61, J63, J65.

K130. *Canadian Journal of Human Sexuality.* Ontario: Sex Information and Education Council of Canada, 1992-. Quarterly.

Formerly *SIECCAN Journal.* Each issue contains original scholarly articles and research reports, book reviews, conference announcements, abstracts of articles published elsewhere, proceedings of the annual Canadian Sex Research Forum, and an unannotated list of books recently received by the SIECCAN library (see A6).

K131. *Contents at a Glance: Sex Studies.* Palo Alto, CA: National Sex Information Network, 1994-.

A monthly journal reproducing the complete table of contents of hundreds of sex related journals and magazines. For more information, contact the National Sex Information Network (see X230).

K132. *Journal of the History of Sexuality.* Chicago: University of Chicago Press, 1990-. Quarterly.

Seeks to foster "scholarly debate and communication among the many individuals working in the history of sexuality." Publishes historical, critical, and theoretical research articles, research and review essays, book reviews, an unannotated bibliography of "Books of Critical Interest," and an events calendar. Covers the history of sexuality from ancient times to the present.

K133. *Journal of Psychology and Human Sexuality*. New York: Haworth Press, 1988-. Quarterly.

Contains scholarly and professional articles about human sexuality written from a range of psychological perspectives, including clinical, counseling, educational, social, experimental, psychoendrocrinology, and psycho-neuroscientific. Articles address theory, research findings, and clinical and educational methods. INDEXED: J15, J37, J40, J46, J52, J60, J63, J64.

K134. *Journal of Sex Research*. Mt. Vernon, IA: Society for the Scientific Study of Sex, 1965-. Quarterly.

Publishes articles by researchers working in all disciplines involved in the scientific study of sexuality, including medicine, law, psychology, sociology, biology, anthropology, and endocrinology. Contains empirical and clinical research reports, theoretical essays, literature reviews, methodological articles, historical articles, and teaching papers. See also X189. INDEXED: J17, J20, J31, J52, J59, J61, J63, J65.

K135. *Society for the Scientific Study of Sex—Newsletter*. Mount Vernon, IA: Society for the Scientific Study of Sex, 1958-. Quarterly.

Contains association news, a conference/meeting calendar, and notes on members' activities. See also X189.

K136. *Topics in Human Sexuality*. Pointe-Claire, Quebec: Trimel Publishing Group, 1989-. 3x/year.

Unable to view. For information contact SIECCAN (see A6) or the publisher: Suite 305, 755 St. Jean Blvd., Pointe Claire, Quebec H9R 5M9.

> SEX ROLES

K137. *Sex Roles: A Journal of Research*. New York: Plenum, 1975-. Monthly.

Scholarly "forum for the publication of original research articles and theoretical manuscripts concerned with the underlying processes and consequences of gender role socialization, perceptions, and attitudes." Contains original articles, critical research reviews, and book reviews. INDEXED: J17, J41, J46, J52, J59, J61, J63, J64.

➤ SEX THERAPY (*See also*: Marriage and Family)

K138. *Journal of Clinical Practice in Sexuality*. East Brunswick, NJ: Gordon L. Deal Inc., 1985-. Monthly.

K139. *Journal of Couples Therapy*. New York: Haworth Press, 1989-. Quarterly.

Professional journal devoted to "understanding the process of achieving a happy relationship." Research and clinical reports on issues of human bonding, intimacy, and intimacy dysfunction in couples; their interaction and daily living as a pair; and the issues that psychotherapy practitioners face in "attempting to help their clients achieve more satisfying and contented commitment and bonding with their most important 'significant other'." Information provided by publisher. INDEXED: J39, J46, J52, J65.

K140. *Journal of Sex and Marital Therapy*. New York: Brunner-Mazel Inc., 1974-. Quarterly.

A clinical and therapeutically oriented professional journal focusing on theory, research, and practice in sex and marital therapy, including information on new therapeutic techniques, research on outcomes, special clinical and medical problems (e.g. sexual dysfunction), and the theoretical parameters of sexual functioning and marital relationships. Includes book reviews. INDEXED: J41, J43, J44, J52, J61.

K141. *Journal of Social Work and Human Sexuality*. New York: Haworth Press, 1982-. Semi-annual.

Human sexuality as it relates to social work practice, research, theory, and education. Publishes research articles, clinical and program reports, and case studies addressing issues of sexual education, counseling, and policy for social work populations (i.e. adolescents, aged, ethnic minorities, institutionalized, mentally ill, handicapped, and others). INDEXED: J20, J51, J52, J64, J65.

K142. *Sexual and Marital Therapy*. Association of Sexual and Marital Therapists. Abingdon, Oxfordshire, U.K.: Carfax Publishing Co., 1986-. 2x/year.

A crossdisciplinary "international journal for everyone professionally concerned with sexual and marital function," including academics, researchers, clinicians, therapists, and counselors. Publishes original research articles, literature reviews, counseling and therapeutic practice accounts, clinical case studies, and book reviews. Takes a "critical stance toward much of the current literature." INDEXED: J41, J59, J52, J65.

➤ SEXUAL ABUSE

K143. *Aegis: Magazine on Ending Violence Against Women.* Washington: Feminist Alliance Against Rape, 1974-1987. Ceased.

Ceased publication with no.42; back issues are available. INDEXED: J1.

K144. *Family Violence and Sexual Assault Bulletin.* Tyler, TX: Family Violence and Sexual Assault Institute, 1985-. Quarterly.

K145. *Journal of Child Sexual Abuse: Research, Treatment and Program Innovations for Victims, Survivors and Offenders.* New York: Haworth, 1992-. Quarterly.

Multidisciplinary journal "devoted to contemporary research, intervention techniques, programs, legal issues and reviews on all aspects of childhood sexual abuse. Intended for researchers, academicians, clinicians, and practitioners, it addresses theoretical, clinical, legal, and empirical issues relating to child and adolescent victims, adult survivors, and offenders.

K146. *Journal of Interpersonal Violence.* Newbury Park, CA: Sage Publications, 1986-. Quarterly.

Devoted to the study and treatment of victims and perpetrators of interpersonal violence, including rape, sexual assault, and child sexual abuse. Articles integrate theory and practice, and focus on the causes, effects, treatments, and prevention of all types of interpersonal violence. Includes therapeutic techniques, program descriptions and evaluations, research and policy analysis, and book and media reviews. Information provided by publisher. INDEXED: J20, J21, J39, J52, J61, J63, J64.

K147. *National Clearinghouse on Marital and Date Rape Newsletter.* Berkeley: National Clearinghouse on Marital and Date Rape, 1982-. Quarterly.

Reports on court decisions, legislation, lobbying activities, statutes, statistics, and other items relating to marital, date, and cohabitation rape. See also X277.

K148. *Sexual Coercion and Assault*. Bellingham, WA: CRU Publishing, Jan. 1986-1991 (ceased). Monthly.

Ceased publication in 1991—back issues are available. Publishes research relevant to coercive sexuality, including rape, spouse abuse, sexual harassment, and child sexual abuse. Also contains abstracts of studies on these topics published in over 800 journals. Book reviews. INDEXED: J20.

K149. *Violence Update*. Newbury Park, CA: Sage Publications, 1991-.

Each 12 page newsletter "brings you concentrated news and information on the latest programs, politics and ideas" in a particular area of interpersonal violence studies. Past issues (still available) have addressed sexual abuse prevention programs, pornography's effect on women, child sexual abuse, treatment of sex offenders, sexual arousal and sexual assault, sexual violence research, and rape trauma. Each includes legal updates, an events calendar, book and resource reviews, and other features.

➤ SEXUAL FREEDOM (*See also*: Sex and the Law; K120, X233)

K150. *Frighten the Horses: A Document of the Sexual Revolution*. San Francisco: Heat Seeking Publications, n.d. Quarterly.

"An intellectually provocative journal that documents the right wing war on erotica as well as the resistance by sexual minorities, including lesbians and gays. News of obscenity trials and repressive legislation shares space on its pages with erotic graphics and essays by Queer Nation and lesbian and gay novelists" (from p.684 of B69).

➤ SEXUAL HEALTH AND MEDICINE (*See also*: Family Planning; Fertility; Sexually Transmitted Diseases)

K152. *British Journal of Sexual Medicine*. London: Inter Medical Communication, 1973-. Monthly.

Unable to view. INDEXED: J15, J43, J51.

K153. *Health and Sexuality*. Washington: Association of Reproductive Health Professionals, 1990-. Quarterly.

Contains brief, non-technical articles on reproductive health issues, organizational news, abstracts, resource reviews, and an events calendar. See also X200.

K154. *Journal of Reproductive Medicine: For Obstetricians and Gynecologists.* St. Louis: Journal of Reproductive Medicine, 1968-. Monthly.

Medical journal devoted to clinical and laboratory aspects of reproductive sciences and neonatology. Publishes articles, case studies and book reviews covering such topics as oral contraception and other contraceptive methods, pediatric and adolescent gynecology and obstetrics, fertility and infertility, and reproductive technologies (e.g. in-vitro fertilization, artificial insemination, surrogate motherhood, embryo transfer). INDEXED: J15, J31, J42, J43, J44, J45.

K155. *Medical Aspects of Human Sexuality.* New York: Cahners Publishing, 1967-. Monthly.

Directed towards physicians and the general public, this non-technical magazine contains articles and research updates on a wide range of sexual problems. Regular features include: Sexuality Update, Vital Statistics, Fertility and Contraception, Questions and Answers (see also F32), Fast Facts, AIDS Research, and STD Briefs. INDEXED: J17, J31, J43, J51, J52.

K156. *MMWR: CDC Surveillance Summaries.* U.S. Centers for Disease Control. Atlanta: Department of Health and Human Services, Public Health Service, CDC, 1983-. Quarterly.

Provides summary analysis of diseases and health problems kept under surveillance by the C.D.C. Includes summaries of new data, trends, and bibliographies of recent publications. Each volume contains 1-9 short reports on a variety of communicable diseases and health concerns, including: abortion, surgical surveillance, birth defects, infant mortality, ectopic pregnancy, toxic shock, maternal mortality, and teenage pregnancy and fertility, among others. For HIV/AIDS (see K15), STDs (see K159), Abortion (see K2). INDEXED: B85, J44, J45.

➤ SEXUALLY TRANSMITTED DISEASES *(See also:* AIDS)

K157. *Morbidity and Mortality Weekly Report.* U.S. Centers for Disease Control. Atlanta: Department of Health and Human Services, Public Health Service, CDC, 1950-. Weekly.

Reports on outbreaks of selected notifiable diseases in the U.S. (e.g. AIDS, syphilis, and gonorrhea) on a state, regional, and national level, including reported deaths in selected cities for the week. Provides current surveillance data (including number of cases, deaths, and historical data), case reports, treatment protocols, statistics. INDEXED: J31, J42, J44, J45.

K158. *International Journal of STD and AIDS.* London: Royal Society of Medicine Services, 1990-. Bimonthly.

K159. *Sexually Transmitted Diseases Surveillance.* U.S. Centers for Disease Control. Atlanta: U.S. Department of Health and Human Services, Public Health Service, CDC, 1989-. Annual.

Continues *Sexually Transmitted Disease Statistics.* See also K156.

K160. *Sexually Transmitted Diseases: Journal of the American Venereal Disease Association.* American Venereal Disease Association. Philadelphia: J.B.Lippincott, 1974-. Quarterly.

Includes both clinical, laboratory, and epidemiologic research reports, and sociological and historical articles on issues relating to sexually transmitted diseases. See also X287. INDEXED: J15, J31, J43, J44.

➤ SINGLES

HOW TO FIND

• Consult the Single Press Association (c/o Singles Scene, 7432 E. Diamond, Scottsdale, AZ 85257; PH: 602/945-6746) for referrals to periodical publishers promoting a positive image of single life.

• Consult *Classified Love Ads: A Directory of Periodicals that Carry Individual Personal Ads Seeking Friendship, Love, Marriage and Similar* (Gibson, LA: Research and Discovery Publications, 1990).

➤ TRANSVESTITE / TRANSSEXUAL

K161. *Chrysalis Quarterly.* Decatur, GA: American Educational Gender Information Service, 1991-. Quarterly.

"Committed to serving the gender community in all its diversity, and especially those segments of the community which have been ignored or only lightly touched on by other publications." Each issue is devoted to the exploration of a single theme, including articles of interest to both consumers and service providers, resource reviews, and an events calendar. See also X290.

K162.   *The TV-TS Tapestry*. Wayland, MA: International Foundation for Gender Education. Quarterly.

Formerly *Tapestry*. Journal intended for all persons interested in crossdressing and transsexualism, including transvestites, transsexuals, their significant others, educators, researchers, and the general public. Includes informative articles and editorials by transvestites, transsexuals, and professionals; a calendar of major TV/TS events worldwide; notices and news; a directory of organizations and services (see p.413); and what the editors claim is the world's largest TV/TS personals listings. Reprints of articles are available (see L23). See also X292.

➤ WOMEN'S SEXUALITY (*See also*: Homosexuality–Lesbians and other specific topics)

HOW TO FIND

• Popular women's magazines (e.g. *Redbook*, *Cosmopolitan*, etc.) often include articles about female sexuality and sexual relationships. Search a popular magazine index for relevant articles (see J6-J8).

K163.   *Eve's Garden*. New York: Eve's Garden, 1983-. Semi-annual.

Magazine focusing on women's sexuality and sexual health. See also L24.

15

BOOKS

Books on sex range from scholarly and professional texts to titles intended for the general public. Varying widely in accuracy, the latter include popularized presentations of research data (e.g. *The Hite Report*), lovemaking guides (e.g. *Joy of Sex*), self help books (e.g. *Becoming Orgasmic*), anecdotal collections of sexual fantasies or experiences (e.g. *My Secret Garden*), encyclopedic texts covering a wide range of topics (e.g. *The Family Book About Sex*), and consumer reference books on sexual/reproductive health related topics (e.g. *The Safe Pregnancy Book*).

With over 7,000 citations added to *Books in Print* each month, a comprehensive bibliography of sex related titles is beyond the scope of this volume—use the resources described under "How to Find" to identify books on a particular topic. Specialized publishers and bookdealers are described below.

● ● ● ●

Listings: Eighteen book dealers and six publishers specializing in books on sex related topics are described below; all distribute mail order catalogs. Organizations and institutions which publish or distribute books or other materials are indicated by a "P" code under "Services" in the descriptive listings beginning on p.321.

227

How to Find

• Search library catalogs (see Ch.8) by author, title, or subject (see Ch.3 THESAURI, for authorized subject headings)—nearly any title held in a U.S. library is available through interlibrary loan. For the most comprehensive coverage, search an on-line catalog such as RLIN (see G4) or OCLC (see G3) which electronically merges the catalogs of hundreds of libraries into a single database. The Library of Congress catalogs (see G1) serve as our National Bibliography, and include books not cataloged elsewhere, as well as records for items submitted to the Library for copyright but not yet published. For older books, consult the print catalogs of the Kinsey Institute's collection (see G6, G7), which cover materials published prior to 1974; or search the card catalogs of older research libraries—the catalogs of the Library of Congress, founded in 1800, and the New York Public Library, founded in 1895, are available on microfilm or in book form in many research libraries. The New York Library of Medicine (see X52) has an archival collection of sex books.

• Browse library shelves for relevant titles. See Ch.9 for details of the classification schemes used to physically arrange sex related materials in libraries.

• The trade bibliographies, *Books in Print*, *Subject Guide to Books in Print*, and *Forthcoming Books in Print* (see B16), provide title, author, and detailed subject access to virtually all books published in the U.S., which are currently in print or forthcoming in the next five months. Consult Sheehy's *Guide* (see B81) for directories of books in print published in other countries. *Cumulative Book Index* (see B17) provides subject, title, and author access to English-language books published worldwide since 1898.

• Request catalogs from specialized publishers, see p.229.

• Browse general bookstores (most sex related titles are shelved in the psychology, gay/lesbian, health, or women's studies sections), or contact specialized bookdealers, most of whom sell via mail order (see "How to Find" Bookdealers, p.229). For older materials, contact antiquarian dealers (see L11, L12).

• Consult subject bibliographies (see Ch.10) and indexes (see Ch.12).

BOOK REVIEWS

• Consult a book review index: *Book Review Digest* (see B23) is a title, author, and subject index; *Book Review Index* (see B24) provides title and author access only. Periodical indexes (see Ch.12) often cite book reviews in a separate section from articles—consult the index's scope notes for details.

• Most journals and newsletters contain book reviews. See especially: *SIECUS Reports* (see K119), *Archives of Sexual Behavior* (see K129), *Journal of Sex Education and Therapy* (see K115), *Journal of Sex Research* (see K134), and other titles listed by topic in Ch.13. The *LAMBDA Book Report: A Review of Contemporary Gay and Lesbian Literature* (see K77) claims to review all new gay and lesbian titles published in the U.S. The newsletters of specialized libraries and archives (e.g. *Link Line*, *Lesbian Herstory Archives Newsletter*) often contain reviews of recent acquisitions; the *Directory of Special Libraries and Information Centers* (see B62) notes any publications in its description of each library.

SPECIALIZED BOOKDEALERS

• Consult the *Directory of Specialized American Bookdealers* (see B19) or the *American Book Trade Directory* (see B18), which includes a "Type of Store Index" listing bookstores by primary specialty (e.g. alternative lifestyles, family studies, gay/lesbian, sexuality). For dealers of out-of-print, antiquarian, or rare books, consult *Buy Books Where—Sell Books Where: A Directory of Out-of-Print Booksellers and Collectors* (see B22), *Directory of American Book Specialists: Sources for Antiquarian and Out-of-Print Titles* (see B21), or the Antiquarian Booksellers of America's *ABAA Membership Directory* (see B20).

• Many organizations and associations sell books and other publications through mail order, and most distribute free catalogs on request (see Ch.30).

PUBLISHERS

• Use the *Encyclopedia of Associations* (see B4) to identify specialized press association which can provide referrals (e.g. Gay and Lesbian Press Association).

• Consult directories of specialized publishers. *Literary Marketplace*, published annually by R.R. Bowker, includes an index of publishers by specialty (e.g. gay/lesbian).

• Request catalogs from the publishers of relevant book series. *Books in Series* (see B15) includes a subject index to series titles, and cites the individual volumes published in each (contact the customer service department of the publisher for a more updated list). For new titles, subject search the series files in RLIN (see G4) or the on-line/on disc versions of *Books in Print* (see B16). The following publish sex related book series: University of Chicago Press (*Studies in the History of Sexuality, The Chicago Series on Sexuality, History and Society*); Prometheus Books (*Chinese Erotic and Sexual Classics Series, New Concepts in Human Sexuality*); Oxford University Press (*Kinsey Institute Series*); Garland Publishing (*Reference Series in Homosexuality*); State University of NY Press (*SUNY Series in Sexual Behavior*); Prometheus Books (*New Concepts in Human Sexuality*); Plenum Press (*Perspectives in Sexuality: Behavior, Research and Therapy*); Elsevier (*Handbook on Sexuality Series*); Praeger (*Series in Sexual Medicine*); Haworth Press (see L10). See B16 for publisher's addresses and phone numbers.

➤ CONSERVATIVE / TRADITIONALISTS

—— BOOKDEALERS

L1.   American Life League: P.O. Box 1350, Stafford, VA 22544. PH: (703)659-4171.

Distribute a free catalog of books, booklets, pamphlets, videos, and other resources on abortion, ethics, infant homicide/euthanasia, the law and the pro-life movement, natural family planning and birth control facts, planned parenthood and other "anti-life groups," population, sex instruction, school based clinics vs. chastity, and secular humanism. See also X2.

L2.   Human Life International: 7845 E. Airpark Rd., Gaithersburg, MD 20879. PH: (301)670-7884.

Distributes a mail order catalog, *Human Life International Pro Life/Family Catalog*, describing available books, pamphlets, and booklets on abortion,

AIDS and homosexuality, chastity vs. sex education, church teachings, contraception, euthanasia and medical ethics, family values, feminism, the new age and "other threats," natural family planning, Planned Parenthood and other "population controllers," post-abortion healing, and pro-life direct action. See also X86.

➤ EROTICA

—— BOOKDEALERS (For women centered erotica see L13, L24)

HOW TO FIND

• Antiquarian bookdealers C.J. Scheiner (see L11) and Ivan Stormgart (see L12) both carry erotic books. Other dealers, while not specializing in such titles, may list erotic works in their catalogs under *curiosa*, *facetiae*, or *erotica*. *Erotica* is used as an index heading in most directories of specialized bookdealers (see B20-B22).

• Most bookstores carry erotica published by mainstream publishers, including erotic classics (e.g. *Fanny Hill, Story of O*), erotic literature (e.g. *Erotica: Women's Writings from Sappho to Margaret Atwood*), and the results of survey research (e.g. *My Secret Garden*). For hard core erotica, visit "adult" bookstores.

—— PUBLISHERS

HOW TO FIND

• The annual *Erotic Writers and Collectors Market* (see p.355) and Valerie Kelly's *How to Write Erotica for Fun and Profit* (New York: Crown, 1986) both include lists of publishers.

➤ GAY / LESBIAN

—— BOOKDEALERS

Many gay/lesbian bookstores nationwide will provide mail order catalogs free on request. Only a few of the larger dealers are listed below.

HOW TO FIND

• The *Gay Yellow Pages* (see p.361), available in national and regional editions, lists bookstores and sources of mail order erotica.

• The Gay and Lesbian Task Force of the American Library Association (see X53) has compiled *Bookstores and Mail Order Firms Specializing in Gay and Lesbian Books: A Directory.*

L3.   A Different Light: 548 Hudson St., New York, NY 10014. PH: (212)989-4850.

Also operates bookstores in San Francisco and Los Angeles. Distributes a quarterly mail order catalog.

L4.   Giovanni's Room: 345 S. 12th St., Philadelphia, PA 19107. PH: (215)923-2960.

Distributes two bimonthly mail order catalogs—one lesbian/feminist and one gay male—describing scholarly and popular fiction/literature, non-fiction, and erotic titles.

L5.   Glad Day Bookshop: 673 Boylston, 2nd Fl., Boston, MA 02116. PH: (617)267-3010.

Compiles, distributes, and regularly updates 11 bibliographies, each listing between 30-200 books and magazines currently available for purchase: *AIDS Bibliography* (15 pages), *Basic Books for the Lesbian and Gay Library, Basic Classics of Gay Fiction, Basic Classics of Lesbian Fiction, Books For and About Teenagers on Homosexuality, Books for High School and College Libraries, Coming Out, Families and Friends of Lesbians and Gays, Gay and Lesbian Parents, Homosexuality and Religion*, and *New Titles* (annotated).

L6.   LAMBDA Rising Bookstores: 1625 Connecticut Ave., NW, Washington, DC 20009. PH: (800)621-6969.

Distributes a free, illustrated catalog, and publishes the *LAMBDA Book Report* (see K77), which claims to review all new gay and lesbian titles published in the U.S.

The following dealers specialize in out-of-print titles:

L7. **Books Bohemian**: Box 17218, Los Angeles, CA 90017. PH: (213)385-6761.

L8. **Elysian Fields**: 80-50 Baxter Ave., #339, Elmhurst, NY 11373. PH: (718)424-2789.

L9. **St. Maur Booksellers**: 820 N. Madison, Stockton, CA 95202. PH: (202)464-3550.

—— PUBLISHERS (*See also*: Women's Sexuality)

Although most major publisher in the U.S. produces at least a few books each year of special interest to gays/lesbians, Haworth Press (see L10) is the only mainstream publisher of significant numbers of gay/lesbian themed scholarly titles (although contact Garland Publishing for a catalog of their new *Reference Series in Homosexuality*). Use the resources discussed below to identify community presses publishing exclusively gay/lesbian titles.

HOW TO FIND

• Consult directories. Forty-seven publishers of gay and lesbian titles are listed in R.R. Bowker's *Literary Marketplace*, available in all libraries. Publishers specializing exclusively in such titles are listed in the *Gay Yellow Pages* (see p.361). The Gay and Lesbian Task Force of the American Library Association (see X53) have compiled, and regularly update, *Publishers of Gay and Lesbian Books*.

• The Gay and Lesbian Press Association (see X244) distributes a directory of publishers specializing in gay and lesbian materials.

L10. **Haworth Press:** Ten Alice St., Binghamton, NY 13904-1580. PH: (800)342-9678.

Publishes *The Haworth Series in Gay and Lesbian Studies*, each volume of which is based on scholarly research but written in language that is readily understandable to the nonspecialist. All disciplines and inter-disciplinary fields that have contributed to gay and lesbian studies are represented, with an emphasis on the social sciences, history, the humanities, the arts, and a broad range of applied/professional fields.

Haworth also publishes the *Research in Homosexuality Series*, consisting of monograph editions of thematic issues of the *Journal of Homosexuality* (see K83). For a complete list of their gay/lesbian journal titles and books, request the *Harrington Park Press Trade Catalog*.

➤ GENERAL

—— BOOKDEALERS

All bookstores carry books on sexual topics, but the following dealers specialize exclusively in such titles. Scheiner (see L11) and Stormgart (see L12) sell out-of-print, antiquarian, and rare books, ranging from recently out-of-print titles priced at less than $10, to rare collector's items selling for thousands. Although their catalogs are intended to identify books available for purchase, the titles they list may also be available through inter-library loan.

L11.   C.J. Scheiner/Erotica and Curiosa: 275 Linden Blvd., Brooklyn, NY 11226. PH: (718)469-1089.

Bookseller specializing in out-of-print, rare, and antiquarian books on sexuality related topics, including erotica. *The Compendium; Being a List of All the Books (Erotica, Curiosa, and Sexology) Listed in our Catalog 1-6 1978-1988* is an alphabetical list of 1,465 titles—current catalogs are available. His complete collection includes over 80,000 books, plus catalogs, magazines, and other print ephemera.

L12.   Ivan Stormgart: P.O. Box 470883, San Francisco, CA 94147-0883. PH: (415)931-6746.

Bookseller specializing in out-of-print books on all aspects of human sexuality, and other controversial literature. At any given time, 10,000 volumes, in 12 different languages, are available for purchase. He distributes catalogs in the following subject areas:

Abortion	Child/teen sexuality
Aging and sexuality	Courtship, marriage and divorce
AIDS	Erotic art
Amazons	Erotic image in photography
Aphrodisiacs	Eugenics
Bibliographies and dictionaries	Female sexuality
Birth control	Fetishism
Censorship and sexual privacy	Flagellation

General catalogues
Homosexuality—clinical
Homosexuality—fiction and art
Humor and limericks
Incest
Jealousy
Male sexuality
Masturbation
Motion picture and erotic theater
Nudism
Phallic worship
Prostitutes, madams and pimps
Religion and sex
S/M
Sex and drugs

Sex in prison
Sex and war
Sex manuals and encyclopedias
Sexual aggression
Sexual anthropology
Sexual revolution
Sexual slavery and harems
Sexuality and the law
Tantra, kundalini and magic
Tattoos
Transsexuals, transvestites, and
  hermaphrodites
Venereal disease
Victorian sexuality
Vintage paperbacks

L13.   The Sexuality Library: 1210 Valencia St., San Francisco, CA 94110. PH: (415)974-8990.

A women run, "personalized bookstore offering carefully selected sexual self-help books, books about sexuality, and erotic books by mail," all of which were "lovingly produced by small publishers and are difficult to find elsewhere. We arrived at our final selection based on several factors: customer response to the previous editions of this catalog, the advice of a panel of sex educators and therapists, feedback from Good Vibrations, customers and recommendations from our staff." The Spring 1992 catalog briefly describes over 250 titles, classified under 15 categories: Adolescent Sexuality, Children's Sexuality, Comics, Erotic Art, Erotic Literature, Female Sexuality, Male Sexuality, Older Adults Sexuality, "On the Light Side," "One of a Kind" (primarily scholarly books), "Parents Corner" (talking to children about sex), "Sex for One," "Sex for Two," Sexual Politics, "Smut Series" (i.e. books with "scandalous sex, anonymous authors, and minimal plot . . . little of lasting literary merit, but plenty of enjoyable rambunctious lechery"). For erotic videos, see W10.

— PUBLISHERS

Most books on sex related issues are published by major publishers. Besides gay/lesbian titles, Haworth Press (see L10) publishes a number of sex related journals and books—request their Journal Catalog, Gender Catalog, and Social Work and Human Sexuality Catalog.

L14.   Down There Press: P.O. Box 2086, Burlingame, CA 94011-2086. PH: (415)550-0912.

"The nation's only independent publisher devoted exclusively to the publication of sexual health books for children and adults . . . [Emphasis] is on books that are innovative, lively and practical in both form and content. [They] concentrate on books that provide basic physiological information along with realistic and non-judgmental techniques for developing good sexual communication."

➤ NUDISM

—— PUBLISHERS

L15.   Elysium Growth Press: 814 Robinson Rd., Topanga, CA 90290. PH: (213)455-1000.

Operated by the Elysium Institute (see X159). "The source for books about the philosophy, history, psychology, art and health of the human body—with and without clothes." Their catalog includes books on nudism, body image, clothing, and body decoration.

➤ REPRODUCTION / PARENTHOOD

—— BOOKDEALERS

L16.   Birth and Life Bookstore: 7001 Alonzo Ave. N.W., P.O. Box 70625, Seattle, WA 98107-0625. PH: (800)736-0631.

IMPRINTS, Birth and Life Bookstore's review newsletter and mail order catalog, is published three times per year. The 30 page, Winter 1992 edition contained nine pages of lengthy reviews plus brief descriptions of over 1,100 additional titles, arranged under the following categories:

Adoption	Education	Infertility
Audio Recordings	Exercise and Yoga	Journals/Baby Books
Breastfeeding	Family Planning	Loss and Grief
Cesarean Birth	Fathers	Midwives
Child Care	Food and Nutrition	Naming Baby
Child Development	For Children	Parenthood
Child Health/Safety	Full-Time Mothering	Periodicals
Circumcision	Grandparents	Play and Toys
Disabled Children	History	Post Partum
Divorce/Step Families	Humor, Gifts, Etc.	Pregnancy and Birth

Premature/Ill Infants	Text and Reference	Vaccines/Immunizations
Sleep Problems (babies)	Toilet Teaching	Video Recordings
Social Comment	Touch and Massage	Women's Health Issues
Teenage Pregnancy	Travel With Children	Working/Child Care
Teens and Preteens	Twins	

L17. **ICEA Book Center**: P.O.Box 20048, Minneapolis, MN 55420. PH: (612)854-8660

A mail order bookstore, operated by International Childbirth Education Association (see X70), selling literature on all aspects of childbirth education, and family centered maternity care.

➤ SEX EDUCATION / FAMILY PLANNING

— BOOKDEALERS

L18. **Planned Parenthood Bookstore**: 2211 E. Madison, Seattle, WA 98112-5397. PH: (206)328-7716

L19. **Planned Parenthood S.E. Pennsylvania, Bookstore and Library**: 1144 Locust St., Philadelphia, PA 19107-5740. PH: (215)351-5590

The bookstore sells books and pamphlets written for educators, parents, clergy, kids, teens, and adults on a range of topics, including conception, birth, sexual abuse prevention, puberty, sexually transmitted diseases, values and decision making, sexual orientation, sex education, and reproductive health. A catalog is available. The library contains professional journals and books addressing the statistical, medical, legal, social, and ethical aspects of sexuality, sexuality education, reproductive health, and family planning, as well as curriculum and other resources for creating, conduction, and evaluating educational programs.

— PUBLISHERS

L20. **Network Publications**: ETR Associates, P.O. Box 1830, Santa Cruz, CA 95061-1830. PH: (800)321-4407

A division of ETR (see X219), this claims to be the largest publishing house in the country specializing in family life and prevention education materials. They publish original titles, and distribute materials produced by over 40 non-profit organizations. Their catalog includes books, displays and models, pamphlets, curriculum, and videos on HIV/AIDS prevention, family life, sex education, sexual abuse and domestic violence, birth control, homosexuality, adolescent relationships, reproductive health, and sexual responsibility, among other topics.

➤ SEX THERAPY

— PUBLISHERS

L21.   Guilford Publications, Inc.: 72 Spring Street, New York, NY 10012. PH: (800)365-7006.

Although not specializing exclusively in the area, Guilford publishes many sex and marital therapy handbooks, including *Principles and Practice of Sex Therapy* (1989), see F31; *Sexual Desire Disorders* (1988); *Erectile Disorders: Assessment and Treatment* (1992); *Intimate Environments: Sex, Intimacy, and Gender in Families* (1989); *Husbands, Wives, and Lovers: The Emotional System of the Extramarital Affair* (1990); *Sexuality and Chronic Illness: A Comprehensive Approach* (1988).

➤ SEXUAL ABUSE

— BOOKDEALERS

Contact organizations listed under "Sexual Abuse" in Ch.30 for referrals to other distributors.

L22.   Womantyme Distribution Company: P.O. Box 50145, Long Beach, CA 90815-6145. PH: (800)247-8903 / (310)429-4802.

Distributes a mail order catalog of recovery materials for women and children, including many titles addressing incest and sexual assault.

➤ TRANSVESTITES AND TRANSSEXUALS

— PUBLISHERS

L23.   Tapestry Publication: Box 367, Wayland, MA 01778. PH: (617)899-2212.

A division of the International Foundation for Gender Education (see X292). Tapestry publishes and distributes how-to books, presentation transcripts, anthologies of pertinent reprints, directories, and other timely material related to the interests of the transvestite and transsexual community. Titles include *Transvestites and Transsexuals: Toward a Theory of Cross-Gender Behavior*; *Legal Aspects of Transsexualism*; *Body Packaging: A Guide to Human Sexual Display*; *Art and Illusion: A Guide to Crossdressing*; *My Husband Wears My Clothes*. Request a full catalog.

➤ WOMEN'S SEXUALITY (*See also*: L14)

—— BOOKDEALERS

HOW TO FIND

• Consult *Feminist Bookstore News*, a bimonthly newsletter listing bookstores, feminist publishers, and new feminist publications. Order from Carol Seajay: Box 882554, San Francisco, CA 94118-2554.

L24.   **Eve's Garden**: 119 West 57th St., New York, NY 10019. PH: (800)848-3837.

Devoted to women's sexual health and happiness, Eve's Garden seeks to provide "women the space to enjoy, expand and celebrate their own sexuality," be that heterosexual, lesbian, or bisexual. Their retail store and mail order catalogs are "filled with books on women's sexuality and health, books on Tantric sex and spirituality, books on enhancing relationships, and a diversified collection of erotic literature written by and for women. You'll also find body massagers, vibrators, safer-sex accessories and many other pleasurable things designed to build sexual self-esteem and encourage women's sexual independence and self growth."

—— PUBLISHERS

HOW TO FIND

• Consult Andrea Clardy's *Words to the Wise: A Writer's Guide to Feminist and Lesbian Periodicals and Publishers* (Ithaca, NY: Firebrand Books, 1990), a directory of 100 publishers of feminist and lesbian books and periodicals.

16

DISSERTATIONS & THESES

Dissertations and theses are valuable for their bibliographic references, concise statements of theoretical perspectives and research methodologies, and extensive literature reviews. As by definition they must make a new and significant contribution to the literature in their field, doctoral dissertations are an especially good source for information on topics that have not been widely addressed previously in the literature.

Some dissertations are published as monographs and purchased by libraries. Others may be borrowed from the degree granting institution through interlibrary loan, or purchased from UMI (see "How to Find").

● ● ● ●

Listings: The following two sex related dissertation catalogs are available through interlibrary loan. See "How to Find" for obtaining updates.

M1. *Vital Research on Homosexuality 1936-1982*. Ann Arbor, MI: UMI, 1982.
214 MA and PHD American dissertations. Updated regularly by UMI.

M2. *Sex in Contemporary Society: A Catalog of Dissertations 1938-1972*. Ann Arbor, MI: Xerox University Microfilm, 1973.
Cites over 400 American and Canadian dissertations.

HOW TO FIND

• UMI Dissertation Services (300 North Zeeb Rd., Ann Arbor, MI 48106-1346. PH: 800/521-0600) offers complete publishing, indexing, and copying services for doctoral dissertations and masters theses. Their comprehensive data base covers all academic disciplines, and cites over one million U.S. doctoral dissertations and over 45,000 masters theses. British dissertations have been included since 1988, those from Canada since 1991. To identify relevant dissertations, (1) search their print or computer readable index, *Comprehensive Dissertations Index* (see B34) and its companion volume, *Dissertation Abstracts International* (the two are combined on disc and on-line); (2) order one of UMI's free subject catalogs (including one on homosexuality); or (3) request a DATRIX Search, a customized subject/keyword search available for $20.

17

GOVERNMENT DOCUMENTS

This chapter focuses on locating documents produced by the U.S. Federal Government, although local, state, regional, foreign, and international governmental organizations and agencies can also be excellent sources of information. The single most prolific publisher in the world, the federal government publishes statistical reports; indexes, directories, bibliographies, handbooks, and other reference materials; pamphlets, posters, and curriculum; journals, newsletters, and magazines; announcements of legislative actions and executive orders; research reports; and more, with items ranging in size from single page fact sheets to multi-volume book sets. Government publications relating to sexuality tend to focus on issues of public policy, public debate and controversy, or public health (i.e. AIDS, abortion, birth defects, contraception for teenagers, family planning, health and vital statistics, sexual orientation discrimination, laws governing sexual behavior, maternal and child health, pornography and obscenity, prostitution, reproductive health, sex education in schools, sexually transmitted diseases, and sex crimes, to name only a few). They range from transcripts of congressional hearings on gays in the military, to a bibliography of sexual assault compiled by the Congressional Research Service, to regulations regarding abortion counseling in federally funded health clinics.

Federal documents are sold through the Government Printing Office (GPO) in Washington and at GPO bookstores nationwide, and are col-

HOW TO FIND

• Check publication catalogs. The Government Printing Office's (GPO) *Monthly Catalog of U.S. Government Publications* (see B53) is a subject classified guide to currently available titles produced by the executive, legislative, and judicial branches, as well as federal agencies, and affiliated independent agencies and commissions. Although comprehensive, it is not exhaustive. For more thorough coverage, consult the government document indexes described below and/or request a publication catalog directly from the federal agency specializing in the area of interest—to identify, see the resources listed under "How to Find" Government Agencies, p.317. For subject bib-liographies issued by the GPO, consult their *Subject Bibliography Index* (see B54).

• Federal Information Centers (see B44) and the National Health Information Center (see B45) provide referrals to relevant publications, as well as to agencies. Information clearinghouses can also provide this service—see p.260 for a partial list of government clearinghouses, and "How to Find" Information Clearinghouses, p.317, for additional resources.

• Consult government document indexes. The following are some of the major titles (see the entry numbers indicated for sex subjects covered); consult N1 and N2 for additional resources. For federal regulations, see *CIS Federal Register Index* (B48). For congressional publications, see *CIS/Index and Abstracts to Publications of U.S. Congress* (B49). For periodicals, see *Index to U.S. Government Periodicals* (B51) and *Guide to U.S. Government Publications* (B50). For statistics, see *American Statistical Index* (B85) and *Statistical Abstracts of the United States* (B90). For Congressional Research Service Reports, see *Major Studies and Issue Briefs of the Congressional Research Service 1916-1989 Cumulative Index* (B52). For Supreme Court decisions, see *Digests of U.S. Supreme Court Reports* (B55). For reference materials, see *Government Reference Books: A Biennial Guide to U.S. Government Publications* (B80).

lected by government depository libraries, where they are classified by Superintendent of Document number. Many universities are depository libraries and their government document collections are, by law, freely accessible to the public, regardless of the institution's general policy towards public access. To locate the nearest GPO bookstores or depository library, contact a Federal Information Center (B44). For further assistance in locating and using government publications, consult a government document librarian or one of the following published research guides:

N1.   Robinson, Judith Schiek. *Tapping the Government Grapevine: The User-Friendly Guide to U.S. Government Information Sources.* 2nd ed. Phoenix: Oryx Press, 1993. Forthcoming.

N2.   Sears, Jean L., and Marilyn K. Moody. *Using Government Publications v.1: Searching by Subjects and Agencies*; *v.2: Finding Statistics and Using Special Techniques.* Phoenix: Oryx Press, 1985.

18

CONFERENCES & MEETINGS

Sponsored by institutions, organizations, and professional associations, conferences and meetings provide a forum for the presentation of the most up-to-date research and thinking on a subject through lectures, panel discussions, interactive workshops, and more informal networking and social events. They often include exhibits of related products, services, and publications. Besides actually attending a conference, one can access the information presented in three ways: obtain audio/video recordings of conference proceedings from the sponsor (e.g. the 120 tapes recorded at the National Council of Family Relation's 1989 conference, *Families and Sexuality*); obtain published conference proceedings (see "How to Find" Conference Proceedings); or contact scheduled speakers directly (see "Conference Speakers," p.312).

The most important sex conferences held in the U.S. are the annual meetings of the American Association of Sex Educators, Counselors, and Therapists (see X183) and the Society for the Scientific Study of Sexuality (see X189), both of which also hold regional meetings throughout the year. The Annual Guelph Conference and Training Institute on Sexuality is the largest annual conference in North America (for more information contact the office of Continuing Education, University of Guelph, Guelph, Ontario, N1G 2W1). The World Congress of Sexuality (see X192) and the International Academy of Sex Research (see X186) both hold annual international conferences. Hundreds of other, more specialized,

HOW TO FIND

• Many organizations (see Ch.30) and all professional associations (see Ch.29) hold annual conventions, conferences, or meetings. The *Encyclopedia of Associations* (see B4) notes their titles, frequency, dates, and locations.

• Most newsletters and journals include calendars of upcoming events. Those in *SIECUS Reports* (see K119), *Society for Scientific Study of Sex—Newsletter* (see K135), and *Contemporary Sexuality* (see K113) are the most comprehensive, noting conferences, symposiums, meetings, and continuing education opportunities on a wide range of sexuality related topics, but they are far from exhaustive. Consult specialized titles for more complete coverage of a particular area (see Ch.14).

CONFERENCE PROCEEDINGS

• To locate collections of papers delivered at or published on the occasion of congresses, symposia, conferences, meetings, etc., as well as general proceedings reports, search library catalogs using the form subdivision *–Congresses* under the appropriate topical subject heading or the name of the conference's sponsor.

• Consult a proceedings index: *Index to Social Sciences and Humanities Proceedings* (see B26); *Proceedings in Print* (see B27); or *Bibliographic Guide to Conference Publications* (see B25).

conferences are held worldwide each year, ranging from primarily social events (e.g. the *National Sexuality Symposium and Expo*), to professional meetings (e.g. the *Clinical Conference on Sexually Transmitted Diseases*), to special interestgatherings (e.g. *Whores Conference, Living in Leather*), to regional professional meetings (Asian Conference of Sexology). As an indication of the diversity of topics addressed in these forums, the following were among the hundreds of conferences held between 1990 and 1992:

> *Annual Conference on Adolescent AIDS and HIV Infection*
> *Annual Conference on Sexual Liberty and Social Repression*
> *Clinical Conference on Sexually Transmitted Diseases*

Conference on Abuse of Persons with Developmental Disabilities
Conference on Child Abuse and Neglect
Conference on Family Life Education
Conference on Women's Reproductive Health Care
International Conference on Orgasm
International Conference on Sexual Assault on Campus
International Conference on Treatment of Sex Offenders
International Symposium on Gender Dysphoria
National Conference Regarding Allegations of Child Sexual Abuse
National Conference on Sexual Compulsivity/Addiction
National Sexuality Symposium and Expo 1992
Postpartum Support International
Sager Symposium in Lesbian/Bisexual/Gay Studies
Symposium on Clergy and Religious as Sexual Abusers
STD World Congress
World Conference on Love, Life, and the Family

Use the resources noted under "How to Find" to locate conferences on a particular subject. Organizations and associations which regularly hold conventions or meetings are indicated by a "C" code under "Services" in the descriptive listings beginning on p.321.

Part VI
Statistical and Survey Data

19

PUBLIC OPINION POLLS

Thousands of public opinion polls are conducted each year. Some are informal, non-scientific surveys of little generalizability (e.g. radio call in talk show polls), while others survey scientifically selected samples and are considered to be quite accurate (e.g. those conducted by professional pollsters such as Gallup or Roper). Polls survey public opinion about social and public policy issues (e.g. "Should gays be allowed in the military?"), assess knowledge (e.g. "Can AIDS be transmitted via mosquitos?"), and quantify personal behavior and attitudes (e.g. "How many partners have you had since 18?," "Do you feel entitled to a good sex life because you contributed to the financial fuel that powers your family?"). Often they are the only source for up-to-date data on such topics.

• • • •

Listings: The following two compendia contain public opinion data on a range of topics, including sex related issues.

P1.   Gilbert, Dennis A. *Compendium of American Public Opinion.* New York: Facts on File, 1988. 438 p.

A compilation of public opinion data gathered between 1984 and 1986,

How to Find

• Search *Public Opinion On-line*, the database of the Roper Opinion Locator Library of the Roper Center for Public Opinion Research (see B77).

• Consult indexes. *American Public Opinion Index* (see B75) provides subject access to questions asked in polls conducted by over 200 organizations. *Statistical Reference Index* (see B91) indexes polls conducted by Gallup and other organizations. (*Gallup Poll Monthly*, see B76, also compiles their own cumulative index.) Magazine and newspaper indexes (see J6-J10), some updated daily, report the results of new polls before they appear in more specialized indexes.

• Consult published compendia of survey data. To identify, search library catalogs using the appropriate subject heading followed by the form subdivision *–Public opinion.*

• Most specialized libraries, including those of the Kinsey Institute (see A4), SIECUS (see A5), and Planned Parenthood (see A7-A14), maintain extensive vertical files which include newspaper and magazine clippings reporting the results of sex related public opinion polls.

with older data included for comparison. Sex subjects covered include: AIDS, abortion, censorship, prostitution, pornography, living together, reproduction, homosexuality, extramarital sex, and premarital sex.

P2.   Niemi, Richard G., John Mueller, and Tom W. Smith. *Trends in Public Opinion: A Compendium of Survey Data*. New York: Greenwood Press, 1989. 325 p.

Charts trends in public opinion on major social issues since the 1940s. The work is based on data gathered in the General Social Surveys conducted annually by the National Opinion Research Center (in which virtually identical questions have been asked every year since 1972), supplemented by older longitudinal data from other sources. Public opinion on the following subjects is discussed under "Sexual and Reproductive Morality": the availability of birth control; birth control information to teens; sex education in public schools; the morality of premarital and extramarital sex; the morality of homosexuality; beliefs about pornography (i.e. whether it provides information on sex, leads to the breakdown of morals, leads to rape, is an outlet for bottled up impulses, should be illegal, and X-rated movie viewing habits); circumstances in which abortion should be allowed (i.e. if serious defect in baby, if want no more kids, if rape, if mother's health endangered, if can't afford, if unmarried and don't wish to marry, or if want for any reason).

20

STATISTICS

Non-Governmental Statistics. Private organizations generate statistics as a service to their clients (e.g. circumcision rates in the U.S. compiled by the Non-Circumcision Education Foundation), or as an offshoot of their primary activities (e.g. statistics on abortion clinic bombings compiled by the National Abortion Federation). The results of scholarly and professional research are often presented in statistical form when published in journal articles or when presented at conferences.

Governmental Statistics. The U.S. Federal Government compiles numerical data on a vast range of topics, with most sex related data falling into one of the following categories: vital statistics from the Census Bureau (see Q3) and the National Center for Health Statistics (see Q6); health statistics from the National Center for Health Statistics and the Centers for Disease Control (see Q4); and criminal justice statistics from the Bureau of Justice Statistics (see Q2). However, all government bodies are required to collect, compile, and disseminate statistics, even if this is not their primary mandate, and many occasionally publish data on sex related topics.

• • • •

Listings: Described below are the four federal agencies primarily responsible for gathering and disseminating government statistics on sex

HOW TO FIND

• Search library catalogs using the subdivision –*Statistics* under names of countries, cities, classes of persons, or topical headings. To identify services that collect numerical data, use the subject heading –*Statistical services*.

• Consult resource guides. *Statistics Sources* (see B89) notes both governmental and non-governmental sources. Planned Parenthood Federation of America's (see X111) *Statistical Sources and Resources*, is a seven page guide to obtaining data in areas of interest to family planning agencies and reproductive health educators, including government and private agencies, publications, and databases. See also, the guides discussed below.

• Consult an information clearinghouse focusing in the area of interest—most collect statistics from both federal and private sources (see p.318).

GOVERNMENT STATISTICS

• Search indexes. For statistics compiled by the federal government, see *American Statistical Index* (see B85). For state and local government statistics, see *Statistical Reference Index* (see B91).

• Consult a research guide. *Using Govt Publications v.2: Finding Statistics and Using Special Techniques* (see N2) is available in most libraries. The Government Printing Office's Subject Bibliography Series (see B54), includes the following free resource guides: *Vital and Health Statistics*, *Education Statistics*, *Statistical Publications*, and *Census of Population Statistics*. *Statistics Sources* (see B89) and *Lesko's Info Power* (see B38) both index statistical sources by subject. The National Health Information Center (see B45) distributes *Health Statistics: A Guide to Government and Private Sources for Gathering Data about Health Issues*, and can provide referrals.

• Consult statistical compendia. Tables in the *Statistical Abstracts of the United States* (see B90) summarize data on a wide range of topics, with sources for additional data indicated in the text and footnotes. Subject specific statistical compilations (e.g. the *Uniform*

Crime Report published by the Bureau of Justice Statistics), many of which are serials, are described in *ASI* (see B85) under issuing agency.

• Contact the federal agency or research center specializing in the area of interest. To identify relevant agencies, see "Government Agencies," p.317. Once identified, contact the public affairs department or use government agency and staff directories (see B38-B43) to contact their statistical office directly. The following directories provide subject access to Federal statistical telephone contacts: *Statistics Sources* (see B89), *Lesko's Info Power* (B38), and *Federal Statistical Specialists: The Official Directory of Names and Numbers* (see B86). For state statistics, request *Listings of Personnel for State Vital and Health Statistics Offices* from the National Center for Health Statistics (see Q6).

• For statistical databases, see *Federal Data Base Finder* (B30).

NON-GOVERNMENT STATISTICS

• Consult statistical indexes. *Statistical Reference Index* (see B91) is the most comprehensive, but even it only indexes a fraction of the statistics compiled by organizations and associations, most of which aren't indexed at all. See also: *State and Local Statistics Sources* (see B88) and *Index to International Statistics* (see B87).

• Each entry in the *Encyclopedia of Associations* (see B4) indicates whether a the organization compiles statistics.

• Research reports containing statistical data are published primarily as journal articles; see Ch.14 for journal titles, and Ch.12 for indexes with which to search for relevant articles. Review articles are especially useful, as they summarize, compare, and evaluate the statistical findings of numerous researchers (see Ch.5).

---

and reproduction related topics. All provide statistical information and research assistance via phone or mail, and publish statistical handbooks and compendia indexed by *ASI* (see B85). Federally supported information clearinghouses, also collect statistical data, including the National Institute of Justice AIDS Clearinghouse (see X36), the Family Life Information

Exchange (see X108), National AIDS Clearinghouse (see X35), National Resource Center on Child Sexual Abuse Information Services (see X273), National Maternal and Child Health Clearinghouse (X134), and the National Sudden Infant Death Syndrome Research Center (see X139).

Non-governmental organizations and associations that collect statistics are indicated with an "S" code under "Services" in the descriptive listings beginning on p.321. See especially the Alan Guttmacher Institute (X253), which compiles statistics on many sex and reproduction related issues, and for adolescent sexuality issues, the Center for Population Options (see X18).

➤ FEDERAL STATISTICAL AGENCIES

Q1.   **Bureau of Justice Statistics**: Department of Justice, 10th and Constitution Ave., NW, Washington, DC 20530. PH: (202)307-6100 / (800)732-3277.

Compiles statistics on criminal offenses, persons arrested, victims, types of crimes, arrests, court cases, etc.; data on public attitudes towards criminal justice topics; and state laws. Their *Uniform Crime Report for the United States* provides a summary analysis of 8 crimes, including forcible rape. SEX STATISTICS COLLECTED: all criminal justice topics, among them: pornography and obscenity, incest, sodomy laws, sexual orientation, sexual offenses, rape, sexual offenders, rape in prisons, AIDS in prisons, and prostitution.

Q2.   **Census Bureau**: Customer Service Branch / Data User Service Division, Washington, DC 20233. PH: (301)763-4100.

Census Bureau data is collected primarily during the decennial census supplemented by monthly Current Population Surveys. A number of research guides are available, including *Factfinder for the Nation*, which details categories of Census Bureau data and how to access them, and *Telephone Contacts for Data Users*, which lists key census bureau personnel and their specialties. SEX STATISTICS COLLECTED: fertility and childbearing (e.g. abortion rates, child spacing, maternal age, birth defects, fetal deaths and defects, teenage pregnancy); marital status by race, age, sex, locale, education; marital history and divorce; and cohabitation patterns, among others. Maintains a division of Natality, Marriage, and Divorce Statistics.

Q3. **Centers for Disease Control**: Office of Public Affairs, 1600 Clifton Rd. NE, 2047 Mail Stop D25, Atlanta, GA 30333. PH: (404)639-3286

Surveys national disease trends and cases. They publish a number of statistical publications, including *Morbidity and Mortality Weekly Report* (see K157) and *MMWR: CDC Surveillance Summaries* (see K156). SEX STATISTICS COLLECTED: AIDS/HIV, abortion, infant and maternal mortality, reproduction, birth defects, ectopic pregnancy, teenage pregnancy and fertility, and sexually transmitted diseases, among others.

Q4. **National Center for Health Statistics**: 6525 Belcrest Rd., Rm. 840, Hyattsville, MD 20782. PH: (301)436-8980.

Major data collection is provided by (1) vital registration (i.e. birth certificates, marriage licenses, and divorce decrees); (2) Health Interview Surveys—data collected through household interviews; (3) Health Examination—data gathered through physical exams and tests; and (4) data from additional surveys conducted throughout the year. SEX STATISTICS COLLECTED: in addition to reproductive and sexual health statistics—family planning, maternal and infant health and mortality, STDs, AIDS, abortion complications, contraceptives and contraception use, diseases of reproductive organs, hysterectomy rates, menopause, infertility, pregnancy, and many others—this is, along with the Census Bureau, the primary source for vital statistics, including fetal death (stillbirths, sudden infant death), live births and abortion, fertility rates and characteristics (e.g. births to unmarried women by age of mother and race), and marriage and divorce.

21

SEXUAL BEHAVIOR SURVEYS

The last comprehensive surveys of American sexual behavior were conducted by Alfred Kinsey and his associates in the 1940s (although see R15, which claims to be the "first broadscale, scientific, nationwide survey since Kinsey"). The publication of *Sexual Behavior in the Human Male*, in 1948, and *Sexual Behavior in the Human Female*, in 1953, marked the first time the subject of American sexual behavior had been presented in a quantitative framework, and although his samples were not representative of the U.S. population as a whole, they have remained the standard source for sexual behavior statistics for over 40 years.

Since then, the results of a number of broadscale sexual behavior surveys have been published in book form, many more journalistic than scientific, and many seeming commercially rather then scientifically motivated. Some, while thought provoking and purporting to be scientific, lack the rigorous research methodologies needed to empirically support their claims. (Consult reviews published in scholarly/professional journals for critiques of a survey's methodological and theoretical weaknesses.) Most scientific surveys of sexual behavior are limited to very specific populations, and are published in journals.

• • • •

Listings: The published reports of the Kinsey studies conducted in the

HOW TO FIND

• To locate book length analysis of data gathered by polls, questionnaires, direct observation, interviews, or other means, search library catalogs using the appropriate subject heading followed by the form subdivision *–Survey*, *–Case studies*, *–Longitudinal studies*, *–Public opinion*, or *–Research*; or use the search term *Sexual behavior surveys* (e.g. *Sexual behavior surveys–United States*). Research reports on particular populations are cataloged according to the following patterns: *College Students–United States–Sexual Behavior*; *Married people–United States–Attitudes*, etc.

• All research reports, whether published as books, dissertations, or journal articles, cite related surveys in their literature review sections. *Sexual Behavior in the Human Male* (see R1) reviews 19 studies of male and female sexual behavior published prior to 1948; *Sexual Behavior in the Human Female* (see R2), an additional 11. See also H108.

• Use magazine and newspaper indexes (see J6-J10) to identify sex surveys conducted by magazines (e.g. *Cosmopolitan*, *Redbook*, *Playboy*), as well as for feature articles discussing the results of more scientific research.

• Surveys published in journals can be located using the indexes described in Ch.12.

1940s are described below. Following is an unannotated list of American sexual behavior surveys published in book form since 1972, plus reprints of three earlier studies (see R10, R31, R32). All are national surveys which purport to be scientific (although some employ questionable methodology). Citations are classified by the population studied (i.e. aged, females, singles, etc.).

➤ KINSEY STUDIES *(See also*: R18, R19)

See U2 for information on custom analysis of raw data collected by Kinsey and his associates, or under the auspices of the Kinsey Institute.

R1.   Kinsey, Alfred C., Wardell B. Pomeroy, and Clyde E. Martin. *Sexual Behavior in the Human Male*. Philadelphia: Saunders, 1948. 804 p.

Narrative and statistical analysis of male sexual outlets and the factors effecting them, drawn from extensive interviews with 5,300 white males. Part I details the history and methodology of the survey. Part II presents data on masturbation, nocturnal emissions, heterosexual petting, premarital intercourse, marital intercourse and non-coital techniques (oral, anal, and manual), extramarital sex, intercourse with prostitutes, homosexuals, and animal contacts. Data is analyzed in terms of age, economic level, marital status, education, social class, religion, and whether rural/urban. For a critical examination of the study, see Cochran's *Statistical Problems of the Kinsey Report on Sexual Behavior in the Human Male* (Washington: American Statistical Association, 1954).

R2.   Kinsey, Alfred C., Wardell B. Pomeroy, Clyde E. Martin, and Paul H. Gebhard. *Sexual Behavior in the Human Female*. Philadelphia: Saunders, 1953. 842 p.

Narrative and statistical analysis of the case histories of 5,940 white females, most between 16-50. Part I details the history and methods of the study and related literature. Part II presents data on sexual behavior, including preadolescent sexual development, masturbation, nocturnal sex dreams, premarital petting, premarital coitus, marital coitus, animal contacts, extramarital coitus, homosexual response and contacts, and total sexual outlets. Part III compares male and female findings in the areas of anatomy and physiology of sexual response and orgasm, psychological factors, neural mechanisms of sexual response, and hormonal factors in sexual response. Statistics are copious and very detailed (e.g. the percentage of women using vaginal insertion in masturbation, breast stimulation in petting, extent of nudity in premarital coitus, coital positions practiced, etc.).

R3.   Gebhard, Paul H., and Alan B. Johnson. *The Kinsey Data: Marginal Tabulations of the 1938-1963 Interviews Conducted by the Institute for Sex Research*. Philadelphia: Saunders, 1979.

Data from over 18,200 case studies compiled between 1938 and 1963. Includes college whites and blacks of both sexes, and non-college whites, but very few non-college blacks (blacks were excluded from R1 and R2). "We have cleaned our samples, more accurately processed the data, and have made new tabulations. These may be compared to our previously published material so the extent of prior error may be estimated and suitable qualifications and corrections made."

➤ ADOLESCENTS *(See also*: Z17, Z18)

How to Find

• The Data Archives on Adolescent Pregnancy and Pregnancy Prevention (see U1), contain data sets from 110 national studies on adolescent sexuality and pregnancy—see their publication catalog for a full description of each. They also publish *Just the Facts: What Science Has Found Out About Teenage Sexuality in the U.S.*

• Planned Parenthood (see X111) and Louis Harris annually conduct a survey of adolescent sexual attitudes and behavior.

• The National Adolescent Student Health Survey (1988), was the first federally funded national survey in more than 20 years to collect data on teen's behavior, knowledge, and attitudes towards health and sex related issues. For information, contact the Association for the Advancement of Health Education (1900 Association Dr., Reston, CA 22091. Ph: 703/476-3400).

R4.   Coles, Robert, and Geoffrey Stokes. *Sex and the American Teenager*. New York: Harper & Row, 1985. 238 p.

R5.   Hass, Aaron. *Teenage Sexuality: A Survey of Teenage Sexual Behavior*. New York: Macmillan, 1979. 203 p.

R6.   Segal, Jay. *The Sex Lives of College Students*. Wayne, PA: Miles Standish Press, 1984. 499 p.

R7.   Sorenson, Robert C. *Adolescent Sexuality in Contemporary America: Personal Values and Sexual Behavior Ages Thirteen to Nineteen*. New York: World Publishing/Times Mirror, 1973. 549 p. Alternative title: *The Sorenson Report*.

➤ AGING

R8.   Brecher, Edward M. *Love, Sex, and Aging: A Consumers Union Report*. Boston: Little, Brown, 1984. 441 p.

R9.   Starr, Bernard D., and Marcella Bakur Weiner. *The Starr-Weiner Report on Sex and Sexuality in the Mature Years*. New York: Stein and Day, 1981. 302 p.

➤ FEMALE SEXUALITY *(See also:* R2, H108)

R10.   Davis, Katheryn Bement. *Factors in the Sex Life of Twenty-two Hundred Women*. New York: Arno Press, 1972, c.1929. 430 p.

R11.   Grosskopf, Dianne. *Sex and the Married Woman*. New York: Simon and Schuster, 1983. 216 p.

R12.   Hite, Shere. *The Hite Report: A Nationwide Study of Female Sexuality*. New York: Macmillan, 1976. 438 p.

R13.   Tavris, Carol, and Susan Sadd. *The Redbook Report on Female Sexuality: 100,000 Married Women Disclose the Good News About Sex*. New York: Delacorte Press, 1975. 186 p.

R14.   Wolfe, Linda. *The Cosmo Report*. New York: Arbor House, 1981. 416 p.

➤ GENERAL SEXUAL BEHAVIOR *(See also:* R1, R2, R3)

R15.   Janus, Samuel, and Cynthia L. *The Janus Report on Sexual Behavior: The First Broadscale Scientific National Survey Since Kinsey*. New York: John Wiley and Sons, 1993.

R16.   Carter, Steven, and Julia Sokol. *What Really Happens in Bed: a Demystification of Sex*. New York: M. Evans, 1989. 333 p.

R17.   Hunt, Morton. *Sexual Behavior in the 1970's*. New York: Dell, 1975.

R18.   Klassen, Albert D., Colin J. Williams, Eugene E. Levitt. *Sex and Morality in the U.S.: An Empirical Inquiry Under the Auspices of the Kinsey Institute*. Middletown, CT: Wesleyan University Press, 1989. 462 p.

> HOMOSEXUALITY: BISEXUAL, GAY, AND LESBIAN

R19.   Bell, Alan P., and Martin S. Weinberg. *Homosexualities: A Study of Diversity among Men and Women*. New York: Simon and Schuster, 1978. 505 p.

R20.   Bell, Alan P., Martin S. Weinerg, and Sue Kiefer Hammersmith. *Sexual Preference: Its Development in Men and Women: Statistical Appendix*. Bloomington, IN: Indiana University Press, 1981. 242 p.

R21.   Hill, Ivan, ed. *The Bisexual Spouse: A Different Dimension in Human Sexuality*. McLean, VA: Barlina Books, 1987. 180 p.

R22.   Jay, Karla, and Allen Young. *The Gay Report: Lesbians and Gay Men Speak Out About Sexual Experiences and Lifestyles*. New York: Summit Books, 1979. 861 p.

R23.   Loulan, JoAnn Gardner, and Mariah Burton Nelson. *Lesbian Passion: Loving Ourselves and Each Other*. San Francisco: Spinsters/Aunt Luce, 1987. 223 p.

R24.   Spada, James. *The Spada Report: The Newest Survey of Gay Male Sexuality*. New York: New American Library, 1979. 339 p.

> MALE SEXUALITY

R25.   Hite, Shere. *The Hite Report on Male Sexuality*. New York: Knopf, 1981. 1129 p.

R26.   McGill, Michael E. *The McGill Report on Male Intimacy*. New York: Holt, Rinehart and Winston, 1985. 300 p.

R27.   Pietropinto, Anthony, and Jacqueline Simenauer. *Beyond the Male Myth: What Women Want to Know about Men's Sexuality: A Nationwide Survey*. New York: Times Books, 1977. 430 p.

R28.   Shanor, Karen. *The Shanor Study: The Sexual Sensitivity of the American Male*. New York: Dial Press, 1978. 274 p.

> MARRIED COUPLES

R29. Ard, Ben Neal, Jr. *The Sexual Realm in Long-term Marriages: A Longitudinal Study Following Marital Partners Over Twenty Years.* San Francisco: Mellen Research University Press, 1990. 177 p.

R30. Blumstein, Philip, and Pepper Schwartz. *American Couples: Money, Work, Sex.* New York: Morrow, 1983.

R31. Dickinson, Robert Latou, and Lura Beam. *A Thousand Marriages: A Medical Study of Sex Adjustment.* Foreword by Havelock Ellis. Westport, CT: Greenwood Press, 1970, c.1931. 482 p.

R32. Hamilton, G.V. *A Research in Marriage.* New York: Garland Publishing, 1986, c.1929. 570 p.

> MASTERS AND JOHNSON

These studies focus on the physiology of sex rather than social or psychological aspects of sexual behavior.

R33. Masters, William H., and Virginia E. Johnson. *Human Sexual Response.* Boston: Little, Brown, 1966. 366 p.

R34. _____. *Human Sexual Inadequacy.* Boston: Little, Brown, 1970. 467 p.

22

RECORDS, LISTS, AND FACTS

HOW TO FIND

• Search library catalogs using the subject headings *sex–miscellanea* or *sex–anecdotes*.

• • • •

S1. Gerber, Albert B. *The Book of Sex Lists*. Secaucus, NJ: L. Stuart, 1981. 319 p.

S2. Rutledge, Leigh W. *Gay Book of Lists*. Boston: Alyson Publishing, 1987. 212 p.

S3. Simon, G.L. *Simon's Book of World Sexual Records*. New York: Pyramid Books, 1975. 416 p.

The author hopes that "this catalog of extremes, firsts, excesses, and the like will inform, entertain, titillate, or simply amuse . . ." Three types of items are included: (1) matters of fact, well attested; (2) matters of fact, poorly attested; and (3) matters of subjective evaluation. It is left up to the reader to decide in which class any particular item belongs. One thousand items are arranged in 8 chapters: Animals and Plants (e.g. most vicious insect coitus; most convincing evidence of female animal orgasm); Human Physiology (e.g. most severe circumcision, longest vulva); Sex Technique, Performance, and Response (e.g. most effective aphrodisiac, first English description of a dildo in action, most sexually active Popes); Deviant Sexuality (e.g. most curious 17th c. account of flagellation, first organization of bestiality as public entertainment); Prudery, Superstition and Law (e.g. oddest forms of marriage, most famous Indian sex cults, longest obscenity law trial); Sexology and Sex Education (e.g. first scientifically observed coitus, first discovered sperm); Contraception and Castration (e.g. first establishment of the eunuch system in China, first instance of artificial insemination); The Arts (e.g. first girlie magazines, largest phallic replica, first topless dress). A revised and updated edition was published in 1983 by Corgi Books Ltd. (61-63 Uxbridge Rd., Ealing, London, W5 55A, United Kingdom).

S4.   Smith, David, and Mike Gordon. *Strange But True Facts About Sex*. Deerhaven, MN: Meadowbrook Press, 1990. 96 p.

S5.   Smith, Robin. *Encyclopedia of Sexual Trivia*. New York: St. Martin's Press, 1992. 192 p.

Part VII
Tools

23

CURRICULA

Use the following resources to identify curricula developed for use in elementary through secondary school sex education programs—puberty education, AIDS/HIV prevention, pregnancy prevention, STD prevention, sexual abuse prevention, sexual health and hygiene—as well as for use with special populations such as church groups, parents, and the disabled.

HOW TO FIND

• Search library catalogs. For works on methods of study and teaching in a particular area, use the appropriate subject heading followed by the form subdivision *–Study and teaching* (e.g. *Midwifery–Study and teaching*); or use *Sex instruction–Curriculum* or *Sex instruction–Methods* as search terms. To locate general sex education resource guides, which may include citations to curricula, search catalogs using the subject heading *Family life education–Bibliography* or *Sex instruction–Bibliography.*

• Search indexes, especially *Resources in Education* (see J30), *ERIC* (see J27), *Education Index* (see J26), *Combined Health Information Database* (see J24), and *Exceptional Children Education Resources* (J28). For AIDS related curricula, see the *AIDS Education Materials*

Database and the *AIDS School Health Education Database* (see J24).

• *El Hi Text Books in Print* cites curricula and teacher development materials, as well as textbooks (see B96). For textbooks see Ch.6.

• Consult specialized libraries and archives. SIECUS (see A5, X223) has the largest collection of curricula in the country, holding over 600 titles on AIDS/HIV, sexual abuse, and sex education, for all ages and populations—all can be photocopied within copyright limitations. *Sexuality and Family Life Education: Curricula and Leader Resources* (1993) briefly describe the most popular items in their collection (see H46). They also distribute *Future Directions: HIV/ AIDS Education in the Nation's Schools*, reviewing 34 curricula in use around the country; *Performance Standards and Checklists for the Evaluation and Development of School HIV/AIDS Education Curricula for Adolescents*; and *Guidelines for Comprehensive Sexuality Education, K-12*, among other titles (see p.82 and X223). Curricula produced by Planned Parenthood or catalogued in their Federation Clearinghouse of Educational Resources, are cited by subject and target population in the Program Data File and Clearinghouse Data File of *LINKLine* (see I6). Planned Parenthood of Arizona (see A12) and Connecticut (see A13) maintain curriculum collections of 350 and 150 titles respectively, and other Planned Parenthoods maintain smaller collections. Information centers focusing on a particular topic (e.g. the Breastfeeding Information Center, the National AIDS Clearinghouse) or population (e.g. the Center for Early Adolescents) may also collect relevant curricula; see Ch.30.

• Many organizations produce or distribute curricula. Those described in this volume are listed primarily under the headings *AIDS, Sex education, Sexual abuse, Childbirth*, and *Adolescent sexuality* in Ch.30, but check under all relevant topics. The National Council on Family Relations (see X131) publishes *Family Life Education Curriculum Guidelines* to assist in the development and assessment of family life/human sexuality education programs across the life span.

• Consult periodicals which review curricula and other educational resources, especially *SIECUS Reports* (see K119), *Family Life Educator* (see K114), *AIDS Education and Prevention* (see K11), and *Journal of Sex Education and Therapy* (see K115).

24

MEASUREMENT TOOLS

Intended for use in primary research, measurement tools—tests, surveys, scales, questionnaires, interview schedules, observation checklists, indexes, coding schemes, and the like—are designed to measure knowledge, attitudes, behavior, and other variables (e.g. the *Mosher Sex Guilt Inventory*, *Cross Gender Fetishes Scale*, *Passionate Love Scale*, *Sex Knowledge and Attitude Test*, *Anticipated Sexual Jealousy Scale*, *Contraceptive Embarrassment Scale*, and the *Sexual Satisfaction Inventory*, to name only a few).

• • • •

Listings: Four compilations of sexuality related instruments are described below. For sex education evaluation tools, see *Handbook for the Evaluation of Programs* (F26).

T1.   Beere, Carole A. *Sex and Gender Issues: A Handbook of Tests and Measures*. New York: Greenwood Press, 1990. 605 p.

Describes 197 measures cited in *ERIC* and/or *Psych Literature* between January 1978 and December 1988. Entries are grouped by subject: breast exam, heterosocial relations, menstruation, menopause, body image and appearance, contraception and abortion, eating disorders, family

How to Find

• Individual measures are not usually cataloged by libraries. For compilations of tests, or books about constructing and administering them, search library catalogs using the appropriate subject heading followed by the subdivision *–Research–Methodology* (e.g. *Sex customs–Research–Methodology*), *–Research–Evaluation*, *–Testing* (e.g. *Sex (Psychology)–Testing*), or *–Methodology*. To locate titles on the evaluation of sex education programs, use *Sex instruction–Methods–Evaluation*. Consult *Library of Congress Subject Headings* (see C1) for terms with which to search for books on specific types of measures (e.g. *Scale analysis (Psychology)*.

• Consult instrument indexes such as *Mental Measurements Yearbook* (see B67) and the on-line database *Health and Psychosocial Instruments* (see B66). Both describe thousands of instruments of all types, including many useful for sex research. The staff at *Health and Psychosocial Instruments* offer phone consultation on all aspects of research methodology, including the identification, development, evaluation, and use of measurement tools. Contact them at P.O. Box 110287, Pittsburgh, PA 15232-0787. PH: (412)687-6850.

• Consult dissertations and journal articles for measurement tools developed and/or employed in the author's research. Dissertations usually reproduce the entire instrument in an appendix; articles may only cite its source.

• Search periodical indexes, especially *Psychological Abstracts* (see J52) and *ERIC* (see J27). "Tests and Scales" may be used as a subheading under primary topical headings (consult the thesaurus) or conduct a keyword search combining relevant subject headings with terms such as *scales*, *measures*, *constructs*, *tests*, *surveys*, and *assessments*.

• Contact the staff at a research center or other organization conducting research in the area of interest (see Ch.30).

violence, heterosocial relations, homosexuality, pregnancy and childbirth, rape and sexual coercion, and sexuality (including sexual experience, sexual functioning, sexual dysfunction, sexual satisfaction, sexual attitudes, sexual arousal, and sex knowledge). Each item is fully described, including information on the development of the instrument, variables, previous subjects, reliability and validity data, appropriate population, scoring, sample items, and a bibliography of studies in which the measure was used. An introductory chapter discusses additional sources for measurement tools.

T2.   Beere, Carole A. *Gender Roles: A Handbook of Tests and Measures*. New York: Greenwood Press, 1990. 575 p.

Describes 211 tests and measures, cited in *ERIC* and/or *Psych Literature* between January 1979 and December 1988. Entries are grouped into seven chapters: gender roles, children and gender, stereotypes, marital and parental roles, employee roles, multiple roles, and attitude towards gender role issues.

T3.   Davis, Clive M., William L. Yarber, and Sandra L. Davis. *Sexuality Related Measures: A Compendium*. Lake Mills, IA: Graphic Press, 1988. 270 p.

Describes 100 scales, questionnaires, inventories, and interview schedules developed to measure a myriad of sexuality-related states, traits, attitudes, behaviors, effects, and outcomes. Citations are grouped into 38 subject categories: abortion, aggression, aging, anxiety, arousal, attitudes, beliefs, contraception, decision making, education, emotions, experience, extramarital, family planning, fantasy, female sexuality, functioning, gender identity, guilt, homophobia, homosexuality, ideology, initiating, involvement, jealousy, knowledge, love, marriage, masturbation, medical, premarital, rape, satisfaction, sexually transmitted diseases, transsexuals, variations, and vasectomy. Brief articles describe the "development and appropriate use of each instrument, giving information on timing, scoring, interpretation, etc. Reliability and validity data are summarized and completely referenced. Most papers include the entire instrument and grant permission for its use in professional setting. The others give illustrative content from the instrument and provide all necessary information to obtain the instrument."

T4.   Touliatos, John, Barry F. Perlmutter, and Murray A. Straus, eds. *Handbook of Family Measurement Techniques*. Newbury Park, CA: Sage Publications, 1990. 797 p.

Describes 976 instruments—identified in an exhaustive review of 60 journals published between 1975 and 1986—developed to measure family variables, including those relating to intimacy and family values; marital relations; love, liking and affection; pregnancy, childbirth and transition to parenthood; and sex. Abstracts include a brief description of the variables measured, reliability and validity data, and complete information on how to obtain the measure.

25

DATA SETS

A data set is a compilation of the raw data gathered in a particular research project. The following two sources make selected data available to researchers wishing to utilize it in current research.

• • • •

U1. **Data Archive on Adolescent Pregnancy and Pregnancy Prevention (DAAPPP):** 685 High St., Suite 2E, Palo Alto, CA 94301. PH: (415)949-3282

A computer archive of social science data from 110 "outstanding studies" of adolescent family life, sexuality, contraception, conception, child-bearing, parenting, and family planning; collectively over 40,000 variables are measured (a subject index to variables is included in *Accessing and Using DAAPPP Files*, below). In addition to the data itself, a typical record includes title and principal investigator, the variables studied, number of cases, and a summary of the study. The entire archive is available on magnetic tapes or on compact disc as the *National Archive on Sexuality, Health, and Adolescence* (NATASHA), and individual data sets can be purchased on floppy disc. Research assistance is provided by *Accessing and Using DAAPPP Files: An Introduction for the Novice*, or archive staff will conduct searches for a fee. The *DAAPPP Catalog of Products* contains full descriptions of all the data sets held in the archive, including bibliographic citations to relevant published research reports.

U2.   Kinsey Institute—Unpublished Codebooks and Related Data: contact The Kinsey Institute Information Services (see A4)

The Kinsey Institute does not distribute its data sets (see Ch.20); however, qualified scholars and researchers may request fee-based computer analysis of specific variables from the following studies, with output available on paper, disk, or via electronic network:

Kinsey Interviews	San Francisco Homosexual Study
Chicago College Youth Study	Chicago Attitude Study
Chicago Homosexual Study	Sexuality Following Spinal Cord
Cross-Cultural Study	Injury

The interview schedules and codebooks necessary to specify variables are available for purchase, as is a bibliography of *Selected, Relevant Published Materials.*

SECTION TWO
NON-PRINT
RESOURCES

Part VIII
Media Resources

26

EDUCATIONAL AUDIOVISUALS

Use the resources discussed in this chapter to identify audiovisual materials—filmstrips, compact discs, videos, films, slides, posters, and the like—for use in elementary to postgraduate sex education programs, as well as adult sex education and therapy. To identify feature films and television programming for use in educational settings, see Ch.27 and Ch.28. For erotic sex education films, see V3, V4, W10.

AIDS/HIV information changes so quickly that the items described in published guides, such as *Learning AIDS* (New York: R.R. Bowker, 1989), are often out-of-date before the book is even released. Consult the resources listed under "How to Find" AIDS/HIV Audiovisuals, p.289, for the most current materials.

● ● ● ●

Listings: Under "Filmographies and Resource Guides" are described the only two sex education filmographies listed in RLIN as of October 1992. Under "Distributor's Catalogs" are described the only two distributors in the U.S. handling exclusively sex related titles. Organizations producing and/or distributing audiovisuals or av resource guides are indicated by an "AV" code under "Services" in the descriptive listings beginning on p.321.

HOW TO FIND

• Consult audiovisual directories, indexes, and databases (see entry numbers indicated for sex subjects covered). *The Video Source Book* (see B11), *Bowker's Complete Video Directory* (see B5), and *Media Review Digest* (see B8) cite both entertainment and educational films and videos; *Film and Video Finder* (see B7), only educational titles. *ERIC* (see J27) and the *Combined Health Information Database* (see J24) describe audiovisuals as well as print materials. The audiovisual file on *LINKLine* (see I6) contains reviews conducted by Planned Parenthood's Education Department through 1992. Although they no longer formally review videos, titles and sources are input into the database from over 30 distributor's catalogs. For compact discs, consult *CD-Roms in Print* (Westport, CT: Meckler).

• Consult topical resource guides. To locate, search library catalogs using the appropriate subject heading (e.g. *Sex instruction, Family life education*) followed by the form subdivision *–Audio-visual materials*, *–Directories–Audio-visual aids*, *–Audio-visual aids–Catalogs*, *–Study and teaching–Audio-visual aids*, or *–Film catalogs*. To locate materials intended for use with a particular population (the aged, children, disabled, etc.), compound the terms above with the subject heading signifying that group (e.g. *Handicapped–Sex instruction–Audio-visual aids*). Audiovisual resources are often discussed in sex education handbooks (e.g. *Sexuality Education: A Resource Book*, see H83); search catalogs for titles using *Sex instruction–Bibliography*.

• Consult the catalogs of libraries and archives with audiovisual collections. The *Directory of Special Libraries and Information Centers* (see B62) includes audiovisuals in its enumeration of each library's holdings. The Kinsey Institute's Audiovisual Archives (see A4) include over 50,000 chronologically arranged films, including commercial erotic films, documentaries dealing with sex and reproduction, and medical films (for catalog information, see notes p.296). See also the *Education Film and Video Locator* (B6)—the catalog of the holdings of members of the Consortium of College and University Media Centers—and the *National Library of Medicine's Audiovisual Catalog*, available in print (see B10) or on-line as AVLINE (see J45).

• Most sex education journals and newsletters include reviews of new audiovisual resources (see especially K113-K119).

• Obtain catalogs from av producers/distributors. While to our knowledge there are only two in the U.S. specializing exclusively in sex related titles (see V3, V4), most health education av distributors include a sex education or family life section in their catalogs. *Sexuality Education: A Resource Book* (see H83) lists the addresses of 56 producers and distributors, and audiovisual directories (see B5-B11) give contact information for those of the films they index. The education department of Planned Parenthood (see X223) and the resource centers at SIECUS (see A5) and the Kinsey Institute (see A4) can also provide referrals, with the latter distributing the guide *Sources of Information and Materials Relating to Human Sexuality: Audiovisual Materials*. For av's produced by the federal government, contact the National Audiovisual Center (see B9), or search the *Monthly Catalog* (B53), where *–audiovisual aids* is used as a subheading.

• Some organizations hold film festivals in which new titles are screened and reviewed. In the National Council of Family Relation's (see X223) annual media competition, films, videos, and filmstrips are judged in 12 categories, including nontraditional family systems, parenting issues, marital and family issues and communication, sexuality and sex role development, human reproduction and family planning, abuse and neglect, and teenage sexuality. Winners are reported in the January issue of *Family Relations* (see K88). Planned Parenthood no longer holds a film festival, but reviews of films screened through 1992 are included in *LINKLine* (see I6).

• Many organizations (see Ch.30) distribute audiovisuals or compile av resource guides (e.g. the International Childbirth Education Association's *Audiovisuals about Birth and Family Life*, see X170). Planned Parenthood affiliated resource centers are especially good sources—see notes under "Filmographies & Resource Guides," p.290.

AIDS/HIV AUDIOVISUALS (*See also*: resources listed above)

• New audiovisuals are reviewed in *AIDS Education and Prevention* (see K1), *California AIDS Clearinghouse Reviewer* (see X33), *AIDS*

Educator (see X39), and other journals.

• The AIDS Information Clearinghouses (see X35) is the central source for AIDS related materials produced or approved by the Federal Government. They distribute an av catalog and provide referrals through their *AIDS Education Materials Database*, portions of which are accessible to the public through J4.

• The Health Information Network (P.O. Box 30762, Seattle, WA 98103. PH: 206/784-5655) has compiled 5 lists (25-50 titles each) of AIDS av's targeting people at risk (including PWA's), health care professionals, schools/kids, the workplace, and the general public.

• AIDS/HIV resource directories (see B1-B3) include the names of av producers/distributors, and information clearinghouses (see X33-X39) can provide additional referrals.

• SIECUS (see A5) distributes the free, *HIV/AIDS Audiovisual Resources: A SIECUS Guide to Selecting, Evaluating, and Using A.V.R.'s*, including posters, films/videos, audio-cassettes, promotional buttons, anatomical models, and wallet cards.

➤ FILMOGRAPHIES AND RESOURCE GUIDES (*See also:* family planning, H34; gay youth, p.328; young adults, H82; young adolescents, H7; special education, H25; childbirth, X79; child sexual abuse, X273; H83)

Many Planned Parenthood resource centers compile and regularly update resource lists of films, filmstrips, slides, videotapes, and other teaching aids (e.g. Planned Parenthood of Minnesota's av catalog describes 102 videos relating to contraception/family planning, family, parenting, pregnancy, reproductive health, sexual abuse, sexuality, sexuality and persons with developmental disabilities, STDs, teenage relationships, and unplanned pregnancy)—see A7-A14 or contact X223 for referrals.

V1. Daniel, Ronald S. *Human Sexuality Methods and Materials for the Education Family Life and Health Professions: An Annotated Guide to the Audiovisuals*. Brea, CA: Heuristicus Publishing Co., 1979. 507 p.

At the time of its publication, this was a comprehensive filmography of sex and family life educational audiovisuals available in the U.S., including multi-media programs, filmstrips, records, audio-cassettes, video-cassettes, 16mm and 8 mm films, and slides. Although compiled over 14 years ago, many of the titles focus on issues not addressed in more recent releases. A lengthy essay on the "Creative and Effective Use of Audio-visuals" begins the work. The 3,100 annotated entries are classified by audience age level and by topic:

abortion	drugs and sex	population control
adolescence	fantasy	pornography
affection	fertility & infertility	premarital sex
alternative life styles	fetal development	prostitution
anatomy & physiology	gender roles	puberty
arousal/response cycle	geriatric sexuality	rape
beauty & sex attraction	homosexuality	reproduction
birth & pregnancy	humor & satire	sex education
birth control	live sex acts	sex crimes
conception	love	sexual medicine
contraception	marriage & family	sexual dysfunction
counseling & therapy	masturbation	variant sexual behaviors
cross-cultural studies	misconceptions/myths	venereal disease
disabled	morality	

V2. Snyder, Susan Utener, and Sol Gordon. *Parents as Sexuality Educators: An Annotated Print and Audiovisual Bibliography for Professionals and Parents 1970-1984.* Phoenix: Oryx Press, 1984. 212 p.

A briefly annotated bibliography of print and audiovisual resources published or revised between 1970 and 1984 (some of which have since been updated). Intended to help professionals assist parents in becoming their children's primary sex educators, it's organized into four chapters for parents—(1) Resources to Assist Parents in their Role as Sexuality Educators; (2) Resources for Selected Audiences; (3) Resources for Special Parent/Family Situations; and (4) A Selected List of General Parenting Materials—and four chapters for professionals—(1) Sexuality Resources for Professionals; (2) Resources for Working with the Family; (3) Resources Appropriate for Special Parent/Family Situations; and (4) Resources for Professionals Who Work with Selected Audiences. Appendixes note the following: sources for professional materials; additional bibliographies, training manuals, and resource guides; recommended reading lists for parents and professionals; organizational information sources; and Spanish-language materials.

➤ PRODUCERS AND DISTRIBUTORS CATALOGS (See also: L22 for sexual abuse)

To our knowledge, Focus International and Multi-Focus are the only distributors in the U.S. carrying exclusively sex related titles. Network Publishing (see L20) distributes audiovisuals produced by ETR (see X219) and over 40 other non-profit organizations, including titles on sexual and reproductive health, and abuse prevention. The Sexuality Library catalog (see W10) includes erotic sex education films made for college human sexuality courses, as well as "How-To" tapes by pornographers. To identify additional producers and distributors, use the resources discussed under "How to Find," p.289.

V3.   Focus International: 14 Oregon Drive, Huntington Station, NY 11746-2627. PH: (800)843-0305 / (516)549-5320 (in N.Y.)

FOCUS distributes sex education films and videos for use in educational and therapeutic settings with children through adult audiences. The 1991 edition of their annual catalog, *Sex Education, Research and Therapy: Film and Video Catalog*, fully describes over 112 videos on the following subjects, as well as reproductive anatomy models and "Teach a Body" dolls. Video tapes are available for either rent or purchase and will be shipped within 24 hours.

Aging	Disability	Safer Sex
AIDS Education	Erotica	Sex Education
Anatomy/Physiology	Family Life Education	Sex Research
Assessment Tools	Family Issues	Sex Roles
Birth	Heterosexuality	Sex Therapy
Birth Control	Homosexuality	Sexual Abuse
Bisexuality	Impotence	Sexual History Taking
Chlamydia	Lesbianism	STDs
Condoms	Male Issues	Vaginismus
Contraception	Masturbation	Women's Issues

V4.   Multi-Focus: 1525 Franklin St., San Francisco, CA 94109-4592. PH: (800)821-0514 / (415)673-5100.

Multi-Focus, formerly the Multi Media Resource Center, is affiliated with the Institute for the Advanced Study of Human Sexuality (see X228). They produce and distribute sex education audiovisuals intended for use by educators, therapists, and counselors working with high school, college, and adult audiences. A SAR Video Package is available for those conducting Sexual Attitude Restructuring seminars. Their 1992 catalog fully describes 200 films, videos, and slides on the following subjects, some of which are "sexual enrichment" films portraying nudity and explicit sexual behavior.

Intro. to Sexuality	Humor/Satire	Sex and Pregnancy
Abortion	Incest	Sex Roles
AIDS and STDs	Massage	Sex Therapy
Anatomy	Masturbation	Teenage Sexuality
Bisexuality	Multiple Partners	Touch
Childbirth	Phone Sex	Vasectomy
Erotica/Fantasy	Physiology	Women's Health
Gender	Prostitution	Women's Sexuality
Heterosexuality	Sex and Disability	Youth
Homosexuality	Sex in Later Life	

—— MODELS AND TEACHING AIDS (*See also*: V3)

Contact SIECUS (see A4) or Planned Parenthood's Education Department (see X223) for referrals to sources of models and other teaching aids for use in sex education programs (e.g. dildos to demonstrate proper condom use, cutaways of the female pelvis to demonstrate the birth process, breast and testicle models used to teach cancer self exams, etc.).

V5. Worthington, George M. *Tactile Media for Sexuality Education*. New York: Planned Parenthood Federation of America, 1984. 3 p.

Briefly annotates distributor's catalogs from which to purchase sex and reproduction related 3-D models and other teaching aids. Although the annotations are now outdated, most of the suppliers are still in business and will send their current catalogs on request. Planned Parenthood also recommends contacting Health Edco at (800)299-3366 ext. 295.

27

ENTERTAINMENT FILMS & VIDEOS

Use the resources in this chapter to identify feature films and
"sexvids"—Robert Rimmer's term for legal, sexually explicit videos (see
W12)—for use in primary research, education, or therapy.

HOW TO FIND

FEATURE FILMS

• *On the Screen: A Film, Television, and Video Research Guide*
(Littleton, CO: Libraries unlimited, 1986), describes hundreds of
resources, including 37 motion picture archives and libraries whose
staff can provide further assistance.

• Popular magazines and newspapers often contain feature articles
about sex in films, as well as film reviews (to locate, search indexes
J1, J6-J10). Each November, Playboy publishes a review of sex in the
previous year's films. To find scholarly articles about sex in the
media, search a humanities index (see J34, J35) or a film studies
index (e.g. *Film Literature Index, International Index to Film
Periodicals*).

• Consult published filmographies or the "concealed filmographies" included in scholarly studies of sex in film. To identify, search library catalogs using the terms *Sex in moving pictures, Homosexuality in moving pictures*, etc. See also, "How to Find" Concealed Bibliographies, p.98.

• Film and video directories (see B5–B11) cite both educational and entertainment titles, but only non-fiction videos are classified by subject.

"SEXVIDS"

• Consult published filmographies. To identify, search library catalogs using the terms *Erotic films–Catalogs* or *Erotic films–Catalogs–Directories. Bowker's Complete Video Directory* (see B5) classifies titles by genre, including "Erotica."

• Consult archive or library catalogs. The Audiovisual Archives of the Kinsey Institute (see A4) include over 6,500 commercial erotic films (8mm, 16mm, and 35mm) dating back to 1911, as well as contemporary commercial erotic videos. There is a print catalog for the Institute's early films, 1911-1960's, which describes the plot, characters, and settings of each, and details, in the form of a checklist, the sexual behaviors portrayed. An in-house computer database for materials received since the 1970s is being developed. The Institute for Advanced Study of Sexuality (see A3) claims to have the finest collection of erotic films and videos in the country—over 100,000 films and 10,000 videos—but the collection is closed except to Institute faculty, students, and alumni.

• Consult commercial guides such as *Hustler Erotic Video Guide* (Beverly Hills: Larry Flynt Publishing), *Best of Erotic Film Guide* (New York: Eton Publishing), and *Adam Film Quarterly* (see K52), all of which review/announce new titles. They can be purchased at newsstands in metropolitan areas, in "adult" bookstores, or directly from the publisher. "Men's" magazines, such as *Penthouse* and *Hustler*, also contain reviews of erotic films.

• Consult distributor's and producer's catalogs. For names and numbers, see: *Adams Film World Guide and Directory of Adult Films* (see W6), *Adams Film World Directory of Gay Adult Videos* (see W7), *X-Rated Videotape Guide* (see W12), and *Erotic Writer's and*

Collector's Market (see p.355). "Adult" bookstores sell illustrated catalogs of major distributors (e.g. Color Climax Corp.'s *Video Index*), and most pornographic magazines and commercial guides (see above) carry advertisements for distributors from whom catalogs can be ordered directly. For much more selective coverage, consult the catalogs of the Sexuality Library (W10), and Eve's Garden (L24).

● ● ● ●

➤ FEATURE FILMS

W1. Limbacher, James L. *Sexuality in World Cinema*. 2 vols. Metuchen, NJ: Scarecrow Press, 1983. 1511 p.

Begins with an essay on the history of film censorship, pornography, and obscenity, followed by an annotated filmography of over 13,000 films classified into 26 topical chapters by the type of sexual activity portrayed: anal sex, bigamy/polygamy, child molestation, adolescent sexuality, "naughty ladies," prostitution, group sex, bestiality, incest, masturbation, nymphomania, lesbianism, gay men, sex toys and fetishism, oral sex, sadomasochism, "sleeping around," sex crimes, breast and penis size, transvestites and hermaphrodites, sexually transmitted diseases, necrophilia, exhibitionism and commercial sex, sexual dysfunction, and reproduction (i.e. contraception, sterility, etc.). Films portraying exclusively "normal" sexual intercourse are not included. Concludes with a 700 item bibliography, and a glossary of sex and media terms.

W2. Hosoda, Craig. *The Bare Facts Video Guide: Where to Find Your Favorite Actors and Actresses Nude on Videotape*. 2nd ed. Santa Clara, CA: Bare Facts, 1991. 225 p.

Each entry includes the actor or actress's name, a selective list of films in which they've appeared, and a brief description of scenes in which they've appeared nude—some of which are sex scenes (e.g. Helen Mirren in *The Cook, The Thief, His Wife and Her Lover*, "In black bra in restroom performing fellatio on Michael"; "Clint Eastwood in *Tightrope*, "Buns, on the bed on top of Becky. Slow pan, red light, covered with sweat"), some of which are not (e.g. Kirk Douglas in *There Was a Crooked Man*, "Brief buns and balls, jumping into a barrel to take a bath in prison").

—— GAY / LESBIAN

HOW TO FIND

• Contact Frameline (346 Ninth St., San Francisco, CA 94103. PH: 415/703-8650), organizers of the San Francisco International Lesbian and Gay Film Festival, and a resource center for information on lesbian and gay media. The Campus Project of the National Gay and Lesbian Task Force (see X119) can also provide guidance on selecting and obtaining films for film festivals, and have compiled an annotated filmography.

• *The Gay Yellow Pages* (see p.361) list distributors and producers under the heading "Films and Videos"—most publish catalogs and many will provide review copies of videos on request.

• If a title is unavailable at your local video store or gay bookstore, contact Lambda Rising (see L6) or Cinevista (353 W. 39th St., New York, NY 10018. PH: 212/947-4373); both distribute gay-themed titles via mail-order.

W3.   Greenblatt, Ellen. "Gay and Lesbian Films and Videos: A Filmography." In *Gay and Lesbian Library Service*, edited by Cal Gough and Ellen Greenblatt, 214-252. Jefferson, NC: McFarland & Co., 1990.

Includes contact information for 30 producers and distributors of domestic, foreign, independent, and commercial films and videos exploring lesbian and gay themes; a filmography of readily available lesbian and gay documentaries, feature films, and shorts; and a bibliography which notes additional sources for filmographies. Contact the Gay and Lesbian Task Force of the American Library Association for updates (see X53).

W4.   Hadleigh, Boze. *The Lavender Screen: the Gay and Lesbian Films: Their Stars, Makers, Characters, and Critics*. Secaucus, NJ: Carol Publishing Group, 1992. 254 p.

W5.   Russo, Vito. "Filmography." In *The Celluloid Closet: Homosexuality in Movies*, 327-345. New York: Perennial Library, 1987. 368 p.

➤ "SEXVIDS"

—— DIRECTORIES AND CATALOGS (*See also*: V4 and W10 for sexually explicit films and videos intended for educational use)

W6.   *Adam's Film World Guide and Directory of Adult Films*. Los Angeles: Knight Publishing. Annual.

A directory of over 200 distributors, manufacturers, producers and others involved in the adult film and video industry. Each entry notes the general content of their films and the availability of a mail-order catalog.

W7.   *Adam's Film World Directory of Gay Adult Video*. Los Angeles: Knight Publishing. Annual.

W8.   **Bijou Video Sales**: 1363 N. Wells Street, Chicago, IL 60610. PH: (800)932-7111.

The largest mail order distributor of gay videos in the country.

W9.   **Femmes Distributor**: 588 Broadway, Suite 1110, New York, NY 10012. PH: (212)226-9330.

To our knowledge, the production company of Candida Royale, a 1970s porn star, is the only erotic video production company in the U.S. dedicated to a feminist approach to heterosexual erotic relations. The films are aimed at women and couples, and portray explicit sex in a "believable caring setting."

W10.   *Sexuality Library Video Catalog*: see L13 for address and phone number.

Erotic videos are included in the general catalog (see L13). They claim that all are "outstanding exceptions to the mediocrity, erotophobia and sexual illiteracy that plague the American screen . . . Each has a spark of originality and creativity that make it noteworthy to the audience that wants more than a nudity and/or intercourse demonstration. Allowing for taste, we think each video listed shows outstanding erotic and educational quality, with enough hot energy to start something cooking in your very own living or bedroom." The Spring 1993 catalog describes over 97 videos classified under the headings: sex and comedy, porn noir, docudrama, erotic drama, compilations, "star vehicles," feminist erotica, lesbian, gay male, bisexual, s/m, and erotic sex education. Each film is briefly described and assigned one or more codes indicating that it's women centered, superior in script and acting, weak in filmmaking but has "killer sex scenes," lesbian themed, portrays unconventional sexual content, displays safer sex techniques, is primarily educational with an erotic component, or is an underground/art picture.

—— FILMOGRAPHIES

W11.   Justice, Keith L. *Adult Video Index '84*. Jefferson, NC: McFarland & Co., 1984. 217 p.

W12.   Rimmer, Robert H. *The X-Rated Videotape Guide*. Crown, 1986.

_____. *The X-Rated Videotape Guide II*. Buffalo, NY: Prometheus Books, 1991.

Reviews thousands of "sexvids," legal, erotic/pornographic videos of the type available in neighborhood video rental stores—illegal, "underground" materials (i.e. those involving minors) are not included. The 1986 volume covers feature films produced between 1970 and 1985. The 1991 volume reviews an additional 1,200 videos made between 1986 and 1991, plus earlier films not previously released on video. Each entry includes a plot summary, special features, credits, and one or more codes indicating sexual content. N codes signify "normal" sex is portrayed: "NL" for normal laughing and bawdy, "NR" for normal romantic or deeply caring, "NN" for normal noncommitted sex without love but with momentary caring, "NM" for normal masturbation. D codes indicate portrayals of "deviational" sex, kinky variations of normal heterosexual sex, group sex, golden showers, anal sex, etc.: "DB" for bondage and discipline, "DS" for sadistic and violent, "DC" for acts involving what appears to be children under 16 (although in actuality, all participants in the films reviewed are over 18). Additional codes indicate bisexuality, soft core movies, and feature actors. Introductory essays discuss the adult film industry, plots of "sexvids," rating videos, and making one's own sexvids, and includes a list of adult film producers/distributors. 500-1000 new adult films are released annually—contact Rimmer for reviews of new films c/o Challenge Press, P.O. Box 2708, Quincy, MA 02269-2708.

W13. Rowberry, John W. *Gay Videos: A Guide to Erotica.* San Francisco: G.S. Press, 1986. 156 p.

W14. Satkin, Jeff, ed. *Atkol Comprehensive Guide to Adult Male Videos.* Plainfield, NJ: Atkol, 1990.

28

TELEVISION

Use the resources in this chapter to identify: (1) sex themed broadcast "fiction"—made for television movies, soap operas, mini series, sitcoms, evening dramas, etc.—for use in educational or clinical settings, or for primary research on sex on television; and (2) news and public affairs programming—evening news broadcasts, news magazines, news specials, talk shows, and the like—which frequently address sexuality related issues, ranging from current social problems and public policy issues (e.g. gays in the military) to sensational talk shows on alternative lifestyles and unusual sexual practices. For an indication of the range of sex topics addressed in broadcast fiction, see the subject headings in the Annenberg Television Script Archive's *Thesaurus of Subject Headings for Television* (see B87). For those addressed in news and public affairs programming, see Journal Graphic's *Transcript/Video Index* (see B89).

HOW TO FIND

• Purchase transcripts or tapes of news and public affairs programming from a transcription service—ordering information is given in the closing credits of shows for which this service is available. Journal Graphics (see B89) currently covers over 120 news and public affairs programs broadcast on ABC, PBS, and CNN, and

---

publishes the *Transcript/Video Index*, providing subject access to transcripts of shows broadcast since 1968. Burrelle's Transcripts (see B92) covers such programming broadcast on CBS and NBC, although Journal Graphics has covered these networks in the past—contact them for details. Broadcast "fiction" is not covered by transcription services but scripts are collected by the Annenberg Television Script Archives (see B87) which provides subject access to the collection through its *TSAR Database*.

• For both broadcast fiction and public affairs programming, search television archive catalogs, which usually provide subject access to the titles in their collections. *On the Screen: A Film, Television, and Video Research Guide* (Littleton, CO: Libraries Unlimited, 1986), describes 27 television and video archives and special libraries, most of which allow some degree of public access. For news broadcasts, see the Vanderbilt Television News Archive's *Television News Index and Abstracts* (see B95).

• Consult with the staff of a media watchdog organization: GLAAD (see X243) monitors portrayals of gays and lesbians in the media, as does the Gay Media Task Force (see X245); the Center for Population Options Media Project (see X241), portrayals of family planning, sexuality, and reproductive health; Women Against Pornography (see X181), portrayals of sexual violence and sex role stereotyping; and the conservative American Family Association (see X240) and Morality in Media (see X176), broadcasts involving sex, profanity, and violence.

• Obtain tapes of television fiction (e.g. *The Cosby Show, The Golden Girls*), for use in educational settings, from the show's producer, identified in its closing credits. Search the *TSAR Database* (see B87) for relevant shows. The Center for Population Options Media Project (see X241) may also suggest programming. Cultural Information Service (P.O. Box 786, Madison Sq. Station, New York, NY 10159. PH: 212/691-5240), emphasizes the value of contemporary culture (books, films, television programs, pop music) as an educational tool. They publish discussion guides for use in home or school, and viewer guides for TV movies and news specials.

Part IX
Human Resources

29

EXPERTS

Experts—individuals with special knowledge about a subject or activity—can clarify confusing points raised in a literature review or provide the information needed directly, eliminating the need for library research altogether; provide information on subjects so new they've not yet been discussed in print, or so specialized little has been written about them; and can provide referrals to other specialists. Thirteen types of experts are briefly discussed below:

Association and Institution Staff. See Chapter 30 for a discussion how to locate various types of organizations and institutions, followed by descriptive listings of nearly 300 organizations, professional associations, self help groups, special libraries, research centers, private businesses, government agencies, etc., all of whom are staffed by experts willing to provide up-to-date information in their area of focus, usually at little or no charge.

Authors and Journalists. Authors of books and professional journal articles can be assumed to have some degree of expertise in the subject matter addressed. Popular magazine and newspaper articles, however, are often written by journalists with little in-depth knowledge of the topic beyond the content of the article itself. Their real value is to provide referrals to the experts with whom they spoke while researching the piece. For "How to Find," see p.308.

HOW TO FIND

AUTHORS AND JOURNALISTS (*See also*: Ch.15)

• Contact an author through his or her most recent publisher. If the book is an older one, check library catalogs and the author index of *Books in Print* (see B16) for any more recent publications.

• Journal articles typically note an address from which to request reprints or correspond with the author. Consult faculty directories or the membership directories of professional associations for the current affiliations of authors of older articles. Contact journalists through the magazine or newspaper in which the article of interest was published.

COMPUTER FORUM USERS

• Each entry in the *Encyclopedia of Associations* lists, under the heading "Telecommunication Services," any electronic bulletin boards or mail services operated by the organization.

• Consult directories. Forums sponsored by *HSX* (see I5) are available through Compuserve (see I2). To identify those available on the Internet network, consult an on-line Internet directory such as ARCHIE, which can be searched by keyword. To access Internet, see Ch.11. A directory of AIDS related bulletin boards is available from the National AIDS Clearinghouse (see X35). Contact Joh Stamford-Chew of Harbor Communications (337 E. Lorraine Ave., Baltimore, MD 21218. PH: 301/366-8423) for a list of gay, lesbian, and mixed electronic computer bulletin board systems. The *Gay Yellow Pages* (see p.361) utilizes the heading "Computer Services/Bulletin Boards."

EDITORIAL BOARDS / BOARDS OF DIRECTORS

• The names of a non-profit organization's board members are noted in its annual report, available on request. The names and affiliations of a journal's editorial board are usually listed in each issue.

EXPERTS CITED IN THE MEDIA

• Be especially alert for media discussions of sexual topics around specially designated days, weeks, and months (e.g. National Condom Week, World AIDS Day), which can be identified using *Chase's Annual Events: Special Days, Weeks and Months* (see B83).

• Transcripts of broadcast public affairs and news programming indicate participant's names and affiliations. See "How to Find" Television, Ch.28.

• Newspaper and magazine articles usually indicate the institutional affiliations of the experts they cite.

EXPERTS TESTIFYING AT GOVERNMENT HEARINGS

• Published reports of congressional hearings include full text of witness testimony. Hearings are indexed in *CIS/Index* (see B49) and its abstracts note each witness's name and affiliation, summarize the subjects they discussed, and cite any print or audiovisual materials they presented. For homosexuality related hearings, see H62.

FACULTY

• Consult *The National Faculty Directory* (see B37) or *The Faculty Directory of Higher Education* (see B36). The latter classifies faculty by subject specialty (including titles of courses taught) but hasn't been updated since 1988.

• Browse college catalogs—available on microfilm in many libraries—for relevant classes, and then contact the sponsoring department for the teacher's name.

• Many professional organizations publish guides to graduate programs in their discipline which list each program's faculty and their research interests.

• Contact the Educators in Sexual Science Special Interest Group of the Society for the Scientific Study of Sex (see X189).

• Purchase a faculty mailing list from CMG Information Services (50 Cross St., Winchester, MA 01890. PH: 800/677-7959). Not a good technique for identifying a single professor, mailing lists are invaluable to those needing to identify faculty teaching in a particular area for research or commercial purposes, including those teaching courses in the following areas: AIDS, sex roles, sexual disorders (psychiatry), sexuality (psychiatry), sex education (elementary), sex education (secondary), human sexuality (psychology), human sexuality (religion), methods and materials for sex education (elementary and secondary), philosophy of love and sexuality, human reproduction, and reproductive biology.

• For gay studies faculty, order the *Student Organization Packet* from the Campus Project of the National Gay and Lesbian Task Force (see X119), which lists gay studies courses and programs throughout the U.S. See also K79.

GOVERNMENT EXPERTS (*See also*: "How to Find" Gov't Agencies, p.317)

• Consult a government personnel directory. For state government staff, see the *State Executive Directory* (B46) or *State Yellow Book* (B47). For federal staff, identify relevant offices using the keyword index of the semi-annual *Federal Staff Directory* (see B42), and then consult the quarterly *Federal Yellow Book: Who's Who in Federal Departments and Agencies* (see B43) for updates of names and numbers. Although names of agency directors and other high ranking staff are listed in these directories, it is rarely necessary to speak with them directly; the operator at the agency's main information number can provide referrals. For statistical experts, see *Federal Statistical Specialists* (see B86). *Lesko's Info Power* (see B38) includes a subject classified directory of over 8,000 federal experts.

• Some government agencies, including the Department of Health and Human Services which directs most federal family planning and reproductive health activities, make their internal phone directories available to the public.

"HANDS ON EXPERTS"

• Organizations and associations that service a particular population can usually provide referrals to individuals with special knowledge in the area (see "How to Find" Organizations, p.318). The *Encyclopedia of Associations* notes if a group operates a speaker's bureau.

• Place an advertisement describing the type of information or person sought in a relevant newspaper, newsletter, or journal (see Ch.14). The back page of New York City's *Village Voice* is an excellent place to run ads seeking those involved in a particular sex practice or alternative sexual lifestyle. (See also: *Classified Love Ads*, p.224).

• Place announcements on relevant computer bulletin boards and forums. See "How to Find" Computer Forum Users, p.308.

PROFESSIONALS IN THE FIELD (*See also*: p.319)

• If the person is prominent in their field, consult biographical directories (see B13, B14).

• Contact researchers affiliated with research centers (see B82, B83) or universities (see "How to Find" Faculty, p.309).

• Consult directories (see Ch.13). The only two directories of sex professionals which are not membership directories—the Institute for the Advanced Study of Human Sexuality's *International Who's Who in Sexology* (San Francisco: Specific Press, 1986), and the Kinsey Institute's *Institute for Sex Research International Directory of Sex Research and Related Fields* (Boston: G.K. Hall, 1976)—are both out-of-date and no updates are planned. Most professional associations (see p.319) compile annual membership directories which typically include information on each member's background, research interests, and current affiliation; see especially those of the American Association of Sex Educators, Counselors, and Therapists (see X183) and the Society for the Scientific Study of Sex (see X189; available to members only). For works on the condition of belonging to an organization, search library catalogs using the organization's name followed by the form subdivision *–Membership*. For works listing names, addresses, and other identifying data, use the group's name followed by the subdivisions *–Directories* or *–Roster*. The *National Family Resources Database* (see J39) and *LINKLine* (see I6) both include directories of experts willing to be contacted by the public.

• Professionals often serve on advisory boards of organizations or publications: HSX (see I5) has assembled a 40 person advisory board; and author Robert Francoeur consulted with 70 sexuality experts in writing the 2nd edition of his textbook, *Becoming a Sexual Person* (their names and affiliations are noted in the text).

"PUBLIC FIGURES"

• For biographies, consult *Marquis Who's Who Publications: Index to All Books* (see B14) or *Gale's Biography and Genealogy Master Index* (see B13).

• Search popular magazine and newspaper indexes (see J1, J6-J10), under the individual's name.

Computer Forum Users. Computer bulletin boards, special interest groups, and other interactive computer systems provide a forum for information exchange worldwide, by allowing people to communicate directly with each other via computer networks and electronic mail (see Ch.11). *HSX* (see I5), available on Compuserve, includes over 30 active forums on sex related topics including For Women Only, I was Abused, I'm Abstaining, Variations I and II (a variety of paraphilias), Gender Line (for transvestites and transsexuals), Gay Adults, Sex-Problem Help, Naturist Lifestyle, Shyness Workshop, Living with AIDS, Man to Man, Teens Talk, Gay Alliance, Sex Ed. for Adults, You and Your Body, Gay Youth, Fantasyland, Singles Club, Formerly Married, and others. Many other forums and bulletin boards are available for free on Internet (e.g. alt.sex.homosexuality). For "How to Find," see p.308.

Conference Speakers. All professional associations and many organizations hold annual conferences or meetings which include speakers who are leaders in their fields, or at least have expertise in the topics of their presentations. Such experts range from John and HoneyBear Rivers speaking on the "ABCs of Swinging" at Lifestyle's 1990 *COUPLES Conference*, to Sue Marx speaking on "Interviewing and Preparing Children for Court" at the *Eighth National Symposium on Child Sexual Abuse*. Preliminary conference programs, as well as those from past meetings, are available directly from the sponsor or may be published in their newsletter/journal. These generally indicate the names, backgrounds, and affiliations of scheduled speakers, as well as the titles of their presentations. To identify relevant conferences, see Ch.18.

Members of Editorial Boards and Boards of Directors. Contact board members of non-profit organizations and institutions (see Ch.30), and the editorial boards of journals. Although not all board members are experts in the area—holding the position for political, financial, or other reasons—they should be able to provide referrals. For "How to Find," see p.306.

Experts Cited in the Media. Experts appearing on television or radio news and public affairs programs or quoted in newspaper or magazine articles have the advantage of being pre-screened for their expertise (to at least some extent) by the journalist or program director. Talk shows and newsmagazines often compile panels of experts presenting differing viewpoints within a single show. For "How to Find," see p.306.

Experts at Private Companies.   Most large companies maintain customer service, public relations, or education departments with staff who can answer questions related to their company's products and services, supply print materials, and/or refer one to others in the company who can provide further assistance. See "How to Find" Businesses, p.316.

Experts Testifying at Government Hearings.   Prior to making policy recommendations, congressional and presidential committees conduct fact-finding hearings (e.g. Meese Commission Hearings on Obscenity and Pornography). Those testifying at such hearings range from recognized "expert witnesses," to lobbyists from public and private interest groups, to elected state, local, and federal officials, to concerned citizens. Witnesses at the 1984 Congressional Hearings on Child Pornography and Pedophilia, for example, included both a convicted child molester, testifying on the operation of child pornography and pedophilia trafficking groups, and a Los Angeles police detective and New Jersey prosecutor, summarizing law enforcement agency programs to curb child porn. For "How to Find," see p.309.

Faculty.   College and university professors may be willing to share syllabi and/or reading lists from their classes, or provide other guidance. Although there are only a few accredited programs specializing directly in sex studies (see X226-X229), and the notes under "Sex Therapy," p.404, and homosexuality studies, p.362, most schools offer introductory human sexuality courses, usually within the sociology, psychology, women's studies, physical education, health, or biology departments, with specialized courses offered in other disciplines (request the catalog of San Francisco State University's interdisciplinary sexuality program, see X229, for an indication of the range of courses that may be available). For "How to Find," see p.307.

Government Experts. (*See also*: "Government Agencies," p.317) Matthew Lesko, an expert on government information sources (see B38), claims that the U.S. government is the richest source of experts in the world, with over 700,000 specialists in the federal government alone, who spend their entire careers studying a particular topic, and who, for the price of a phone call, will provide information about it to the public. For "How to Find," see p.310.

"Hands On" Experts.   People whose expertise stems from having first hand experience with the activities or issues under examination can provide a perspective on the topic often lacking in more traditional

information sources. Children of gay parents, for example, can provide information on the impact of being raised by gay parents on one's own sexual identity; those involved in "swinging" or polyfidelitous lifestyles, on handling jealousy in non-monogamous relationships, etc. For "How to Find," see p.310.

Professionals in the Field. Professionals currently working in the field (i.e. educators, therapists, researchers, physicians, etc.) can provide referrals, research guidance, background information, and other assistance. Be especially cognizant with these types of experts that their time is money, and unless you are willing to pay for their services, they are doing you a favor: enclose a S.A.S.E. with all inquiries, suggest they call back collect, etc. For "How to Find," see p.311.

Public Figures. Some researchers, educators, and therapists achieve public prominence because they host radio or television talk shows, write newspaper or magazine columns, or publish controversial books which receive a great deal of media attention (e.g. Dr. Ruth, Dr. Joyce Brothers, Shere Hite). For "How to Find," see p.311.

30

ORGANIZATIONS & INSTITUTIONS

Hundreds of organizations and institutions collect up-to-date materials on sex related topics—much of it difficult or impossible to obtain elsewhere—and disseminate it in response to mail or phone queries, usually at little or no cost. Collectively, they produce and distribute bibliographies, directories, catalogs, pamphlets, audiovisuals, curriculum, books, and periodicals; maintain libraries, referral services, and data bases; compile statistics and monitor legislative activities; sponsor conferences; make policy recommendations and set professional standards; and interact with groups and individuals with similar interests and concerns. Seven types of organizations and institutions are briefly described below, with descriptive listings of nearly 300 beginning on p.321.

Archives and Special Collections (See also: Ch.1). Some archives are autonomous institutions (e.g. the Lesbian Herstory Archive), while others are held in the special collections department of a larger library (e.g. the Bullough Collection on Human Sexuality at California State University at Northridge's Oviatt Library). Some collections are continually expanded; others contain strictly historical materials. For "How to Find," see p.316.

Businesses (See also: Ch.14 for bookstores and publishers; Ch.26 & Ch.27 for audiovisual distributors). For information on a particular product, or

How to Find

• Consult directories (see Ch.13). *SEXPERTS U.S.A.: Information Sources in Human Sexuality, Reproduction, and Related Topics* (Palo Alto, CA: National Sex Information Network) is an annual directory of organizations, businesses, government agencies, and institutions providing information to the public on a wide range of sex related topics—order from X230. *The Gay Yellow Pages* (see p.361) is a comprehensive, subject classified directory of gay and lesbian groups, but includes no descriptions of their activities, services, etc.

ARCHIVES AND SPECIAL COLLECTIONS *(See also: Ch.1)*

• Consult directories. General library directories (see B60, B62) describe the special collections held by each institution. See also, *Subject Collections: A Guide to Special Book Collections and Subject Emphasis as Reported by University, College, Public, and Special Libraries and Museums in the United States and Canada* (B61).

• New special collections are noted in library and book trade publications (e.g. *College and Research Libraries News, AB Bookmans Weekly, Publishers Weekly, Library Journal*), many of which are indexed by *ACCESS: The Supplementary Index of Periodicals* (see J6).

• For published descriptions of special collections, search library catalogs using the term *Libraries–Special collections–* followed by the appropriate topical subject heading (e.g. *Libraries–Special Collections–Erotica; Libraries–Special collections–Sex oriented periodicals*).

BUSINESSES

• Consult directories. *Brands and Their Companies* (see B64) cross references manufacturers with the brand names of the products they produce, indicating, for example, that Carter Wallace manufactures Trojans condoms. *Health Device Sourcebook* (see B65) indexes companies by the products they manufacture and/or distribute (e.g. tampons, sanitary pads, pap smear kits, penile prostheses, condoms, diaphragms, cervical caps, breast implants, etc). For titles of other specialized business directories, consult *Directory of Directories* (see B33).

GOVERNMENT AGENCIES

• Consult directories. The *United States Government Manual* (B40) is the official handbook of the federal government, covering the creation, organization, authority, activities, and chief officials of the legislative, judicial, and executive branches. *Washington Information Directory* (see B41) provides similar information, but is organized by subject and includes non-profit organizations in the Washington, D.C. area. *Lesko's Info Power* (see B38) provides a detailed subject index to government sources. For a detailed breakdown of an agency's structure, consult staff directories (see B39-B43). If you're unsure with whom to talk, look for the office of public affairs, public information, consumer affairs, or press/public liaisons, their staff can provide referrals. For the most up-to-date contact information, call the U.S. Government Operator at (202)555-1272. To identify directories produced by the federal government, consult *Government Reference Books* (see B80).

• To identify relevant state agencies, consult staff directories (see B46, B47), contact the state's information office for referrals (call directory assistance for the number), or contact the office of a state legislator (all maintain staff who field constituents' inquiries).

• Call a referral agency. For general information, contact a Federal Information Center (see B44) which will provide referrals to a specific program or to the public information office of the department or agency with jurisdiction over the area of interest. For referrals to health information sources, contact the National Health Information Center (see B45). For referrals to criminal justice information sources, contact the National Criminal Justice Reference Service (see X217). Federal information clearinghouses also provide referrals (see p.260 for a partial list; contact a referral agency for additional names).

• Contact your congressperson—all maintain local offices whose primary purpose is to serve their constituents.

INFORMATION CLEARINGHOUSES (*See also*: for federal clearinghouses, see Gov't Agencies, above)

• Consult *Clearinghouse Directory: A Guide to Information Clearinghouses and Their Resources, Services and Publications* (see B59).

The *Encyclopedia of Associations* contains more entries and is updated more frequently, but descriptions are more brief.

ORGANIZATIONS AND ASSOCIATIONS

• Consult the *Encyclopedia of Associations* (see B4) which fully describes thousands of organizations of all types. Gale Research also publishes specialized directories (e.g. of legal associations).

• For local organizations, consult the telephone white pages under keywords, and the yellow pages under relevant headings.

• Contact the American Society of Association Executives (1575 Eye St., Washington, DC 20005. PH: 202/626-2772), for referrals.

PROFESSIONAL ASSOCIATIONS (*See also*: p.319)

• Consult *The Encyclopedia of Associations* (see B4). In addition to those associations made up exclusively of sex professionals, many scholarly associations have specialized task forces or divisions (e.g. the Sexual Behavior Division of the Society for the Study of Social Problems)—look under the name of the main association. The Society for the Scientific Study of Sex (see X189) maintains liaisons to the anthropology, psychology, biological sciences, and social, economic, and political science sections of the American Association for the Advancement of Science—they may also be able to provide referrals.

• Search library catalogs for works discussing two or more societies or institutions related to a particular subject, using the Library of Congress form subdivision *–Societies* under classes of persons or topical headings. To locate membership directories, see p.311.

• A *Directory of Gay and Lesbian Professional Groups* is available from the Gay and Lesbian Task Force Clearinghouse of the American Library Association (see X53), and the *Gay Yellow Book* (see p.361) lists such groups under "Business and Professional Associations."

RESEARCH CENTERS

• Consult the *Research Centers Directory* (see B83) for non-profit research centers, and the *Governmental Research Centers Directory* (see B82) for those affiliated with the federal government.

the issues surrounding the use of that product, contact the public affairs or customer service department of the company that manufacturers and/or markets it. They will answer questions over the phone, send print materials, or provide referrals to experts in the company who can provide further assistance. This is an especially relevant source for those interested in pharmaceuticals (e.g. the sexual side effects of drugs), contraceptives (e.g. how condoms are tested), sexually related medical devices (e.g. penile implants used in treating impotence), and "female hygiene" products (e.g. toxic shock syndrome or the treatment of PMS). For "How to Find," see p.316.

Government Agencies (*See also*: Ch.17; Ch.20 for federal statistical agencies; "Gov't Experts" p.313). Although the U.S. Department of Health and Human Services (which includes the Centers for Disease Control, Food and Drug Administration, and National Institutes of Health) directs most federal family planning and reproductive health activities, sex related topics are addressed by agencies throughout the government. All have public affairs offices whose sole purpose is to field inquiries from the public by answering questions directly, sending publications, or providing referrals. For "How to Find," see p.317.

Information Clearinghouses. Information clearinghouses are organizations (or units within an organization) which collect up-to-date materials on specific subjects and disseminate them to the public, usually at little or no cost. They generally maintain libraries and databases, produce bibliographies and other reference materials, and provide referrals. Some are sponsored by the federal government (e.g. the National AIDS Clearinghouse), others are private (e.g. Intinet Resource Center's Clearinghouse on non-monogamy). For a partial list of the federal clearinghouses described in Ch.30, see p.260. For "How to Find," see p.317.

Organizations and Associations. Non-profit advocacy groups, organizations, activist organizations, professional associations, educational organizations, support groups, and the like—are an often overlooked source for print and non-print information on virtually any sexual topic imaginable, much of it unavailable elsewhere. For professional associations, see below. For "How to Find," see p.318.

Professional Associations. The American Association of Sex Educators, Counselors and Therapists (AASECT) (see X183) and the Society for the Scientific Study of Sex (SSSS) (see X189) are the two largest professional organizations of sex educators, counselors, therapists, and researchers in the U.S., but there are others that specialize in specific aspects of sexuality (e.g. Society for the Philosophy of Sex and Love), sex related committees or divisions of more general associations (e.g. the Sexuality and Family Psychology Division of the American Psychology Association), and associations of professionals in related fields (e.g. American College of Obstetricians and Gynecologists, American Academy of Matrimonial Lawyers). A comprehensive list of all professional associations that deal in some way with sex related issues is beyond the scope of this volume. Consult the *Encyclopedia of Associations* for descriptions of associations of the following professionals (see "How to Find," p.318, for additional resources):

For childbirth and pregnancy: childbirth educators, midwives, nurse midwives, obstetrics, gynecologists, ovulation teachers, natural family planning teachers, and pediatricians.

For scholarly research: anthropologists, philosophers, sociologists, psychologists, biologists, folklorists, etc.

For educators: physical education teachers, health education teachers.

For therapy and counseling: clinical social workers, psychiatrists, psychoanalysts, psychologists, marriage and family therapists.

For medicine: psychiatrists, obstetricians, gynecologists, urologists, public health specialists, epidemiologists, embryologists, endocrinologists, geneticists, dermatologists (for treatment of STDs).

For law: matrimonial and family law specialists, civil rights lawyers.

There are also many gay and lesbian professional organizations, some made up of gay and lesbian professionals (e.g. Gay Pilots Association, High Tech Gays), others more generally concerned with gay and lesbian issues within a particular profession (e.g. Association for Gay, Lesbian, and Bisexual Issues in Counseling).

Research Centers. Research centers are usually affiliated with universities or government agencies, although some are autonomous institutions. Researchers in such centers are generally working on the cutting edge of their fields and can provide the most up-to-date information available, although it may be more technical than desired. Many maintain libraries. For "How to Find," see p.318.

•   •   •   •

Listings: Nearly 300 organizations, institutions, government agencies, and businesses are described below. (For bookstores and publishers, see Ch.15; for audiovisual distributors, see Ch.26 and Ch.27; for libraries, see Ch.1.) All (1) provide services or information to the public at little or no charge; (2) are national in scope unless offering a unique focus or service; and (3) are accessible by phone or mail. Inclusion of an organization does not constitute endorsement of its mission or activities. Due to space constraints, I have emphasized umbrella organizations, information clearinghouses, and other key organizations and institutions in each subject area. Specialized directories with which to locate additional groups are described in "How to Find" boxes under many headings, and in the entries themselves. A "D" code under "Services" indicates the group distributes a directory that may not be listed by title. See also the sources listed under "How to Find" (p.316-318), or contact the National Sex Information Network (see X230) for referrals.

Entries are arranged by subject (see the table of contents for details) with extensive cross references. Organizations' names are indexed in the Name Index, their publications in the Title Index.

The sample entry below indicates the information included in most entries:

ENTRY NUMBER   NAME   ADDRESS/PHONE
   ↓   ↓   ↓

X1.   **Gay Mens Health Crisis** 129 E. 20th St., New York, NY 10011. PH: (212)897-6664.

[SERVICES: AV,L,P,R,S,SB,SG] Description. (EA)
      ↑   ↑
   SERVICE CODES (see below)   DIRECTORY CODES (see below)

Whenever possible, the descriptions are based on information supplied directly by each organization[1], either in the form of solicited literature or

---

[1] Descriptions of the following programs were drawn from *Health Information Resources in the Federal Government Fifth Edition, 1990* (Washington DC: ODPHP National Health Information Center, 1990): X24, X35, X44, X89, X90, X102, X103, X108, X130, X134, X135, X138, X139, X197, X201, X204.

their responses to my questionnaire. They emphasize each organization's information services, and do not fully describe their other services and activities. These are partially indicated by the following codes listed under "Services" at the beginning of each entry:

Service Codes:

AV	Audiovisuals	DB	Database	R	Referrals
B	Bibliographies	L	Resource Center	S	Statistics
C	Conference		or Library	SB	Speakers Bureau
D	Directories	P	Publications	SG	Support Groups

Contact information is subject to change. The following codes (appearing in parentheses at the end of each entry) indicate a source from which updated phone and address listings can be obtained. Federal Information Centers are a telephone reference service; the others are print directories published annually with inter-edition updates. If the most current edition is not available in your library, call telephone reference at the Library of Congress (see A1) for assistance. If a group isn't listed in a directory, call the Kinsey Institute Information Services (see A4) or SIECUS (see A5) for updates.

Directory Codes

EA   *Encyclopedia of Associations* (see B4)
FIC   Federal Information Centers (see B44)
RC   *Research Centers Directory* (see B83)
SL   *Directory of Special Libraries and Information Centers* (see B62)

▶ ABORTION (*See also*: Bioethics, Conservative/Traditionalists, Women)

HOW TO FIND

• To locate local facilities providing abortion information and services, as well as those supporting other alternatives to unplanned pregnancies, consult telephone yellow pages under "Abortion," "Family Planning," "Clinics," "Pregnancy," and "Women."

—— ANTI-ABORTION (*See also*: Conservative/Traditionalists; X247)

X1.   **Alternatives to Abortion International**: c/o Women's Health and Education Foundation, 1213 1/2 S. James Rd., Columbus, OH 43227-1801. PH: (614)239-9433.

[SERVICES: D,R,P] Coalition of service groups providing emotional, medical, legal, and social support services to pregnant women and girls who choose to continue their pregnancies. (EA)

X2.   **American Life League**: c/o America's Family Center, P.O. Box 1350, Stafford, VA 22554. PH: (703)659-4171.

[SERVICES: AV,C,L,P] A pro-life, pro-family organization with over 250,000 members and an $8.2 million annual budget. Their primary goal is to educate the public on "life" issues and to "promote the social welfare and defend the human rights of persons born and preborn—from fertilization, without regard to age, health or condition of dependency." Maintains a resource center with over 17,000 leaflets, booklets, flyers, books, and audiovisuals opposing abortion, tax subsidized birth control organizations (i.e. Planned Parenthood), sex and profanity on television and radio, school based sex education programs and clinics, and other issues. Operates the American Life Lobby, dedicated to passing the Human Life Amendment to the U.S. Constitution (see also X10,X11). Publishes *All About Issues* (see K35), and distributes a wide variety of educational materials (see L1). (EA, SL)

X3.   **Americans United for Life**: 343 S. Dearborn, Suite 1804, Chicago, IL 60604. PH: (312)786-9494.

[SERVICES: L,P,R] Serves as the legal arm of the pro-life movement. Maintains a legal resource center. Publishes *AUL Insights*, providing analysis of court cases and legislation; the monograph series, *AUL Studies in Law, Medicine and Society*; and *Lex Vitae*, a quarterly report of relevant litigation and legislation nationwide. (EA)

X4.   American Victims of Abortion: 419 7th St., NW, Suite 500, Washington, DC 20004. PH: (202)626-8800.

[SERVICES: P,R,SB] Seeks to increase public awareness of post-abortion syndrome and provide support for all those who feel they have been negatively affected by the procedure. (EA)

X5.   Diocese of Allentown Pro-Life Library: 1135 Stefko Blvd., Bethlehem, PA 18017. PH: (215)691-0380.

[SERVICES: L,P] Contains 700 volumes, 600 audio tapes, and hundreds of pamphlets, newspaper clippings, and other materials addressing bio-ethical issues, abortion, and sexuality from a Catholic perspective. (SL)

X6.   Feminists for Life of America: 811 E. 47th St., Kansas City, MO 64110. PH: (816)753-2130.

[SERVICES: C,P,SB] Disseminates current literature on pro-life feminism. Publishes *Sisterlife*, a quarterly newsletter; and the book *Prolife Feminism: Different Views*. (EA)

X7.   National Right to Life Committee: 419 7th St., NW, Suite 500, Washington, DC 20004. PH: (202)626-8800.

[SERVICES: AV,B,C,L,P,S,SB] Conducts education, outreach, and lobbying on pro-life issues, with over 3,000 local groups nationwide. Distributes a periodically updated bibliography of more than 70 antiabortion/prolife books, plus some "so revealing of how pro-abortionists think and operate [they're] very much worth reading." Their information clearinghouse includes over 1,000 books, pamphlets, brochures, and audiovisuals, as well as over 20,000 items in vertical files. Publications include the biweekly *National Right to Life News*; a full publications catalog is available on request. (EA, SL)

X8.   U.S. Coalition for Life: P.O. Box 315, Export, PA 15632. PH: (412)327-7379.

[SERVICES: D,R,P] Serves as an information clearinghouse on abortion, genetic engineering, government sponsored family planning, and other population control activities, to a network of over 22,000 pro-life, anti-abortion organizations, institutions, and government agencies. Operates an international document reprint service. Publishes *Pro-life Reporter* (quarterly). (EA)

X9. **Women Exploited by Abortion**: RR 1, Box 821, Venus, TX 76084-9514. PH: (214)366-3600.

[SERVICES: C,L,P,R,S,SG] Christian group of women who regret having had abortions. Provides information on post-abortion syndrome. (EA)

The following two congressional committees hold jurisdiction over the proposed Human Life Amendment to the U.S. Constitution. Contact the National Committee for a Human Life Amendment (1511 K St., NW, #335, Washington, DC 20005. PH: 202/393-0703) for more information.

X10. **House Judiciary Committee/Subcommittee on Civil and Constitutional Rights**: 806 O'Neil Bldg. (300 N.J. Ave., SE) Washington, DC 20515. PH: (202)226-7680.

X11. **Senate Judiciary Committee/Subcomittee on the Constitution**: SD-524, Washington, DC 20510. PH: (202)224-5573.

—— "PRO-CHOICE" (*See also*: Family Planning; Women; X113, X246, X253)

X12. **American Civil Liberties Union/Reproductive Freedom Project**: 132 W. 43rd St., New York, NY 10036. PH: (212)944-9800.

[SERVICES: P] Conducts litigation relevant to abortion rights. Publishes the bimonthly *Reproductive Rights Update* (see K4).

X13. **National Abortion Federation**: 1436 U St., NW, Suite 103, Washington, DC 20009. PH: (800)772-9100.

[SERVICES: C,L,P,R,S] A professional association of abortion service providers, pro choice organizations, and individuals dedicated to ensuring that safe, legal abortion services are available to all women who want them. Provides information on the medical, legal, and social aspects of abortion; sets standards of abortion care; tracks educational, public policy, and legislative developments relating to abortion and other reproductive health issues; and maintains a legal issues clearinghouse (including statistics on violence against abortion providers). Their national toll-free hotline provides guidelines for choosing an abortion facility and referrals to abortion clinics nationwide. Publications include the annual *National Abortion Federation Membership Directory*, a geographically arranged directory of over 310 abortion clinics, medical practices, hospitals, and research centers, including services offered and type of facility; and *National Abortion Federation Update*, a newsletter containing an events calendar, book reviews, and news and research updates. (EA, SL)

X14.   National Abortion Rights Action League (NARAL): 1101 14th St., NW, 5th Fl., Washington, DC 20005. PH: (202)408-4600.

[SERVICES: C,P,S,SB] The largest pro-choice advocacy organization in the country. Monitors public policy, and coordinates political actions to keep abortion legal and accessible to all women. Publications include: *NARAL Newsletter*, providing updates on abortion related legislation; *Who Decides? A State by State Review of Abortion Rights* (annual); *Who Decides? A Reproductive Rights Issues Manual*, containing NARAL position statements, discussion of relevant issues, and supporting facts and references; and *Congressional Votes on Abortion*, published annually since 1978. (EA)

X15.   Religious Coalition for Abortion Rights: 100 Maryland Ave., NE, Suite 307, Washington, DC 20002. PH: (202)543-7032.

[SERVICES: AV,C,L,P,SB] Ecumenical coalition of religious organizations—representing 36 different denominations—concerned that abortion remains legal. Monitors legal, regulatory, and religious efforts to restrict access to abortion, and distributes the position papers of various religious organizations in regards to abortion rights. Their quarterly newsletter on reproductive rights and religious freedom includes an events calendar, book reviews, and articles on religious and legislative activities. (EA)

—— RU-486 (*See also*: Anti-Abortion; Family Planning; Women's Health)

X16.   Reproductive Health Technologies Project: 1601 Connecticut Ave., NW, Suite 801, Washington, DC 20009. PH: (202)328-2200.

Promotes education and dialogue about RU-486 (the French "abortion pill") and other abortifacient and contraceptive drugs.

➤ ADOLESCENT SEXUALITY (*See also*: Family Planning; X108, X111, X223, X253)

X17. **Center for Early Adolescence**: University of North Carolina at Chapel Hill, D2 Carr Mill Town Center, Carrboro, NC 27510. PH: (919)966-1148.

[SERVICES: AV,C,D,L,P,R,S] Provides information and conducts research on issues relating to 10-15 year old youth. Operates the CEA Information System, an information clearinghouse with a 10,000 item, multi-disciplinary collection of books, periodicals (130 current subscriptions), organization publications, and program materials on all aspects of early adolescence, including adolescent health and sexuality. Publications include: bibliographies, resource lists, and curriculum; *Common Focus* (see K7); *Early Adolescent Sexuality: Resources for Professionals, Parents and Young Adolescents* (see H7); and *Early Adolescence: A Resource Directory*. (EA, SL)

X18. **Center for Population Options**: 1025 Vermont Ave., NW, Suite 210, Washington, DC 20005. PH: (202)347-5700.

[SERVICES: B,D,C,L,P,S] Devoted to the reduction of unintended teenage pregnancies and other adolescent sexuality and fertility related issues, through public education, research, training and technical assistance, and media programs. Disseminates information on adolescent pregnancy prevention and childbirth, adolescent sexuality, school based clinics, family planning, condom availability, adolescent reproductive health, sex education, the impact of portrayals of sex on television on adolescents, and other fertility related issues. Provides technical assistance to those planning, implementation, and evaluating sex education programs in the U.S., and through their International Clearinghouse on Adolescent Fertility, worldwide. Their resource center, open to the public by appointment, contains over 2,500 books, subscriptions to 150 journals and newsletters, vertical files, and a wide variety of educational materials. Publications include pamphlets, curriculum, reports, and books for teens, professionals, and parents on the subjects of sex education, youth and the media (e.g. *Sexuality and Television in the '80's*), teen pregnancy and public policy (e.g. *Adolescents and Abortion, Teen Pregnancy and Too-Early Childbearing: Public Costs, Personal Consequences*), HIV/AIDS prevention (e.g. *Resources for Educators*), adolescent fertility in developing countries (e.g. *Spanish Language Sexuality Education Material for Adolescents*), and school-linked youth health centers. They publish three newsletters: *Options* (quarterly) on public policy, *Passages* (quarterly) on international issues, and *Clinic News* (quarterly) on issues relating to school based clinics. Their *Get the Facts* series of fact sheets covers statistics, emerging trends, and available resources on a range of issues, including childbearing and educational attainment, contraceptive use, males and teen pregnancy, sexuality, pregnancy and parenthood, substance use and sexual risk-taking, abortion, AIDS/HIV, condom use, sexually transmitted diseases, the media and adolescent sexuality, parent-child communication about sex, school-linked health clinics, sex education, teen pregnancy in Africa, teen pregnancy and STDs in Latin America, and young women and AIDS. (EA, RC, SL)

—— GAY YOUTH

HOW TO FIND

• Consult Katherine Whitlock's *Bridges of Respect: Creating Support for Lesbian and Gay Youth* (Philadelphia, PA: American Friends Service Committee, 1989), a 97-page resource guide for adults working with lesbian or gay youth, describing print, audiovisual, and organizational resources on homophobia, stereotyping, and diversity, as well as those addressing the religious, educational, legal, social service, and health issues of gay youth.

X19.   Hetrick-Martin Institute: 401 West St., 2nd. Fl., New York, NY 10014. PH: (212)633-8920.

[SERVICES: L,P,R,SB] Affiliated with the Harvey Milk School, a public gay/lesbian high school in New York City. Provides information on the needs of gay and lesbian youth, and coordinates gay youth services. Maintains a 100 volume library. Operates a speakers bureau. (EA)

X20.   National Gay Alliance for Young Adults: P.O. Box 19712, Dallas, TX 75219. PH: (817)381-0343.

[SERVICES: C,P,R] Operates *Youthscan*, a database of information on gay youth and related issues. Sponsors National Gay Youth Awareness Week. Publishes *NGAYA Newsletter* (monthly). (EA)

X21.   National Gay Youth Network: P.O. Box 846, San Francisco, CA 94101-0846.

[SERVICES: C,P,R] A network of gay youth support groups, organizations serving gay youth, and gay student unions. Publications include: *We Are Here: Guide for Young Lesbians and Gays*, a national resource guide containing articles and a bibliography; *Gay Youth Community News*, a newspaper containing resource listings and book reviews; and a 7 page directory of switchboards and hotlines. Send a S.A.S.E. for a full publications list. (EA)

—— TEEN PREGNANCY *(See also*: Family Planning; U1, X1, X17, X18, X108, X111)

HOW TO FIND

• Consult Dominique Treboux's *TAPP Sources: A National Directory of Teenage Pregnancy Prevention* (Metuchen, NJ: Scarecrow Press, 1989), a 557-page, geographically arranged directory of over 500 teenage pregnancy prevention services. Entries include type of program, target population, fees, parental notification policies, and services.

X22.   Adolescent Pregnancy Prevention Clearinghouse: Children's Defense Foundation, 122 C St., NW, Washington, DC 20001. PH: (202)628-8787.

[SERVICES: AV,C,P,S] Provides advocacy, policy analysis, and education on issues relating to children and teenagers. Publishes a bimonthly monograph series on adolescent pregnancy and prevention efforts (see K6), containing research data, descriptions of effective programs, strategies for reaching high risk students, and information relating to pregnant students, sex education, the impact of teen pregnancy on adolescent lives, and related topics.

X23.   National Organization of Adolescent Pregnancy and Parenting: 4421-A East-West Highway, Bethesda, MD 20814. PH: (301)913-0378.

[SERVICES: C,P,R] Provides information, advocacy, and public education on preventing and resolving problems associated with adolescent sexuality, pregnancy, and parenting. Monitors relevant legislation. Publications include: the *National Directory of Adolescent Pregnancy and Parenting Programs*, and the *NOAPP Network Newsletter*, containing legislative updates, resource reviews, and program reports. (EA)

X24.   Office of Adolescent Pregnancy Programs: HHH Building, Rm.736 E, 200 Independence Avenue, SW, Washington, DC 20201. PH: (202) 245-7473.

A program of the federal Department of Health and Human Services. Seeks to discover new approaches to providing care services for pregnant adolescents and adolescent parents, emphasizing primary prevention strategies based on reaching adolescents before they become sexually active. Encourages the active involvement of the adolescent's family in addressing issues related to teen pregnancy, and promotes the postponement of teenage sexual activity. Adoption is promoted as a positive option to early parenting. Supports research in adolescent sexual behavior, adoption, and early childbearing (FIC).

➤ ADOPTION *(See also*: Fertility; X1)

X25.   National Adoption Center: 1218 Chestnut St, 2nd Fl., Philadelphia, PA 19107. PH: (215)925-0200 / (800) TO-ADOPT.

[SERVICES: L,P,R,SB) Maintains 7,000 volume library. (EA)

X26.   National Adoption Information Clearinghouse: 1400 Eye St., NW, Suite 1275, Washington, DC 20005. PH: (202)842-1919.

[SERVICES: AV,B,DB,L,R,S,SB] A service of the U.S. Health and Human Services Department. Provides information on all aspects of adoption, including international adoption, interracial adoption, adoption by gay couples, and adoption of children with special needs. Maintains a bibliographic database of books, journal and magazine articles, documents, and other publications from which custom bibliographies are compiled on request. Publications include: *National Adoption Directory*, a state by state listing of agencies and support groups; *National Adoption Training and Education Directory*; and *National Crisis Pregnancy Centers Directory*. (EA, FIC)

X27. **National Committee for Adoption Inc.**: 1930 17th St., NW, Washington, DC 20009-6207. PH: (202)328-1200.

[SERVICES: C,P,R,S,SB] Works for the regulation of adoption to insure protection of birth parents, children, and adoptive parents. Maintains a 2,000 volume library and extensive vertical files covering all aspects of adoption and related issues (e.g. maternity services, infertility). Operates the National Adoption Hotline: (202)328-8072. Publishes the *Adoption Factbook: U.S. Data, Issues, Regulations and Resources* (1989). (EA)

➤ AGING AND SEX (*See also*: Disability and Illness)

X28 and X29, while not focusing exclusively on sexuality, provide information on all aspects of aging, including menopause and the effects of estrogen replacement therapy, human sexual functioning and aging, the aging reproductive system, sexuality and the older person, and the effects of disability and illness on sexuality.

HOW TO FIND

• Consult the *Encyclopedia of Senior Citizens Information Sources* (Detroit: Gale Research, 1987) a subject classified directory of over 13,500 associations, federal agencies, research centers, databases, and publications.

X28. **National Gerontology Resource Center**: American Association of Retired Persons, 601 E St., NW, Washington, DC 20049. PH: (202)434-2277.

[SERVICES: B,DB,L,P,R] (EA,RC)

X29. **National Institute of Aging/ National Institute of Health**: 9000 Rockville Pike, Bldg. 31, Rm. 5C35, Bethesda, MD 20205. PH: (301)496-1752.

[SERVICES: B,DB,P,R] Conducts and supports biomedical, psychological, social, behavioral, and economic research and training relating to the aging process and the diseases and other special problems and needs of the aged. (FIC).

—— GAY AND LESBIAN

X30. National Association for Lesbian and Gay Gerontology: 1853 Market St., San Francisco, CA 94103. PH: (415)626-7000.

Publishes *Resource Guide: Lesbian and Gay Aging*.

X31. Senior Action in a Gay Environment (SAGE): 208 W. 13th St., New York, NY 10011. PH: (212)741-2247.

[SERVICES: C,P,S,SB] Volunteer organization providing care and support services for gay and lesbian seniors, and public education, professional training, and advocacy on issues of lesbian and gay aging. Publishes *SAGE Bulletin* (monthly), and *SAGE News* (semi-annually). (EA)

—— WOMEN (*See also*: Menstruation/Menopause; Women's Health)

X32. National Action Forum for Mid-life and Older Women: P.O. Box 816, Stonybrook, NY 11790.

[SERVICES: P,R] Serves as an international network and resource exchange for those interested in issues effecting women over 40. Publishes *Hot Flash Newsletter* (1981-), a quarterly newsletter addressing the health and social concerns of mid-life and older women through research news and announcements, book and resource reviews, conference announcements, and editorials. (EA)

➤ AIDS (*See also*: Sexually Transmitted Diseases; X237, X238)

X33. California AIDS Clearinghouse: P.O. Box 1830, Santa Cruz, CA 95061-1830. PH: (408)438-4822.

[SERVICES: AV,DB,L,P,R,S] A division of ETR (see X219). Trains AIDS educators, conducts research, and produces and distributes educational resources (see Network Publications, L20). Their library, open to the public by appointment, includes 2,500 books, 250 audiovisual programs, and other educational resources. Maintains databases of AIDS organizations and AIDS education materials. Publishes *California AIDS Clearinghouse Review*. (EA)

X34. Gay Mens Health Crisis: 129 E. 20th St., New York, NY 10011. PH: (212)897-6664.

[SERVICES: AV,L,P,R,S,SB,SG] Provides emotional and physical support,

How to Find

• For referrals, contact the clearinghouses described in this section, especially the National AIDS Clearinghouse (see X35) with its 8,000 entry Resource Database.

• Consult directories. See B1-B3, or search the on-line directory included in *AIDSQuest* (J11). To identify local resources, consult the biennial *AIDS/HIV Record: Directory of Key AIDS Program Officials in Federal, State, County and City Governments* (Washington, DC: Bio Data Publishers) and *Local AIDS Services: The National Directory* (Washington, DC: U.S. Conference of Mayors), an annual listing of over 2,500 organizations, including local health departments, community based organizations, AIDS treatment and evaluation units, and AIDS information hotlines. It includes a bibliography of state and local directories.

• The federal government's AIDS prevention and control efforts are coordinated by the Centers for Disease Control. Standards for testing vaccines and insuring the safety of the blood supply are set by the FDA's Center for Biologics Evaluation and Research. New AIDS treatments and drugs are approved by the FDA's Center for Drug Evaluation and Research. The Public Health Service develops AIDS/HIV public policy. The National Institute of Health's National Institute of Allergy and Infectious Diseases coordinates AIDS research efforts. Contact X35 for referrals to specific programs.

and legal, financial and health care advocacy for HIV and AIDS infected people (not limited to gay men), and their families. Conducts public education programs and develops and distributes audiovisuals, booklets, and brochures addressing various aspects of AIDS (e.g. general information, risk reduction, medical and psychological issues, testing, health insurance and legal concerns). Publishes *GMHC News*, and *The Volunteer*, a bimonthly newsletter containing updated political, medical, and clinical information on AIDS, new resources, and an events calendar. (EA)

X35.   National AIDS Clearinghouse (NAIC): P.O. Box 6003, Rockville, MD 20849-6003. PH: (301)217-0023 / (800)458-5231.

[SERVICES: AV,B,C,DB,L,P,R] Operated by the Centers for Disease Control, the clearinghouse identifies and responds to the needs of health professionals involved in the development and delivery of AIDS programs; provides the general public access to AIDS information; provides technical assistance to organizations involved in the fight against AIDS; assists in the development and assessment of resources; and distributes government approved educational materials. Operates the National AIDS Hotline (800-342-AIDS), which disseminates current information on HIV/AIDS to the public, and provides referrals to AIDS programs, materials, and services, including books and monographs, newsletters, pamphlets, databases and other electronic media (request the *Directory of AIDS Related Databases and Bulletin Boards*), library services and clearinghouses, educational meetings, information dissemination services, and national and local organizations. Referrals are drawn from two on-line databases: (1) *Resource Database*—a directory of over 8,000 programs, projects, and organizations, updated daily; and (2) *Educational Materials Database* (1984-)—a bibliographic database citing over 5,000 HIV/AIDS educational items, including bibliographies, comic books, brochures, directories, policy and procedural manuals, pamphlets, audiovisuals, teacher's guides, reports, and curricula; selected records are available on the *Combined Health Information Database* (see J24). Distributes free educational materials, including pamphlets, booklets, posters, audiovisuals, and displays; request the catalog of *HIV/AIDS Materials for Professionals*. A full publications catalog is available on request. The NAIC Resource Center is open to the public. (FIC)

X36.   National Institute of Justice AIDS Clearinghouse: Box 6000-AIQ, Rockville, MD 20850. PH: (301)251-5500.

[SERVICES: B,P,R,S] A centralized source for information on AIDS as it relates to criminal justice, operated by the National Criminal Justice Reference Service.

X37.   National Minority AIDS Council: 300 Eye St., NE, #400, Washington, DC 20002. PH: (202)544-1076.

Provides information on AIDS and minorities, and monitors relevant legislation. (EA)

X38.   National Resource Center on Women with AIDS: Center for Women Policy Studies, 2000 P St., NW, Suite 508, Washington, DC 20036. PH: (202)872-1770.

[SERVICES: AV,B,D,P,R,SB] Publications include a *Guide to Resources on Women and AIDS*, an annual directory of local, state, and national organizations and educational programs; and *Policy Papers* summarizing current research and policy developments, and making policy recommendations. (EA)

X39.   San Francisco AIDS Foundation: P.O. Box 6182, San Francisco, CA 94101-6182. PH: (415)864-5855.

[SERVICES: AV,P,R,S,SB,SG] Provides information and referrals; conducts public education on HIV/AIDS prevention; and provides support services to people with AIDS. Operates the AIDS Clinical Trials Information Service, providing up-to-date information on more than 200 HIV/AIDS clinical trials and the drugs being testing. Publications include *AIDS Educator* (semi-annual), a free catalog of AIDS education materials. (EA)

—— PEOPLE WITH AIDS

X40.   National Association of People with AIDS: 1413 K St., NW, 10th Fl., Washington, DC 20005. PH: (202)898-0414.

[SERVICES: P,R,S,SB] Publishes *NAPWA News Monthly*. (EA)

X41.   People With AIDS Coalition (PWA Coalition): 31 W. 26th St., New York, NY 10010. PH: (800)828-3280.

[SERVICES: D,L,P,R,S,SB] Publishes *PWA Coalition Newsletter* (monthly) and the *NYC Metropolitan AIDS Resource Directory*. (EA)

▶ ALCOHOL AND DRUGS (*See also*: Maternal and Child Health)

X42 and X43 (university based) and X44 (operated by the federal government) will compile custom bibliographies on any alcohol or drug related topic on request.

X42.   Center for Alcohol Studies: Information Services Division, Rutgers University, Piscataway, NJ 08903.

[SERVICES: B,DB] Operates the *Drug Information and Alcohol Use Data Base*.

X43.   Drug Information Services: University of Minnesota, 3-160 Health Sciences Center, Unit F, 308 Harvard Suite, SE, Minneapolis, MN 55455. PH: (612)624-6492.

[SERVICES: B,DB]

X44.   National Clearinghouse for Alcohol and Drug Information: P.O. Box 2345, Rockville, MD 20852. PH: (301)468-2600.

[SERVICES: AV,B,DB,L,P,R,S] Gathers and disseminates current information on alcohol and drug related subjects. Conducts subject searches of its on-line database IDA (*Information on Drugs and Alcohol*), which includes both prevention materials and traditional bibliographic resources. Their library is open to the public and contains materials on all aspects of alcohol and drug abuse. (FIC)

—— GAY AND LESBIAN

X45.   International Advisory Council on Homosexual Men and Women in Alcoholics Anonymous: P.O. Box 90, Washington, DC 20044-0090. PH: (310)436-7884.

[SERVICES: C,P,R,SG] Network of gay and lesbian A.A. groups worldwide. Publishes *Directory of AA Meetings for Gays/Lesbians*. (EA)

X46.   National Association of Lesbian/Gay Alcoholism Professionals: 204 W. 20th St., New York, NY 10011. PH: (212)713-5074.

[SERVICES: B,C,L,P,SB] A network of individuals and organizations working with chemically dependent gays and lesbians. Their information clearinghouse distributes reprints of articles on addiction as it pertains to homosexuality. Publishes: *NALGAP Annotated Bibliography* (see H16); *National Directory of Facilities and Services for Gay Alcoholics*; and *NALGAP Reporter*, a quarterly newsletter. (EA)

➤ ALTERNATIVE LIFESTYLES (*See also*: Non-Monogamy; Nudism; Sadomasochism; Sexual Freedom)

X47.   All Together: c/o Lloyd M. Levin, 120 Eastman, Suite 207, Arlington Heights, IL 60004. PH: (708)398-5525.

[SERVICES: L,S,SB] Central resource for people engaging in or researching alternative lifestyles, including "gays, swingers, cohabitants, bisexuals,

---

HOW TO FIND

• *Alternative Lifestyles* (see p.338), includes full descriptions of 10 special collections on alternative lifestyles.

• *The 1990/91 Directory of Intentional Communities: A Guide to Cooperative Living* (Stelle, IL: Community Publications Cooperative, 1990), describes 350 intentional communities worldwide. Those involved in sexually alternative lifestyles are indexed by "sexual relationship predominating." The directory was also published as issue no.77/78 of *Communities Magazine* (Stelle, IL: Communities Publication Coop).

---

singles, divorced people, new women." Maintains a clipping file of book reviews and newspaper and magazine articles on alternative lifestyles. (EA)

X48.   **Center for Communal Studies**: University of Southern California, 8600 University Blvd., Evansville, IN 47712. PH: (812)464-1727.

[SERVICES: C,DB,L] Promotes the establishment of cooperative communal living groups and public understanding and acceptance of "intentional communities." Their research collection covers 90 historical and 350 contemporary communal groups, making it the most comprehensive collection on modern communal living in the U.S. Publishes the *Directory of Intentional Communities* every 2-3 years. (EA)

X49.   **The Lifestyle Organization**: 2641 W. LaPalma, Suite A, Anaheim, CA 92801. PH: (714)821-9953.

[SERVICES: C,D,L,P,R] Membership organizations of persons engaged in alternative sexual lifestyles, including those involved in communes and "swinging." Holds two annual conventions: *Couples* and the *International Lifestyles Convention*, both of which include exhibits of related products, services, books, publications, and organizations. Participation lists, programs, abstracts, and audio cassettes of presentations are available for conferences held since 1977. Publishes *NASCA Inside Report: For Those Who Want More Than Just One Bite* (see K97). See also X155. (EA)

➤ ARCHIVES AND SPECIAL COLLECTIONS

The following archives contain materials on a range of sexuality topics. (See also the specialized libraries described in Ch.1.) Topic-specific archives are described under relevant subject heading.

HOW TO FIND

• Jefferson P. Selth's *Alternative Lifestyles: A Guide to Research Collections on Intentional Communities, Nudism and Sexual Freedom* (Westport, CT: Greenwood, 1985) fully describes 36 libraries and special collections in the U.S. "which would be useful to the research in three kinds of alternative lifestyles: the contemporary secular intentional community, nudism and sexual freedom." It includes detailed descriptions of their history, holdings, public access, services, and bibliographic access.

X50.   Bullough Collection on Human Sexuality: Oviatt Library Special Collection Department, California State University, Northridge, 18111 Nordhoff St., Northridge, CA 91330. PH: (818)885-2832.

[SERVICES: L] 1,800 books and other materials on all aspects of human sexuality, with especially strong collections in prostitution, homosexuality, and transvestism. (SL)

X51.   Center for the Study of Human Sexuality: Montclair State College, Upper Montclair, NJ 07043. PH: (201)655-4336.

[SERVICES: L] A general collection on all aspects of sexuality, including artistic, sociological, biological, psychological, and anthropological.

X52.   New York Academy of Medicine: 2 E. 103rd St., New York, NY 10029. PH: (212)876-8200.

A private, non-lending, research library, open to the public without fee. The collection includes four categories of books on sexuality related topics: contemporary books, emphasizing the medical and psychiatric aspects of sexuality, shelved with the main collection; 2,200 volumes by major authors (largely psychology of sex and marriage, and erotica), most published between 1900 and 1939; approximately 600 volumes published between 1950 and 1977; and approximately 100 oversized books. (See also H55). All are cataloged, but many of the older items are now in storage, with access granted on a case-by-case basis. Contact the Acting Librarian for more information. (See p.338 for a description of the unique history of the collection.)

—— GAY AND LESBIAN ARCHIVES

HOW TO FIND

• Consult directories (see B61, B62). *Lesbian Periodicals Index* (see H59) lists 46 libraries and archives with extensive holdings of lesbian periodicals and other items. The Gay and Lesbian Task Force of the American Library Association distributes the directory *Gay and Lesbian Archives and Libraries in North America* (see X53). The *Directory of the International Association of Lesbian and Gay Archives and Libraries* (Toronto, Ontario: International Association of Lesbian and Gay Archives and Libraries, 1987) describes 12 libraries nationwide. F17 also discusses such collections.

X53. **American Library Association / Social Responsibilities Round Table / Gay and Lesbian Task Force Clearinghouse**: c/o ALA, Office of Library Outreach Services, 50 Huron, Chicago, IL 60611. PH: (800)545-2433.

[SERVICES: B,C,L,P] Supports the dissemination of materials concerning gays and lesbians into libraries and to library patrons. Maintains a 2,000 volume information clearinghouse and publishes the *GLTF Newsletter* (see K76); bibliographies on homosexuality, lesbianism, feminism, and gay rights; and many directories and resource guides, including *Gay and Lesbian Archives and Special Collections in North America*, *Gay Resources for Religious Study*, *Gays and Lesbians/Libraries & Archives: A Checklist of Publications 1972-1989*; *Publishers of Gay and Lesbian Books*; *Recipients of the Gay/Lesbian Book Award 1971-1989*, *Gays and Lesbians on Stage: How to Find Gay/Lesbian Plays*; *Bookstores and Mail Order Firms Specializing in Gay and Lesbian Books: A Directory*. A complete publication list is available on request. See also, p.121. (EA,SL)

X54.   Blanche M. Baker Memorial Library: 3340 Country Club Drive, Los Angeles, CA 90019. PH: (213)735-5252.

[SERVICES: B,L] Affiliated with the ONE Institute (see X122). The library, founded in 1953, holds over 24,000 volumes, an extensive periodical collection (with 250 current subscriptions), 350 feet of vertical files, and 60 drawers of primary documents on homosexuality, lesbianism, and the homophile and gay liberation movement. Open by appointment. (SL)

X55.   Homosexual Information Center—Library / Archive: 151 Monroe St., Bossier City, LA 71111-4539. PH: (318)742-4709.

[SERVICES: B,C,L,P,R,SB] Collects materials on homosexuality, civil liberties, prostitution, and sexual freedom, dating back to the beginnings of the U.S. homosexual rights movement in the 1940s. Holdings include 9,800 books and bound periodicals, plus manuscripts, documents, clippings, pamphlets, legal briefs, and court opinions. Publishes a newsletter, reading lists, subject heading guides, and *A Selected Bibliography of Homosexuality*, citing materials reflecting all perspectives (i.e. pro, con, religious, political, medical, etc.). The *Directory of Homosexual Organizations and Publications: A Field Guide to the Homosexual Movement in the United States and Canada with Topical Index* was issued regularly from the early 1960s to 1985; back issues provide a historical record of the development of the homosexual rights movement in this country. For more information and referrals, contact the Information Center: Box 8252, Universal City, CA 91608. (SL)

X56.   International Gay/Lesbian Archives: 626 N. Robertson, West Hollywood, CA 90038. PH: (213)854-0271.

X57.   Labadie Collection: Dept. of Rare Books and Special Collections, University of Michigan, Ann Arbor, MI 48109.

A collection of over 40,000 serials and pamphlets representing the homosexual protest movement prior to its official designation as "gay/lesbian liberation." The catalog of the collection is accessible on-line as a file in the University of Michigan's on-line library catalog.

X58.   Lesbian and Gay Archives / Naiad Press Inc.: Box 10543, Tallahassee, FL 32302. PH: (904)539-5965.

[SERVICES: L] Holds over 300 videotapes, 18,000 books, thousands of bound periodicals, manuscripts, newspaper clippings, and more. Currently subscribes to 62 journals and 111 newsletters. (SL)

X59. **Lesbian Herstory Educational Foundation Archive**: Box 1258, New York, NY 10116. PH: (212)874-7232.

[SERVICES: B,DB,L,P] Claiming to be the largest and oldest lesbian archive in the world, the foundation is dedicated to documenting, collecting, and preserving all aspects of lesbian history and culture, including evidence of both lesbian oppression and liberation. In 1989 the collection contained over 6,000 books and 13,000 periodicals titles; 12,000 photographs; 500 unpublished papers; ephemera (e.g. posters, art work, buttons, T-shirts); 12,000 photographs, films, records, videotapes, and audiotapes; 30 file drawers organized by topic (e.g. Butch/Fem, Lesbians in Africa, Lesbian Theater, etc.); and a collection of letters, diaries, snapshots, and other memorabilia. A database is under development. The archives are open to the public by appointment. (EA,SL)

X60. **Quatrefoil Library**: 1619 Dayton Ave., Suite 105, St. Paul, MN 55104-6208. PH: (612)641-0969.

[SERVICES: L] A private lending library in St. Paul, Minnesota holding over 5,000 books, newspapers, and magazines published since 1946, as well as videotapes, audiotapes, and sound recordings. Members have circulation privileges. (SL)

▶ BIOETHICS (*See also*: specific topics [e.g. Abortion, Fertility, etc.]; X250)

X61. **National Reference Center for Bioethic Literature**: Kennedy Institute of Ethics, Georgetown University, Washington, DC 20057. PH: (800)MED-ETHX.

[SERVICES: B,D,DB,L,P] Collects materials on contemporary biomedical issues in the fields of ethics, philosophy, medicine, science, law, religion, and the social sciences. Among the topics addressed are sexuality, contraception, abortion, population, reproductive technologies, genetics, and fetal experimentation (see J16 and H19 for more details). The library includes over 16,000 books; over 80,000 journal and newspaper articles and 200 periodical subscriptions; laws, regulations, and court decisions; and government publications. They maintain the biographical database BIOETHICSLINE (see J16) and the Bioethics Curriculum Clearinghouse, an international collection of syllabi from universities and health centers.

Publications include the quarterly *Scope Note Series* (1982-), each issue of which includes an introductory essay and annotated bibliography on a particular biomedical ethics topic; *Bibliography of Bioethics* (see H19); *New Titles in Bioethics*, a quarterly update of new books on biomedical, philosophical, religious, and applied ethics; *International Directory of Bio-Ethics Organizations* (1987), a geographically arranged directory of 124 organizations (56 in the U.S. and 68 elsewhere) concerned with bioethical issues; and *Kennedy Institute of Ethics Journal* (see K20). (EA,SL,RC)

➤ BISEXUALITY

X62.   Bay Area Bisexual Network: 2404 California St., Box 24, San Francisco, CA 94115. PH: (415)564-BABN.

[SERVICES: B,C,D,P,R,SB] Publishes *Anything that Moves: Beyond the Myths of Bisexuality* (see K22) and a bibliography.

X63.   East Coast Bisexual Network at the Center: 338 Newbury, Boston, MA 02115. PH: (617)BIS-MOVE.

[SERVICES: D,P,R,SG] Publishes the biannual *International Directory of Bisexual Groups*, a comprehensive list of bi groups and their publications worldwide.

X64.   National Bisexual Network (BiNet): c/o The Center, 584 Castro St., Box 441, San Francisco, CA 94114. PH: (415)775-1990

[SERVICES: C,P,R].

➤ CHILDBIRTH

— ALTERNATIVE CHILDBIRTH

The following organizations provide education and training for parents and childbirth educators/birth assistants, educate the public on alternative childbearing techniques and family centered maternity care, and seek to reform childbirth practices and the treatment of mothers and newborns. All provide information on the various childbirth practices and techniques available to parents in hospitals, birth centers, and the home.

X65. **American Society for Psychoprophylaxis in Obstetrics (ASPO/LAMAZE)**: Connecticut Ave., NW, Suite 700, Washington, DC 20036. PH: (800)368-4404.

[SERVICES: C,P,R,S] 5,000 members including parents, physicians, nurse-midwives, LAMAZE certified childbirth educators, and other professionals interested in the Lamaze method of childbirth preparation. Serves as an international information clearinghouse on the theory and application of psychoprophylaxis in obstetrics. Publishes *Genesis*, a bimonthly newsletter which includes book and film reviews. (EA)

X66. **Association for Child Birth at Home International**: P.O. Box 430, Glendale, CA 91209. PH: (213)663-4996.

[SERVICES: C,L,P,R,SB] 30,000 parents, midwives, childbirth educators, and others supporting home births. Maintains a 500 volume reference library, and provides international resource referrals. (EA)

X67. **Childbirth Education Foundation**: P.O. Box 5, Richboro, PA 18954. PH: (215)357-2792.

[SERVICES: AV,B,C,D,L,P,R,S,SB] (EA)

X68. **Informed Homebirth/Informed Birth and Parenting**: P.O. Box 3675, Ann Arbor, MI 48106. PH: (313)662-6857.

[SERVICES: AV,C,P,R] (EA)

X69. **International Association of Parents and Professionals for Safe Alternatives in Childbirth**: Rt. 1, Box 646, Marble Hill, MO 63764. PH: (314)238-2010.

[SERVICES: AV,C,DB,P,R] 30,000 parents, nurses, physicians, midwives, social workers, and childbirth educators in 20 countries, dedicated to "exploring, examining, implementing, and establishing family-centered childbirth programs which meet the needs of families as well as provide the safe aspects of medical science." Publishes the annual *NAPSAC Directory of Alternative Birth Services and Consumer Guide*, and *NAPSAC News*, a quarterly newsletter. (EA)

X70. **International Childbirth Education Association**: P.O. Box 20048, Minneapolis, MN 55420. PH: (612)854-8660.

[SERVICES: A,C,D,P] 12,000 cesarean educators, childbirth educators, counselors, homebirth specialists, nurses, nurse-midwives, obstetricians, gynecologists, parent educators, pediatricians, physical therapists, and others involved in family centered maternity care. Operates a mail order bookstore (see L17). Publishes the annual *ICEA Membership Directory*; *ICEA Newsletter*, containing an events calendar, and research updates on issues relating to parent education, pregnancy, labor, and birth; and the *International Journal of Childbirth Education* (see K29). (EA)

—— BIRTH PSYCHOLOGY

X71.   Association for Birth Psychology: 444 E. 82nd St., New York, NY 10028. PH: (212)988-6617.

[SERVICES: C,L,P] Interdisciplinary, multi-professional association of pediatricians, midwifes, psychologists, nurses, psychotherapists, social workers, counselors, obstetricians, sociologists, and others interested in birth psychology (i.e. the experience of birth, and the relationship between birth experiences and personality development). Seeks to establish birth psychology as an autonomous field of study and encourages multi-disciplinary research and theory. Maintains resource lists. Publishes *Birth Psychology Bulletin*, a semiannual journal covering the period from conception through the first year of life, including book reviews, case studies, research reports, and an events calendar. (EA)

X72.   International Society of Prenatal and Perinatal Psychology and Medicine: Engelbrektsgatania, S-114, 32 Stockholm, Sweden. PH: 8-213419. FAX: 8-202743.

[SERVICES: C,P,S] Conducts research on psychological experiences and influences before, during, and immediately after birth. Maintains a subject classified, international bibliography and document center containing data, research reports, publications, and audiovisuals. Correspondence is conducted in English.

—— CESAREAN BIRTHS

X73.   C/Sec (Cesarean/Support Education and Concerns): 22 Forest Rd., Framingham, MA 01701. PH: (508)877-8266.

[SERVICES: AV,B,C,D,P,R] Offers information and support services to parents and professionals regarding cesarean childbirth, cesarean prevention, and vaginal birth after cesarean. Publications include: *C/Sec Newsletter* (quarterly), containing resource lists, book reviews, an events calendar, and research updates; a periodic membership list; *Preventing Unnecessary Cesareans: A Guide to Labor Management and Detailed Bibliography*; *Labor and Vaginal Delivery After Cesarean Birth: A Survey of Contemporary Opinion*, consisting of 47 abstracts from the professional literature on vaginal birth after cesarean; and *Frankly Speaking: A Book for Cesarean Parents*, which includes a six page resource list of organizations, print resources, and audiovisuals. (EA)

X74.   Cesarean Prevention Movement: P.O. Box 152, Syracuse, NY 13210. PH: (315)424-1942.

[SERVICES: C,L,P,R,S] Concerned with increasing cesarean birth rates in the U.S. Promotes vaginal birth after cesarean and cesarean prevention. Publishes *The Clarion*, a quarterly newsletter containing articles, book reviews, and organization news. (EA)

—— POST-PARTUM DEPRESSION

X75.   Depression After Delivery (D.A.D.): P.O. Box 1282, Morrisville, PA 19067. PH: (215)295-3994.

[SERVICES: C,P,R] Information clearinghouse on postpartum adjustment problems (i.e. depression, blues, anxiety, postpartum psychosis). (EA)

X76.   Marce Society: c/o Dr. Michael O'Hara, Department of Psychology, University of Iowa, Iowa City, IA.

[SERVICES: C,P] Seeks to improve the understanding, prevention, and treatment of child-bearing related mental illness. Publishes *Marce Bulletin*, containing news, articles, and reviews of recent scientific research.

X77.   Postpartum Support International: 27 N. Kellogg Ave., Santa Barbara, CA 93111. PH: (805)967-7636.

[SERVICES: C,P,R,SG] An umbrella organization of postpartum depression self-help groups. Works to increase awareness among the public and professionals of the emotional changes women often experience during pregnancy and postpartum, and provides current information on the diagnosis and treatment of postpartum mental illness and other mental health issues related to childbearing. Publishes *PSI News*. (EA)

—— PROFESSIONAL ASSOCIATIONS

X78.   American College of Nurse Midwifes: 1522 K St., NW, Suite 1000, Washington, DC 20005. PH: (202)289-0171.

[SERVICES: C,D,P] (EA)

X79.   American Society of Childbirth Educators: P.O. Box 1630, Sedona, AZ 86336. PH: (602)284-9897.

[SERVICES: C,D,P] (EA)

X80.   Midwives Alliance of North America: P.O. Box 1121, Bristol, VA 24203. PH: (615)764-5561.

[SERVICES: C,D,P] (EA)

X81.   National Association of Childbirth Assistants: 205 Copco Ln., San Jose, CA 95126. PH: (408)225-9167.

[SERVICES: D] (EA)

➤ CIRCUMCISION

X82.   National Organization of Circumcision Information Resource Centers (NOCIRC): P.O. Box 2512, San Anselmo, CA 94979. PH: (415)488-9883.

[SERVICES: C,L,P,R,S,SB,SG] Umbrella organization of circumcision information centers nationwide. Provides information on the historical, cultural, religious, medical, legal, and ethical aspects of routine infant circumcision and female genital mutilation, with the ultimate goal of eradicating both practices. Sponsors an annual International Symposium on Circumcision. Publishes a bi-annual membership directory, and *NOCIRC Newsletter*, containing statistics, medical and legal information on routine infant circumcision in the U.S., audiovisual and book reviews, research study announcements, and a directory of support groups.

X83.   UNCircumcision Information and Resources Center: c/o Jim Bigelow, 315 Congress Ave., Pacific Grove, CA 93950.

[SERVICES: P,R,SG] Provides information on foreskin restoration and reconstruction. Publishes *The Joy of Uncircumcision: Restoring Your Birthright for Maximum Sexual Pleasure*. For information on support groups for men interested in or undergoing foreskin restoration, send a S.A.S.E. to R. Wayne Griffiths, 3205 Northwood Drive, Suite 209, Concord, CA 94520. (EA)

X84. Non-Circumcision Educational Foundation: P.O. Box 5, Richboro, PA 18954. PH: (215)357-2792.

[SERVICES: AV,C,L,P,S,SB] Opposed to routine infant circumcision and other medical procedures on newborns it considers to be unnecessary. Maintains an extensive library on infant circumcision, childbirth, and infant/newborn care. (EA)

X85. Population Crisis Committee—Library: Draper Fund, 1120 19th St., NW, Suite 550, Washington, DC 20036. PH: (202)659-1833.

[SERVICES: L] Library includes a special collection on female circumcision. (EA,SL)

➤ CONSERVATIVE / TRADITIONALISTS (*See also*: Abortion–Anti-Abortion; Bioethics; X2, X225, X247, X250)

HOW TO FIND

• Consult the annual *Guide to the American Right: Directory and Bibliography* (Olathe, KS: Laird Wilcox), a geographically arranged listing of over 2,000 conservative and right wing organizations and publishers. Entries include the special interests of each, and their major political or philosophical affiliations.

X86. Human Life International: 7845 E. Airpark Rd., Gaithesburg, MD 20879. PH: (301)670-7884.

[SERVICES: C,L,P,S,SB] 500,000 members. "International research, educational, and service program offering positive alternatives to the worldwide anti-life/anti-family movement. It aims to explore and clarify all dimensions of the human life issue through research, publications, and sponsored conferences, national and international—with particular emphasis on Christian sexuality, natural family planning, and all forms of mechanical and medical fertility control means and programs, including abortion, infanticide, and euthanasia." Compiles statistics on contraception, sterilization, abortion (including post-abortion stress), euthanasia, sex education, marriage preparation, natural family planning, and chastity promotion in 111 countries. Their library holds over 1,000 volumes and 70 subscriptions addressing sociological, philosophical, and theological perspectives on these issues. Distributes pro-life, pro-family literature, videos, and films through their *Human Life International Pro-Life/Family Catalog* (see L2). Publishes *HLI Reporter* (monthly) and *Sorrows Reward*, a quarterly newsletter reporting worldwide research on post-abortion syndrome. (SL, EA)

X87.   Human Life Center: University of Steubenville, Steubenville, OH 43952. PH: (614)282-9953.

[SERVICES: B,DB,L,P,R,SB] Resource center for pro-life individuals and organizations, supporting Christian moral and social teaching on marriage and family issues, sexuality, family planning, abortion, and related subjects. Maintains a 4,000 volume library which includes an extensive collection of pro-life organizations' publications. Publishes *Human Life Issues* (see K36) and *International Review* (see K38). (EA,SL,RC)

X88.   National Pro Family Coalition: 717 2nd St., NE, Washington, DC 20002. PH: (202)546-3003.

[SERVICES: R] Coalition of 2,000 local, state, and national pro-family, pro-decency, pro-morality, and pro-life organizations seeking to achieve a "just and humane society functioning in accordance with the moral imperatives of the Judeo-Christian ethic." (EA)

➤ CONTRACEPTIVE METHODS (*See also*: Family Planning; Maternal and Child Health; Population; Women's Health; X18, X170, X197)

X89.   Contraceptive and Reproductive Evaluation Branch / Contraceptive Development Branch: Center for Population Research, 9000 Rockville Pike, Bldg. 6100, Bethesda, MD 20814. PH: (301)496-4924 (evaluation); (301)496-1661 (development).

Branches of the National Institute of Child Health and Human Development's Center for Population Research (see X197). The Contraception Evaluation Branch supports programs to study the safety and effectiveness of fertility control methods—including drugs, devices

> ## HOW TO FIND
>
> • To locate manufacturers of contraceptive devices, consult the *Medical Devices Register, Thomas Manufacturer's Register* (both available in libraries), or the *Health Device Sourcebook* (see B65).
>
> • A customer service number is indicated on the package of most over-the-counter contraceptives (i.e. sponges, condoms, spermicides).

and surgical procedures—and provides ongoing surveillance of their effectiveness; call for referrals to the staff person examining a particular birth control method. The Contraceptive Development Branch works to develop new methods of fertility control. (FIC)

X90.   Food and Drug Administration / Office of Consumer Affairs: 5600 Fishers Lane (HFE-88), Rockville, MD 20857. PH: (301)443-3170.

[SERVICES: B,DB,L,P,R,S] The Office of Consumer Affairs is responsible for handling consumer inquiries of the Food and Drug Administration. Inquiries are referred to the appropriate agency offices for reply or are answered by OCA staff, utilizing data from agency offices and agency publications. For more technical information, they will provide referrals to specific FDA programs, such as the Center for Drug Evaluation and Research, National Center for Drugs and Biologics, Bureau of Medical Devices, etc. These and other FDA programs develop, implement, and evaluate standards for the safety, effectiveness, and labeling of drugs and medical devices; coordinate research and evaluation of drugs and medical devices, including maintaining surveillance over contraceptive drugs (e.g. spermicides, birth control pills) and contraceptive devices (e.g. condoms, sponges); and assist in legal actions concerning medical devices (e.g. Dalkon Shield). Maintains a library open to the public. (FIC)

— CONDOMS

X91.   Condom Resource Center: P.O. Box 30564, Oakland, CA 94604. PH: (510)891-0455.

[SERVICES: P] Coordinates National Condom Week (Feb.14-21). Acts as a resource center on all aspects of condom education.

X92.   Condom Sense: 2487 Burnt Leaf Lane, Decatur, GA 30033. PH: (404)634-2570.

—— CONTRACEPTIVE DEVICES *(See also*: X90; p.349)

X93.   International Dalkon Shield Victims Education Association: 527 Pioneer Bldg., Seattle, WA 98104. PH: (206)329-1371.

[SERVICES: C,P,SB] Provides support for women who have been made sick or injured through use of the Dalkon Shield I.U.D.; advocacy; and public education. (EA)

—— CONTRACEPTIVE DRUGS *(See also*: X90)

HOW TO FIND

• Contact contraceptive drug manufacturers. *Directory of Hormonal Contraceptives* (London: International Planned Parenthood Federation, 1988) is a directory of the 10 major manufacturers of hormonal contraceptives worldwide. (Order from A8.) Entries include drug's brand names, hormonal composition, and availability. All manufacturers maintain education/customer service departments that can provide additional information. For information on Norplant implants—the new hormonal contraceptive inserted in capsule form under the skin of the woman's upper arm—contact the American manufacturer, Wyeth-Ayerst Laboratories in Philadelphia, or X170.

—— NATURAL FAMILY PLANNING *(See also*: X109)

There are a number of both religiously based and non religiously based organizations promoting natural family planning; X94 can provide referrals to both.

X94.   Fertility Awareness Services: 2857 NW Tyler, P.O. Box 986, Corvallis, OR 97339. PH: (503)753-8530.

[SERVICES: B,L,P,S] An information clearinghouse on all methods of fertility awareness, providing education and counseling on fertility awareness for birth control or achieving pregnancy. Publishes the *Fertility Awareness and Natural Family Planning Resource Directory* and many pamphlets and books.

—— STERILIZATION

X95.   Association for Voluntary Surgical Contraception Inc.: 122 E. 42nd St., New York, NY 10168. PH: (212)351-2500.

[SERVICES: AV,C,L,P,S,SB] Seeks to make safe, effective, voluntary surgical contraception available worldwide. Operates an information clearinghouse on all aspects of voluntary sterilization, including research on related medical, legal, educational, psychological, ethical, socio-economic, and public health issues. Their library holds over 3,000 volumes, over 80 feet of vertical files, and subscribes to over 100 journals and other serials. Provides annual estimates of male and female voluntary sterilization in the United States. Publishes *AVSC News*, a quarterly newsletter containing updates on research, legal issues, and new sterilization technologies. (EA, SL)

▶ CONTROVERSIAL ISSUES / PUBLIC AFFAIRS (*See also*: X61) Many sexuality issues fall within the public affairs arena, including abortion, AIDS, adolescent sexuality, birth control, censorship, child abuse, gay rights, marriage, pornography, rape, prostitution, reproductive technologies, sexual freedom, sodomy laws, sex education, and sexually transmitted diseases—see the resources listed under the topic of interest.

HOW TO FIND

• Consult the *Encyclopedia of Public Affairs Information Sources* (Detroit: Gale Research, 1988), a bibliographic guide to approximately 8,000 citations for publications, organizations, and other sources of information on nearly 300 public affairs subjects.

• Dushkin's *Taking Sides: Clashing Views on Controversial Issues* series (Guilford, CT: Dushkin Publishing) includes volumes on human sexuality (edited by Robert Francoeur and in its 4th edition), bioethical issues, and moral issues, among others. Each provides students with carefully considered and sharply opposed viewpoints in the form of pro and contra essays. Each chapter includes a concise introduction to the issue, a summary postscript, a bibliography of suggested readings, and a list of relevant organizations.

➤ CROSS CULTURAL RESEARCH

HOW TO FIND

• Contact the World Association of Sexology (see X192) or the International Academy of Sex Research (see X186) for information on organizations of sex professionals worldwide (e.g. Asian Federation for Sexology).

• Consult the annual *Encyclopedia of Associations: International Organizations* (Detroit: Gale Research).

X96.   Human Relations Area Files Inc.: 755 Prospect St., New Haven, CT 06511. PH: (202)777-2334.

[SERVICES: B,L,P] "An international, not-for-profit research and educational organization which facilitates the comparative study of human behavior, society, and culture" by maintaining and disseminating the HRAF Cultural Information Archive, a collection of historical and descriptive data on the cultures of the world. For sex subjects covered in the archives, see the *Outline of Cultural Materials*, C7. Constantly expanding, the collection currently holds over 780,000 pages of information from 7,000 source documents, on over 340 cultures of the world, including ethnic, national and religious groups. The entire collection is available on microfiche in many libraries (see J14) and a portion of it—1,000 anthropological, sociological, and psychological articles focusing on all aspects of life in 60 selected societies worldwide during the 19th c. and 20th c.—is available on compact disc as the *Human Relations Area Files Data Archives*. Five volumes, each consisting of two CDs, are planned, including v.1 Human Sexuality/Marriage. (EA, SL)

➤ DISABILITY AND ILLNESS *(See also:*Aging; Reproductive Health; Women's Health; D9, D10)

X101-X103 provide information on all aspects of disability and illness, including sex and reproduction. The Xandria Collection (see X265) distributes a special edition of their catalog of sexual aids directed towards disabled people and couples. Many medical associations (see p.386) distribute specialized literature (e.g. *Sexuality and Cancer: For the Woman Who Has Cancer and Her Partner* [from the American Cancer Society],

Sex, Courtship, and the Ostemate [from the United Ostomy Association]).

HOW TO FIND

- SEICUS's bibliography *Sexuality and the Developmentally Disabled* (see H46), includes a list of relevant organizations and hospital based training programs.

X97.   **Coalition on Sexuality and Disability**: 122 E. 23rd St., New York, NY 10010. PH: (212)242-3900.

[SERVICES: C,P,R,SB] Provides professional training, information, and advocacy regarding sexuality and sexual health care for people with any type of disability or illness which interferes with sexual functioning. Publications include: *Coalition Newsletter* (quarterly) (see K47); and *The Sexual Rights of Persons with Developmental Disabilities*. (EA)

X98.   **Planned Parenthood of SE Pennsylvania**: 1144 Locust St., Philadelphia, PA 19107-5740. PH: (215)351-5590.

X99.   **Sexuality and Developmental Disability Network**: SIECCAN, 850 Coxwell Ave., East York, Ontario M4C 5R1, Canada. PH: (416)466-5304.

X100.   **Task Force on Sexuality and Disability**: American Congress of Rehabilitation Medicine, 130 S. Michigan Ave., Suite 1310, Chicago, IL 60603. PH: (804)786-9055.

X101.   **National Center for Youth with Disabilities**: University of Minnesota, Adolescent Health Program, Box 721-UMHC, Harvard St. at E. River Rd., Minneapolis, MN 55455. PH: (800)333-6293.

[SERVICES: B,DB,L,P,R,S] Works with adolescents and young adults with chronic illness and developmental disabilities. Maintains the National Resource Library on Youth with Disabilities. Publishes *CYDLINE Reviews*, an annotated bibliography series; and *Connections*, a quarterly newsletter reporting current research on key issues and reviews of educational programs and resources. (EA)

X102.   National Information Center for Children and Youth with Disabilities: P.O. Box 1492, Washington, DC 20013. PH: (800)999-5599 / (703)893-6061.

[SERVICES: DB,P,R] National information clearinghouse authorized by Congress under the Education for Handicapped Act to assist parents, educators, caregivers, advocates, and others working to improve the lives of children and youth with physical, mental, or emotional disabilities. Services include responding to specific questions, referrals to organizations or other resources, and technical assistance to parents and professional groups. Develops and distributes fact sheets and issues briefs on current topics, and *NICHY: News Digest*, each quarterly issue of which focuses on a single topic, and other publications. (EA, FIC)

X103.   National Rehabilitation Information Center: 8455 Colesville Rd., Suite 935, Silver Spring, MD 20910-3319. PH: (800)346-2742.

[SERVICES: DB,L,P,R] A service of the U.S. Department of Education's National Institute on Disability and Rehabilitation. An information clearinghouse on all types of disabilities, including sensory, physical, mental, psychiatric, and developmental ones. Their library holds research reports, conference proceedings, books, journals, and audiovisuals. Creates custom bibliographies from commercially available databases and their own on-line database, REHABDATA (accessible to the public through BRS). Publishes fact sheets, resource guides, research reports, and technical publications, including a *Directory of Libraries and Information Specialists in Disability and Rehabilitation* and the *NARIC Guide to Disability and Rehabilitation Periodicals*. (EA, FIC)

— SOCIAL

X104.   Handicap Introductions: 1215 Brigantine Rd., Manahawkin, NJ 08050. PH: (609)660-0606.

[SERVICES: SB] Dating/introduction service for the physically disabled. (EA)

▶ EROTICA (*See also*: for producers of erotic films, see Ch.27)

See "Pornography" for organizations concerned with the social and legal issues relating to pornography, obscenity, and censorship.

HOW TO FIND

• The Kinsey Institute Archives (see A4, especially p.10) hold a 25,000 item erotica collection, which includes videos and films (see also p.296), books, magazines, comic books and pamphlets, vulgar songs, bawdy songbooks, and art from around the world. F20 contains a complete description of the collection. (See also p.200, p.203.)

• *Erotic Writer's and Collector's Market* (Sun Valley, NV: Michael Drax), published semi-annually, includes a directory of publishers and producers of erotica, videos, audio tapes, and computer software, and sex clubs nationwide. To order: Box 20593, Sun Valley, NV 89433.

X105. **Adult Video Association**: 270 N. Canon Dr., Suite 1370, Beverly Hills, CA 90210. PH: (818)882-6323.

[SERVICES: C,P,R,SB] Trade organization for those involved in the "adult" video industry, including performers, distributors, producers, directors, and retailers. Dedicated to preserving the right of adults to create, distribute, and enjoy adult entertainment. Provides legal information and referrals. (EA)

X106. **Fans of X Rated Entertainment (F.O.X.E.)**: 8033 Sunset Blvd., Suite 851, Los Angeles, CA 90046. PH: (213)650-7121 / (213)656-6545.

Worldwide anti-censorship and fan participation organization for those who like to watch adult video tapes. Dues help support the legal activities of the Adult Video Association (see X105). Director William Margold has been involved in the X-rated film/video industry as an actor, producer, director, and activist, and can provide information and referrals on all aspects of the industry.

▶ FAMILY PLANNING (*See also*: Adolescent Sexuality–Teen Pregnancy; Contraception; Population; Reproduction; X197, X253; p.367)

X107. **Family Health International**: P.O. Box 13950, Research Triangle Park, NC 27709. PH: (914)544-7040.

[SERVICES: DB,L,P,S] Conducts, analyzes, and disseminates research on contraception and family planning, with the goal of increasing availability,

---

HOW TO FIND

• Under the heading "Birth Control" in the *Directory of Special Libraries and Information Centers* are listed a number of archives holding materials on the history of the U.S. birth control movement.

• Consult directories. The *World List of Family Planning Addresses* (New York: International Planned Parenthood Federation, 1991-) is a geographically arranged, annual directory of national family planning associations in over 150 countries—order from A8. *Non-Governmental Organizations in International Population and Family Planning* (Washington: Population Crisis Committee, 1988) describes 100 population and family planning organizations worldwide.

---

acceptance, safety, effectiveness, and ease of use of family planning methods. Maintains a library on reproductive medicine, AIDS, breast cancer, contraception, population, and family planning, holding over 5,500 books, 9,000 reprints and unpublished documents, and 800 volumes of periodicals (with over 700 current subscriptions). Annual publication catalog. (EA, SL)

X108. Family Life Information Exchange: P.O. Box 37299, Washington, DC 20013-7299. PH: (301)585-6636.

[SERVICES: B,DB,P,R,S] Federally contracted program under the jurisdiction of the Department of Health and Human Services' Office of Population Affairs. Collects and disseminates information and statistics on family planning and related topics, including adolescent pregnancy, reproductive health, STDs, contraception, and adoption. Although its primary clients are federally supported service agencies, it also provides information to family planning service providers, educators, trainers, and consumers throughout the U.S. Their 5,000 volume research library is open to the public by appointment. Publishes *Adolescent Family Life Project Summaries*, containing summaries of demonstration projects, summaries of adolescent family life prevention curricula, and summaries of research projects on adolescent sexual behavior, adoption, adolescent pregnancy and parenting. It also distributes patient and professional education materials produced by the DHHS. (FIC)

X109. Los Angeles Regional Family Planning Council—Library: 3600 Wilshire Blvd., Suite 600, Los Angeles, CA 90010-5614. PH: (213)386-5614.

[SERVICES: AV,B,L] The library holds over 1,500 books, 400 audiovisual programs, and extensive vertical files; and currently subscribes to 70 journals. Materials address issues of reproductive health, sexually transmitted diseases, birth control, family life education, and natural family planning. They distribute film and audiovisual catalogs and annotated bibliographies. (SL)

X110. National Family Planning and Reproductive Health Association: 122 C St., NW, Suite 380, Washington, DC 20001. PH: (800)5NF-PRHA.

[SERVICES: C,P] National communication network of advocacy organizations, institutions, and individuals concerned with the maintenance and quality of family planning and reproductive health services. Monitors government policy and regulations. (EA)

X111. Planned Parenthood Federation of America: 810 7th Ave., New York, NY 10019. PH: (212)541-7800.

[SERVICES: C,L,P,S] Conducts research, training, education, and advocacy, with the goal of making effective means of voluntary fertility control safe, legal, and accessible to all who need them. Operates over 800 clinics nationwide providing family planning service and education on sexually transmitted diseases, contraception, abortion, sterilization, prenatal care, and maternal health. Maintains the Katherine Dexter McCormick Library (see A7). Publications include *Planned Parenthood Affiliates, Chapters, and State Public Affairs Offices Directory*, a geographically arranged directory including descriptions of the services each provides (i.e. medical, educational, public affairs); the bimonthly newsletter *LINK Line* (see K58); annotated bibliographies on *Adolescent Sexuality* (1991) (see H9), *Men and Sexuality* (1985), *School Sexuality Education: Opposition and Answers* (1985), *Evaluating Sexuality Education Programs* (1984), and *Sexually Transmitted Diseases* (1983); White Papers (PPFA position statements); *First Facts: A Manual For Sexuality Educators*; National Family Sexuality Education Month materials, including *Guidebook for National Family Sexuality Education Week*; *AIDS and Adolescents: A Resource Listing for Parents and Professionals* (1989), citing publications, videos, curricula, programs and hotlines; and *Statistical Sources and*

Resources (1991), which identifies governmental and private sources of statistical data in subject areas of interest of family planning agencies and reproductive health educators. The Washington office (2010 Massachusetts Ave., NW, #500, Washington, DC 20036. PH: 202/785-3351) works with the Guttmacher Institute (see X253) to monitor legislation and conduct research on fertility related topics, including international population control, family planning, contraception, and abortion. See also X223. (EA)

X112.   Population Affairs / Public Health Service: 200 Independence Ave., SW, Washington, DC 20201. PH: (202)245-0151.

Coordinates, monitors, and evaluates federal research on population, population education, family planning, and adolescent family life services and programs. Operates two programs: the Office of Adolescent Family Life, which coordinates all aspects of DHHS programs in the areas of adolescent pregnancy prevention and care; and the Office of Family Planning, which coordinates DHHS funding and support of U.S. domestic family planning services and provides project grants for family planning services, training, research, and distribution of information (FIC).

X113.   Transnational Family Research Institute: 8307 Whitman Dr., Bethesda, MD 20817. PH:(301)469-6313.

[SERVICES: C,L,P] Works to increase understanding of the demographic, epidemiological, psychological, and psychosocial aspects of fertility regulating behavior, including couple communication regarding fertility, and the relationship between abortion and contraception. Seeks to improve delivery of family planning services, prevent adolescent pregnancy, and further consumer acceptance of fertility regulation. Operates the International Reference Center for Abortion Research. Publishes *Abortion Research Notes* (see K1). (RC)

➤ FERTILITY AND INFERTILITY *(See also*: Maternal and Child Health; Reproductive Medicine; Reproductive Technologies; Women's Health; X197)

The Census Bureau (see Q2) and the National Center for Health Statistics (see Q4) can provide statistics and other data on the fertility of American women, including number of children, birth expectations, child spacing patterns, etc.

X114. American Fertility Society: 2140 11th Ave. S., Suite 200, Birmingham, AL 35205-2800. PH: (205)933-8494.

[SERVICES: AV,C,P] A professional association of gynecologists, obstetricians, urologists, reproductive endocrinologists, researchers, and others interested in reproductive health. Provides up-to-date information on all aspects of infertility, reproductive endocrinology, conception control, and reproductive biology to their members and the general public. Affiliated societies focus on reproductive endocrinology, reproductive surgery, and assisted reproductive technologies. Publishes the journal *Fertility and Sterility* (see K62), the quarterly newsletter *Fertility News*, and bibliographies. (EA)

X115. National Infertility Network Exchange (NINE): P.O. Box 204, East Meadow, NY 11554. PH: (516)794-5772.

[SERVICES: B,C,P,R,SG] A national, non-profit organization for individuals and couples with impaired fertility. NINE supports the decision to use legal means and/or medical treatment to build families, as well as the decision to remain child-free.

X116. Resolve Inc.: 1310 Broadway, Somerville, MA 02144-1731. PH: (800)662-1016.

[SERVICES: B,C,D,P,R,S,SB] Provides information, education, referrals, advocacy, and support to individuals with infertility problems, as well as associated professionals. Operates an international infertility information clearinghouse containing materials on reproductive options and technological advances. Supports the right of infertile individuals to build their families through a variety of methods, including adoption, artificial insemination by donor, in-vitro fertilization, and surrogacy. Sponsors National Infertility Awareness Week in October. Distributes over 100 fact sheets and briefs on all aspects of infertility (eg. semen analysis, overviews of new technologies, religious perspectives on infertility, adoption, sexuality and marriage, early menopause, etc.); a comprehensive, annotated bibliography—updated biennially—of books and articles on the medical and emotional aspects of infertility; *Referral List of IVF Clinics* (annual); *Referral Lists of Physicians*; and the *Resolve National Newsletter* (5/year), containing information on related medical, emotional, and legal issues, a conference calendar, book reviews, and research reports. (EA)

➤ FETISHES (*See also*: Pedophilia; Sadomasochism; Transvestites)

HOW TO FIND

• Magazines catering to specific fetishes often carry advertisements for related organizations. To find relevant periodicals, see p.200 and p.203; for additional titles, see p.355. *Fetish Times* (see K63) lists groups interested in everything from bondage to foot worship.

X117.   National Leather Association: P.O. Box 17463, Seattle, WA 98107. PH: (206)789-8990.

[SERVICES: C,P,R,SB,SG] A worldwide communication, support, and educational network of individuals and organizations supporting the right of consenting adults to participate in non traditional sex practices, especially those involving S/M, leather, and fetishism. Sponsors the annual Living in Leather Conference. Publishes *First Link*, a monthly newsletter containing an events calendar, NLA news, and political information. Works to preserve records of the history, traditions, and culture of those in the "leather/sm/fetish community." (EA)

➤ GAYS AND LESBIANS (*See also*:Adolescent Sexuality–Gay Youth; Sex and Religion; Sex and Law; for publishers and bookdealers, see p.232-233; for archives and libraries, see X53-X60; X132, X243-X245, X261)

As there are hundreds of gay and lesbian political, academic, religious, community, athletic, and benevolent organizations in the United States, and a plethora of excellent, comprehensive directories for locating them (see "How to Find," p.361), we have listed only a few referral organizations below, with a selection of more specialized organizations listed under relevant topics throughout this chapter.

X118.   Fund for Human Dignity: 1734 14th St., NW, Washington, DC 20009-4309. PH: (202)332-6483.

Seeks to educate the public about gay and lesbian life, with the goal of eliminating homophobia, increasing pride among gays and lesbians, and increasing the visibility of the gay and lesbian community. Operates a national clearinghouse of educational materials on gay/lesbian life, homophobia, and AIDS/HIV. (EA)

HOW TO FIND

• Consult directories. The *Encyclopedia of Associations* (see B4), available in all libraries, describes many gay and lesbian organizations of all types. The *Gay Yellow Pages: A Classified Directory of Gay Services and Businesses in U.S.A. and Canada* (New York: Gay Yellow Pages) is a comprehensive annual directory available in national and regional editions. (Local directories are noted under "Publications" in the regional editions.) Modeled after the telephone yellow pages, it contains names, addresses, phone numbers, and in some cases display advertising, for over 8,000 gay and lesbian related organizations, institutions, and businesses. Updated contact information can be obtained between editions directly from the publisher (Box 292, Village Station, New York, NY 10014. PH: 212/674-0120). Entries are classified under the following headings:

Academic: Students, Teachers, Alumni
AIDS/HIV Support, Education, and Advocacy
Alcohol, Substance Abuse, and Other Addictions
Archives, Libraries, and History Projects
Broadcast Media
Business and Professional Associations
Business and Finance
Computer Services/Bulletin Boards
Distributors
Education and Research
Ethnic and Nationality Resources and Publishers
Family/Youth/Age Related Resources
Film and Video
Health Care
Legal Services and Resources

Mailing List
Mail Order Clothing
Mail Order Erotica
Mail Order: gifts, cards, novelties
Meeting/Contact
Military Resources
Movements: Political, Social, Support
Music and Records
Performance/Theater
Political Organizations
Prisoners Resources
Publications: Directory, Bibliography, Guides and Travel
Publishers
Real Estate
Recreation: Social, Outdoor, Sport, Hobby, Special Interest
Religious Organizations & Publishers
Switchboards and Helplines
Transsexual/Transgender Services
Travel

• Gay and lesbian magazines and newspapers usually carry announcements of national and local organization's activities, see p.204.

X119.   National Gay and Lesbian Task Force: 1734 14th St., NW, Washington, DC 20009-4309. PH: (202)332-6483.

[SERVICES: AV,B,C,L,P,R,S,SB] Seeks to eliminate prejudice and discrimination based on sexual orientation. Operates a number of ongoing projects: anti-violence, campus, lesbian/gay families, media, privacy and legislative. (EA).

X120.   Parents and Friends of Lesbians and Gays Federation: P.O. Box 27605, Washington, DC 20038. PH: (202)638-4200.

[SERVICES: C,P,R,SB,SG] Provides support and referrals for parents and friends of gays and lesbians nationwide. A similar organization, the National Federation of Parents and Friends of Lesbians and Gays (8020 Eastern Ave., NW, Washington, DC 20012. PH: 202/726-3223) distributes the annual *Parents and Friends of Gays International Directory*, listing over 780 self help and support groups, organizations, counselors, religious, social and community services serving parents, friends and families of gays, lesbians, and bisexuals. (EA)

—— GAY AND LESBIAN STUDIES

HOW TO FIND

• For referrals to other gay and lesbian studies programs, contact the Campus Project of the National Gay and Lesbian Task Force (see X119).

X121.   Lesbian and Gay Studies Center/Yale University: Department of History, P.O. Box 2585, Yale Station, New Haven, CT 06520. PH: (203)432-1370.

Center for the study of the variety of human sexuality, particularly studies of homosexuality. Sponsors and cosponsors conferences on AIDS, history of homosexuality, and homosexual representations in contemporary art.

X122.   ONE Institute of Homophile Studies: 3340 Country Club Drive, Los Angeles, CA 90019. PH: (213)735-5252.

Has offered classes and lectures in Homophile Studies since 1956, and since 1961 has been accredited by the state of California to grant MA and

PhD degrees in Homophile Studies. Operates the Blanche Baker Memorial Library (see X54).

➤ IMPOTENCE

HOW TO FIND

• Urologists can provide information on the diagnosis and treatment of erectile dysfunction. Contact the American Urological Association for referrals: 1120 N. Charles St., Baltimore, MD 21201. PH: (301) 727-1100.

• Richard B. Manning's *Impotence: How to Overcome It: The Authoritative Layman's Guide to Sexual Potency* (Health Prolink and Thirty Three Publishing, 1989) includes a list of 150 support groups, research/treatment institutions, and penile implant manufacturers.

X123. **Impotence Institute of America / Impotence Anonymous / I-Anon**: 119 S. Ruth St., Maryville, TN 37801-5746. PH: (615)983-6064.

[SERVICES: P,R,S,SG] I-Anon provides support for partners of impotent males. Impotence Anonymous provides medical and psychological referrals to impotent men, including referrals to support groups. The Impotence Institute of America informs and educates the public on the causes and treatment of impotence. (EA)

X124. **Potency Restored**: 8630 Fenton St., Suite 218, Silver Spring, MD 20910. PH: (301)588-5777.

[SERVICES: C,P,R,SG] Provides information on inflatable penile implant surgery and support for impotent men who are considering or have undergone the procedure. (EA)

X125. **Recovery of Male Potency (ROMP)**: 27211 Lasher Rd., #208, Southfield, MI 48034. PH: (313)357-1216 / (800)TEL-ROMP.

[SERVICES: C,P,R,S,SG] Hospital based self-help group for impotent men and their partners. Also provides medical information on the causes, testing, treatment (i.e. device implantation, drugs, therapy), and emotional aspects of impotence. (EA)

➤ LACTATION AND BREASTFEEDING

X126.   Human Lactation Center: 666 Sturges Hwy., Westport, CT 06880. PH: (203)259-5995.

[SERVICES: B,C,DB,L,P] Disseminates information and conducts research on human lactation, maternal/infant feeding behavior and nutrition, and related issues. Maintains a 6,000 volume library (with 70 current journal subscriptions) and a museum of items related to infant feeding (e.g. animal skin milk carrying containers, breastfeeding promotion posters, etc.). Operates a database on lactation, maternal behavior, and lactation amenorrhea. Publications include the journal *Lactation Review*, and the book *Only Mothers Know: Infant Feeding Practices in Traditional Cultures*. (EA,SL,RC)

X127.   International Lactation Consultants Association: 201 Brown Ave., Evanston, IL 60202-3601. PH: (708)260-8874.

[SERVICES: C,P] An association of organizations, lactation consultants, and others interested in lactation and breastfeeding. Reviews films, conducts public education and research, and sets professional standards for lactation consultants. Publishes the *Journal of Human Lactation* (see K25). (EA)

X128.   LaLeche League International—Breastfeeding Information Center and Library: P.O. Box 1209, 9616 Minneapolis Ave., Franklin Park, IL 60131-8209. PH: (800)La-Leche.

[SERVICES: B,C,DB,L,P,R] Promotes breastfeeding worldwide. The Information Center is open to the public (with a fee) and contains pamphlets and booklets, 200 books, and over 7,500 published research reports. The Breastfeeding Information Database can be used to compile custom bibliographies. Publications include the journals *Breastfeeding Abstracts* (see K24) and *New Beginnings* (K26), and the *La Leche League Directory*. For a full listing of books, videos, and products available via mail order, request the *La Leche League International Catalog*. (EA,SL)

➤ LANGUAGE

X129.   International Maledicta Archives: P.O. Box 14123, Santa Rosa, CA 95402-6123. PH: (707)523-4761.

[SERVICES: B,C,DB,L,P] "The Archives, begun in 1965, contain books, some 15,000 pages of published research, and 5,000 bibliographical file cards of maledicta-related material from some 200 languages and dialects from the past 5,000 years." Much of the material is sex related. Director, Dr. Reinhold Aman, who will provide research assistance by phone or mail, also operates the International Research Center on Verbal Aggression, and coordinates the International Maledicta Society, made up of 3,000 professors of folklore, linguistics, English, sociology, anthropology, and psychology, and others interested in verbal aggression in all languages, dialects, culture, religions, and ethnic groups. Publishes *Maledicta: The International Journal of Verbal Aggression* (see K85). See also p.60 and p.126. (EA)

➤ MARRIAGE AND FAMILY (*See also*: X234, X239, X260)

HOW TO FIND

• The *Encyclopedia of Associations* (see B4) lists hundreds of organizations under family related headings (e.g. *parents, family, divorce, singles, adoption, marriage, fathers, mothers, multiple births, children*, etc.).

• John Touliatos' *Graduate Study in Marriage and the Family: A Guide to Masters and Doctoral Programs in the U.S. and Canada* (Fort Worth, TX: Human Sciences Publications, 1989), is a geographically arranged directory to graduate programs in family studies, and marriage and family therapy.

X130.   Family Information Center: National Agriculture Library, Rm. 304, Dept. of Agriculture, 10301 Baltimore Blvd., Beltsville, MD 20705. PH: (301)344-3719.

[SERVICES: L] Provides information services to professionals concerned with the strengths, well being, economics, and social environment of the family unit and its individual members; acquires print and audiovisual resources; and distributes the resource lists *Pathfinders* and *Special Reference Briefs*. They can identify a library holding a particular book, journal, or audiovisual, and if necessary, lend books and audiovisuals through interlibrary loan or provide photocopies of materials not available elsewhere. The center is part of the U.S. Dept. of Agriculture's National Agriculture Library, and is open to the public. (FIC)

X131.   National Council on Family Relations: 3989 Central Ave. NE, Suite 550, Minneapolis, MN 55421. PH: (612)781-9331.

[SERVICES: B,C,D,L,P,R,S,SB] The oldest multidisciplinary family organization in the U.S., the Council serves all marriage and family professionals, including psychologists, counselors, family life educators, marriage and family therapists, clergy, sociologists, nurses, physicians, attorneys, social workers, home economists, psychiatrists, and others dedicated to strengthening marriage and the family through research, education, therapy/counseling, and other family programs and services. (The *Human Resources Bank*, a file in the Family Resource Database, see J39, notes those members willing to be contacted by the general public.) Activities include development and distribution of educational resources, and maintenance of the print index *Inventory of Marriage and Family Literature* (see J40) and the on-line database *Family Resource Database* (see J39). Publications include *Family Life Education Curriculum Guidelines*, and the journals *Family Relations* (see K88) and the *Journal of Marriage and the Family* (see K91), among others. Sponsors an annual conference; 120 tapes from the 1989 conference, "Families and Sexuality," are available from Custom Audio Tapes at PH: (800)798-0986. (EA,SL)

—— GAY AND LESBIAN *(See also: X239)*

X132.   Gay and Lesbian Parents Coalition International: P.O. Box 50360, Washington, DC 20091. PH: (202)583-8029.

[SERVICES: B,C,P,R,SB,SG] An information clearinghouse on issues relating to gay and lesbian parenting. Provides advocacy and support for gay fathers and lesbian mothers through a network of local parent groups. Publications include the *Network* newsletter, containing articles, interviews with gay/lesbian parents, legal news, updates on ongoing research and education projects, a resource directory, and other features; *Bibliography on Gays and Lesbians and their Families*, which cites books, videos, and articles in both popular magazines and scientific journals; and *Books for Children of Gay and Lesbian Parents*. (EA)

➤ MASTURBATION

X133.   Betty Dodson: P.O. Box 1933, Murray Hill, New York, NY 10156. PH: (212)679-5667.

Ms. Dodson leads workshops on masturbation for men and women.

➤ MATERNAL AND CHILD HEALTH (*See also*: Alcohol and Drugs; Reproductive Health; Population; Women's Health)

HOW TO FIND

• The annual *Directory of Training Courses in Family Planning and Maternal and Child Health* (New York: United Nations Population Fund) describes short term training courses to be offered worldwide. Entries include sponsoring institution or organization, telephone number, contact person, course title, language of instruction (courses are offered in Bahasa Malaysia, Diola, Kinyarwarda, Urdu, among many others), subjects covered, skills learned, entrance requirements, etc. To order, contact the U.N. Population Fund: 220 E. 42nd St., New York, NY 10017.

X134. **National Maternal and Child Health Clearinghouse**

National Center for Education in Maternal and Child Health
38th and R St., NW, Washington, DC 20057. PH: (202)625-8400 (Center) (202)625-8410 (Clearinghouse)

[SERVICES: B,D,DB,L,R,S] The National Center for Education in Maternal and Child Health (NCEMCH) responds to information requests from consumers and professionals, provides technical assistance, and develops educational and reference materials which are distributed through the Clearinghouse. The NCEMCH Resource Center is open to the public, and contains professional literature (over 8,000 volumes and 70 journal subscriptions), patient education materials, curricula, audiovisuals, and information about organizations and programs. Major content areas include pregnancy and childbirth, child and adolescent health, nutrition, high-risk infants, chronic illness and disability, human genetics, women's health, and maternal and child health services and programs. Their monthly newsletter *MCH Program Interchange*, addresses a different topic in each issue, and includes announcements of new publications.

The National Clearinghouse for Maternal and Child Health is the centralized source for materials and information in the areas of maternal, infant, child, and adolescent health, human genetics, and pregnancy care, including materials from federal and state agencies, professional and voluntary organizations, and grantees of the Maternal and Child Health Bureau. Clearinghouse staff respond to phone and mail inquiries and disseminate over 500 publications—many of them free—including news-letters, bibliographies, booklets, brochures, resource guides, and other educational materials; for a complete listing, request the *National Center for Education in Maternal and Child Health and National Maternal and Child Health Clearinghouse Publications Catalogs*. Directories include a directory of clinical genetic service centers; *Reaching Out: A Directory of National Organizations Related to Maternal and Child Health*, a subject classified, annual directory of over 500 national and international voluntary organizations, support groups, self help clearinghouses, and federal maternal/child health information centers; *Starting Early: A Guide to Federal Resources in Maternal and Child Health* (1988), a directory of federal agencies and federally supported organizations which distribute print and non-print resources on prenatal, infant, maternal, and adolescent health, including audiovisuals, posters, pamphlets, educational software, and curriculum; and *Healthy Mother, Healthy Babies—Directory of Educational Materials*, which fully describes each group's mission, services, and products. (FIC)

X135.   National Institute of Child Health and Human Development: Office of Research Reporting, National Institutes of Health, 9000 Rockville Pike, Bethesda, MD 20892. PH: (301)496-5133.

Conducts and supports basic and clinical research in maternal and child health and the population sciences, including research in all phases of human development, from maturation of sperm and egg cells through fetal and child development; reproductive biology and contraception; fertility and infertility; developmental biology and nutrition; mental retardation; pediatric, adolescent and maternal AIDS; and developmental disabilities, mental retardation, and congenital defects. Consumer materials are available on maternal and child health, cesarean childbirth, oral contraception, precocious puberty, premature birth, pregnancy, smoking and pregnancy, and vasectomy, among other topics. Professional materials are available on sudden infant death syndrome, pregnancy and genetics, and other topics. A complete publications catalog is available on request. NICHD maintains two research centers: Center for Population Research (see X197) and the Center for Research for Mothers and Children, which seeks to increase the likelihood of pregnancies and births producing healthy babies by supporting research and training in the biomedical and behavioral sciences. (FIC)

X136.   American Foundation for Maternal and Child Health: 439 E. 51st St., 4th Fl., New York, NY 10022. PH: (212)759-5510.

[SERVICES: L,P,S] Maintains an interdisciplinary research library focusing on the perinatal and birth period and its effect on infant development. Affiliated with the Women's Health Network (see X297). (EA)

—— BIRTH DEFECTS *(See also*: X134)

X137.   March of Dimes Birth Defects Foundation: 1275 Mamaroneck Ave., White Plains, NY 10605-5298. PH: (914)428-7100.

[SERVICES: C,S,L,P] Works to prevent birth defects, low birth weight babies, and infant mortality. Monitors relevant legislation and regulations. Develops and distributes educational materials to health professionals and the public. Maintains a library holding 1,700 bound periodical volumes and 108 current subscriptions (the journal holdings list is published semi-annually), 2,500 books and vertical files on birth defects, obstetrics and pediatrics, and maternal and child health. Publishes *Genetics in Practice*, a newsletter reporting current clinical research in genetics. (EA, SL)

X138.   National Institute of Environmental Health Sciences: P.O. Box 12233, Research Triangle Park, NC 27709. PH: (919)541-3345.

[SERVICES: B,P] This division of the National Institutes of Health, supports and conducts research on the interaction between humans and potentially toxic or harmful agents in their environments, including the effects of toxic substances on reproduction. (FIC)

—— INFANT DEATH AND ILLNESS

X139.   National Sudden Infant Death Syndrome Resource Center: 8201 Greensboro Dr., Suite 600, McLean, VA 22102. PH: (703)821-8955.

[SERVICES: B,L,P] Operated by the U.S. Health and Human Services Department, the clearinghouse was established in 1980 to provide information and educational materials on sudden infant death syndrome (SIDS), apnea, infant mortality, perinatal grief and loss, and related issues. They respond to information requests from professionals, families with SIDS related deaths, and the general public, by sending written materials and making referrals to state and local programs, organizations, support groups, and individuals. The clearinghouse maintains a reference library of materials covering etiology, epidemiology, research, counseling, effects on families, training of emergency personnel, legal aspects, treatment, and prevention of SIDS. The clearinghouse also compiles annotated bibliographies on a variety of topics, and publishes fact sheets, catalogs, directories and other educational and resource materials, including *Directory of Sudden Infant Death Syndrome Programs and Resources*, a geographically arranged directory of 110 private organizations and federal, state, and local government agencies providing information and counseling on SIDS. Their quarterly newsletter, *Information Exchange*, promotes the exchange of information among SIDS groups nationwide. (FIC, SL)

X140.   Pregnancy and Infant Loss Center: 1421 E. Wayzata Blvd., #40, Wayzata, MN 55391. PH: (612)473-9372.

[SERVICES: B,C,P,R] Distributes bibliographies on miscarriage, stillbirth, newborn death, infertility, childlessness, high risk birth, adoption, death and dying, and children and death, among other topics. Sponsors Pregnancy and Infant Loss Awareness Month each October. (EA)

The following five groups provide information and resources on stillbirth, miscarriage, ectopic pregnancy, and newborn/infant death, and provide bereavement support to parents grieving the loss of their baby.

X141.   Intensive Caring Unlimited: 910 Bert Lane, Philadelphia, PA 19118. PH: (215) 233-4723.

X142.   National Share Office: St. Elizabeths Hospital, 211 S. 3rd St., Belleville, IL 62222. PH: (618)234-2415.

X143.   Parent Care: 9041 Colgate St., Indianapolis, IN 46268-1210. PH: (703)836-4678.

X144.   Resolved Through Sharing: La Crosse Lutheran Hospital, 1910 S. Ave., La Crosse, WI 54601. PH: (608)791-4747.

X145.   UNITE: c/o Jeanes Hospital, 7600 Central Ave., Philadelphia, PA 19111. PH: (215)728-3777.

➤ MEN

X146.   Fatherhood Project: Families and Work Institute, 330 7th Ave., 14th Fl., New York, NY 10001. PH: (212)268-4846.

[SERVICES: DB,R] National research center and information clearinghouse on father related topics, including those of single, step, expecting, homosexual, teen, divorced, new, and adoptive fathers. Encourages the development of nurturing male roles in childrearing. (EA,RC)

X147.   Society for the Study of Male Psychology and Physiology: c/o Jerry Bergman, 321 Iuka, Montpellier, OH. PH: (419)485-3602.

180 psychologists, psychiatrists, biologists, sociologists, and others interested in the study of male behavior and physiology alone and in relation to women. Maintains a 6,000 volume library on male psychology, physiology, sex roles, homosexuality, and other topics.

➤ MENSTRUATION / MENOPAUSE (*See also*: Women's Health)

HOW TO FIND

• Most manufacturers of tampons and sanitary napkins operate educational and/or customer service departments. Tambrands, for example, operates a health education hotline, (800)628-1352, for teachers, students, and parents, which answers questions and distributes free educational materials on puberty and menstrual health. Identify other manufacturers using business directories (see B65 and notes on p.316), or directly from packages of feminine hygiene products; most indicate a customer service number on the outside of the package or on the insert. The FDA (see X90) also provides information on tampons, toxic shock syndrome, etc.

X148.   Hysterectomy Education Resources and Service Foundation (HERS Foundation): 422 Bryn Mawr Ave., Bala-Cynwyd, PA 19004. PH: (215)667-7757.

[SERVICES: AV,C,L,P,R,S,SB] Provides information on hysterectomies and alternate treatments. The quarterly *HERS Newsletter* reports on relevant popular, medical, and scientific literature. (EA)

X149.   **Menstrual Health Foundation**: P.O. Box 3248, Santa Rosa, CA 95402. PH: (707)829-2744.

[SERVICES: P] Non-profit educational corporation dedicated to "creating a new way of thinking about menarche, menstruation, and menopause—the Menstrual matrix—through education, so that women of all ages are empowered and strengthened by their fertility and menstrual cycle." Offers "menstrual well being" education.

X150.   **North American Menopause Society**: University Hospital of Cleveland, Dept. of OB/GYN, 2074 Abington Rd., Cleveland, OH 44106. PH: (216)844-3334.

[SERVICES: C,R] Physicians, researchers, scientists, and health care professionals interested in the study of the climacteric in men and women. Provides referrals to menopause care providers. (EA,RC)

X151.   **Society for Menstrual Cycle Research**: 10559 N. 104th Pl., Scottsdale, AZ 85258. PH: (602)451-9731.

[SERVICES: C,P] Physicians and other health care professionals, psychologists, sociologists, educators, and others interested in women's menstrual health. Promotes and disseminates interdisciplinary research on the menstrual cycle. Publishes books, including *The Menstrual Cycle: A Synthesis of Interdisciplinary Research* and *The Menstrual Cycle: Research and Implications for Women's Health*. (EA)

➤ MISCELLANEOUS

X152.   **Consortium for Sex Research in Space and the Future**: 513-515 Broadway, #3AR, New York, NY 10012. PH: (212)941-1309.

X153.   **The Not Naughty Network**: NSS Seminars Inc., P.O. Box 620123, Woodside, CA 94062. PH: (415)851-4751.

[SERVICES: C,P] "An association of people who believe in sex-positive, respectful and loving relationships," which seeks to "promote a positive view of human sexuality and its potential for good in our lives." Publishes *The Not Naughty News*, a quarterly journal containing an events calendar and articles addressing a wide range of sexuality, relationship, and communication related topics. Sponsors the annual Fall Fantasy Ball (an erotic costume ball), and the National Sexuality Symposium and Expo, "an open forum where people expand their understanding about relationships and the beauty of being the sexual loving human beings that they are," through speakers, social events, and exhibits.

➤ NON-MONOGAMY (*See also*: Alternative Lifestyles)

How to Find

• Both *Emerge Playcouple* (see K94) and *NASCA Inside Report* (see K97) include directories of swing clubs and organizations worldwide, as well as classified/display advertising. *Loving More* (see K96) contains listings of established families, groups, and organizations interested in group marriage or other forms of adult, multiple, committed relationships.

X154. Intinet Resource Center: P.O. Box 2096-G, Mill Valley, CA 94942. PH: (415)507-1739.

[SERVICES: C,L,P,R,SB,SG] Operates an information clearinghouse on "ethical non-exclusive relationships" and other alternatives to the traditional nuclear family. Works to increase public awareness of the "joys and benefits of responsible alternatives to monogamy" and provides a communication network of people and organizations exploring "new paradigms for sexual love" which encourage and support "appropriate, healthy, responsible, spiritual, and compassionate sexual practices." Publishes the book *Love Without Limits: Responsible Nonmonogamy and the Quest for Sustainable Intimate Relationships*, which includes a resource list of over 200 books, films, videos, computer conferences, seminars, and organizations dedicated to ethical nonmonogamy, tantric sex, spiritual and personal growth, and family and community. Resources are updated in the quarterly newsletter, *Floodtide*. A 200 volume library on multiple adult relationships is open to members only. (EA)

X155. North American Swing Club Association: P.O. Box 7128, Buena Vista, CA 90622. PH: (714)821-9953.

[SERVICES: C,DB,L,P,R,S,SB] Information clearinghouse and resource center on swinging—"engaging in sexual activity with someone other than one's spouse/primary partner, with the full knowledge and consent of that spouse/primary partner." Their archives on swinging, swinging organizations, and related social and sexual research (known as the Robert McGinley Collection) date back to 1969, and include materials on swinging's legal, social, and medical aspects. (The archives are fully described in *Alternative Lifestyles*, see p.338.) Publishes a guide to *Etiquette in Swinging*; *Emerge Playcouple* (see K94), a newsletter "dedicated to helping couples to achieve happiness, romance, adventure and excitement in their erotic relationship, and a sense of freedom and fulfillment in their lives"; and *International Directory: Swing Clubs and Publications*, an annual directory of over 350 heterosexual swing clubs, conventions, publications, companies, organizations, tours, and special events, classified by product or service. Intraedition updates will be provided from their computer database of affiliated clubs. (EA)

X156. Paradise Educational Partnership (PEP): P.O. Box 6306, Captain Hook, HI 96704. PH: (808)929-9691.

[SERVICES: C,D,P,R] Formerly known as the Polyfidelity Education Project. A nationwide, non-profit educational corporation publishing materials and information related to polyfidelity—"a sexually fidelitous marriage of more than two adults in which all partners are valued equally." Publishes the newsletter *Loving More: A Group Marriage Journal and Network* (see K96); and the book *Loving More: The Polyfidelity Primer*, which describes the theory and essentials of the lifestyle. Sponsors an annual conference. (EA)

➤ NUDISM

X157. American Nudist Research Library: 4425 S. Pleasant Hill Rd., Kissimmee, FL 32741. PH: (305)933-2866 / 933-4874.

[SERVICES: AV,B,L,P] Contains over 40,000 items, including foreign and American journals, books, films, audio-cassettes, primary documents of the American nudist movement, and other materials. (SL)

X158. American Sunbathing Association: 1703 N. Main St., Kissimmee, FL 34744. PH: (407)933-2064.

[SERVICES: C,L,P,R,SB] Promotes "improved health, physically, psychologically, and spiritually through nudism and the realization that true modesty is not related to the wearing of clothes." Publishes *The Bulletin*

How to Find

• *Alternative Lifestyles* (see p.338) contains full descriptions of 6 nudism collections, including X157, X159, X161.

• Consult *INF World Naturism Handbook* (Berchem/Antwerpen, Belgium: International Naturist Federation), a geographically arranged directory of 800 nudist clubs, resorts, beaches, centers, and related organizations and businesses worldwide. Available in the U.S. from X158. Directories are also published by X159, X162.

(11x per year), a newspaper on nudist facilities and organizations, and the international nudist movement; the semi-annual *North American Guide to Nude Recreation*; and *Solution*, a quarterly newsletter addressing legal issues of nudism. (EA)

X159. Elysium Institute: 5436 Fernwood Ave., Los Angeles, CA 90027. PH: (213)455-1000.

[SERVICES: C,L,P] Operates Elysium Fields, a clothing optional family resort, and Elysium Growth Press (see L15). Publications include the *Journal of the Senses* (see K98), and *Nudist-Naturist Factfinder: Nude Living Factfinder and Directory*, which answers the questions most often asked by newcomers to the nudist lifestyle, and includes a bibliography and directory of nudist/naturist facilities and groups worldwide. They can provide information on the annual TANR (Trade Association for Nude Recreation) conference. (SL)

X160. Institute for Nudist Studies: P.O. Box 328, Sunnymead, CA 92388.

[SERVICES: B,L] A partial list of the holdings of the Institute for Nudist Studies is available for purchase.

X161. Johnson Archives of Nudism: 16401 Otsego St., Encino, CA 91436.

Largest collection on nudism in the U.S. A 90 page, fully annotated *Catalog of the Johnson Archives of Nudist Literature*, citing books, pamphlets, and periodicals in the collection, is available from the American Nudist Research Library (see X157).

X162.   Naturist Society: P.O. Box 132, Oshkosh, WI 54902. PH: (414)426-5009.

[SERVICES: C,D,P] Believes "body acceptance is the idea, nude recreation is the way." Publishes *Nude and Natural* ("the world's best magazine of body acceptance and nude recreation"); and the 240 page *World Guide to Nude Beaches and Recreation* (1991), which describes thousands of nudist beaches and resorts throughout the U.S., Canada, Europe, Asia, Central and South America, and the Caribbean. (EA)

X163.   Naturists and Nudists Opposing Pornographic Exploitation: P.O. Box 2085, Rancho Cordova, CA 95741. PH: (408)427-2858.

[SERVICES: P,SB] Organization of former nudists who now believe that the lifestyle sexually exploits women and children under the guise of nudism. (EA)

X164.   Nudist Information Center: P.O. Box 4321, N. Las Vegas, NV 89030. PH: (702)648-9990.

[SERVICES: R] Answers questions about nudist lifestyles and nudist facilities. Affiliated with X158. (EA)

➤ PEDOPHILIA *(See also*: Fetishes)

X165.   North American Man/Boy Love Association: 537 Jones St., #8418, San Francisco, CA 94102.

[SERVICES: P] A political organization supporting consensual, inter-generational relationships between men and boys. Seeks to educate society about the positive aspects of such relationships. Publishes *NAMBLA Bulletin* (see K99). For books, contact the Book Dept.: P.O. Box 174, Midtown Station, New York, NY 10018. PH: (212)807-8578.

X166.   Rene Guyon Society: 256 S. Robertson Blvd., no. 5020P, Beverly Hills, CA 90211.

[SERVICES: P,SB] Advocates change in the statutory rape laws so as to abolish laws prohibiting sex between a young person and a person more than 10 years older. According to their entry in the *Encyclopedia of Associations* (see B4), they act as a voice for "those advocating consenting child bisexuality protected both vaginally and anally with condoms by age eight," believing that such experiences could eliminate "neurotic problems such as crime, dope abuse, AIDS, suicide, divorce, alcoholism, obesity, reckless driving, and gambling." (EA).

➤ POPULATION STUDIES (*See also*: Family Planning; Fertility)

All of the following organizations conduct research and disseminate information on issues such as population trends, family planning, abortion, and contraception. Descriptions focus on each organization's information services, and do not fully describe their activities.

X167. **Association for Population/Family Planning Libraries and Information Centers**: c/o Population Council Library (see X170)

[SERVICES: AV,B,D,L,P,R] "A body of resource people who can assist in finding the appropriate organization or person for seeking an answer on a specific topic" in population/family planning fields and related public health areas. Publications include: *Union List of Population/Family Planning Periodicals*; *Guide to Population/Family Planning Information Sources*; *Tools for Population Information: Indexing and Abstracting Services*; *Population and Related Organizations: International Address List*; and fact sheets, statistics, research reprints, bibliographies, and teaching tools. Sponsors an annual conference and film festival. (SL)

X168. **Carolina Population Center**: University of North Carolina at Chapel Hill, CB no.8120, Chapel Hill, NC 27516-3997. PH: (919)962-3081.

[SERVICES: B,L] Maintains an extensive international collection on population, including "reasonably complete coverage" of family planning and reproductive behavior. The collection includes books, conference proceedings, book chapters, journals (375 current subscriptions), reprints, government documents, technical reports, annual reports, and bibliographies. Library holdings from 1984-1990 are included on POPLINE (see J49), and an in-house computer catalog is updated monthly; custom searches of either are available for a fee. (SL)

X169. **Center for Population and Family Health at Columbia University—Library and Information Programs**: 60 Haven Ave., New York, NY 10032. PH: (212)305-6960.

[SERVICES: L,P,S] The center conducts research in population and family planning, including adolescent fertility, maternal and child health, barriers to effective family planning, social and personal determinates and consequences of reproductive behavior, sterilization, adolescent pregnancy, and contraceptives. The library subscribes to over 200 serials, and holds over 7,000 books and 30,000 published and unpublished documents, reports, reprints, etc. Maintains a special collection on the evaluation of family programs in developing countries; see also *Fertility Modification Thesaurus* (see C10). (RC,SL)

X170.   The Population Council: One Dag Hammarskjold Plaza, New York, NY 10017. PH: (212)339-0532.

[SERVICES: B,L,P] International, nonprofit organization "applying science and technology to the solution of population problems in developing countries." Conducts social, health science, and biomedical research on population policy, family planning and fertility, STDs, AIDS, maternal and child health, reproductive health and child survival, women's roles and status, demography, the development and introduction of new contraceptive methods, reproductive physiology, and the economic and environmental consequences of rapid population growth. Their library contains over 20,000 books, 350 journal subscriptions, and 6,000 reprints, pamphlets, and other items. A *Catalogue of the Population Council Library* was published by G.K. Hall in 1979. Publishes *Studies in Family Planning* (see K61), among other titles. (EA,SL)

X171.   Population Information Program: Population Center, Johns Hopkins University, 111 Market Place, Suite 310, Baltimore, MD 21202-4024. PH: (410)659-6300.

[SERVICES: DB,L] The Population Center conducts research on population, demography, family planning, reproductive health, adolescent fertility, contraceptive development, and reproductive biology. The Information Program provides accurate, up-to-date information on new developments in these areas, and related legal, health, and public policy issues. Maintains the on-line database *POPLINE* (see J49), custom searches of which are available on request. Their library, open to the public by appointment, contains over 13,000 volumes, 150,000 documents, and subscribes to over 500 journals and other serials. (SL,RC)

X172.   Society for the Study of Social Biology: East-West Population Institute, 1777 East-West Rd., Honolulu, HI 96848.

[SERVICES: C,P] Association of biological, behavioral, and social science scholars concerned with the advancement and dissemination of knowledge about the biocultural and sociocultural forces affecting human behavior and the structure and composition of human populations. Publishes *Social Biology* (see K101).

➤ PORNOGRAPHY AND CENSORSHIP

—— FEDERAL ACTIVITIES (*See also*: X217)

The U.S. Customs Service and U.S. Postal Service are the federal agencies primarily responsible for regulating pornography and obscenity.

X173. **Child Exploitation and Obscenity Section**: Justice Department, Main Justice Bldg., Washington, DC 20530. PH: (202)514-5780.

Enforces federal obscenity and child pornography laws. Operates a document clearinghouse containing briefs, pleadings, and other materials for use by federal, state, and local prosecutors.

X174. **Child Pornography Protection Unit**: U.S. Customs Service, Treasury Department, 1301 Constitution Ave., NW, Washington, DC 20229. PH: (202)566-8005.

A clearinghouse for information on child pornography investigations conducted by the customs service.

X175. **Inspection Service, U.S. Postal Service**: Main Justice Building 20530, 475 L'Enfant Plaza, SW, Washington, DC 20260. PH:(202)268-4267 / (800)654-8896.

Monitors the distribution of obscene materials through the mails.

—— ANTI-PORNOGRAPHY (CONSERVATIVE)

The Children's Legal Foundation (also known as Citizens for Decency Through Law), was the largest anti-pornography organization in the U.S. until it ceased operation in October 1992. They are referring all queries to the National Family Legal Foundation (see X178).

X176. **Morality in Media Inc.**: 475 Riverside Dr., New York, NY 10115. PH: (212)870-3222 / (212)929-4083.

[SERVICES: C,L,P,SB] A national, interfaith organization dedicated to the "moral and legal battle against pornography. [They] focus on pornographic magazines and videos, cableporn, and dial-a-porn, although naturally [they] are also concerned about the decadent messages of some TV, rock music, advertising, etc." They work for the constitutional elimination of the illegal traffic in pornography, through "vigorous enforcement of obscenity laws" and public education on the "problem of illegal pornography." They believe that "if morality and decency are to be preserved, our country's obscenity laws—federal, state and local—must be aggressively enforced to eliminate obscenity from our society." Towards this end, MIM operates the National Obscenity Law Center, a legal clearinghouse which collects and abstracts information on all reported obscenity cases since 1808, and their attorneys assist in the preparation of obscenity cases nationwide. Publishes *Obscenity Law Bulletin* (see K104), and *Morality in Media Newsletter* (1962-), a bimonthly newsletter reporting on obscenity laws, court cases, and ongoing anti-pornography actions. (EA)

X177.   National Coalition Against Pornography: 800 Compton Rd., Suite 9224, Cincinnati, OH 45231-9964. PH: (513)521-6227.

[SERVICES: AV,C,P,S,SB] Coalition of religious groups, lay organizations, and individuals working for the elimination of obscenity and pornography. Seeks strict upholding of obscenity and child protection laws. Sponsors the annual Conference on Obscenity and Child Protection. (EA)

X178.   National Family Legal Foundation: 5353 N 16th St., Suite 400, Phoenix, AZ 85016. PH: (602)265-1513.

—— ANTI-PORNOGRAPHY (FEMINIST) (*See also*: H70)

X179.   Citizens for Media Responsibility Without Law: P.O. Box 2085, Rancho Cordova, CA 95741-2085. PH: (408)427-2858.

Advocates for freedom of speech, press, and sexual expression, and encourages public rejection of pornography rather then government suppression of it. Denounces sexual exploitation of women in beauty pageants and advertisements, and portrayals of sexual violence towards women in pornography. (EA)

X180.   Feminists Fighting Pornography: P.O. Box 6731, Yorkville Station, New York, NY 10128. PH: (212)410-5182.

Publishes the annual magazine *Backlash Times* (see K102). (EA)

X181. **Women Against Pornography**: 321 W. 47th St., New York, NY 10036. PH: (212)307-5055.

[SERVICES: L,P,R,S,SB] A 10,000 member feminist organization seeking to change public opinion regarding pornography so it's no longer viewed as socially acceptable. Provides tours of New York City's Times Square, which they consider the "porn capital of the country." Operates a task force on sexual abuse and pornography. Monitors art, films, books, and advertisements for sexual violence and sex role stereotyping; findings are published in the *Women Against Pornography News* (see K105). (EA)

—— ANTI-CENSORSHIP *(See also:* X179-X181, X242)

X182. **National Coalition Against Censorship**: 2 W. 64th St., Rm. 402, New York, NY 10023. PH: (212)724-1500.

[SERVICES: C,P] A coalition of 42 national, non-profit groups dedicated to preserving and advancing freedom of thought, inquiry, and expression. Publishes *Meese Commission Exposed.*

➤ PROFESSIONAL ASSOCIATIONS *(See also:* X79-X81, X225, X260)

X183 and X189 are the two major U.S. professional associations in the sex field (see also p.319). Contact X192 and X186 for groups worldwide.

X183. **American Association of Sex Educators, Counselors, and Therapists (AASECT)**: 435 N. Michigan Ave., Suite 1717, Chicago, IL 60611. PH: (312)644-0828.

[SERVICES: C,D,P,R] A not-for-profit, interdisciplinary professional organization devoted to the promotion of sexual health through the development and advancement of the fields of sexual therapy, counseling, and education, including certification of sexual health professionals. Sponsors a national conference annually and regional meetings throughout the year. Publishes *Contemporary Sexuality* (see K113), the *Journal of Sex Education and Therapy* (see K115), and the *AASECT National Register* (see p.404).

X184. **Council of Associations for Sexual Science, Health and Education (CASSHE)**: c/o Beverly Whipple, 1523 Franklin St., San Francisco, CA 94109.

A cooperative council of professional organizations in the sexuality field.

X185. Division of Family Psychology / American Psychology Association: c/o Dr. William R. Fishburn, 3821 Shenandoah Pl. NE, Albuquerque, NM 87111.

[SERVICES: C,D,P] Psychologists with academic, research, or clinical interests in family/marital/sex psychology and therapy. Focuses on the study and application of family theory and practice to such areas as premarital, marital, divorce, and remarriage counseling; health and illness; sexuality and the family; the family and work; and family violence and abuse. Has a task force on Sexuality and Family Psychology. Publishes *The Family Psychologist*. (EA)

X186. International Academy of Sex Research: c/o Kenneth J. Zucker, Child and Family Studies Center, Clarke Institute of Psychiatry, 250 College St., Toronto, Ontario, M5T 1R8 Canada. PH: (416)979-2221 ext.2271.

X187. Society for the Philosophy of Sex and Love: c/o Alan Soble, University of New Orleans, Philosophy Department, New Orleans, LA 70148. PH: (504)286-6257.

[SERVICES: C,P] Philosophers, psychologists, sociologists, educators, and physicians interested in the philosophical dimensions of human sexuality, love, and related topics such as the family, marriage, and sex roles. Provides bibliographic referrals. Their annual newsletter contains a membership directory. (EA)

X188. Society for the Psychological Study of Lesbian and Gay Issues / American Psychology Association 1200, 17th St., NW, Washington, DC 20036. PH: (202)955-7727.

A division of the American Psychology Association which "seeks to advance the contribution of psychological research in understanding lesbian and gay issues; to promote the education of psychologists in matters of lesbian and gay concerns; and to inform psychologists and the general public of relevant research, educational and service activities." Maintains an Ad hoc Committee on Psychology and AIDS. (EA)

X189. Society for the Scientific Study of Sex: P.O. Box 208 Mt. Vernon, IA 52314. PH: (319)895-8407.

[SERVICES: C,P] Founded in 1957, the Society is an international organization dedicated to advancing knowledge of sexuality through the production of quality research, the application of sexual knowledge in educational, clinical and other settings, and the communication of accurate information about sexuality to professionals, policy makers, and the general public. As such, the Society provides an international, inter-disciplinary forum for communication, collaboration, and critical evaluation among all sexuality professionals who are committed to a serious, scholarly, and scientific approach to acquiring and disseminating knowledge of sexuality, including biologists, physicians, nurses, therapists, psychologists, sociologists, anthropologists, historians, educators, and theologians. In 1992, there were six special interest groups: Sexual Aggression, Feminist Perspectives on Sexual Science, Gay-Lesbian-Bisexual Interests, Cross-Cultural Research in Sexuality, Educators in Sexual Science, and the Consortium of Sex Educators in Health Professions. Sponsors a national conference each November, and regional meetings throughout the year. Publishes *The Society Newsletter* (see K135); a *Membership Handbook and Directory* (available to members only–mailing labels are available for purchase); *The Journal of Sex Research* (see K134); *Annual Review of Sex Research* (see K128). (EA)

X190. **Society of Sex Therapists and Researchers (STAR):** c/o Dr. R. Taylor Segraves, 19910 S. Woodland, Shaker Heights, OH 44122. PH: (212)459-3634.

X191. **Society for the Study of Social Problems (SSSP) / Sexual Behavior Division:** 901 McClung Tower, University of Tennessee, Knoxville, TN 37996-0490. PH: (615)974-6021.

[SERVICES: C,D,P] Members of SSSP are practitioners and advocates interested in the application of scientific methods and theory, especially from the social sciences, to the study of social problems and the formation of public policy. Maintains 16 special problems divisions, including this one on sexual behavior.

X192. **World Association of Sexology:** c/o Dr. Eli Coleman, General Secretary, Program in Human Sexuality, University of Minnesota, 1300 S. 2nd St., Minneapolis, MN 55454. PH: (612)625-1500.

Sponsors an annual conference.

➤ PROSTITUTION

Sex Works (see H74) includes statements from six prostitution groups worldwide: WHISPER, English Collection of Prostitutes, U.S.PROstitutes Collective, COYOTE, The Red Thread, and the International Committee for Prostitutes Rights.

—— ARCHIVES *(See also*: X50, X194)

X193.   **Walton Collection/ Cleveland Public Library, Social Sciences Dept.**: 325 Superior Ave., Cleveland, OH 44114.

[SERVICES: L] Holds 300 19th century, English and French language publications on prostitution. (SL)

—— PROSTITUTES ORGANIZED

X194.   **Call Off Your Old Tired Ethics (COYOTE)**: 2269 Chestnut St., #452, San Francisco, CA 94123. PH: (415)474-3037.

[SERVICES: C,L,R] A prostitutes rights organization with the goal of (1) repealing existing prostitution laws; (2) empowering prostitutes; (3) providing public information on the reality vs. myths of prostitution; (4) providing education to prostitutes on AIDS and other sexually transmitted diseases; and (5) working to end the stigma associated with prostitution. Regularly conduct "everything you always wanted to know about sex work but didn't know who to ask," panel discussions for the general public. COYOTE's archives are housed at the Schlessinger Library at Radcliff University, where they are only accessible with special permission. See also COYOTE-Los Angeles: 1626 N. Wilcox Ave. #580, Hollywood, CA 90028. PH: (213)738-8028.

X194A.   **Prostitutes of New York (PONY)**: 25 West 45th St., #1401, New York, NY 10036. PH: (212)713-5678.

X195.   **PRIDE (PRostitution to Independence, Dignity and Equality)**: c/o Family and Children Services, 414 S. 8th Ave., Minneapolis, MN 55404. PH: (612)340-7634.

[SERVICES: R,SG] Self help advocacy program run by former prostitutes for women attempting to get out of the business. "Believe prostitution is a culturally sanctioned system of oppression, dehumanizing and demeaning to everyone involved in it."

X196. Women Hurt in Systems of Prostitution Engaged in Revolt (WHISPER): P.O. Box 8719, Lake St., Minneapolis, MN 55408. PH: (612)644-6301.

[SERVICES: L,P,SB,SG] Committed to "ending the sexual enslavement of women" in prostitution. Provides public education on prostitution as a form of violence against women and offer support services for women attempting to leave the sex industry. Publishes *WHISPER Newsletter* (quarterly). (EA)

➤ REPRODUCTION (*See also*: Abortion; Childbearing; Contraception; Family Planning; Lactation; Fertility; Menstruation; Reproductive Health; Maternal and Child Health; Reproductive Technologies; Women's Health)

HOW TO FIND

• The *Research Centers Directory* (see B83) lists many entries under "Human Reproduction," most focusing on reproductive medicine and genetic research.

X197. Center for Population Research: National Institute of Child Health and Human Development, 9000 Rockville Pike, Bldg. 6100, Rm.8B07, Bethesda, MD 20814. PH: (301)496-1101.

Develops fertility regulating methods and evaluates the safety and effectiveness of contraceptive methods. Supports fundamental biomedical research on the reproductive processes influencing human fertility and infertility, including behavioral and social science research on the reproductive motivation of individuals, the causes and consequences of population change, the diagnosis and treatment of reproductive diseases and disorders, and healthy fetal development. (EA)

X198. Society for the Study of Reproduction: 309 W. Clark St., Champaign, IL 61820. PH: (217)356-3182.

[SERVICES: C,P] Over 1,400 OB/GYNs, urologists, physiologists, zoologists, veterinarians, animal husbandry specialists, and other researchers interested in the study of human and animal reproduction. Publishes *Biology of Reproduction* (see K107). (EA)

➤ REPRODUCTIVE HEALTH AND MEDICINE (*See also*: Disability
& Illness; Fertility; Sexually Transmitted Diseases; Women's Health)

HOW TO FIND

• As sexology has not been declared a distinct medical specialty,
study and research in sexual medicine is conducted by a range of
specialists: psychiatrists (sex therapy), public health specialists (the
prevention of diseases); embryologists (fetal development); endocrinologists (hormones, fertility problems); obstetricians (the management
of pregnancy, labor and post perineum period); urologists (diseases
of the male genital tract, impotence); gynecologists (diseases of the
female genital tract); and dermatologists (STDs), among others.
Contact a local medical society or the American Medical Association
(515 N. State St., Chicago, IL 60610. PH: 312/464-4818) for
assistance in identifying the medical specialty dealing with the area
of interest. Specialized medical associations are listed by keywords
in the *Encyclopedia of Associations* (see B4).

• Organizations focusing on a particular illness or condition often
distribute print or audiovisual materials (see p.353). To identify,
consult *Encyclopedia of Health Information Sources* (Detroit: Gale
Research, 1987), a "bibliographic guide to approximately 13,000
publications, organizations, and other sources of information on more
than 450 health-related subjects."

X199.   American College of Obstetricians and Gynecologists: 409
12th St., SW, Washington, DC 20024-2188. PH: (800)762-2264.

[SERVICES: C,D,L,P] Professional association of OB/GYNs. Publishes a
series of six page technical bulletins, each reporting the latest research and
clinical findings on some aspect of OB/GYN; request a free list of titles.
Their library, open to the public by appointment, holds over 8,000 books
and reprints, and currently subscribes to 300 journals and newsletters. The
collection is especially strong in abortion, STDs, OB/GYN, sex education,
contraception, and the history of obstetrics and gynecology. (EA,SL).

X200.   Association of Reproductive Health Professionals: 2401 Pennsylvania Ave., NW, Washington, DC 20037. PH: (202)863-2475.

[SERVICES: C,P] Also known as the Association of Planned Parenthood

Physicians. 600 physicians, scientists, educators, and others interested in reproductive health issues including abortion, prevention of STDs, sexuality, contraception, family planning, maternal and child health, etc. Publishes *Health and Sexuality* (see K153). (EA)

X201. **Cancer Information Service**: National Cancer Institute, Building 31, Rm. 10A24, 9000 Rockville Pike, Bethesda, MD 20892. PH: (800)4-CANCER.

[SERVICES: B,P,R] Provides information on the diagnosis and treatment of cancers of all types, including those of the breast, genitals, and reproductive organs, and the carcinogenic effects of DES. (FIC)

X202. **Division of Reproductive Health / Center for Chronic Disease Prevention and Health Promotion / CDC**: 1600 Clifton Rd., NE, Atlanta, GA 30333. PH: (404)488-5191.

Consists of several branches: Behavioral Epidemiology and Demographic Research, Pregnancy and Infant Health, Statistics and Computer Resources, and Women's Health and Fertility. Call for referrals to specific programs. (FIC)

X203. **International Society of Reproductive Medicine**: c/o Donald C. McEwen, 11 Furman Ct., Rancho Mirage, CA 92270. PH: (619)340-5080.

Association of researchers in reproductive medicine, endocrinology, gynecology, obstetrics, and laypersons interested in population problems. (EA)

X204. **National Library of Medicine** (NLM): 8600 Rockville Pike, Bethesda, MD 20894. PH: (301)496-6095 (reference desk).

In support of its mission to collect, preserve, and disseminate biomedical information, NLM has assembled the largest collection of biomedical literature in the world, with comprehensive holdings in over 40 biomedical fields, as well as the nation's largest medical history collection. Included are books, journals, technical reports, and other print and audiovisual materials. NLM's services include computer based literature retrieval (they maintain 40 specialized databases on the MEDLARS system, see J45) and interlibrary loan. They publish numerous catalogs, guides, and indexes, including *Index Medicus* (see J44), the *NLM Audiovisuals Catalog* (see B10), and a series of subject bibliographies (see p.143). (FIC,SL)

➤ REPRODUCTIVE TECHNOLOGIES (*See also*: Bioethics; Fertility and Infertility; Women's Health)

HOW TO FIND

• Elizabeth Noble's *Having Your Baby by Donor Insemination: A Complete Resource Guide* (Boston: Houghton Mifflin Co., 1988) includes a list of related organizations and facilities.

• The Federal Office of Technology Assessment's *Infertility: Medical and Social Choices* (Washington: Government Printing Office, 1988), examines scientific, legal, economic, and ethical considerations of new and established reproductive technologies. It includes a list of over 190 facilities performing surrogate mother matching, in-vitro fertilization, and gamete intrafallopian transfer (GIFT).

X205.   **Society for Assisted Reproductive Technologies**: c/o American Fertility Society, 2140 11th Ave. S., Suite 200, Birmingham, AL 35205. PH: (205)933-8494.

[SERVICES: C,P,R] An association of institutions and organizations which conduct assisted reproductive procedures. Collects and disseminates information on human in-vitro fertilization techniques and related topics. (EA)

X206.   **Feminist International Network of Resistance to Reproductive and Genetic Engineering**: c/o Janice Raymond, Women's Studies Dept., University of Massachusetts, Amherst, MA 01003. PH: (413)367-2287.

X207.   **National Coalition Against Surrogacy**: 1130 17th St., NW, Suite 630, Washington, DC 20036. PH: (202)466-2823.

Works to bar surrogate contracts in the U.S. and for protection of the rights of surrogate mothers.(EA 11885)

—— SUPPORT GROUPS

X208.   **Donors Offspring**: P.O. Box 37, Sarcoxie, MO 64862. PH: (417)548-3679.

Self help support group for individuals involved in artificial fertilization, including donors, recipients, surrogate parents, offspring, parents of donor or recipient, and fertility experts and professionals. (EA)

X209. **National Association of Surrogate Mothers**: 8383 Wilshire Blvd., Suite 750D, Beverly Hills, CA 90211. PH: (213)655-2015.

X210. **Parents of Surrogate-Born Infants and Toddlers in Verbal Exchange (POSITIVE)**: P.O. Box 204, East Meadow, NY 11554. PH: (516)794-5772.

Provides peer support for parents of surrogate born children and answers inquiries nationwide. (EA)

➤ SADOMASOCHISM (*See also*: Fetishes; D8)

X211. **Eulenspiegel Society**: Box 2783, Grand Central Station, New York, NY 10163. PH: (212)633-8376 / 477-6588.

[SERVICES: C,D,P,SB,SG] A membership organization of people interested in dominant and submissive role playing. Advocates "freedom for sexual minorities and particularly the rights of those whose sexuality emphasizes D/S or dominant/submissive fantasies and urges." Seeks to "foster consciousness raising and understanding among our members and the public at large through public forums and workshops on D/S, dissemination of Society publications and literature, by providing speakers for all forms of media, colleges and other audiences, and by giving support to other sexual liberation movements." Conducts weekly public lectures on such topics as "Giving a Real Spanking," "Bondage Workshop," "Spouse Abuse and S/M," "S/M and Catholicism," "Dominant Women in History," "Japanese Bondage," and "The Emergence of S/M from the Underground: From Perversion to Acceptance." Publishes *The Eulenspiegel Society Newsletter* (see K112), which includes a national directory of non-profit/non-commercial clubs and support groups, including mixed groups (straight, bi-, and gay), dominant men/submissive women, men only, women only, and crossdressers/transvestites).

➤ SEX ADDICTION

X212. **National Council on Sexual Addiction and Compulsivity**: P.O. Box 20249, Wickenburg, AZ 85358.

A private, non-profit organization dedicated to promoting public understanding, awareness, and recognition of sexual addictions and compulsions. Comprised of service providers, allied health professionals, educators, members of the recovering community, and other concerned citizens. Provides education, information, and referral services throughout the professional and lay communities. Sponsors the *Interdisciplinary Conference on Sexual Addiction, Compulsion and Trauma.*

The following four groups provide support and referrals to sex addicts and their families, and information on sex addiction to the general public. All are twelve step programs developed to assist men and women desiring to stop living out patterns of addictive sexual and emotional behavior, including compulsive sexual behavior practiced alone or with others, desperate attachment to one person, and sexually self destructive thoughts or behavior, including fantasy, pornography, adultery, masturbation, incest, or criminal sexual activity. All are open to people of any age, sexual preference, or gender orientation.

X213.   **Co-Dependents of Sex Addicts**: P.O. Box 14537, Minneapolis, MN 55414. PH: (612)537-6904.

X214.   **Sex Addicts Anonymous**: P.O. Box 3038, Minneapolis, MN 55403. PH: (612)339-0217.

X215.   **Sex and Love Addicts Anonymous**: P.O. Box 119, New Town Br., Boston, MA 02258. PH: (617)332-1845.

X216.   **Sexaholics Anonymous**: P.O. Box 300, Simi Valley, CA 93062. PH: (805)581-3343.

➤ SEX CRIMES *(See also*: Sex and Law; Sex Therapy; Sexual Abuse)

X217.   **National Criminal Justice Reference Service**: Box 6000, Rockville, MD 20850. PH: (800)851-3420.

[SERVICES: B,DB,P,R] International information clearinghouse and reference center operated by the National Institute of Justice. Their goal is to increase understanding of the causes, effects, and prevention of crime, and the operation of the criminal justice system. The National Institute of Justice has experts on nearly every aspect of criminal justice. For referrals, contact the Office of Communication and Research

Utilization of the National Institute of Justice (see B44). Topical bibliographies are available and custom bibliographies are compiled from the *National Criminal Justice Reference Service Database* (see J22). Maintains a library of over 100,000 books, reports and articles, on such topics as sex establishments (brothels, massage parlors), morals-decency crimes, prostitutes, pornography, profiles of sex offenders, treatment of sex offenders, causes of sex offenses, sex offense investigations, incest, rape, indecency, sexual assault on prisoners, sodomy, autoerotic death, sexual addictions, and sexual assault trauma, to name only a few. Items are classified using terms from the *National Criminal Justice Thesaurus*. See also the Bureau of Justice Statistics, Q1.

➤ SEX EDUCATION (*See also*: X183)

X218. **ERIC Clearinghouse on Counseling and Personnel Services**: University of Michigan, 2108 School of Education Bldg., Ann Arbor, MI 48109-1259. PH: (313)764-9492.

[SERVICES: B,DB,L,P] A unit of the U.S. Department of Education's ERIC network of information clearinghouses which collect and disseminate educational documents. Materials on sex education, family living, and teenage pregnancy and parenting, are among those collected by this clearinghouse. Call (800)USE-ERIC for research assistance. (RC)

X219. **ETR Associates**: P.O. Box 1830, Santa Cruz, CA 95061-1830. PH: (408)438-4060.

[SERVICES: AV,C,L,P] A national non-profit whose programs, projects, and services focus on family life education, sexuality education, health education, reproductive health, AIDS, adolescent pregnancy, child sexual abuse prevention education, and substance abuse prevention education. They conduct training and research, and develop and distribute educational and professional materials, including pamphlets, books, curricula, films, and videos (see Network Publications, L20). Operates the California AIDS Clearinghouse (see X33).

X220. **Exodus Trust**: 1523 Franklin St., San Francisco, CA 94109. PH: (415)928-1133.

[SERVICES: AV,P] Formerly known as the National Sex Forum. A non-profit California trust, affiliated with the Institute for the Advanced Study of Human Sexuality (see X228), which has "as its sole and exclusive purpose to perform educational, scientific, and literary functions relating to sexual, emotional, mental and physical health." They offer continuing education courses, and produce educational audiovisuals, products, books and other print materials for use in sex education, therapy, and counseling (see MultiFocus V4). Exodus developed the Sexual Attitude Restructuring (SAR) process, "a revolutionary method for educating adults about what people do sexually and how they feel about it."

X221. International Council of Sex Education and Parenthood: c/o Patricia Schiller, 5010 Wisconsin Ave., NW, Washington, DC 20016. FAX: (202)686-2523.

[SERVICES: AV,C,L,P,SB] Supports training, research, and program development in family life and sex education. Develops curriculum and training materials. Maintains a library.

X222. National Coalition to Support Sexuality Education: c/o SIECUS. See X225 for address.

A coalition of more than 60 non-profit organizations supporting comprehensive sexuality education for children and youth. Advocates for sexuality education policy at the federal and state level, and monitors federal, state, and local actions; assists national youth organizations in developing sex education policies and programs; develops national strategies for countering anti-sex education movements and assuring local implementation of sexuality education initiatives. Publications include *Sex Education 2000: A Call to Action*, outlining 13 goals for the next decade.

X223. Planned Parenthood Federation of America—Education Department: 810 7th Ave., New York, NY 10019. PH: (212)261-4629.

[SERVICES: AV,P,R,S] Planned Parenthood has provided reproductive health care and sex education in the U.S. for 75 years. The Education Department provides information, consulting, training, resource referrals and technical assistance to students, professionals, the media, and PPFA affiliates and volunteers, on issues relating to sexuality and reproductive health. They offer an extensive professional development program for those seeking assistance in program development, implementation, evaluation, and personnel training. In an effort to build support for their Comprehensive School Sexuality Education (CSSE) initiative, they hold national forums, conduct lobbying activities, and provide on-site technical assistance. Sponsors National Family Sexuality Education Month in October. Maintains the Federation Clearinghouse of Educational Resources, available on *LINKLine* (see I6). See also A4 and X111.

X224. Sex Education Coalition: P.O. Box 3101, Silver Springs, MD 20918. PH: (301)593-8557.

X225. Sex Information and Education Council of United States (SIECUS): 130 W. 42nd St., Suite 2500, New York, NY 10036. PH: (212)819-9770.

[SERVICES: AV,C,L,P,R] The premier source in the U.S. for information on sex education. SIECUS "affirms that sexuality is a natural and healthy part of living and advocates for the rights of individuals to make responsible sexual choices." They develop, collect, and disseminate information to professionals and the general public (see also A5); promote comprehensive education about sexuality through public speaking, lobbying efforts, workshops, seminars, and publications; and provide consulting services and technical assistance with program planning and curriculum development. Publications include the *SIECUS Report* (see K119; back issues and reprints also available), regularly updated bibliographies (see H46), and fact sheets, position statements, booklets, pamphlets, and reports, including *Talk About Sex: A Booklet for Young People on How to Talk About Sexuality and AIDS*; *Guidelines for Comprehensive Sexuality Education, Kindergarten Through Twelfth Grade*; *Winning the Battle: Developing Support for Sexuality and HIV/AIDS Education*; *Communication Strategies for HIV/AIDS and Sexuality: A Training Manual for Mental Health and Health Professionals*; *Performance Standards and Checklist for the Evaluation and Development of School HIV/AIDS Education Curricula for Adolescents*; *How to Talk to Your Children About AIDS*; *Messages About Sexuality: How to Give Yours to Your Child*, among others (see also p.82, p.276, p.290)—an annotated publications catalog is available on request. SIECUS Fact Sheet #4 *The Far-Right and Fear-Based Abstinence-Only Programs* lists the major Far-Right organizations opposing comprehensive sexuality education. (EA,SL)

— TRAINING

The following programs train sex educators. For others, as well as for information on continuing education programs, contact AASECT (see

X183) and the Society for the Scientific Study of Sex (see X189).

X226. Human Sexuality Program / School of Education, University of Pennsylvania: Philadelphia, PA 19104. PH: (215)898-7394.
Offers MS, EdD, and PhD degrees in human sexuality education.

X227. Human Sexuality Program / Dept. of Health Education, New York University: 35 West 4th St., 12th Fl., New York, NY. PH: (212)998-5780.
Offers MA, EdD, and PhD degrees in health education, with an emphasis on human sexuality education.

X228. Institute for the Advanced Study of Human Sexuality: 1523 Franklin St., San Francisco, CA 94109. PH: (415)928-1133.
[SERVICES: L] A private, non-traditional graduate school of sexology offering Masters of Human Sexuality, Doctor of Human Sexuality, PhD, and EdD degrees, as well as professional certification programs, continuing education, and independent study programs.

X229. Human Sexuality Program / San Francisco State University: Psychology Bldg., 1600 Holloway Ave., San Francisco, CA 94132.
Offers an interdisciplinary undergraduate minor and an individualized MA program in Human Sexuality Studies.

➤ SEX INFORMATION SERVICES

Although most organizations provide sex information services to the public, few have this as their primary mission. See also SIECUS (see A5) and the Information Services of the Kinsey Institute (see A4).

X230. National Sex Information Network: 3805 Bohemian Hwy., Box 902, Occidental, CA 95465. PH: (415)326-1155.
[SERVICES: B,DB,L,P,R] Devoted to assisting the general public in accessing free and low cost information on sex, reproduction, and related topics, although they also serve professionals, students, the media, and others seeking sex related resources. Publications include a quarterly newsletter providing updates of new resources; the annual directory

SEXPERTS U.S.A.: Information Sources in Human Sexuality, Repro-duction, and Related Topics, describing hundreds of organizations, libraries, government agencies, information clearinghouses, research centers, and businesses providing services to the public; *Contents at a Glance: Sex Studies* (see K131) and *Contents at a Glance: Gay and Lesbian Studies* (see K64). They maintain a computer-readable database of organizational, institutional, governmental, and corporate publications.

X231.   San Francisco Sex Hotline: P.O. Box 881254, San Francisco, CA 94188-1254. PH: (415)621-7300 (M-F 3:00-9:00 p.m.)

A non-profit, volunteer organization dedicated to providing the public—through a telephone hotline—with basic, factual, non-judgmental information and referrals concerning all aspects of human sexuality. A 50 hour volunteer training is offered twice a year for a fee.

➤ SEX AND THE LAW *(See also:* Abortion; Pornography; Prostitution; Reproductive Technologies; B48, X176, X259, X270)

HOW TO FIND

• Law libraries can provide research guidance, and some offer phone or mail reference services; consult the American Association of Law Library's *AALL Directory and Handbook* for referrals. The AALL also maintains a standing committee on Lesbian and Gay Issues.

• Consult *Encyclopedia of Legal Information Sources* (Detroit: Gale Research, 1992).

Many aspects of sexuality are regulated by local, state, and/or federal laws and regulations, including marriage, dissolution and annulment, adultery, prostitution, pornography and obscenity, illegitimacy, artificial insem-ination and surrogate parenthood, bigamy, abduction, seduction, incest, nudity, rape, child molestation, oral and anal sex, bestiality, age of consent, homosexuality, sex offenders, and sexual "perversions" (i.e. voyeurism, exhibitionism). There are also laws and regulations governing such sex and reproductive health related issues as contraception, abortion, sterilization, sex education, sexually transmitted diseases, and paramedical personnel (e.g. midwives, sex therapists), birth defects, etc. (See also F28.)

X232.   American Civil Liberties Union: 132 W. 43rd St., New York, NY 10036. PH: (212)944-9800.

[SERVICES: C,P,R] Works to uphold the constitutional rights set forth in the Bill of Rights, including freedom of speech, press, assembly, due process of law, and equality before the law, through advocacy, litigation, and public education. Maintains a 3,000 volume library. Ongoing projects include, the Task Force on AIDS, the First Amendment Project, the Reproductive Freedom Project (see X12), and the Gay/Lesbian Rights Project. Publications include: *The Rights of Lesbians and Gay Men: The Basic ACLU Guide to a Gay Person's Rights.*

X233.   Committee to Preserve our Sexual and Civil Liberties: Box 1592, San Francisco, CA 94101-1592.

[SERVICES: C,P] Educational corporation working for "open and positive attitudes toward sexuality, the right to consensual sexual expression, and the rights of sexual minorities." Founded to fight the closure of San Francisco bathhouses and sex clubs, ostensibly for AIDS related health reasons, it now works on behalf of all sexual civil liberties, including sexual expression issues (pornography and erotica, erotic performances, censorship, S/M, sexual clubs); civil rights and sexual orientation issues (discrimination due to sexual orientation, prostitution, transsexuality and transvestism, age of consent); and medical issues (abortion, AIDS and other STDs, circumcision, contraception, sterilization). Publishes the *Journal of Sexual Liberty*, a monthly newsletter. Sponsors the annual Sexual Liberty and Social Repression Conference.

X234.   Institute for the Study of Matrimonial Laws: c/o Sydney Siller, 11 Park Pl., Suite 1116, New York, NY 10007. PH: (212)766-4030.

[C,L,P,S] Studies divorce, alimony, child custody, and visitation laws with the goal of encouraging rational and objective laws that reflect contemporary life. Collects and studies statistics in the areas of alimony, divorce, child custody, and other matrimonial problems. Maintains a 10,000 volume library of books and other documents. (EA)

X235.   National Committee for Sexual Civil Liberties: 98 Olden Ln., Princeton, NJ 08540. PH: (609)924-1950.

[SERVICES: P] An association of civil liberties lawyers and scholars working to "dismantle the entire structure of criminality and discrimination surrounding private sexual conduct between consenting adults," including repeal of adultery, fornication and sodomy laws, regulations and laws which discriminate on the basis of sexual orientation, and laws punishing the distribution, importation, or sale of pornographic materials to adults. Publishes the *Sexual Law Reporter*, quarterly. (EA)

X236. Sexual Sanity: P.O. Box 471061, San Francisco, CA 94147. A new group organizing for sexual civil liberties.

—— SEXUAL ORIENTATION

In addition to those described below, there are a number of specialized groups which focus on a particular legal issue (e.g. X239; the Committee to Fight Exclusion of Homosexuals from Armed Forces). For referrals, see the *Encyclopedia of Associations*, or consult X119 or X238.

X237. Human Rights Campaign Fund: 1012 14th St., NW, 6th Fl., Washington, DC 20005. PH: (202)628-4160.

[SERVICES: C,P,S,SB] Provides information on issues affecting the lesbian and gay community and related legislative activity, and seeks to exert the power of lesbian and gay Americans on national politics and legislation through bi-partisan political action, lobbying, and grassroots mobilization. Collects relevant polling data and research. Their publications monitor and review relevant legislation and the actions of legislators on issues affecting the gay and lesbian community: *Momentum* (quarterly); *Capitol Hill Update*; *Weekly Legislative Report*; *AIDS Policy Report*; *Presidential Bulletin*; *Congress in Review*; and *Votes of the Congress* (reporting the voting records of each Congressperson on pertinent issues). Also operates a number of computer bulletin boards.

X238. LAMBDA Legal Defense and Education Fund Inc.: 666 Broadway, 12th Fl., New York, NY 10012-2317. PH: (212)995-8585.

[SERVICES: B,L,P,R,S] Seeks to protect and advance the legal rights of gay men and lesbians by educating the public about discrimination based on sexual orientation, and pursuing test-case litigation nationwide in such areas as sexual orientation discrimination in the military, immigration, and employment; AIDS and HIV related issues; parenting and relationship issues; sodomy statutes; domestic partner benefits; and constitutional rights. Publishes the *LAMBDA Update* (see K121); a regularly updated AIDS bibliography; *AIDS Update*, a bimonthly newsletter on AIDS related legal issues; and legal briefs, information packets, and litigation manuals, including *Legalizing Lesbian and Gay Marriage*, *AIDS Legal Guide Domestic Partnership Packet*, among others; and a regularly revised *AIDS Bibliography*.

X239.   Lesbian Mothers National Defense Fund: P.O. Box 21567, Seattle, WA 98111. PH: (206)325-2643.

[SERVICES: P,R,S,SB] Non-profit volunteer resource network providing information, attorney referrals, and emotional support for lesbians on issues of custody and visitation, childbearing, donor insemination, and adoption. Distributes copies of psychological studies and legal articles pertaining to lesbian mothers and child custody by gay/lesbian parents to lesbians preparing for custody battles and others with interest in the area. The following are among the titles available (a complete catalog is available on request): *The Impact of Parental Homosexuality in Child Custody Cases: A Review of the Literature*; *Lesbian Mothers and Their Children: An Annotated Bibliography of Legal and Psychological Materials*; *Sexual Identity of 37 Children Raised by Homosexual or Transsexual Parents*; *Artificial Insemination Packet*; *A Lesbian and Gay Parents Legal Guide to Child Custody*. (EA)

➤ SEX IN THE MEDIA *(See also*: Conservative/Traditionalist; Pornography; X2, X176, X242)

X240.   American Family Association: P.O. Drawer 2440, Tupelo, MS 38803. PH: (601)844-5036.

[SERVICES: S,SB] Supports a "biblical ethic of decency in American society with primary emphasis on television and other media." Encourages its members to protest shows portraying "violence, immorality, profanity, and vulgarity" and to support those that are "clean, constructive, wholesome, and family oriented." Compiles statistics on scenes from television broadcasts involving sex, profanity and violence. (EA)

X241.   Center for Population Options Media Project: 12023 1/2 Ventura Blvd., #2, Studio City, CA 91604. PH: (818)766-4200.

[SERVICES: S,SB] Encourages the film and television industry to present more positive, accurate, and responsible images of family planning, sexuality, and other reproductive health issues. See also X18. (EA)

X242.   Parents Music Resource Center: 1500 Arlington Blvd., Arlington, VA 22209. PH: (703)527-9466.

[SERVICES: L,P,S,SB] Concerned about rock music lyrics, videos, and stage shows which "glorify graphic sex and violence and glamorize the use of drugs and alcohol." Does not support, condone, or accept censorship, but advocates that records be voluntarily labeled "Explicit Lyrics–Parental Advisory," when appropriate. Maintains extensive files on popular, rock, and rap music groups which include transcripts of offensive lyrics, interviews, and reviews. Collects studies relating to the effects of music on adolescents. (EA)

—— GAY AND LESBIANS IN THE MEDIA

X243.   Gay and Lesbian Alliance Against Defamation: 80 Varick St., No. 3E, New York, NY 10013. PH: (212)807-1700.

Seeks to replace bigoted and misinformed representations of gays and lesbians in the media with positive images. Monitors portrayals of gays and lesbians in the media. Publishes *GLAAD Bulletin* (see K125). (EA)

X244.   Gay and Lesbian Press Association: P.O. Box 8185, Universal City, CA 91608-0815. PH: (818)902-1476.

X245.   Gay Media Task Force: 71-426 Estellita Dr., Rancho Mirage, CA 92270. PH: (619)568-6711.

Monitors the media for portrayals of gays and lesbians, and works to promote accurate representations of gays and lesbians in nonfiction and the media. Serves as a resource to the media on issues relating to the gay and lesbian community. (EA).

➤ SEX AND RELIGION (*See also*: Anti-Abortion; Conservative / Traditionalists)

X246.   Catholics for a Free Choice: 1436 U St., NW, No. 301, Washington, DC 20009-3916. PH: (202)638-1706.

[SERVICES: C,L,P,SB] Catholics supporting the right to legal abortion and family planning, while at the same time working to reduce the incidence

---

HOW TO FIND

• The American Theological Library Association (820 Church St., 3rd floor, Evanston, IL 60201) will provide referrals to a theology library in your area.

---

of abortion, and to increase women's choices in childbearing and child-rearing through advocacy of social and economic programs for women, families, and children. Publishes *Conscience: A News Journal of Prochoice Catholic Opinion* (see K126), a bimonthly journal discussing ethical questions relating to human reproduction and sexuality. (EA)

X247.   Catholics United for Life: c/o Dennis Musk, 3050 Gap Knob Rd., New Hope, KY 40052. PH: (502)325-3061.

[SERVICES: C,L,P] Distributes information on Catholic moral and social teachings regarding marriage, sexuality, natural family planning, alternatives to abortion, family life, and other pro-life issues. Their 10,000 volume library is open to the public. (EA,SL)

X248.   CORPUS, National Association of Resigned/Married Priests: P.O. Box 2649, Chicago, IL 60690. PH: (312)764-3399.

[SERVICES: C,P] 12,000 resigned Roman Catholic priests who retain their commitment to the priesthood and the Church, non-resigned priests, and laypersons advocating the acceptance of married priests in all aspects of the Roman Catholic Church. (EA)

X249.   Institute for the Study of American Religion: P.O. Box 90709, Santa Barbara, CA 93190-0709. PH: (805)893-3250.

[SERVICES: L] An independent, educational/research organization dedicated to furthering the study of small American religious bodies, although they collect materials from all religious families represented in the U.S.— including over 1,300 currently active bodies and hundreds more which are now defunct—as well as from the main bodies of organized dissent, and special interest groups within larger denominations (e.g. Dignity, an organization of gay Catholics). Open to the public, their library/archive contains more than 20,000 volumes and 400 periodicals, as well as pamphlets, leaflets, magazine and newspaper clippings, and ephemera.

Research assistance is provided by mail. They compile *The Churches Speak Series* (see F30), which includes a number of sex related titles, the *Encyclopedia of American Religions*, and other reference books.

X250.   The Pope John XXIII Medical-Moral Research and Education Center: 186 Forbes Rd., Braintree, MA 02184. PH: (617)848-6965.

[SERVICES: C,L,P] Dedicated to analyzing current and emerging medical-moral and ethical issues from the perspective of Catholic teaching and the Judeo-Christian heritage. Publications include the journal *Ethics and Medics* (see K18) and two handbooks: *Handbook of Critical Life Issues* and *Handbook on Critical Sexual Issues: The Latest Medical-Moral Research on Issues of Human Sexuality and Sexual Ethics in Light of the Teachings of the Catholic Church.*

—— GAY AND LESBIAN

Gay and lesbian religious groups range from Affirmation of Gay and Lesbian Mormons to Witches/Pagans for Gay Rights. Some, such as Dignity, are supportive of gay lifestyles, believing that homosexuals can be sexually active without breaking God's laws. Others, such as Courage, also a Catholic organization, use support groups and prayers to encourage homosexual members to live celibate lives. Still others seek to change their members' sexual orientation (e.g. the Homosexual Anonymous Fellowship Service), believing that "there is no such thing as a homosexual, only men and women, created by God heterosexually, who because of the broken world we live in, are confused over their sexual identity." Space restrictions prevent us from describing all such groups; see *Encyclopedia of Associations* or *Gay Yellow Pages* (see p.361) for listings.

X251.   Dignity: 1500 Massachusetts Ave., NW, Suite 11, Washington, DC 20005. PH: (202)861-0017.

Gay and lesbian Catholics and others who believe that gays and lesbians can be sexually expressive in ethical, responsible ways. Publications include *Theological Pastoral Resources: A Collection of Articles on Homosexuality from a Catholic Perspective.* (EA)

X252.   Universal Fellowship of Metropolitan Community Churches: 5300 Santa Monica Blvd., Suite 34, Los Angeles, CA 90029.

[SERVICES: L] A Christian group primarily ministering to homosexual communities. Publishes a semiannual *Directory of Congregations and Clergy*. The Metropolitan Community Church in Houston, Texas, maintains a 10,000 volume library on all aspects of homosexuality (1919 Decatur, Houston, TX 77007. PH: 713/861-9149).

➤ SEX RESEARCH (*See also*: Professional Associations; X170, X263)

Many organizations listed in this chapter conduct research; see under the relevant subject headings.

X253.   Alan Guttmacher Institute: 11 5th Ave., New York, NY 10003. PH: (212)254-5656.

[SERVICES: C,P,S] Monitors federal activities, compiles statistics, and conducts research, public policy analysis, social science research analysis, and public education on issues of reproductive health and reproductive rights, including family planning, sex education, abortion, population, fertility and infertility, maternal and child health care, pregnancy, teen pregnancy, contraceptive development and use, reproductive health services, and related health and social policy issues. Findings are communicated to policy makers and the public through numerous publications, including *Family Planning Perspectives* (see K56); *International Family Planning Perspectives* (see K57); *Washington Memo* (20/year), which tracks legislation; *State Reproductive Health Monitor: Legislative Proposals and Actions* (quarterly); and *Abortion Services in the United States: Each State and Metropolitan Area* (annual), among others. They also distribute specialized publications for the media, general public, government, family planning clinicians and personnel, gynecologists, sex education teachers, social scientists, and related organizations. (EA, RC)

X254.   Center for Research and Education in Sexuality: San Francisco State University, Psychology Building, Rm. 502, San Francisco, CA 94132. PH: (415)338-1137.

Interdisciplinary research and education center affiliated with the Human Sexuality Studies program at San Francisco State University. Seeks to integrate research from the humanities, as well as the behavioral, social, and biological sciences into the study of human sexuality. Director John P. DeCecco edits the *Journal of Homosexuality* (see K83) and Haworth Press's *Gay and Lesbian Studies Series* (see L10). (RC)

X255. **Institute for Advanced Study of Human Sexuality**: 1523 Franklin St., San Francisco, CA 94109. PH: (415)928-1133.

Conducts research on erotology and sexual behavior and attitudes. See also, A3, V4, X220, X228. (RC)

X256. **The Kinsey Institute for Research in Sex, Gender, and Reproduction**: Indiana University, 313 Morrison Hall, Bloomington, IN 47405. PH: (812)855-7686.

[SERVICES: C,DB,P,L,R,S] Formerly known as the Institute of Sex Research, this independent, non-profit research organization was established by Alfred Kinsey (see Ch.21), and currently conducts research on American sexual behavior, sexual identity, sexual and psychological development, and biomedical and psychobiological approaches to sex, gender, and reproduction. Custom analysis of data collected by the Institute since the 1940s is available (see U2). Maintains the Kinsey Institute Library and Information Services (see A4). (RC)

X257. **Masters and Johnson Institute**: 24 S. Kings Highway Blvd., St. Louis, MO 63108. PH: (314)361-2377.

X258. **Office of Psychohormonal Research**: Johns Hopkins University, School of Medicine, 1235 E. Monument St., Suite LL20, Baltimore, MD 21202. PH: (301)955-3740.

Conducts longitudinal psychohormonal research on endocrine, genital, and sexological syndromes. Maintains a 2,000 volume library on sexology and psychoendocrinology. (RC)

X259. **Program in Psychiatry, Law and Human Sexuality**: UCLA Neuropsychiatric Institute, 760 Westwood Plaza, Los Angeles, CA 90024. PH: (213)206-8716.

[SERVICES: C,P] Affiliated with the International Academy of Sex Research (see X186), this research program examines the interface between psychiatry, law and human sexuality, including studies of sexual privacy laws. Publishes *Archives of Sexual Behavior* (see K129). (RC)

▶ SEX THERAPY *(See also*: X183, X185, X188, X189, X190, X282)

HOW TO FIND

• Many medical schools offer sex therapy training programs, including University of Chicago Medical Center, SUNY Downstate Medical Center, New York University Medical Center, University of Minnesota Medical School, Mt. Sinai, Cornell, University of California at Los Angeles, University of California at San Francisco, and others.

• SEICUS compiles and regularly updates a *Sexual Dysfunction Clinics Directory*, describing 65 centers nationwide that have treatment programs for sexual dysfunctions, paraphilias, gender dysphoria, sexual compulsions, sex offenders, and survivors of sexual abuse. Centers with training programs for professionals are highlighted. Order from X225.

• *AASECT National Register*, a geographically arranged directory of certified sex therapists, educators, counselors, and supervisors, is available from AASECT (see X183).

X260.   American Association for Marital and Family Therapy: 1100 17th St., NW, Washington, DC 20036. PH: (202)452-0109.

Membership association of marriage and family therapists providing education and referral services to the public.

X261.   Association for Gay, Lesbian and Bisexual Issues in Counseling: Box 216, Jenkintown, PA 19046.

[SERVICES: C,D,P] Counselors concerned with lesbian and gay issues. Provides referrals to gay counselors.

X262.   International Professional Surrogates Association: P.O. Box 74156, Los Angeles, CA 90004. PH: (213)469-4720.

[SERVICES: C,P,R,SB] Operates a referral and information phone line for therapists and clients, and provides training for therapists and sex surrogates (individuals who work, in conjunction with therapists, as sexual partners for clients seeking to improve sexual functioning and skills). (EA)

X263. **Johns Hopkins Hospital Sexual Disorders Clinic**: Johns Hopkins Hospital, Meyer Bldg. Rm. 4-181, 600 N. Wolfe St., Baltimore, MD 21205. PH: (301)955-6292.

[SERVICES: C,R,SB] Also known as the National Institute for the Study, Prevention, and Treatment of Sexual Trauma. Conducts research on the bio-correlates and treatment of sexual disorders, including pedophilia, sadism, transvestism, voyeurism, exhibitionism, compulsive rape, and other psychosexual disorders. Evaluates the effects of various treatments on sex offenders, offers therapy, and provides referrals. (RC)

➤ SEX TOYS *(See also:* L24)

Vibrators, dildos, and other sex aids can be purchased via mail order from X264, X265, and Eve's Garden (see L24)—all guarantee anonymity. X264 and L24 are directed primarily toward women (both heterosexual and lesbian), although many of their products are non-gendered.

X264. **Good Vibrations**: 1210 Valencia St., San Francisco, CA 94110. PH: (415)550-7399.

A retail store and mail order catalog offering a highly selective collection of sex toys of all types.

X265. **Xandria Collection, Lawrence Research Group**: P.O.Box 319005, San Francisco, CA 94131. PH: (800)242-2823.

A mail order distribution company of sex toys and novelty items. Also publishes a special catalog for disabled individuals and couples.

➤ SEXUAL ABUSE AND COERCION *(See also*: Sex Crimes; L22)

X266. **National Victims Resource Center**: Dept. F, P.O. Box 6000, Rockville, MD 20850. PH: (800)627-NVRC.

Information clearinghouse operated by the U.S. Department of Justice's Office of Victims of Crimes. Distributes publications and maintains a database of over 7,000 victim related books and articles, including items on sexual abuse.

HOW TO FIND

• Consult directories. Jane Roberts Chapman's *Directory of Information Resources on the Victimization of Women* (Chevy Chase, MD: Response) is a directory of libraries, clearinghouses, on-line databases, and other resources providing information on abused women and children. Order from Response: P.O. Box 2462, Ada, OK 74820. Linda Webster's *Sexual Assault and Child Sexual Abuse: A National Directory of Victim/Survivor Services and Prevention Programs* (Phoenix: Oryx Press, 1989) fully describes over 2,200 facilities and programs for survivors of domestic violence, sexual assault, child and adolescent sexual abuse, and incest. Introductory notes include statistical information on services and programs.

—— CHILD SEXUAL ABUSE AND INCEST (*See also*: J18; p.403)

HOW TO FIND

• Kay Clark's *Sexual Abuse Prevention Education: An Annotated Bibliography* (Santa Cruz, CA: Network Publications, 1986) includes a directory of organizations and consultants who can provide assistance in establishing child abuse prevention programs, and/or who distribute audiovisuals for use in such programs.

X267.   Children of the Night: P.O. Box 4343, Hollywood, CA 90078. PH: (818)908-0850.

[SERVICES: R,SB] Provides support and protection to street children involved in pornography and/or prostitution. Maintains biographical archives and operates a speakers bureau.

X268.   Committee for Children: 172 20th Ave., Seattle, WA 98122. PH: (206)322-5050 / (800)634-4449.

[SERVICES: AV,C,P,S,SB] Dedicated to the prevention of child exploitation and sexual abuse through education, professional training, community education, and curriculum development (preschool through high school). Maintains an information clearinghouse on legislation regarding child and adolescent victims of sexual abuse. Distributes print and audiovisual materials; for a complete listing, request their semiannual catalog, *No More Victims, No More Victimized: Catalog of Prevention Education Resources*. (EA)

X269. **Incest Survivors Resource Network International**: P.O. Box 7375, Las Cruces, NM 88006-7375. PH: (505)521-4260.

[SERVICES: C,R] Specializes in providing information on female offenders/male victims, emotional incest, incest survivors as part of the overall adult child movement, and traumatic stress disorders in incest survivors. (EA)

X270. **National Association of State VOCAL (Victims of Child Abuse Laws) Organizations**: P.O. Box 1314, Orangeville, CA 95662. PH: (916)863-7470.

[SERVICES: C,L,P,SB] According to its entry in the *Encyclopedia of Associations*, this is a "national association of state and local support groups for men and women who believe they have been unjustly harmed by existing child abuse laws." Maintains a 1,000 volume library. Conducts public education and advocacy. (EA)

X271. **National Center for the Prosecution of Child Abuse**: 1033 N. Fairfax St., Suite 200, Alexandria, VA 22314. PH: (703)739-0321.

An information clearinghouse seeking to improve the investigation and prosecution of child abuse cases by providing technical assistance and training to prosecutors, including training in how to deal directly with child victims of physical or sexual abuse. Publishes the *National Directory of Child Abuse Prosecutors*, a geographic listing of over 800 prosecutors and district attorneys specializing in child abuse cases. (EA)

X272. **National Committee for Prevention of Child Abuse**: 332 S. Michigan Ave., Suite 1600, Chicago, IL 60604-4357. PH: (312)663-3520.

[SERVICES: AV,C,P,R] Committed to the prevention of all forms of child abuse, including sexual abuse—"the exploitation of a child for the sexual gratification of an adult, as in rape, incest, fondling of the genitals, exhibitionism, or pornography." The NCPCA's Research Center functions as a clearinghouse, and operates a computerized reference system on the incidence, origins, nature, effects and treatment of child abuse. Publications include *Self Help and the Treatment of Child Abuse*, which discusses the nature of self help groups and describes a wide range of programs; and *Selected Child Abuse Information and Resources Directory*, a guide to locating facts and services in the field. (EA)

X273. **National Resource Center on Child Sexual Abuse Information Services**: 107 Lincoln St., Huntsville, AL 35801. PH: (205)533-KIDS / (800)KIDS-006 (Information Service).

[SERVICES: B,C,DB,L,P,R,S] Funded by the National Center on Child Abuse and Neglect, the primary goal of the National Resource Center is to advance knowledge and improve skills in the field of child sexual abuse, by pulling together a vast network of information comprising the expertise and experience of outstanding leaders in the field, and providing an array of services that help professionals better investigate, manage, and treat child sexual victimization cases. They provide information, training, referrals, and technical assistance to professionals and the public. Publishes *Directory of Child Sexual Abuse Treatment Programs*; regularly updated bibliographies in more than 42 subject areas; *Think Tank Reports*, a monograph series; *Statistics on Child Sexual Abuse*; the quarterly newsletter, *Roundtable*; and others. (FIC)

X274. **Parents United International Inc.**: c/o Institute for Community as Extended Family, 232 E. Gish Rd., San Jose, CA 95112. PH: (800)422-4453 / (408)453-7616.

[SERVICES: C,P,R,SB,SG] A national, self-help organization for those who are, or have been, involved in intrafamilial sexual abuse, including spouses of offenders, children who have been molested, adults molested as children, family members (e.g. siblings, step parents, spouses), and, unlike other such groups, offenders themselves. Works closely with social service agencies and the judicial system to ensure that child molestation cases are handled in the most humanistic manner possible. Operates two support organizations: Daughters and Sons United, for children age 5-18 and their families, and Adults Molested as Children. (EA)

X275. **Survivors of Incest Anonymous**: P.O. Box 21817, Baltimore, MD 21222-6817. PH: (410)433-2365.
[SERVICES: C,P,R,SB,SG] A 12 step recovery program, with 80 local

groups, for adult survivors of child sexual abuse who are not themselves abusing a child. Incest is defined very broadly as "any sexual behavior [penetration not necessary] imposed on a person by a member of her or his immediate or extended family," including blood relatives, step-relatives, in-laws, and family friends. Publishes a bimonthly *Meeting Directory*, and the bimonthly *SIA World Service Directory*. (EA)

X276. VOICES (Victims of Incest Can Emerge Survivors) in Action: P.O. Box 148309, Chicago, IL 60614. PH: (800)7VOICE8 / (312)327-1500.

[SERVICES: C,P,R,S,SB,SG] A communication and peer support network intended to help adult victims of incest and child sexual abuse become survivors, as well as support their partners, families, and other pro survivors (i.e. people who give emotional support to survivors). Acts as a liaison between survivors and medical, legal, and social service agencies. Serves as an information clearinghouse and resource and referral service for the public. Sponsors special interest committees and support groups, including ones on pornography, ritual abuse, male survivors, multiple personality disorders, and female perpetrators. Publishes *The Chorus*, a bimonthly newsletter containing feature stories, book reviews, conference listings, a directory of self help groups, organizational news, and feature stories. (EA)

—— RAPE

In responding to our questionnaire, Women Against Rape expressed the following reservations about their organization being listed in a directory on human sexuality: "Rape is a violent, not a sexual crime. For too long, rape has been looked at as a sexual act which has continued to allow society to excuse it as a part of the natural order and to blame women for its occurrence." Any of the organizations described below can provide materials addressing this issue.

X277. National Clearinghouse on Marital and Date Rape: Women's History Research Inc., 2325 Oak St., Berkeley, CA 94708. PH: (510)524-1582.

[SERVICES: L,P,S,SB] Provides information and education on marital rape. Maintains an extensive library on marital, date, and cohabitation rape, and related legislative and prosecution efforts, including legal briefs and court testimony; sociological, psychological, and legal research studies; journals

---

HOW TO FIND

• Contact local rape crisis centers in your area for information; check the telephone yellow pages. The Washington, D.C. Rape Crisis Center (P.O.Box 21005, Washington, DC 20009) was one of the first such centers in the U.S., and may be able to provide local referrals.

---

and newsletters (10 current subscriptions); dissertations; newspaper and magazine clippings; and audiovisuals. The collection is housed at the University of Illinois' Women's Studies Library; a *Bibliographic Guide to the Files on Marital Rape* is available. Publications include a newsletter (see K147), and a *State Law Chart: Marital Rape Laws by State*. Phone consultation and document searching are available for a fee. (EA,SL)

X278. National Coalition Against Sexual Assault: P.O. Box 21378, Washington, DC 20009. PH: (202)483-7165.

[SERVICES:C,P,R,S] A network of organizations and individuals working against sexual assault. Sponsors Sexual Assault Awareness Month in April. (EA)

X279. People Organized to Stop Rape of Imprisoned People: P.O. Box 632, Ft. Bragg, CA 95437. PH: (707)964-0820.

[SERVICES: L,P,S,SB] An activist organization working to prevent rape, sexual slavery, forced prostitution, and sexual harassment in U.S. jails. Provides statistics on prison rape. (EA)

X280. Rape Crisis Center—Library: St. Vincent's Hospital, 153 W. 11th St., New York, NY 10011. PH: (212)790-8068.

[SERVICES: L,R] A collection of legal, medical, and political resources on rape, including rape trauma syndrome, incest, sex offenders, and rape in special populations (e.g. elderly, disabled, men, date/marital rape).

X281. Violence and Traumatic Stress Research and Training: NIMH, Parklawn Bldg., Rm. 18-105, 5600 Fishers Lane, Rockville, MD 20857. PH: (301)443-3728.

Formerly the National Center for the Prevention and Control of Rape.

Supports research on the causes of rape, sexual assault, and other violent assaults, the mental health consequences to offenders and survivors, and the treatment of survivors and offenders. *National Directory: Rape Prevention and Treatment Resources.* (FIC)

—— SEX OFFENDERS (*See also*: Sex Therapy; X263, X270, X271, X274)

X282. **Association for the Behavioral Treatment of Sexual Abusers**: P.O. Box 866, Lake Oswego, OR 97034. PH: (503)233-2312.

[SERVICES: P,R,SB] Association of 250 professionals working with sex offenders and/or victims of sexual assault. Offers training and consultation in treatment of sex offenders, and instruction in the use of penile plethysmograph, a device used to determine changes in penis size. Sponsors the Annual Research and Treatment Conference focusing on current research and clinical practices in the treatment and assessment of sexual deviancy. (EA)

X283. **Molesters Anonymous**: c/o Batterers Anonymous, 16913 Lerner Ln., Fontana, CA 92335. PH: (714)355-1100.

[SERVICES: C,P,R] A 12 step group for child molesters. (EA)

—— SEXUAL HARASSMENT

X284. **Association for the Sexually Harassed**: P.O. Box 27235, Philadelphia, PA 19118. PH: (215)952-8037.

[SERVICES: L,R,S,SB,SG] Provides information, education, and policy recommendations on "harassment that takes the form of unwelcome exposure to physical contact, pornography, sexual jokes, requests for dates, and demeaning comments, made by male or female, which causes an individual's environment or work place to become intimidating, hostile, or offensive." Disseminates research on sexual harassment related to post traumatic stress syndrome. Maintains a collection of newsclippings on sexual harassment. Conducts surveys and collects statistics. (EA)

➤ SEXUAL FREEDOM (*See also*: Alternative Lifestyles; Gay and Lesbian; Non-Monogamy; Nudism; Sex and Law)

The Sexual Freedom League, founded in 1964 by Jefferson Poland, is no longer active. The special collections department of the University of California at Berkeley's Banckroft Library (U.C. Berkeley, Berkeley, CA

94720) houses the Jefferson Poland/Sexual Freedom Papers documenting the sexual freedom movement in the U.S. in the 1960s and 1970s. See p.338 for a full description of the collection.

➤ SEXUALLY TRANSMITTED DISEASES

X285.   American Foundation for the Prevention of Venereal Disease: 799 Broadway, Suite 638, New York, NY 10003. PH: (212)759-2069.

[SERVICES: P] Provides information and educational materials to the public on the prevention of sexually transmitted diseases. (EA)

X286.   American Social Health Association: P.O. Box 13827, Research Triangle Park, NC 27709. PH: (919)361-8400.

[SERVICES: C,L,P,R,S,SB] Dedicated to the prevention, control, and eventual elimination of sexually transmitted disease, through public and professional education, research, and public policy. Operates a number of information hotlines answering questions and providing referrals relating to the prevention, exposure, risk, testing, and treatment of STDs: National AIDS hotline (800)342-AIDS (under contract with the Centers for Disease Control); National STD Hotline (800)227-9822; and the Herpes Resource Center Hotline (919)361-8488. Sponsors the Herpes Resource Center (see X289) and a special program on genital warts. The STD Hotline provides information and referrals on all STDs, including yeast infections, pelvic inflammatory disease, syphilis, gonorrhea, herpes, genital warts, and chlamydia, among others.

X287.   American Venereal Disease Association: P.O. Box 1753, Baltimore, MD 21203-1753. PH: (301)955-3150.

[SERVICES: C,P] Supports and disseminates clinical and laboratory research on the diagnosis, pathology, treatment, and control of venereal disease, with the primary goal of reducing their incidence. Publishes *Sexually Transmitted Diseases* (see K160). (EA)

X288.   Centers for Disease Control/ Center for Prevention Services/ Division of Sexually Transmitted Diseases: Bldg. 1, Rm. 4037, Atlanta, GA 30333. PH: (404)329-3343.

Collects statistics and epidemiological information on reportable STDs.

Publishes a *Resource List for Information Materials on STDs* and a *Directory of STD Clinics Resource List.*

X289. Herpes Resource Center: c/o American Social Health Association. See X286 for address. PH: (919)361-8488 (hotline).

[SERVICES: AV,B,P] Provides accurate, up-to-date information on herpes simplex viruses. Maintains educational programs for public and medical professionals, and offers a range of services through local groups nationwide, including rap groups, medical lectures, telephone hotlines, newsletters, and outreach activities. Call the hotline for local referrals. Publishes *Helper*, a quarterly newsletter reporting the latest research.

➤ TRANSVESTITES AND TRANSSEXUALS

HOW TO FIND

• Organized geographically and by category, the "IFGE Directory of Organizations and Services," included in each issue of *TV-TS Tapestry* (see K162), lists transvestite and transsexual relevant non-profit organizations; professional, medical and psychological health services; computer bulletin boards; commercial and professional publications and services; library and information services; and research centers. The directory can be purchased in booklet form from X292.

X290. American Educational Gender Information Service (AEGIS): P.O. Box 33724, Decatur, GA 30033. PH: (404)939-0244.

[SERVICES: B,P,R,SB,SG] Formerly known as the Montgomery Medical and Psychological Institute. An information clearinghouse on gender dysphoria and other gender issues. Provides research assistance, bibliographic recommendations, and worldwide referrals to support groups, gender clinics, physicians (including surgeons who perform sex reassignment), and others. Publishes a bibliography (see H35), and *Insights*, a quarterly magazine. (EA)

X291. Finding Our Own Ways: P.O. Box 1545, Lawrence, KS 66044.

[SERVICES: P,S,SB,SG] Support group and resource clearinghouse for asexual individuals (those who regard themselves as neither male or female). Publishes an annual membership directory, and *Finding Our Own Ways*, a bimonthly newsletter containing fiction, reviews, and articles relating to gender identification, asexuality, celibacy, and sex roles. (EA)

X292.   International Foundation for Gender Education: Box 367, Wayland, MA 01778. PH: (617)894-8340.

[SERVICES: B,C,DB,L,P,R,SB,SG] Serves as an international, information and referral resource on transvestites and transsexuality for the transvestite/transsexual community (including transsexuals, and male to female and female to male cross dressers), their friends and families, professionals serving the community, and the general public. They "serve all persons regardless of race, religion, sex, age, politics, financial status, sexual orientation, gender, mode or degree of gender expression, and all sincere persons who respect themselves and who respect others." Coordinates a communication network of over 200 organizations and services serving the gender community, and can provide referrals to support groups and gender dysphoria clinics worldwide. Annually sponsors a female-male issues conference, a mental health professional conference, and a transsexual issues conference. Maintains a research library, open to "any persons who wish to expand their knowledge of our community," holding hundreds of books, biographical archives, tapes, and other materials. Publications include: *TV-TS Tapestry Journal* (see K162); a directory (see p.413); *IFGE Update*, a periodic newsletter; a glossary of terminology used in the community (see p.60); *Legal Aspects of Trans- sexuality, Information for the Female to Male Cross Dresser and Transsexuals*, and other publications on special topics (e.g. wives, clothing and makeup, religion, counseling, hormones, etc.); and scholarly and professional literature. See also L23. (EA)

X293.   J2CP Information Service: P.O. Box 184, San Juan Capistrano, CA 92693-0184. PH: (714)248-5843.

[SERVICES:B,L,P,R] Referral and information service on transsexuality, gender dysphoria syndrome, and sex reassignment surgery. Provides national referrals to professionals (physicians, psychiatrists, lawyers, etc.), support groups, and gender reassignment programs. Their library, which is not open to the public, contains the former holdings of the Janus Information Facility, Erickson Educational Foundation, John Augustus Foundation, Renaissance, and the ACLU Transsexual Rights Committee.

It includes a 700 volume special collection on legal issues. Information packets and bibliographies are available. (SL)

X294.   John Augustus Foundation: P.O. Box 11341, Santa Ana, CA 92711. PH: (714)472-4101.

[SERVICES: C,DB,P,R,S,SB] Conducts and disseminates medical, psychological, and legal research on gender dysphoria and sexual identity conflict. Maintains a computerized data base. (EA)

X295.   Renaissance Education Inc.: P.O. Box 552, King of Prussia, PA 19406. PH: (215)630-1437.

[SERVICES: B,C,P,R,SB,SG] Provides support, education, referrals, and information to transvestites and transsexuals, their families, professionals, and others interested in transgender behavior. Publishes a series of background papers providing general information about transgendered behavior (e.g. *Myths and Misconceptions About Crossdressing*; *Understanding Transsexuals*; *Spouses and Significant Others*); a bibliography; and *Renaissance News*, a monthly newsletter. (EA)´

X296.   Society for the Second Self: P.O. Box 4067, Visalia, CA 93278. PH: (209)688-9246.

[SERVICES: C,P,R,SB,SG] Also known as the Tri Ess Sorority. Membership is limited to heterosexual male crossdressers—"men who have a compulsive desire to dress in the clothing normally reserved for women," who are not transsexuals, fetishists, homosexuals, or sadomasochists, and their wives or woman friends. An advisory board of medical and psychological authorities provides research assistance and advice, and works to educate the public concerning crossdressers. Publishes *Femme Mirror*, a quarterly magazine; a periodic directory; and materials for spouses, including the periodical *Women Associated with Crossdressers*, and the book *The Transvestite and His Wife*. (EA)

➤ WOMEN'S SEXUAL AND REPRODUCTIVE HEALTH (*See also*: specific topics [e.g. Abortion, Fertility, Menstruation]; L24, X264)

X297.   National Women's Health Network: 1325 G St., NW, Washington, DC 20005. PH: (202)347-1140.

[SERVICES: B,C,L,P,R,S,SB] Monitors federal health policy and operates the Women's Health Information Clearinghouse, providing resources and

HOW TO FIND

• Consult directories. The *Women's Information Directory* (Detroit: Gale Research) is a comprehensive, biennial directory of information resources for and about women in the U.S., including national, state, and local organizations; publishers and booksellers; newsletters, magazines and other directories; special libraries; electronic and video resources; women's studies programs, and much more. Descriptive entries are classified by type of resource, with subject and title indexes. *Library and Information Sources on Women: A Guide to Collections in the Greater N.Y. Area* (New York: Feminist Press at the City University of New York, 1988), describes resources on a range of women related issues, all of which respond to phone and mail inquiries. Beth Stafford's *Directory of Women's Studies Programs and Library Resources* (Phoenix: Oryx Press, 1990), describes 400 women's studies programs, including supporting library holdings.

referrals on all aspects of women's health care. Publishes the *National Women's Health Network News*, a bimonthly newsletter. Compiles and distributes (for $5.00 each) lengthy information packets on over 50 women's health topics, including the following:

Abortion	Depression	PID
AIDS	Diethylstilbestrol (DES)	Postpartum Depression
Breast Cancer	Endometriosis	Pregnancy/Childbirth
Breast Implants	Estrogen Replacement	Premenstrual Syndrome
Breastfeeding	Therapy	Reproductive Technology
Cervical Cancer	Fibroids	RU-486
Cesarean Childbirth	Fibrocystic Disease	STDs
Contraceptives	Home Pregnancy Tests	Sterilization
–Cervical Cap	Hysterectomy	Tamoxifen
–Diaphragm	Infertility	Teen Pregnancy
–Intrauterine Device	Interstitial Cystitis	Toxic Shock Syndrome
–New Methods	Lesbian Health Issues	Urinary Tract infections
–Norplant	Mammography	Vaginitis
–Pill	Menopause	Women and Alcohol
–Spermicide	Osteoporosis	Women and Disabilities
–Sponge	Ovarian Cysts	Women and Smoking
Depo-Provera	Pap Smears	Yeast Infections

X298. **Women's Health Information Center**: Boston Women's Health Collective, 47 Nichols Ave., Watertown, MA 02172. PH: (617)924-0271.

A project of the Boston Women's Health Book Collective, a not-for-profit organization devoted to education about women and health, best known for writing *The New Our Bodies Ourselves* (see F34). Open to the public, the information center includes an extensive collection of books, periodicals, and newspaper and magazine clippings on all aspects of women health, including sexuality, birth control, abortion, reproduction, and sexually transmitted diseases. They distribute free and low cost materials to women and organizations in the U.S. and other countries.

Appendixes

APPENDIX 1
LIBRARY OF CONGRESS SUBJECT HEADINGS

Beginning on p.424 is an alphabetically arranged list of over 2,900 Library of Congress subject headings and cross references used to locate information on the sex related subjects listed on p.422.[1] A list of general terms begins on p.423. The cross references provide referrals to authorized terms (e.g. Genitals *use* Generative organs), as well as to the broader term encompassing a subject for which a particular term has not been designated (e.g. pederasty *use* anal intercourse, sexual abuse *use* sex crimes).

Although we have attempted to compile a comprehensive listing of relevant subject headings as of August 1992, it is not exhaustive in all areas. Consult the most recent edition of *Library of Congress Subject Headings* (see C1, available in all libraries) for terms we've overlooked, new terms (5,000-10,000 new headings are added annually), revisions (e.g. in the 14th edition *sexology–research* replaced *sex–research*, *sadomasochism* replaced *sexual masochism*, *sex addiction* replaced *sexual addiction*), and for hierarchical relationships between headings (i.e. broader, narrower, and related terms).

There are thousands of "floating subdivisions" specifiying time periods, geographical areas, groups of people, formats, or aspects of a topic (e.g. *–Statistics*, *–Treatment*, *–United States*, *–19th Century*, *–Prisoners*) which can be compounded with subject headings to further refine searches. (Terms used to indicate a particular type of materials [e.g. *–Bibliography*] are listed under "How to Find" throughout this volume.) In the listings that follow we have only included those compound headings listed together in *Subject Headings*; they are not the only subdivisions that can be used with each heading. Floating subdivisions are listed in *Subject Headings*, and a more convenient listing, *Free Floating Subdivisions: An Alphabetical Index*, can be purchased from the Cataloging Distribution Service of the Library of Congress (Ph: 202/707-6100). Most libraries using the Library of Congress system keep a copy of the index in their cataloging

---

[1] The material in this Appendix may not be reproduced, in any form, without written permission from the author. *Sex in Library of Congress Terms: A Thesaurus of Subject Headings Used to Locate Information About Sex* (see C3) is available from the National Sex Information Network (see Z277) in a soft cover, spiral bound format.

Subjects Represented in Headings

1. GENERAL TERMS

2. REPRODUCTION
Human reproduction
Menstruation. Menopause
Family planning. Population
Birth control. Contraceptives
Sterilization
Infertility. Reproductive technologies
Fertility. Conception. Sex preselection
Abortion
Pregnancy. Prenatal care
Pregnancy complications. Fetal disease
Childbirth. Postpartum
Childbirth complications. Infant death
Lactation. Breast feeding
Reproductive medicine

3. ANATOMY AND PHYSIOLOGY
Sexual differentiation
Puberty
Sex hormones
Sexual response cycle
Male sexual and reproductive organs
Male diseases and surgery
Female sexual and reproductive organs
Female diseases and surgery
Sex related medicine

4. COMMERCIAL SEX
Sex related businesses
Pornography
Prostitution. Prostitutes

5. SEX EDUCATION

6. SEX ROLE
Body image. Nudity. Beauty. Clothing
Sex roles

7. SEX AND LAW. SEX CRIMES
Commercial sex and law
Marriage and family law
Obscenity Law. Pornography and law
Reproduction related law
Sex education and law

Sex offenders
Sexual behavior and law

8. SEXUAL ABUSE
Child sexual abuse. Incest
Rape. Sexual abuse
Sexual harassment

9. SEX IN CULTURE
Art
Language. Folklore
Literature. Poetry. Popular literature
Motion Pictures. Television
Music
Performing arts

10. RELATIONSHIPS
Emotions. Love
Single people. Dating. Courtship
Engagement. Marriage. Married people
Family. Parents. Children
Relationship problems. Therapy. Divorce
Non-marital relationships
Alternative Lifestyles

11. SEXUAL DISORDERS
Psychosexual disorders. Sexual deviation
Sexual dysfunction
Sex therapy and counseling
Sexually transmitted diseases
AIDS

12. HOMOSEXUALITY
Bisexuality. Homosexuality
Gays. Lesbians. Bisexuals

13. SEXUAL BEHAVIOR
Sexual attraction. Sexual arousal
Sex customs and rites
Individuals. Cultures. Special groups
Types of sexual behavior

14. MORAL / ETHICAL ASPECTS
Sexual ethics. Bioethics
Sex and religion

department, where it's generally unavailable to the public. The following subdivisions are of special note:

–Marriage or *–Marriage customs and rites* under groups of people, ethnic groups, and groups of Indians (e.g. *Indians of North America–Marriage customs and rites*; *Afro-Americans–Marriage*; *Handicapped–Marriage*).

–Sex counseling under groups of people (e.g. *Ostomates–Sex counseling*).

–Sexual behavior under classes of persons, ethnic groups, and names of individual persons (e.g. *Shakespeare William 1564-1616–Sexual behavior*).

–Religious aspects under most topical headings (e.g. *Abortion–Religious aspects*). Topical headings can also be compounded with *(Jewish law)*, *(Islamic law)*, *(Canon law)*, etc.

–Law and legislation and/or *–Legal status, laws, etc.* under topical headings (e.g. *Unmarried couples–Legal status, laws, etc.*, *Clitoridectomy–Law and legislation*).

–Erotic aspects under topical headings (e.g. *Hair–Erotic aspects*)

–Language under classes of persons (e.g. *Gays–Language*), *–Slang* under individual languages or subjects (e.g. *Sex–Slang*), and *–Obscene words* under languages (e.g. *English language–Obscene words*).

NOTE: Entries are arranged alphabetically, ignoring the words "in," "and," "of," "the," etc. Headings with punctuation are ordered as follows:

> Abortion
> Abortion, Induced
> Abortion–Complications
> Abortion (Islamic law)
> Abortion applicants
> Abortion in the press
> Abortion services

GENERAL TERMS

Sex
Sex (Biology)
Sex (Psychology)
Sex–Information services
Sex–Moral and ethical aspects *use* Sexual ethics
Sex–Moral and religious aspects *use* Sexual ethics
Sex–Mythology
Sex–Physiological aspects *use* Sex (Biology)

Sex–Psychological aspects *use* Sex (Psychology)
Sex–Research *use* Sexology–Research
Sex–Statistics
Sex behavior surveys *use* Sexual behavior surveys
Sex customs
Sex research *use* Sexology–Research
Sex surveys *use* Sexual behavior surveys
Sexology
Sexology–Research

Sexual behavior *use* Sex
Sexual behavior *use* Sex customs
Sexual behavior *use* Sexual ethics
Sexual behavior, Psychology *use* Sex
(Psychology)

Sexual behavior surveys
Sexual psychology *use* Sex (Psychology)
Sexuality *use* Sex

ALPHABETICAL LIST OF LIBRARY OF CONGRESS SUBJECT HEADINGS AND CROSS REFERENCES

-A-

Abdominal delivery *use*
Cesarean section
Abdominal hysterectomy
use Hysterectomy
Abdominal pregnancy
Abnormalities, Human
Abortifacients
Abortion
Abortion, Induced
Abortion, Septic *use*
Septic abortion
Abortion, Spontaneous
use Miscarriage
Abortion, Therapeutic
Abortion–Complications
Abortion–Finance
Abortion–Finance–Law
and legislation
Abortion–Government
policy
Abortion–Government
policy–Citizen
participation
Abortion–Law and
legislation
Abortion–Moral and
ethical aspects
Abortion–Religious
aspects
Abortion (Canon law)
Abortion (Jewish law)
Abortion applicants
Abortion clinics *use*
Abortion services
Abortion counseling

Abortion counseling–Law
and legislation
Abortion facilities *use*
Abortion services
Abortion in the press
Abortion rights movement
use Pro-choice
movement
Abortion seekers *use*
Abortion applicants
Abortion services
Abortion services–
Employees
Abortion services–Law
and legislation
Abortion services–Strikes
and lockouts *use*
Strikes and lockouts–
Abortion services
Abstinence, Sexual *use*
sexual abstinence
Abuse of persons *use*
Offenses against the
person
Abuse, Sexual *use* Sex
crimes
Abused children
Abused gay men
Abused lesbians
Abused wives
Abused wives–legal
status, laws, etc.
Abused wives–services
for
Abusive boyfriends *use*
Abusive men
Abusive Fathers

Abusive men
Accessory organs of the
uterus *use* Adnexa uteri
ACDs *use* Adult children
of divorced parents
Achondroplasia
Acknowledgment of
children
ACOSAs *use* Adult
children of sex addicts
Acquaintance rape
Acquired immune
deficiency syndrome
use AIDS (Disease)
Acquired
immunodeficiency
syndrome *use* AIDS
(Disease)
Acquired immunological
deficiency syndrome
use AIDS (Disease)
Active birth *use* Active
childbirth
Active childbirth
Addiction, Lust *use* Sex
addiction
Addiction, Sex *use* Sex
addiction
Addictive sex *use* Sex
addiction
Addicts, Sex *use* Sex
addicts
Adenomyosis *use*
Endometriosis
Adnexa uteri
Adolescence

Adolescent boys–Sexual
behavior *use* Teenage
boys–Sexual behavior
Adolescent boys–Sexual
behavior *use* Youth–
Sexual behavior
Adolescent child
molesters *use* Teenage
child molesters
Adolescent fathers *use*
Teenage fathers
Adolescent girls–Sexual
behavior *use* Teenage
girls–Sexual behavior
Adolescent girls–Sexual
behavior *use* Youth–
Sexual behavior
Adolescent pregnancy *use*
Teenage pregnancy
Adolescent prostitution
use Prostitution,
Juvenile
Adolescent sex offenders
use Teenage sex
offenders
Adopted children *use*
Children, Adopted
Adoptees
Adoption
Adoption–Corrupt
practices
Adoption–Law and
legislation
Adult child sexual abuse
victims
Adult children of divorced
parents
Adult children of
dysfunctional families
Adult children of problem
families *use* Adult
children of
dysfunctional families
Adult children of sex
addicts

Adult survivors of child
sexual abuse *use* Adult
child sexual abuse
victims
Adultery
Adultery–Biblical
teaching
Adultery–Law and
legislation
Adults sexually abused as
children *use* Adult
child sexual abuse
victims
Adventuresses *use*
Femmes fatales
Advertising–Condoms
Advertising–Marriage *use*
Matrimonial
advertisements
Advertising–Sex oriented
businesses
Aedeagus
Affection *use* Love
Affections, Alienation of
use Alienation of
affections
Afro-Americans–Marriage
Afro-American gays
Afro-American
homosexuals *use* Afro-
American gays
Afro-American lesbians
Age of consent
Aged–Sexual behavior
Aged gay men
Aged lesbians
AIDS (Disease)
AIDS (Disease)–Fear of
AIDS (Disease)–
Prevention
AIDS (Disease) in
adolescence
AIDS (Disease) in
children
AIDS (Disease) in infants
AIDS (Disease) in mass
media

AIDS (Disease) in
pregnancy
AIDS antibodies *use* HIV
antibodies
AIDS memorial quilt *use*
NAMES Project AIDS
memorial quilt
AIDS phobia *use* AIDS
(Disease)–Fear of
AIDS-related complex
AIDS vaccines
Alcoholism in pregnancy
Algolagnia *use*
Sadomasochism
Alienation of affections
Alimony
Amenorrhea
Amenorrhea, Lactation
Amenorrhea, Primary *use*
Menarche
American erotic literature
use Erotic literature,
American
American erotic poetry
use Erotic poetry,
American
American erotic prints *use*
Erotic prints, American
American erotic stories
use Erotic stories,
American
American gays' writings
use Gays' writings,
American
American lesbians'
writings *use* Lesbians'
writings, American
American love songs *use*
Love songs, American
Amniocentesis
Amnioscopy
Amniotic fluid embolism
Amniotic liquid
Amniotic liquid–
Examination

Amniotic liquid embolism
    use Amniotic fluid
    embolism
Anal eroticism *use* Anus
    (Psychology)
Anal intercourse
Anal sphincter *use* Anus
Andrenogenital syndrome
Androgenic hormones *use*
    Androgens
Androgens
Androgynous behavior
    use Androgyny
    (Psychology)
Androgyny (Psychology)
Anemia in pregnancy
Anesthesia in obstetrics
Anesthesia in urology
Animosity, Sexual *use*
    Sexual animosity
Animosity between the
    sexes *use* Sexual
    animosity
Annulment of marriage
    use Marriage–
    Annulment
Anorgasmia *use*
    Anorgasmy
Anorgasmy
Anovulants, Oral *use* Oral
    contraceptives
Anovulation
Antenatal diagnosis *use*
    Prenatal diagnosis
Antenuptial contracts
Anti-abortion movement
    use Pro-life movement
Anti-gay bias *use*
    Homophobia
Anti-homosexual bias *use*
    Homophobia
Antifertility drugs *use*
    Contraceptive drugs
Antifertility vaccines
Anus
Anus (Psychology)
Aphrodisiacs

Aphrodite (Greek deity)
Applicants for abortion
    use Abortion applicants
Arousal, Sexual *use*
    Sexual excitement
Art, Erotic *use* Erotic art
Art, Immoral *use* Erotic
    art
Art and homosexuality
    use Homosexuality and
    art
Art and morals
Artificial impregnation
    use Artificial
    insemination
Artificial insemination,
    Human
Artificial insemination,
    Human–Law and
    legislation
Artificial penis *use* Penile
    prostheses
Assault, Criminal *use*
    Rape
Astrology and birth
    control
Astrology and childbirth
Astrology and divorce
Astrology and
    homosexuality
Astrology and marriage
Athletes, Gay *use* Gay
    athletes
Atraumatic abortion *use*
    Menstrual regulation
Attachment behavior
Attraction, Interpersonal
Augmentation
    mammaplasty
Authors, English–Sexual
    behavior
Autoerotic asphyxia
Autoerotic death
Autoeroticism *use*
    Masturbation
Autoimmune diseases in
    pregnancy

Aversion disorders,
    Sexual *use* Sexual
    aversion disorders
Aversion, Sexual *use*
    Sexual aversion
    disorders

-B-

Baby switches *use* Infants
    switched at birth
Babies switched at birth
    use Infants switched at
    birth
Babies, Test tube *use*
    Fertilization in vitro,
    Human
Bachelors
Bacterial vaginitis
Bartholin's gland
Basal body temperature
    method of birth control
    use natural family
    planning–Temperature
    method
Bashfulness
Bastardy *use* Illegitimacy
Battered gay men *use*
    Abused gay men
Battered lesbians *use*
    Abused lesbians
Battered wives *use*
    Abused wives
Bawdy poetry
Bawdy songs
Beauty *use* Beauty,
    Personal
Beauty, Personal
Beauty, Personal in
    literature
Beauty culture
Behavioral embryology
Behavioral methods of
    birth control *use*
    Natural family planning
Belly button *use* Navel
Belly dancing

Bereavement

Berit milah

Bestiality

Bestiality (Law)

Betrothal

Betrothal–Law *use*
Betrothal–Law and
legislation

Betrothal–Law and
legislation

Bi-racial children *use*
Children of interracial
marriage

Bi-racial dating *use*
Interracial dating

Bible–Homosexuality *use*
Homosexuality in the
Bible

Bible–Scatology *use*
Scatology in the Bible

Bigamy

Bigamy–law and
legistlation

Bigamy (Islamic law)

Billings ovulation method
of birth control *use*
Natural family
planning–Ovulation
method

Bioethics

Biological parents *use*
Birthparents

Biology–Moral and
ethical aspects *use*
Bioethics

Biomedical ethics *use*
Bioethics

Biracial children *use*
Children of interracial
marriage

Biracial dating *use*
Interracial dating

Birth *use* Childbirth

Birth *use* Labor
(Obstetrics)

Birth *use* Parturition

Birth, Multiple

Birth, Premature *use*
Infants (Premature)

Birth, Wrongful *use*
Wrongful birth

Birth (in religion,
folk-lore, etc.) *use*
Childbirth–Folklore

Birth (in religion, folk-
lore, etc.) *use*
Childbirth–Mythology

Birth (in religion, folk-
lore, etc.) *use*
Childbirth–Religious
aspects

Birth attendants *use*
Midwives

Birth attendants *use*
Obstetricians

Birth certificates

Birth control

Birth control (Canon law)

Birth control–Cross-
cultural studies

Birth control–Federal aid
use Federal aid to birth
control

Birth control–Finance

Birth control–Law and
legislation

Birth control–Moral and
ethical aspects

Birth control–Religious
aspects

Birth control and
astrology *use* Astrology
and birth control

Birth control clinics

Birth control clinics–
Access for the
physically handicapped

Birth control clinics–
Utilization

Birth control devices *use*
Contraceptives

Birth control pills *use* Oral
contraceptives

Birth control pills, Male
use Oral
contraceptives, Male

Birth control vaccines *use*
Antifertility vaccines

Birth customs

Birth customs–Religious
aspects

Birth intervals

Birth parents *use*
Birthparents

Birth rate *use* Fertility,
Human–Statistics

Birth-rate *use* Childbirth–
Statistics

Birth records *use*
Registers of births, etc.

Birth weight, Low

Birthing *use* Childbirth

Birthing customs *use*
Birth customs

Birthparents

Births, Registers of *use*
Registers of births, etc.

Bisexual marriage *use*
Bisexuality in marriage

Bisexuality

Bisexuality–Mythology

Bisexuality–Religious
aspects

Bisexuality (Biology) *use*
Hermaphroditism

Bisexuality in marriage

Black market–Infants *use*
Adoption–Corrupt
practices

Blastocyst

Blood–Transfusion,
Intrauterine

Blood coagulation
disorders in pregnancy

Blood diseases in
pregnancy

Blues, Postpartum *use*
Postpartum depression

Body, Human

Body image

Body-marking
Bondage (Sexual
  behavior)
Bondage (Sexual
  behavior) in motion
  pictures
Bondage (Sexual
  behavior) in television
Bondage (Sexual
  behavior) on television
  use Bondage (Sexual
  behavior) in television
Book-plates, Erotic use
  Erotic bookplates
Boy preferences of parents
  use Sex of children,
  Parental preferences for
Boys–Sexual behavior
Bras use Brassieres
Breast
Breast–Adenosis use
  Breast–Fibrocystic
  disease
Breast–Biopsy, Needle
Breast–Cancer
Breast–Cancer–Surgery
Breast–Care and hygiene
Breast–Cysts
Breast–Diseases
Breast–Diseases–
  Diagnosis
Breast–Dysplasia use
  Breast–Fibrocystic
  disease
Breast–Examination
Breast–Fibrocystic disease
Breast–Radiography
Breast–Size augmentation
  use Augmentation
  mammaplasty
Breast–Size reduction use
  Reduction
  mammaplasty
Breast–Surgery
Breast–Tuberculosis
Breast–Tumors

Breast–Ultrasonic
  imaging
Breast in art
Breast augmentation
  surgery use
  Augmentation
  mammaplasty
Breast feeding
Breast feeding (in
  religion, folklore, etc.)
  use Breast feeding–
  Folklore
Breast feeding (in
  religion, folklore, etc.)
  use Breast feeding–
  Religious aspects
Breast feeding–Folklore
Breast feeding–
  Immunological aspects
Breast feeding–Religious
  aspects
Breast feeding in art
Breast feeding promotion
Breast implants
Breast implants–
  Complications
Breast prosthesis
Breast pump
Breast reconstruction
Breast reduction surgery
Breast ultrasonography
Breast ultrasound
Bridal crowns
Bridal customs use
  Marriage customs and
  rites
Bride price
Bride purchase use Bride
  price
Bridewealth use Bride
  price
Brokage, Marriage use
  Marriage brokerage
Broken homes
Brokerage, Marriage use
  Marriage brokerage

Brokers, Marriage use
  Marriage brokerage
Brothels use Prostitution
Brothers and sisters
Buggery use Bestiality
  (Law)
Buggery use Sodomy
Bundling

-C-

C section use Cesarean
  section
Caesarean section use
  Cesarean section
Calendar method of birth
  control use Natural
  family planning–
  Calendar method
Call girls use Prostitutes
Camp followers
Candidiasis, Vaginal use
  Candidiasis,
  Vulvovaginal
Candidiasis, Vulvovaginal
Candlemas
Caps, Cervical use
  Cervical caps
Carbohydrate metabolism
  disorders in pregnancy
Cardiovascular diseases in
  pregnancy
Carnal desire use Lust
Castration
Castration complex
Castration of criminals
  and defectives use
  Castration
Castration of criminals
  and defectives use
  Sterilization, Eugenic
Catamenial receptors use
  Sanitary napkins
Catamenial receptors use
  Tampons
Catholic Church–Clergy–
  Sexual behavior

Catholic gays
Cavernitis, Fibrous *use* Penile induration
Celibacy
Cenogamy *use* Group marriage
Censorship
Ceremonial purity *use* Purity, Ritual
Cervical caps
Cervical mucus method of birth control *use* Natural family planning–Ovulation method
Cervical mucus *use* Cervix mucus
Cervix mucus
Cervix uteri
Cesarean-born children
Cesarean section
Cesarean section–Complications
Cesarean section–Nursing
Cesarean section–Prevention
Chancroid
Change of life *use* Climacteric
Change of life in men *use* Climacteric, Male
Change of life in women *use* Menopause
Change of sex *use* Sex change
Chastity
Chastity, Vow of
Chastity (Islamic law)
Chastity belts
Cheesecake photography *use* Glamour photography
Chicana lesbians *use* Mexican American lesbians

Chicken porn *use* Children in pornography
Child abuse
Child birth *use* Childbirth
Child marriage
Child molesters
Child molesting
Child molesting–Investigation
Child molesting–Religious aspects
Child placing *use* Adoption
Child pornography *use* Children in pornography
Child prostitution *use* Prostitution, Juvenile
Child sexual abuse *use* Child molesting
Child sexual abuse victims, Adult *use* Adult child sexual abuse victims
Child sexual abuse victims *use* Sexually abused children
Childbirth
Childbirth–Cross-cultural studies
Childbirth–Folklore
Childbirth–Mythology
Childbirth–Religious aspects
Childbirth–Religious aspects–Christianity
Childbirth–Statistics
Childbirth–Study and teaching
Childbirth and astrology *use* Astrology and childbirth
Childbirth education *use* Childbirth–Study and teaching

Childbirth educators *use* Childbirth teachers
Childbirth at home
Childbirth in literature
Childbirth in middle age
Childbirth teachers
Childlessness
Children
Children, Adopted
Children, Cesarean-born *use* Cesarean-born children
Children–Parental sex preferences *use* Sex of children, Parental preferences for
Children–Sexual behavior
Children of divorced parents
Children and erotica
Children of gay parents
Children of homosexual parents *use* Children of gay parents
Children of interracial marriage
Children in pornography
Children in pornogaphy–Law and legislation
Children of prostitutes
Children and prostitution *use* Prostitution, Juvenile
Children and sex
Children and sex–Cross cultural studies
Children of single parents
Chlamydia infections
Chlamydia infections–Diagnosis
Chlamydial infections *use* Chlamydia infections
Choice of sex of offspring *use* Sex preselection
Chordee
Choriocarcinoma
Chorionic gonadotropins

Chorionic vilius sampling

Chorionic villi

Chosen child syndrome
    use Emotional incest

Chromosome
    abnormalities

Church work with
    divorced people

Church work with families

Church work with gays

Church work with gays–
    Baptists, Catholic
    Church etc.

Church work with
    homosexuals use
    Church work with gays

Church work with married
    people

Church work with
    prostitutes

Church work with
    remarried people

Churching of women

Circumcision

Circumcision–Religious
    aspects

Circumcision–Religious
    aspects–Judaism

Civil marriage

Clandestine marriages
    (Canon law) use
    Clandestinity (Canon
    law)

Clandestinity (Canon law)

Clean and unclean use
    Purity, Ritual

Cleanliness, Ritual use
    Purity, Ritual

Clergy–Sexual behavior

Clerical celibacy use
    Celibacy

Climacteric

Climacteric, Female use
    Menopause

Climacteric, Male

Climaterium virle use
    Climacteric, Male

Climax, Sexual use
    Orgasm

Clitoridectomy

Clitoridectomy–Law and
    legislation

Clitoris

Clitoris–Surgery

Clothes, Maternity use
    Maternity clothes

Clothing and dress

Clothing, Maternity use
    Maternity clothes

Clubbed penis use Penis–
    Curvatures

Coaching during natural
    childbirth (Obstetrics)
    use Natural childbirth
    Coaching

Cohabitation use
    Unmarried couples

Coital cephalgia use
    Sexual headache

Coital headache use
    Sexual headache

Coitus interruptus

Coitus interruptus–
    Complications

Coitus reservatus use
    Coitus interruptus

Coitus use Sexual
    intercourse

College Students–Sexual
    behavior

College students, Gay use
    Gay college students

Colpohysterectomy use
    Hysterectomy, Vaginal

Coming out (Sexual
    identity) use Coming
    out (Sexual orientation)

Coming out (Sexual
    orientation)

Commercial sex use Sex
    oriented businesses

Common law marriage

Common law marriage
    (Canon law)

Communal living

Communal marriage use
    Group marriage

Communal settlements
    use Communal living

Communes use
    Communal living

Communicable diseases in
    pregnancy

Communicable diseases in
    the fetus

Communication in birth
    control

Communication in
    divorce mediation

Communication in the
    family

Communication in family
    planning use
    Communication in
    birth control

Communication in
    marriage

Communication in sex

Communism and family

Communism and love

Communism and sex

Communities, Gay use
    Gay communities

Commuter marriage

Companionate marriage
    use Marriage,
    Companionate

Compatibility tests,
    Marriage use Marriage
    compatibility tests

Complications of
    pregnancy use
    Pregnancy–
    complications

Compliments

Compulsive sex use Sex
    addiction

Compulsory sterilization
    use Sterilization,
    Eugenic

Conception

Conception–Date of
Conception–Mythology
Conception–Prevention
    use Contraception
Conception–Religious
    aspects
Conception–Religious
    aspects–Catholic
    Church
Conception (in religion,
    folklore, etc.) *use*
    Conception–Mythology
Conception (in religion,
    folklore, etc.) *use*
    Conception–Religious
    aspects
Concubinage
Concupiscence *use* Lust
Condom industry
Condoms
Condoms–Advertising *use*
    Advertising–Condoms
Condoms–Complications
Condoms–Tariff *use*
    Tariff on condoms
Confession stories
Confessional stories *use*
    Confession stories
Conjugal violence
Connective tissue diseases
    in pregnancy
Consanguinity
Consanguinity (Islamic
    law)
Consanguinity (Law)
Contraception
Contraception,
    Immunological
Contraception, Male *use*
    Male contraception
Contraception–
    Complications
Contraception–Failures
Contraception–Religious
    aspects

Contraceptive agents,
    Male *use* Male
    contraceptives
Contraceptive devices *use*
    Contraceptives
Contraceptive devices,
    Male *use* Male
    contraceptives
Contraceptive drug
    implants
Contraceptive drugs
Contraceptive drugs,
    Implantable *use*
    Contraceptive drug
    implants
Contraceptive drugs,
    Injectables
Contraceptives
Contraceptives,
    Intravaginal *use*
    Contraceptives,
    Vaginal
Contraceptives, Male *use*
    Male contraceptives
Contraceptives, Oral *use*
    Oral contraceptives
Contraceptives, Postcoital
Contraceptives, Vaginal
Contraceptives–Failures
    use Contraception–
    Failures
Contraceptives industry
Cooperative living *use*
    Communal living
Copper intrauterine
    contraceptives
Copulation *use* Sexual
    intercourse
Cord umbilical *use*
    Umbilical cord
Corpus luteum
Corpus luteum hormone
    use Progesterone
Corpus luteum-
    stimulating hormone
    use Progesterone
Cosmetics

Cotyledon (Anatomy) *use*
    Placenta
Coumestrol
Counseling, Divorce *use*
    Divorce counseling
Counter culture *use*
    Communal living
Counter culture *use* Life
    style
Couples, Gay male *use*
    Gay male couples
Couples, Gay *use* Gay
    couples
Couples, Lesbian *use*
    Lesbian couples
Couples, Married *use*
    Married people
Couples, Unmarried *use*
    Unmarried couples
Couples psychotherapy
    use Marital
    psychotherapy
Couples therapy *use*
    Marital psychotherapy
Courtesans
Courting *use* Courtship
Courtly love
Courtship
Cousin marriage *use*
    Cross-cousin marriage
Couvade
Craniotomy
Crimes against women *use*
    Women–Crimes against
Crimes of passion
Crimes passionnel *use*
    Crimes of Passion
Crimes without victims
Criminal assault *use* Rape
Cross-cousin marriage
Cross-cultural dating *use*
    Interethnic dating
Cross-dressers *use*
    Transvestites
Cuckolds
Cults, Fertility *use*
    Fertility cults

Cunnilingus *use* Oral
intercourse
Curvatures of the penis
use Penis–Curvatures
Custody of children
Cystic disease of breast
use Breast–Fibrocystic
disease
Cytomegalic inclusion
disease

-D-

Dalkon Shield
(Intrauterine
contraceptive)
Dancers, Exotic *use*
Stripteasers
Date abuse *use* Dating
violence
Date-beating *use* Dating
violence
Date of Conception *use*
Conception–Date of
Date rape *use*
Acquaintance rape
Dating, Bi-racial *use*
Interracial dating
Dating, Biracial *use*
Interracial dating
Dating, Interethnic *use*
Interethnic dating
Dating, Interracial *use*
Interracial dating
Dating (Social customs)
Dating (Social customs)–
Religious aspects
Dating etiquette *use*
Dating (Social
customs)
Dating violence
Decolletage
Defender of the bond *use*
Defender of the
marriage bond
Defender of the marriage
bond

Defloration
Delayed menarche *use*
Menarche
Delivery (Obstetrics)
Demography
Depression, Postnatal *use*
Postpartum depression
Depression, Postpartum
use Postpartum
depression
Desertion and non-support
Desire
Detection of ovulation *use*
Ovulation–Detection
Determination of sex,
Diagnostic *use* Sex
determination,
Diagnostic
Determination of sex,
Genetic *use* Sex
determination, Genetic
Development,
Psychosexual *use*
Psychosexual
development
Developmental genetics
Deviation, Sexual *use*
Sexual deviation
Diabetes in pregnancy
Diagnosis, Obstetrical *use*
Obstetrics–Diagnosis
Diagnostic sex
determination *use* Sex
determination,
Diagnostic
Diaphragms, Vaginal
Differentiation disorders,
Sex *use* Sex
differentiation
disorders
Dirty jokes
Dirty songs *use* Bawdy
songs
Disabled–Sexual behavior
use Handicapped–
Sexual behavior

Disorders, Psychosexual
use Psychosexual
disorders
Disorders, Sexual aversion
use Sexual aversion
disorders
Disorders of sexual
differentiation *use* Sex
differentiation
disorders
Displaced homemakers
Displacement of the
uterus *use* Uterus–
Displacements
Divorce
Divorce, No-fault *use* No-
fault divorce
Divorce–Religious aspects
Divorce–Law and
legislation
Divorce (Canon law)
Divorce (Islamic law)
Divorce a mensa et thoro
use Separation (Law)
Divorce from bed and
board *use* Separation
(Law)
Divorce in literature
Divorce mediation
Divorce practice *use*
Divorce suits
Divorce proceedings *use*
Divorce suits
Divorce records
Divorce settlements
Divorce suits
Divorce suits (Canon law)
Divorce therapy
Divorced fathers
Divorced men
Divorced mothers
Divorced parents
Divorced parents' adult
children *use* Adult
children of divorced
parents

Divorced parents' children
  use Children of
  divorced parents
Divorced people
Divorced people–
  Counseling of
Divorced persons *use*
  Divorced People
Divorced women
Divorcees *use* Divorced
  women
Domestic relations
Domestic relations
  (Islamic law)
Dower (Islamic law)
Dowry
Dowry (Islamic law)
Dowry insurance *use*
  Insurance, marriage
  endowment
Drag queens *use*
  Transvestites
Drawing, Erotic *use* Erotic
  drawing
Drug abuse in pregnancy
Drug implants,
  Contraceptive *use*
  Contraceptive drug
  implants
Drug use in pregnancy
Drugs and sex
Ductus deferens *use* Vas
  deferens
Duration of pregnancy *use*
  Pregnancy–Duration
Dysmenorrhea
Dysphoria, Gender *use*
  Gender identity
  disorders

-E-

Early abortion *use*
  Menstrual regulation
Early marriage *use*
  Teenage marriage
Eclampsia

Eclectic obstetrics *use*
  Obstetrics, Eclectic
Ectodermal dysplasia
Ectopic pregnancy
Edipus complex *use*
  Oedipus complex
Education and
  homosexuality *use*
  Homosexuality and
  education
Ejaculation
Elderly gay men *use* Aged
  gay men
Elderly lesbians *use* Aged
  lesbians
Electra complex
Electrohysterography
Ellis-van Creveld
  syndrome
Elopement
Embracing *use* Hugging
Embryology
Embryology,
  Experimental
Embryology, Human
Embryopathies *use* Fetus–
  Diseases
Emergencies,
  Gynecologic *use*
  Gynecologic
  emergencies
Emmenagogues
Emotional incest
Emotions
Emotions in infants
Endearment, Terms of *use*
  Love names
Endocrine aspects of
  human reproduction
  use Human
  reproduction–
  Endocrine aspects
Endocrine aspects of sex
  differentiation *use* Sex
  differentiation–
  Endocrine aspects

Endocrine gland diseases
  in pregnancy
Endocrine glands
Endocrine gynecology
Endogamy and exogamy
Endometriosis
Endometrium
Endoscopic surgery *use*
  Hysteroscopic
  sterilization
Engagement *use* Betrothal
Engineering, Genetic *use*
  Genetic engineering
English language–
  Obscene words
English language–Slang
Entertainers–Sexual
  behavior
Eonism *use* Transvestism
Epididymis
Epilepsy in pregnancy
Episiotomy
Equitable distribution of
  marital property
Erotic art
Erotic art–Law and
  legislation *use*
  Obscenity (Law)
Erotic art–Primitive
Erotic art–Private
  collections
Erotic bookplates
Erotic comic books, strips,
  etc.
Erotic drawing
Erotic fiction *use* Erotic
  stories
Erotic films
Erotic films–History and
  criticism
Erotic films–Production
  and direction
Erotic folklore *use*
  Scatology
Erotic folklore *use* Sex–
  Folklore
Erotic literature

Erotic literature, American
Erotic painting
Erotic painting–20th
  century
Erotic photography *use*
  Photography, Erotic
Erotic poetry
Erotic poetry, American
Erotic prints
Erotic prints, American
Erotic proverbs
Erotic quotations *use* Sex–
  Quotations, maxims,
  etc.
Erotic sculpture
Erotic songs
Erotic stories
Erotic stories, American
Erotic symbolism *use* Sex
  symbolism
Erotic wood-engraving
Erotic wood-engraving–
  20th century
Erotica
Erotica and children *use*
  Children and erotica
Eroticism *use* Sexual
  excitement
Erythroblastosis fetalis
Escorts (Dating service)
Estradiol
Estrogen
Estrogen replacement
  therapy for menopause
  use Menopause–
  Hormone therapy
Ethics, Sexual *use* Sexual
  ethics
Eugenic sterilization *use*
  Sterilization, Eugenic
Eugenics
Ex-prostitutes
Examinations, Premarital
  use Premarital
  examinations
Excitement, Sexual *use*
  Sexual excitement

Excretion–Folklore
Executives–Sexual
  behavior
Exhibitionism
Exotic dancers *use*
  Stripteasers
Expectant mothers *use*
  Pregnant women
Expectant parent classes
  use Childbirth–Study
  and teaching
Exposure of person *use*
  Indecent exposure
Extra-marital sex *use*
  Adultery
Extra-uterine pregnancy
  use Ectopic pregnancy
Extraction, Menstrual *use*
  Menstrual regulation
Extrauterine pregnancy
  use Ectopic pregnancy

-F-

Failures of contraception
  use Contraception–
  Failures
Fallopian pregnancy *use*
  Tubal pregnancy
Fallopian tubes
Fallopian tubes–Ligature
  use Tubal sterilization
Fallopian tubes–Surgery
Families *use* Family
Family
Family–Health and
  hygiene
Family–Study and
  teaching
Family demography
Family group therapy
Family life education
Family in literature
Family in motion pictures
Family planning *use* Birth
  control

Family planning, Natural
  use Natural family
  planning
Family planning services
  use Birth control clinics
Family psychotherapy
Family relationships *use*
  Family
Family size
Family therapists
Family therapy *use*
  Family psychotherapy
Family violence
Fantastic films
Fantasy
Fascism and sex
Fathers and daughters
Federal aid to birth
  control
Federal aid to infant
  health services
Federal aid to maternal
  health services
Fellatio *use* Oral
  intercourse
Female change of life *use*
  Menopause
Female climacteric *use*
  Menopause
Female generative organs
  use Generative organs,
  Female
Female homosexuality *use*
  Lesbianism
Female homosexuals *use*
  Lesbians
Female husbands *use*
  Woman-to-woman
  marriage
Female impersonators
Female impersonators in
  motion pictures
Female infertility *use*
  Infertility, Female
Female-male relationships
  use Man-woman
  relationships

Female offenders

Female offenders–
Rehabilitation

Female orgasm

Female pimps *use*
Procuresses

Female prostitution *use*
Prostitution

Female sex hormone *use*
Hormones, Sex

Female sterility *use*
Infertility, Female

Female sterilization *use*
Sterilization of women

Feminine beauty
(Aesthetics)

Femininity (Psychology)

Femmes fatales

Femmes fatales in art

Femmes fatales in motion
pictures

Femmiphilliacs *use*
Transvestites

Fertility cults

Fertility, Human

Fertility, Human–
Endocrine aspect

Fertility, Human–
Hormonal aspects *use*
Fertility, Human–
Endocrine aspect

Fertility, Human–
Immunological aspects

Fertility, Human–
Nutritional aspects

Fertility, Human–
Statistics

Fertilization (Biology)

Fertilization, Human *use*
Conception

Fertilization, Laboratory
use Fertilization in
vitro

Fertilization, Test tube *use*
Fertilization in vitro

Fertilization age *use*
Gestational age

Fertilization in vitro

Fertilization in vitro,
Human

Fertilization in vitro,
Human–Law and
legislation

Fertilization in vitro,
Human Religious
aspects

Fertilization in vitro,
Human (Islamic law)

Fetal age *use* Gestational
age

Fetal alcohol syndrome

Fetal anoxia

Fetal death

Fetal distress

Fetal growth disorders

Fetal malnutrition

Fetal monitoring

Fetal presentation

Fetal propitiatory rites

Fetal stillbirth *use* Fetal
death

Fetal ultrasonic imaging
use Fetus–Ultrasonic
imaging

Fetal ultrasonography *use*
Fetus–Ultrasonic
imaging

Fetal ultrasound *use*
Fetus–Ultrasonic
imaging

Fetal wastage *use* Fetal
death

Feticide *use* Abortion

Fetishism

Fetus

Fetus, Death of the *use*
Fetal death

Fetus–Effect of drugs on

Fetus–Ultrasonic imaging

Fetus–Diseases

Fetus–Diseases–Diagnosis

Fetus–Effect of radiation
on

Fetus–Nutrition

Fetus–Research–Law and
legislation

Fibrocystic disease of
breast *use* Breast–
Fibrocystic disease

Fibrous cavernitis *use*
Penile induration

Filiation (Law) *use*
Paternity

First love

First loves

First trimester of
pregnancy *use*
Pregnancy–Trimester,
First

Fistula, Uterine

Foetus *use* Fetus

Forensic gynecology

Forensic obstetrics

Foreskin

Former prostitutes *use* Ex-
prostitutes

Fornication

Fornication–Law and
legislation *use*
Fornication

Fortune hunters *use*
Gigolos

Free love

Free-to-choose movement
use Pro-choice
movement

Freedom-of-choice
movement *use* Pro-
choice movement

Friendship

Frigidity (Psychology)

Frozen human embryos

-G-

Gain of weight in
pregnancy *use* Pregnant
women–Weight gain

Galactorrhea *use*
Lactation disorders

Gametes

Gametes–effects of
radiation on
Gametogenesis
Gang rape
Garden of love in art
Gay accommodations
Gay artists
Gay athletes
Gay bars
Gay Catholics *use*
Catholic gays
Gay clergy
Gay college students
Gay communities
Gay couples
Gay couples, Female *use*
Lesbian couples
Gay family
Gay fathers
Gay Games
Gay lib *use* Gay liberation
movement
Gay liberation movement
Gay librarians
Gay libraries
Gay male couples
Gay men
Gay military personnel
Gay Mormons *use*
Mormon gays
Gay parents
Gay parents' children *use*
Children of gay parents
Gay people *use* Gays
Gay persons *use* Gays
Gay politicians
Gay rights movement *use*
Gay liberation
movement
Gay teenagers
Gay women *use* Lesbians
Gay youth
Gaye family *use* gay
family
Gays
Gays, Afro-American *use*
Afro-American gays

Gays, Female *use*
Lesbians
Gays, Hispanic American
use Hispanic American
gays
Gays, Male *use* Gay men
Gays, Mexican American
use Mexican American
gays
Gays–Attitudes
Gays–Employment
Gays–Identity
Gays–Travel
Gays–United States
Gays in the Armed Forces
Gays and libraries *use*
Libraries and gays
Gays in military service
Gays' writings
Gays' writings, American
Geishas
Gender (Sex) *use* Sex
Gender dysphoria *use*
Gender identity
disorders
Gender identity
Gender identity disorders
Gender role *use* Sex role
Generative organs, Female
Generative organs,
Female–Blood-vessels
Generative organs,
Female–Cancer
Generative organs,
Female–Cancer–
Diagnosis
Generative organs,
Female–Diseases
Generative organs,
Female–Diseases–
Diagnosis
Generative organs,
Female–Examination
Generative organs,
Female–Innervation
Generative organs,
Female–Radiography

Generative organs,
Female–Secretions
Generative organs,
Female–Surgery
Generative organs,
Female–Surgery–
Complications
Generative organs,
Female–Tumors
Generative organs,
Female–Ultrasonic
imaging
Generative organs,
Female–X-ray
examination *use*
Generative organs,
Female–Radiography
Genetic determination of
sex *use* Sex
determination, Genetic
Genetic engineering
Genetic sex determination
use Sex determination,
Genetic
Genital herpes *use* Herpes
genitalis
Genital organs *use*
Generative organs
Genitalia *use* Generative
organs
Genito-urinary organs *use*
Genitourinary organs
Genitourinary organs
Genitourinary organs–
Abnormalities
Genitourinary organs–
Diseases
Geriatric gynecology
Geriatric urology
Gestagens *use*
Progestational
hormones
Gestation *use* Pregnancy
Gestation age *use*
Gestational age
Gestational age

Gestational mothers *use*
Surrogate mothers
Gestogens *use*
Progestational
hormones
Gestosis *use* Toxemia of
pregnancy
Gigolos
Girdles of chastity *use*
Chastity belts
Girl preferences of parents
use Sex of children,
Parental preferences for
Girl victims of crimes *use*
Girls–Crimes against
Girlie magazines
Girls, Crimes against *use*
Girls–Crimes against
Girls–Crimes against
Girls–Sexual behavior
Girly magazines *use* Girlie
magazines
Glamour photography
Gland, Prostate *use*
Prostate
Glandula prosta *use*
Prostate
Gonadal dysgenesis *use*
Turner's syndrome
Gonads
Gonorrhea
Gonosomes *use* Sex
chromosomes
Graafian follicle
Granuloma venereum
Gravid uterus *use* Uterus,
Pregnant
Gravida *use* Pregnant
women
Grooming for women *use*
Beauty, Personal
Grooming, Personal *use*
Beauty, Personal
Group marriage
Group psychotherapy
Group rape *use* Gang rape
Group sex

Gryposis penis *use*
Chordee
Guardian and ward
Guardian and ward
(Islamic law)
Gynaegamy *use* Woman-
to-woman marriage
Gynandromorphism
Gynecologic emergencies
Gynecologic nursing
Gynecologic surgery *use*
Generative organs,
Female–Surgery
Gynecology
Gynecology, Operative
use Generative organs,
Female–Surgery
Gynecology–Law and
legislation
Gynecology–Social
aspects
Gynegamy *use* Woman-
to-woman marriage
Gynoplasty

-H-

Hair–erotic aspects
Handicapped–Marriage
Handicapped–Sexual
behavior
Happiness
Harassment, Sexual *use*
Sexual harassment
Harassment of women,
Sexual *use* Sexual
harassment of women
Harem
Harlot *use* Prostitutes
Hating men *use* Misandry
Hatred of males *use*
Misandry
Health of women *use*
Women–Health and
hygiene
Heart diseases in
pregnancy

Hedonism
Hemorrhage, Uterine *use*
uterine hemorrhage
Hermaphroditism
Herpes genitalis
Herpes simplex, Genital
use herpes genitalis
High risk pregnancy *use*
Pregnancy–
complications
Hispanic American gays
Hispanic American
lesbians
History and sex *use* Sex
and history
HIV (Viruses) infection
use HIV infections
HIV antibodies
HIV disease vaccines *use*
AIDS vaccines
HIV infections
Home birth *use* Childbirth
at home
Home childbirth *use*
Childbirth at home
Home delivery
(Obstetrics) *use*
Childbirth at home
Homebirth *use* Childbirth
at home
Homes, Broken *use*
Broken homes
Homophile movement *use*
Gay liberation
movement
Homophobia
Homosexual couples *use*
Gay couples
Homosexual couples,
Male *use* Gay male
couples
Homosexual liberation
movement *use* Gay
liberation movement
Homosexual parents *use*
Gay parents
Homosexuality

Homosexuality, Female
use Lesbianism
Homosexuality, Male
Homosexuality–Folklore
Homosexuality–Law and
legislation
Homosexuality–
Mythology
Homosexuality–Religious
aspects
Homosexuality (in
religion, folklore, etc.)
use Homosexuality–
Mythology
Homosexuality (in
religion, folklore, etc.)
use Homosexuality–
Religious aspects
Homosexuality (in
religion, folklore, etc.)
use Homosexuality–
Folklore
Homosexuality and art
Homosexuality in art
Homosexuality in the
Bible
Homosexuality and
education
Homosexuality and
employment *use* Gays–
Employment
Homosexuality in
literature
Homosexuality in motion
pictures
Homosexuals *use* Gays
Homosexuals, Females
use Lesbians
Homosexuals, Male *use*
Gay men
Homosexuals' writings,
American *use* Gays'
writings, American
Homosexuals' writings *use*
Gays' writings
Honeymoon

Hormonal aspects of
fertility *use* Fertility–
Endocrine aspects
Hormonal aspects of
human reproduction
use Human
reproduction–
Endocrine aspects
Hormonal aspects of sex
differentiation *use* Sex
differentiation–
Endocrine aspects
Hormone replacement
therapy for menopause
use Menopause–
Hormone therapy
Hormones, Sex
Hormones, Sex–Receptors
Host mothers *use*
Surrogate mothers
Hot tubbing *use* Hot tubs
Hot tubs
Househusbands
HTLV-III infections *use*
HIV infections
HTLV-III-LAV infections
use HIV infections
Hugs *use* Hugging
Human artificial
insemination *use*
Artificial insemination,
Human
Human assisted
reproduction *use*
Human reproductive
technology
Human blastogenesis
Human chromosome
abnormalities
Human embryo
Human embryo, Frozen
use Frozen human
embryos
Human embryo–Effect of
drugs on
Human embryo–
Preservation

Human embryo–
Transplantation
Human embryo
implantation *use*
Human embryo–
Transplantation
Human embryo transfer
use Human embryo–
Transplantation
Human Embryology *use*
Embryology, Human
Human fertility *use*
Fertility, Human
Human fertilization *use*
Conception
Human fertilization in
vitro *use* Fertilization
in vitro, Human
Human in vitro
fertilization *use*
Fertilization in vitro,
Human
Human males *use* Men
Human population *use*
Population
Human population
genetics
Human reproduction
Human reproduction–
Effect of chemicals on
Human reproduction–
Endocrine aspects
Human reproduction–
Hormonal aspects *use*
Human Reproduction–
Endocrine aspects
Human reproduction–
Immunological aspects
Human reproduction–Law
and legislation
Human reproduction–
Mythology
Human reproduction–
Nutritional aspects
Human reproduction–
Regulation

Human reproduction–
Religious aspects

Human reproduction–
Technological
innovations *use* Human
reproductive
technology

Human reproduction
(Islamic law)

Human reproduction
technology industry

Human reproductive
technology

Human reproductive
technology–Law and
legislation

Human reproductive
technology–Religious
aspects

Human reproductive
technology–Religious
aspects–Christianity

Human reproductive
technology industry

Human T-lymphotropic
virus III infections *use*
HIV infections

Husband and wife

Husband and wife
(Islamic law)

Husbands

Hybridity of races *use*
Miscegenation

Hygiene, Sexual

Hygiene, Social *use*
Hygiene, Sexual

Hymen (Gynecology)

Hypersexuality *use* Sex
addiction

Hypertension in
pregnancy

Hypnotism in obstetrics

Hypogonadism

Hypospadias

Hypotension in pregnancy

Hysterectomy

Hysterectomy, Abdominal
use Hysterectomy

Hysterectomy, Vaginal

Hysterectomy–
Complications

Hysterectomy–Nursing

Hysterosalpingography

Hysteroscopic sterilization

Hysteroscopy

-I-

Ideal beautiful women *use*
Feminine beauty
(Aesthetics)

Identity (Psychology)

Illegitimacy

Illegitimacy (Islamic law)

Illegitimate children

Illicit sexual intercourse
use Fornication

Image, Body *use* Body
image

Immaculate Conception

Immoral literature *use*
Literature, Immoral

Immunocontraception *use*
Contraception,
Immunological

Immunological
contraception *use*
Contraception,
Immunological

Impediments to marriage

Impersonators, Female *use*
Female impersonators

Impersonators, Male *use*
Male impersonators

Impersonators of men *use*
Male impersonators

Impersonators of women
use Female
impersonators

Implantable contraceptive
drugs *use*
Contraceptive drug
implants

Implantation of human
embryo *use* Human
embryo–
Transplantation

Implantation of ovum *use*
Ovum implantation

Implants, Contraceptive
drug *use* Contraceptive
drug implants

Impotence

Impotence (Islamic law)

Inadequate corpus luteum
use Luteal phase
defects

Inadequate luteal phase
use Luteal phase
defects

Inbreeding

Incest

Incest, Emotional *use*
Emotional incest

Incest–Mythology

Incest–Religious aspects

Incest (Roman law)

Incest in literature

Incest in popular culture

Incest victims

Indecent assault

Indecent exposure

Indecent liberties *use*
Indecent assault

Indians of North
America–Marriage
customs and rites

Indians of North
America–Sexual
behavior

Induced abortion *use*
Abortion

Induced ovulation *use*
Ovulation–Induction

Induction, Menstrual *use*
Menstrual regulation

Induction of ovulation *use*
Ovulation–Induction

Induration, Penile *use*
Penile induration

Infancy *use* Infants

Infant (Premature)

Infant care *use* Infants–
Care

Infant care leave *use*
Parental leave

Infant development *use*
Infants–Development

Infant health services

Infant health services–
Federal aid *use* Federal
aid to infant health
services

Infant health services–
Finance

Infant health services–
Utilization

Infant Mortality
Awareness Day

Infant and mother *use*
Mother and infant

Infant sudden death *use*
Sudden infant death
syndrome

Infant switches *use* Infants
switched at birth

Infant welfare *use*
Maternal and infant
welfare

Infanticide

Infants

Infants–Care

Infants–Development

Infants–Medical care *use*
Infant health services

Infants–Nutrition

Infants (Newborn)

Infants (Newborn)–
Diseases–Psychological
aspects

Infants (Newborn)–Effect
of drugs on

Infants (Newborn)–
Identification

Infants (Stillborn) *use*
Stillbirth

Infants, Sale of *use*
Adoption–Corrupt
practices

Infants switched at birth

Infertility

Infertility, Female

Infertility, Male

Infertility–Religious
aspects

Infibulation

Infibulation–Law and
legislation

Infidelity, Marital *use*
Adultery

Inflatable penis *use* Penile
prostheses

Inheritance and succession
(Islamic law)

Inhibin

Initiation rites

Initiations

Injectable contraceptives
use Contraceptive
drugs, Injectable

Inmates of institutions–
Sexual behavior

Innocence (Psychology)

Insurance, marriage
endowment

Interactions, Sperm *use*
Sperm-ovum
interactions

Intercountry adoption

Intercourse, Anal *use* Anal
Intercourse

Intercourse, Oral *use* Oral
intercourse

Intercourse, Sexual *use*
Sexual intercourse

Interethnic dating

Interfaith marriage

Interfaith marriage (Canon
law)

Interfaith marriage in
literature

Intergenerational relations

Intermarriage

Intermarriage–Law and
legislation

International adoption *use*
Intercountry adoption

Interpersonal attraction

Interpersonal
communications

Interpersonal relations

Interracial adoption

Interracial dating

Interracial marriage

Interracial marriage,
Children of *use*
Children of interracial
marriage

Intersexuality *use*
Hermaphroditism

Interviewing in child
abuse

Intimacy (Psychology)

Intrauterine contraceptive
devices *use* Intrauterine
contraceptives

Intrauterine contraceptives

Intrauterine
contraceptives,
Medicated

Intrauterine
contraceptives–
Complications

Intrauterine
contraceptives–
Mechanism of action

Intrauterine contraceptives
industry

Intrauterine death *use*
Fetal death

Intrauterine devices *use*
Intrauterine
contraceptives

Intrauterine diagnosis *use*
Prenatal diagnosis

Intravaginal
contraceptives *use*
Contraceptives,
Vaginal

Involuntary sterilization
  use Sterilization,
  Eugenic
IUD (Contraceptive) *use*
  Intrauterine
  contraceptives
IUDs (Contraceptives) *use*
  Intrauterine
  contraceptives
IVF (Reproduction) *use*
  Fertilization in vitro

-J-

Jealousy
Jewish gays
Joy
Judicial separation *use*
  Separation (Law)
Jus primae noctis
Juvenile prostitution *use*
  Prostitution, Juvenile
Juvenile sex offenders *use*
  Teenage sex offenders

-K-

Kiddie porn *use* Children
  in pornography
Kidney diseases in
  pregnancy
Kings and rulers–
  Mistresses
Kissing
Kissing–Folklore
Kissing–Religious aspects
Kissing in motion pictures
Klinefelter's syndrome
Klinefelter's syndrome in
  children

-L-

Labor, Induced
  (Obstetrics)
Labor, Missed (Obstetrics)
  use Prolonged
  pregnancy

Labor, Painless
  (Obstetrics) *use* Natural
  childbirth
Labor, Premature
Labor, Services *use* Labor,
  Premature
Labor (Obstetrics)
Labor (Obstetrics)–
  Endocrine aspects
Labor (Obstetrics)–
  Hormonal aspects *use*
  Labor (Obstetrics)–
  Endocrine aspects
Labor (Obstetrics)–
  Regulation
Labor (Obstetrics)–
  Complications
Lactation
Lactation disorders
Lamaze method of
  childbirth *use* Natural
  childbirth
Lasciviousness *use* Lust
Late fetal death *use*
  Stillbirth
Law and literature
Law and sex *use* Sex and
  law
Lechery *use* Lust
Legal cruelty
Legitimacy (Law) *use*
  Illegitimacy
Legitimation of children
Length of pregnancy *use*
  Pregnancy–Duration
Lesbian athletes
Lesbian clergy
Lesbian couples
Lesbian libraries
Lesbian love *use*
  Lesbianism
Lesbian ministers *use*
  Lesbian clergy
Lesbian mothers
Lesbian nuns
Lesbian teachers
Lesbianism

Lesbianism–Religious
  aspects
Lesbianism in motion
  pictures
Lesbians
Lesbians, Hispanic
  American *use* Hispanic
  American lesbians
Lesbians, Mexican
  American *use* Mexican
  American lesbians
Lesbians–Travel
Lesbians–United States
Lesbians' writings
Lesbians' writings,
  American
Leydig cells
Liability for prenatal
  diagnosis *use* Wrongful
  birth
Liability for unwanted
  pregnancy *use*
  Wrongful birth
Libraries, Gay *use* Gay
  libraries
Libraries, Lesbian *use*
  Lesbian libraries
Libraries and gays
Library services to gays
  use Libraries and gays
Licentiousness *use* Lust
Life sciences ethics *use*
  Bioethics
Life style
Lifestyle *use* Life style
Ligation, Tubal *use* Tubal
  sterilization
Limericks
Lingerie
Liquor amnii *use*
  Amniotic liquid
Literature, Immoral *use*
  Pornography
Literature, Immoral–Law
  and legislation *use*
  Obscenity (Law)

Literature, Sex instruction
  use Sex instruction
  literature
Literature and
  homosexuality use
  Homosexuality and
  literature
Literature and morals
Live birth use Childbirth
Living alone
Living together use
  Unmarried couples
Lobolo use Bride price
Lord's Supper–Admission
  of remarried persons
Loss of loved ones by
  death use Bereavement
Loss of loved ones by
  separation use
  Separation
  (Psychology)
Love
Love, Courtly use Courtly
  love
Love, Maternal
Love, Paternal
Love, Platonic use
  Platonic love
Love–Religious aspects
Love–Religious aspects–
  Christianity
Love–Terminology
Love (Buddhism) use
  Love–Religious
  aspects–Buddhism
Love (Theology) use
  Love–Religious
  aspects–Dowry
Love addiction use
  Relationship addiction
Love in art
Love-hate relationships
Love in literature
Love-letters
Love in motion pictures
Love names use Love–
  Terminology

Love philters use
  Aphrodisiacs
Love philtres use
  Aphrodisiacs
Love poetry
Love potions use
  Aphrodisiacs
Love songs
Love songs, American
Love stories
Love's longings use
  Lovesickness
Lovemaking use Sexual
  intercourse
Lover's malady use
  Lovesickness
Lovers (Mistresses) use
  Mistresses
Lovesickness
Low-cut neckline use
  Decolletage
Lusalo
Lust
Lust–Religious aspects
Lust–Religious aspects–
  Christianity
Lust addiction use Sex
  addiction
Luteal hormone use
  Progesterone
Luteal inadequacy use
  Luteal phase defects
Luteal insufficiency use
  Luteal phase defects
Luteal phase
Luteal phase defects
Luteal phase deficiency
  use Luteal phase
  defects
Luteal phase dysfunction
  use Luteal phase
  defects
Luteal phase inadequacy
  use Luteal phase
  defects
Lymphogranuloma
  venereum

-M-

Machismo
Maiden aunts
Male birth control pills
  use Oral
  contraceptives, Male
Male change of life use
  Climacteric, Male
Male climacteric use
  Climacteric, Male
Male contraception
Male contraceptive agents
  use Male
  contraceptives
Male contraceptive
  devices use Male
  contraceptives
Male contraceptives
Male couples, Gay use
  Gay male couples
Male-female relationships
  use Man-woman
  relationships
Male gays use Gay men
Male homosexuality use
  Homosexuality, Male
Male impersonators
Male impersonators in
  motion pictures
Male infertility use
  Infertility, Male
Male menopause use
  Climacteric, Male
Male nude
Male oral contraceptives
  use Oral
  contraceptives, Male
Male orgasm
Male prostitution use
  Prostitution, Male
Male rape
Male rape victims
Male sex hormone use
  Hormones, Sex
Male sterility use
  Infertility, Male

Male striptease

Males, Human *use* Men

Malnutrition in children

Malnutrition in pregnancy

Malnutrition in pregnancy–United States–Prevention

Malpractice by obstetricians *use* Obstetricians–Malpractice

Malthusianism

Mammaplasty *use* Breast reconstruction

Mammography

Man and wife *use* Husband and wife

Man-woman relationships

Marital communication *use* Communication in marriage

Marital condition *use* Marital status

Marital counseling *use* Marriage counseling

Marital infidelity *use* Adultery

Marital property

Marital psychotherapy

Marital rape *use* Rape in marriage

Marital separation *use* Separation (Law)

Marital settlement agreements *use* Divorce settlements

Marital status

Marital status–Statistics

Marital therapy *use* Marital psychotherapy

Marriage

Marriage, Bisexual *use* Bisexuality in marriage

Marriage, Child *use* Child marriage

Marriage, Companionate

Marriage, Medical examination for *use* Premarital examinations

Marriage, Mixed *use* Intermarriage

Marriage, Mixed (Canon law) *use* Interfaith marriage (Canon law)

Marriage, Mixed, in literature *use* Interfaith marriage in literature

Marriage, Promise of *use* Betrothal

Marriage, Temporary *use* Temporary marriage

Marriage–Annulment

Marriage–Annulment (Canon law)

Marriage–Compatibility tests *use* Marriage compatibility tests

Marriage–Law and legislation *use* Marriage law

Marriage–Parental consent

Marriage–Prohibited degrees *use* Consanguinity

Marriage–Prohibited degrees *use* Marriage law

Marriage–Sermons

Marriage–United States

Marriage (Canon law)

Marriage (Islamic law)

Marriage advertisements *use* Matrimonial advertisements

Marriage age

Marriage age–Law and legislation *use* Age of consent

Marriage age–Religious aspects

Marriage in art

Marriage brokerage

Marriage celebrants

Marriage compatibility tests

Marriage counseling

Marriage customs and rites

Marriage guidance *use* Marriage counseling

Marriage law

Marriage in literature

Marriage in motion pictures

Marriage in moving-pictures *use* Marriage in motion pictures

Marriage proposals

Marriage psychotherapy *use* Marital psychotherapy

Marriage sermons *use* Marriage–Sermons

Marriage service

Marriage and spiritualism

Marriage with deceased wife's sister

Married men *use* Husbands

Married people

Married people–Counseling of *use* Marriage counseling

Married persons *use* Married people

Married women

Married women (Islamic law)

Masculinity (Psychology)

Masochism

Masochism in literature

Masochism in motion pictures

Mass media in birth control

Mass media in breast feeding promotion

Mass media and sex
Massage parlors
Masturbation
Masturbation–Religious
    aspects
Mate selection
Maternal age
Maternal and child health
    services use Maternal
    health services
Maternal deprivation in
    infants
Maternal-fetal exchange
Maternal-fetal medicine
    use Obstetrics
Maternal health care use
    Maternal health
    services
Maternal health services
Maternal health services–
    Federal aid use Federal
    aid to maternal health
    services
Maternal health services–
    Finance
Maternal health services–
    Law and legislation
Maternal and infant health
    services use Infant
    health services
Maternal and infant
    welfare
Maternal love use Love,
    Maternal
Maternal metabolism
Maternal mortality use
    Mothers–Mortality
Maternal nutrition use
    Mothers–Nutrition
Maternal weight gain use
    Pregnant women–
    Weight gain
Maternally acquired
    immunity use
    Maternal-fetal
    exchange

Maternity care use
    Maternal health
    services
Maternity clothes
Matrimonial actions
Matrimonial actions
    (Canon law)
Matrimonial
    advertisements
Matrimonial regime use
    Husband and wife
Matrimony use Marriage
Mechanism of action of
    intrauterine
    contraceptives use
    Intrauterine
    contraceptives–
    Mechanism of action
Meconium aspiration
    syndrome
Mediation, Divorce use
    Divorce mediation
Mediation therapy
Medical examinations for
    marriage use Premarital
    examinations
Medical genetics–Law
    and legislation
Medicated intrauterine
    contraceptives use
    Intrauterine
    contraceptives,
    Medicated
Medicine, Perinatal use
    Perinatology
Melancholic love use
    Lovesickness
Men
Men, Gay use Gay men
Men–Psychology
Men–Sexual behavior
Men–Socialization
Men-hating use Misandry
Men rape victims use
    Male rape victims

Men-women relationships
    use Man-woman
    relationships
Menarchal delay use
    Menarche
Menarche
Menopause
Menopause, Male use
    Climacteric, Male
Menopause–Estrogen
    replacement therapy
    use Menopause–
    Hormone therapy
Menopause–Hormone
    replacement therapy
    use Menopause–
    Hormone therapy
Menopause–Hormone
    therapy
Menorrhagia
Menses use Menstruation
Menstrual cycle
Menstrual cycle–
    Psychological aspects
Menstrual disorders use
    Menstruation disorders
Menstrual extraction use
    Menstrual regulation
Menstrual induction use
    Menstrual regulation
Menstrual regulation
Menstruation
Menstruation–Cross-
    cultural studies
Menstruation–Folklore
Menstruation–Mythology
Menstruation (in religion
    folklore etc.) use
    Menstruation–Folklore
Menstruation (in religion
    folklore etc.) use
    Menstruation–
    Mythology
Menstruation disorders
Menstruation inducing
    agents use
    Emmenagogues

Mental illness in
pregnancy
Mentally handicapped–
Marriage
Mentally handicapped–
Sexual behavior
Mentally ill–Family
relationships
Metabolism in pregnancy
Mexican American gays
Mexican American
lesbians
Middle age–Sexual
behavior *use* Middle
aged persons–Sexual
behavior
Middle aged lesbians
Middle aged persons–
Sexual behavior
Middle aged women–
Sexual behavior
Midtrimester of pregnancy
use Pregnancy–
Trimester, Second
Midwifery *use* Obstetrics
Midwives
Mifepristone
Milk–Secretion *use*
Lactation
Milk, Human
Milk fever
Milk production
Milk secretion *use*
Lactation
Misandry
Miscarriage
Miscegenation
Miscegenation–Law and
legislation
Misogyny
Missed labor (Obstetrics)
use Prolonged
pregnancy
Mistresses
Mixed marriage *use*
Intermarriage

Mixed race children *use*
Children of interracial
marriage
Mole, Uterine *use*
Pregnancy, Molar
Molesting of children *use*
Child molesting
Moral condition
Morals *use* Moral
condition
Morals and art *use* Art and
morals
Morals offenses *use*
Crimes without victims
Mormon gays
Morning after pills *use*
Contraceptives,
Postcoital
Mother and child health
services *use* Maternal
health services
Mother goddesses
Mother and infant
Mother love *use* Love,
Maternal
Mother's age at birth *use*
Maternal age
Mothers
Mothers–Medical care *use*
Maternal health
services
Mothers–Mortality
Mothers–Nutrition
Mothers and sons
Multilateral marriage *use*
Group marriage
Multiple birth *use* Birth,
Multiple
Multiple marriage *use*
Bigamy
Multiple marriage *use*
Polygamy
Multiple pregnancy *use*
Pregnancy, Multiple
Music and erotica
Music and morals
Myometrium

-N-

Nakedness *use* Nudity
NAMES Project AIDS
memorial quilt
Napkins, Sanitary *use*
Sanitary napkins
Natality *use* Fertility,
Human
National Breast Cancer
Awareness Month
Natural childbirth
Natural childbirth–
Coaching
Natural family planning
Natural family planning–
Basal body temperature
method *use* Natural
family planning–
Temperature method
Natural family planning–
Billings ovulation
method *use* Natural
family planning–
Ovulation method
Natural family planning–
Calendar method
Natural family planning–
Cervical mucus method
use Natural family
planning–Ovulation
method
Natural family planning–
Ovulation method
Natural family planning–
Religious aspects
Natural family planning–
Rhythm method *use*
Natural family
planning–Calendar
method
Natural family planning–
Temperature method
Natural parents *use*
Birthparents
Nature worship
Naturism *use* Nudism

Navel
Neck of the uterus *use*
Cervix uteri
Necrophilia
Necrophilism *use*
Necrophilia
Neonatal intensive care
Neonatal intensive care–
Law and legislation
Neonatology
Neonatology–Law and
legislation
Neurosyphilis
Nidation *use* Ovum
implantation
No-fault divorce
Nocturnal emissions
Non-victim crimes *use*
Crimes without victims
Nonconsensual sexual
intercourse *use* Rape
Nongonococcal urethritis
use Urethritis,
Nongonococcal
Nonspecific urethritis *use*
Urethritis,
Nongonococcal
Nude *use* Nudity
Nude in art
Nude culture *use* Nudism
Nude photography *use*
Photography of the
nude
Nudism
Nudist camps
Nudity
Nudity–Religious aspects
Nudity culture *use*
Nudism
Nudity in dance
Nudity in motion pictures
Nudity in the performing
arts
Nullity of marriage *use*
Marriage–Annulment
Nuns, Lesbian *use*
Lesbian nuns

Nuptiality *use* Marriage
Nurse midwives *use*
Midwives
Nutrition in pregnancy *use*
Pregnancy–Nutritional
aspects
Nutrition and sex *use* Sex
(Biology)–Nutritional
aspects
Nymphomania

-O-

Obscene literature
Obscene literature *use*
Literature, Immoral
Obscene words *use*
Words, Obscene
Obscenities (Words) *use*
Words, Obscene
Obscenity (Law)
Obsession, Sexual *use* Sex
addiction
Obstetrical diagnosis *use*
Obstetrics–Diagnosis
Obstetrical emergencies
Obstetrical endocrinology
Obstetrical extraction
Obstetrical forceps
Obstetrical pharmacology
Obstetrical practice
Obstetrical research *use*
Obstetrics–Research
Obstetrical ultrasonic
imaging *use*
Ultrasonics in
obstetrics
Obstetrical ultrasonics *use*
Ultrasonics in
obstetrics
Obstetrical
ultrasonography *use*
Ultrasonics in
obstetrics
Obstetrical ultrasound *use*
Ultrasonics in
obstetrics

Obstetricians
Obstetricians–Attitudes
Obstetricians–Legal status
laws etc.
Obstetricians–Malpractice
Obstetrics
Obstetrics, Eclectic
Obstetrics, Homeopathic
Obstetrics, Operative *use*
Obstetrics–Surgery
Obstetrics–Apparatus and
instruments
Obstetrics–Case studies
Obstetrics–Cases clinical
reports statistics *use*
Obstetrics–Case studies
Obstetrics–Diagnosis
Obstetrics–Immunological
aspects
Obstetrics–Law and
legislation
Obstetrics–Practice
Obstetrics–Psychosomatic
aspects
Obstetrics–Research
Obstetrics–Research–
United States
Obstetrics–Social aspects
Obstetrics–Study and
teaching
Obstetrics–Surgery
Obstetrics–Surgery–
Complications
Occlusion of the vas
deferens *use* Vas
occlusion
Oedipus complex
Offenders, Female *use*
Female offenders
Offenders, Sex *use* Sex
offenders
Offenses against the
person
Offenses against public
morality *use* Crimes
without victims

Office romance *use* Sex in the workplace

Old gay men *use* Aged gay men

Older child adoption

Older gay men *use* Aged gay men

Older lesbians *use* Middle aged lesbians

Omphalos *use* Navel

Onanism *use* Coitus interruptus

Onanism *use* Masturbation

Oogenesis

Open adoption

Operative obstetrics *use* Obstetrics–Surgery

Oral anovulants *use* Oral contraceptives

Oral contraceptives

Oral contraceptives, Female *use* Oral contraceptives

Oral contraceptives, Male

Oral contraceptives– Social aspects

Oral intercourse

Oral sex *use* Oral intercourse

Orgasm

Orgasmic cephalgia *use* Sexual headache

Orgasmic dysfunction *use* Anorgasmy

Orgies *use* Group sex

Orientation, Sexual *use* Sexual orientation

Ostomates–Sex counseling

Ovaries

Oviduct

Oviductal pregnancy *use* Tubal pregnancy

Ovulation

Ovulation–Detection

Ovulation–Induction

Ovulation–Regulation

Ovulation–Time determination *use* Ovulation–Detection

Ovulation of birth control *use* Natural family planning–Ovulation method

Ovum

Ovum implantation

Ovum-sperm interactions *use* Sperm-ovum interactions

-P-

Pacamama (Goddess)

Pads, Sanitary *use* Sanitary napkins

Paedophilia *use* Pedophilia

Painless labor (Obstetrics) *use* Natural childbirth

Painting, Erotic *use* Erotic painting

Palimony

Panders *use* Pimps

Panders *use* Procuresses

Pap smear *use* Pap test

Pap test

Papanicolaou test *use* Pap test

Paramours (Mistresses) *use* Mistresses

Paraphilia *use* Psychosexual disorders

Paraphilia *use* Sexual deviation

Parasitic diseases in pregnancy

Parent and child

Parent and child (Law)

Parental leave

Parental preferences for sex of children *use* Sex of children, Parental preferences for

Parenthood, Preparation for *use* Childbirth– Study and teaching

Parenting, Part-time

Parenting–Study and teaching

Parents

Parents, Adolescent *use* Teenage parents

Parents, Single *use* Single parents

Parents of gays

Parents of sexually abused children

Parents without partners *use* Single-parent family

Parovarium

Partner surrogates (Sex therapy) *use* Sex surrogates

Parturition

Paternal love *use* Love, Paternal

Paternity

Paternity–Criminal provisions

Paternity–Testing *use* Paternity testing

Paternity testing

Pathology, Gynecological

Pederasty *use* Anal intercourse

Pederasty *use* Sodomy

Pediatric AIDS *use* AIDS (Disease) in children

Pediatric gynecology

Pediatric pharmacology

Pediatric urology

Pedophilia

Pedophilics *use* Child molesters

Pelvic examination *use* Pelvis–Examination

Pelvioscopy *use* Pelvis– Examination

Pelvis

Pelvis–Examination

Penetration, Sperm *use* Sperm-ovum. interactions

Penile curvatures *use* Penis–Curvatures

Penile induration

Penile prostheses

Penis

Penis, Clubbed *use* Penis–Curvatures

Penis–Abnormalities

Penis–Cancer

Penis–Curvatures

Penis–Diseases

Penis–Surgery

Penis lunatus *use* Chordee

Penis plastica *use* Penile induration

Penis sheaths

Penis sheaths (Costumes)

People, Divorced *use* Divorced people

People, Married *use* Married people

People, Remarried *use* Remarried people

People, Single *use* Single people

People, Unmarried *use* Single people

Peptide hormones

Perinatal cardiology

Perinatal care

Perinatal death

Perinatal hematology

Perinatal medicine *use* Perinatology

Perinatal pharmacology

Perinatology

Personal beauty *use* Beauty, Personal

Personal relations *use* Interpersonal relations

Persons, Divorced *use* Divorced People

Persons, Married *use* Married people

Persons, Remarried *use* Remarried people

Persons, Single *use* Single people

Persons, Unmarried *use* Single people

Perversion, Sexual *use* Sexual deviation

Peyronie's disease *use* Penile induration

Phallicism

Phallicism in art

Phallus *use* Penis

Pharmacology, Perinatal *use* Perinatal pharmacology

Pheromones

Philters *use* Aphrodisiacs

Phimosis

Photography, Erotic

Photography of the nude

Physically handicapped–Marriage

Physically handicapped–Sexual behavior

Pill, Birth control *use* Oral contraceptives

Pill, The *use* Oral contraceptives

Pimps

Pin-up art *use* Pinup art

Pinup art

Pituitary gland

Placenta

Placenta–Diseases

Placenta–Diseases–Diagnosis

Placenta–Radiography

Placenta–Tumors

Placenta praevia

Placental hormones

Placental proteins *use* Placental proteins

Planned parenthood *use* Birth control

Planned parenthood services *use* Birth control clinics

Platonic love

Pleasure

Plural births *use* Birth, Multiple

PMS (Gynecology) *use* Premenstrual syndrome

Politicians–Sexual behavior

Polyandry

Polygamy

Polygamy (Islamic law)

Polygamy (Jewish law)

Polygamy and Christianity

Population

Population–Law and legislation

Population–Statistics

Population assistance

Population assistance, American

Population biology

Population control *use* Birth control

Population forecasting

Population genetics

Population policy

Population policy–Moral and ethical aspects

Population policy–Religious aspects

Population policy–Religious aspects–Baptists, Catholic Church, etc.

Population policy–Religious aspects–Buddhism, Christianity, etc.

Population psychology

Population research

Populations, Human *use* Population

Pornography

Pornography–Social aspects

Pornography in mass media *use* Sex in mass media

Post services period *use* Puerperium

Post-cesarean vaginal birth *use* Vaginal birth after cesarean

Postal service–Law and legislation

Postal service–Laws and regulation *use* Postal service–Law and legislation

Postcoital contraceptives *use* Contraceptives, Postcoital

Postnatal care

Postnatal depression *use* Postpartum depression

Postnatal psychiatric disorders *use* Postpartum psychiatric disorders

Postpartum blues *use* Postpartum depression

Postpartum care *use* Postnatal care

Postpartum complications *use* Puerperal disorders

Postpartum depression

Postpartum period *use* Puerperium

Postpartum psychiatric disorders

Postpartum sexual abstinence *use* Sexual abstinence, Postpartum

Pre-eclampsia *use* Preeclampsia

Pre-menstrual syndrome *use* Premenstrual syndrome

Precocious puberty

Preeclampsia

Preeclamptic toxemia *use* Preeclampsia

Preemptive abortion *use* Menstrual regulation

Preferences of parents for sex of children *use* Sex of children, Parental preferences for

Pregnancy

Pregnancy, Abdominal

Pregnancy, Adolescent *use* Teenage pregnancy

Pregnancy, Complications of *use* Pregnancy–Complications

Pregnancy, Ectopic *use* Ectopic pregnancy

Pregnancy, Extra-uterine *use* Ectopic pregnancy

Pregnancy, Imaginary *use* Pseudocyesis

Pregnancy, Molar

Pregnancy, Multiple

Pregnancy, Protracted *use* Prolonged pregnancy

Pregnancy, Teenage *use* Teenage pregnancy

Pregnancy, Tubal *use* Tubal pregnancy

Pregnancy, Unwanted

Pregnancy–Complications

Pregnancy–Duration

Pregnancy–First trimester *use* Pregnancy–Trimester, First

Pregnancy–Immunological aspects

Pregnancy–Length *use* Pregnancy–Duration

Pregnancy–Midtrimester *use* Pregnancy–Trimester, Second

Pregnancy–Nutritional aspects

Pregnancy–Prevention *use* Birth control

Pregnancy–Psychological aspects

Pregnancy–Second trimester *use* Pregnancy–Trimester, Second

Pregnancy–Signs and diagnosis

Pregnancy–Third trimester *use* Pregnancy–Trimester, Third

Pregnancy–Trimester, First

Pregnancy–Trimester, Second

Pregnancy–Trimester, Third

Pregnancy in adolescence *use* Teenage pregnancy

Pregnancy Man (Legendary character) *use* Pregnant Man (Tale)

Pregnancy in mentally ill women

Pregnancy in middle age

Pregnancy in physically handicapped women

Pregnancy proteins

Pregnancy termination *use* Abortion

Pregnancy toxemia *use* Toxemia of pregnancy

Pregnant girls in the schools *use* Pregnant schoolgirls

Pregnant Man (Tale)

Pregnant mentally ill women *use* Pregnancy in mentally ill women

Pregnant middle aged women *use* pregnancy in middle age

Pregnant schoolgirls

Pregnant women

Pregnant women–Anthropometry

Pregnant women–Care use
Prenatal care
Pregnant women–
Clothing use Maternity
clothes
Pregnant women–Diseases
use Pregnancy–
complications
Pregnant women–
Employment
Pregnant women–
Employment–Law and
legislation
Pregnant women–
Nutrition use
Pregnancy–Nutritional
aspects
Pregnant women–
Psychology use
Pregnancy–
Psychological aspects
Pregnant women–
Radiography
Pregnant women–Surgery
Pregnant women–
Surgery–Complications
Pregnant women–Tobacco
use
Pregnant women–Weight
gain
Pregnant women–Wounds
and injuries
Preimplantation genetic
diagnosis
Premarital counseling use
Marriage counseling
Premarital examinations
Premarital sex
Premature ejaculation
Premature infants use
Infants (Premature)
Premature labor use
Labor, Premature
Premenstrual syndrome
Premenstrual tension use
Premenstrual syndrome
Prenatal care

Prenatal diagnosis
Prenatal diagnosis,
Liability for use
Wrongful birth
Prenatal influences
Prenatal malnutrition use
Fetal malnutrition
Prenatal malnutrition use
Malnutrition in
pregnancy
Prenuptial contracts use
Antenuptial contracts
Preselection of sex use
Sex preselection
Presidents–United States–
Mistresses
Preterm infants use Infants
(Premature)
Preterm labor use Labor,
Premature
Prevention of rape use
Rape–Prevention
Priapism
Primary amenorrhea use
Menarche
Primitive erotic art use
Erotic art–Primitive
Prisoners–Sexual behavior
Privacy, Right of
Pro-abortion movement
use Pro-choice
movement
Pro-choice movement
Pro-life movement
Problem families
Procreation use
Reproduction
Procurers use Pimps
Procurers use Procuresses
Procuresses
Progestagens use
Progestational
hormones
Progestational hormones
Progestational hormones,
Synthetic
Progesterone

Progestins use
Progestational
hormones
Progestogens use
Progestational
hormones
Prohibited books
Prolactin
Prolapse of the cord use
Umbilical cord–
Prolapse
Prolapse of the umbilical
cord use Umbilical
cord–Prolapse
Prolapse of the uterus use
Uterus–Prolapse
Prolapsus uteri use
Uterus–Prolapse
Prolonged pregnancy
Promiscuity
Promotion of breast
feeding use Breast
feeding promotion
Prophylactics (Birth
control) use Condoms
Prostata use Prostate
Prostate
Prostate gland use
Prostate
Prostitutes
Prostitutes–Personality
use Prostitutes–
Psychology
Prostitutes–Psychology
Prostitutes in art
Prostitutes in literature
Prostitutes' children use
Children of prostitutes
Prostitution
Prostitution, Female use
Prostitution
Prostitution, Juvenile
Prostitution, Male
Prostitution–Religious
aspects
Prostitution in the press

Prostitution as a theme in
literature *use*
Prostitutes in literature
Protracted pregnancy *use*
Prolonged pregnancy
Proxenetes *use* Pimps
Proxenetes *use*
Procuresses
Pseudocyesis
Pseudopregnancy *use*
Pseudocyesis
Psittacosis
Psychiatric disorders
Postpartum *use*
Postpartum psychiatric
disorders
Psychic masochism *use*
Masochism
Psychological child abuse
Psychology, Sexual *use*
Sex (Psychology)
Psychosexual
development
Psychosexual disorders
Psychotherapist and
patient–Sexual
behavior
Puberty
Puberty rites
Puerperal care *use*
Postnatal care
Puerperal convulsions
Puerperal disorders
Puerperal psychiatric
disorders *use*
Postpartum psychiatric
disorders
Puerperal psychoses
Puerperal septicemia
Puerperal state *use*
Puerperium
Puerperium
Puerperium–Nutritional
aspects
Purity, Ceremonial *use*
Purity, Ritual
Purity, Ritual

-Q-

Quadruplets
Quintuplets

-R-

Racial amalgamation *use*
Miscegenation
Radio in birth control
Radio in family planning
use Radio in birth
control
Radiography in obstetrics
Radioisotopes in
obstetrics
Radioisotopes in urology
Rape
Rape–Investigation
Rape–Prevention
Rape (Islamic law)
Rape in marriage
Rape in marriage–
Religious aspects
Rape victims
Rapists
Reanastomosis of the vas
deferens *use*
Vasovasostomy
Records of births etc. *use*
Registers of births etc.
Rectum
Reduction mammaplasty
Registers of births etc.
Regulation of human
reproduction *use*
Human reproduction–
Regulation
Regulation of ovulation
use Ovulation–
Regulation
Rejection (Psychology)
Relations, Interpersonal
use Interpersonal
relations
Relationship addiction

Relationships,
Interpersonal *use*
Interpersonal relations
Relationships, Love-hate
use Love-hate
relationships
Relationships,
Man-woman *use* Man-
woman relationships
Relaxin
Remarriage
Remarriage–Religious
aspects
Remarriage–Religious
aspects–Christianity
Remarriage (Islamic law)
Remarried people
Reproductive
endocrinology
Reproductive
immunology *use*
Human reproduction–
Immunological aspects
Reproductive organs *use*
Generative organs
Reproductive toxicology
Reproductive wastage *use*
Fetal death
Reversal of sexual
sterilization *use*
Sterilization reversal
Reversal of vasectomy *use*
Vasovasostomy
Rhythm method (Birth
control) *use* Natural
family planning–
Calendar method
Rhythm method of birth
control *use* Natural
family planning–
Calendar method
Ribald songs *use* Bawdy
songs
Right-to-choose
movement *use* Pro-
choice movement

Right-to-life movement
(Anti-abortion
movement) *use* Pro-
choice movement
Ritual purity *use* Purity,
Ritual
Romances (Love stories)
use Love stories
RU486 (Drug) *use*
Mifepristone
Rubella in pregnancy
Runaway husbands

-S-

Sadism
Sadism in literature
Sadism in motion pictures
Sadism in moving-
pictures *use* Sadism in
motion pictures
Sado-masochism *use*
Sadomasochism
Sadomasochism
Safe sex in AIDS
prevention
Sale of infants *use*
Adoption–Corrupt
practices
Sanitary napkins
Sanitary pads *use* Sanitary
napkins
Scatology
Scatology in art
Scatology in the Bible
Scatology in literature
School-age fathers *use*
Teenage fathers
Scopophilia
Scrotum
Sculpture, Erotic *use*
Erotic sculpture
Second trimester of
pregnancy *use*
Pregnancy–Trimester
Second

Secret marriage *use*
Elopement
Secretory phase
(Menstrual cycle) *use*
Luteal phase
Seduction
Seduction (Canon law)
Seduction in literature
Seductresses *use* Femmes
fatales
Semen
Semen banks *use* Sperm
banks
Seminal vesicles
Sensuality
Sensuality in dance *use*
Sexuality in dance
Sensuousness *use*
Sensuality
Sentimentalism in
literature
Separate maintenance
Separation (Law)
Separation (Psychology)
Septic abortion
Sertoli cells
Service, Marriage *use*
Marriage service
Services childbirth *use*
Natural childbirth
Services labor *use* Labor,
Premature
Sex
Sex, Oral *use* Oral
intercourse
Sex–Cause and
determination *use* Sex
preselection
Sex–Cause and
determination *use* Sex
determination,
Diagnostic
Sex–Cause and
determination *use* Sex
determination, Genetic
Sex–Fiction *use* Erotic
stories

Sex–Folklore
Sex–Information services
Sex–Juvenile literature
use Sex instruction for
children
Sex–Moral and ethical
aspects *use* Sexual
ethics
Sex–Moral and religious
aspects *use* Sexual
ethics
Sex–Mythology
Sex–Nutritional aspects
use Sex (Biology)–
Nutritional aspects
Sex–Physiological aspects
use Sex (Biology)
Sex–Poetry *use* Bawdy
poetry
Sex–Poetry *use* Erotic
poetry
Sex–Psychological
aspects *use* Sex
(Psychology)
Sex–Quotations, maxims,
etc.
Sex–Religious aspects
Sex–Research *use*
Sexology–Research
Sex–Songs and music *use*
Erotic songs
Sex–Statistics
Sex–Study and teaching
use Sex instruction
Sex (Biology)
Sex (Biology)–Nutritional
aspects
Sex (Gender) *use* Sex
Sex (Physiology) *use* Sex
(Biology)
Sex (Psychology)
Sex (Psychology)–
Endocrine aspects
Sex (in religion, folklore,
etc.) *use* Sex–
Mythology
Sex addiction

Sex addiction–Patients
  use Sex addicts
Sex addiction–Religious
  aspects
Sex addicts
Sex addicts' adult children
  use Adult children of
  sex addicts
Sex in advertising
Sex appeal *use* Sexual
  attraction
Sex in art
Sex in the arts *use* Sex in
  art
Sex behavior surveys *use*
  Sexual behavior
  surveys
Sex bias *use* Sexism
Sex in the Bible
Sex in business *use* Sex in
  the workplace
Sex businesses *use* Sex
  oriented businesses
Sex change
Sex, Change of *use* Sex
  change
Sex change–Law and
  legislation
Sex of children, Parental
  preferences for
Sex chromosome
  abnormalities
Sex chromosome
  abnormalities in
  children
Sex chromosomes
Sex control (Preselection)
  use Sex preselection
Sex counseling
Sex crimes
Sex crimes (Canon law)
Sex crimes in the press
Sex criminals *use* Sex
  offenders
Sex customs
Sex customs–Cross-
  cultural studies

Sex determination,
  Diagnostic
Sex determination,
  Genetic
Sex differences
  (Psychology)
Sex differentiation
Sex differentiation
  disorders
Sex differentiation–
  Endocrine aspects
Sex disorders *use* Sexual
  disorders
Sex in dreams
Sex and drugs *use* Drugs
  and sex
Sex distribution
  (Demography)
Sex education *use* Sex
  instruction
Sex educators
Sex in espionage
Sex fantasies *use* Sexual
  fantasies
Sex glands *use* Gonads
Sex hanging *use*
  Autoerotic asphyxia
Sex headache *use* Sexual
  headache
Sex hormones *use*
  Hormones, Sex
Sex hygiene *use* Hygiene,
  Sexual
Sex identity (Gender
  identity) *use* Gender
  identity
Sex industry *use* Sex
  oriented businesses
Sex instruction
Sex instruction–Juvenile
  literature *use* Sex
  instruction for
  teenagers
Sex instruction–Juvenile
  literature *use* Sex
  instruction for children

Sex instruction–Law and
  legislation
Sex instruction–Religious
  aspects
Sex instruction for the
  aged
Sex instruction for boys
Sex instruction for
  children
Sex instruction for
  children–Religious
  aspects
Sex instruction for gay
  men
Sex instruction for girls
Sex instruction for the
  handicapped
Sex instruction for
  homosexual men *use*
  Sex instruction for gay
  men
Sex instruction for
  lesbians
Sex instruction literature
Sex instruction for men
Sex instruction for the
  mentally handicapped
Sex instruction for
  mentally handicapped
  children
Sex instruction for the
  physically handicapped
Sex instruction for the
  sick
Sex instruction for
  teenagers
Sex instruction for women
Sex instruction for youth
Sex instruction for youth–
  Law and legislation
Sex instruction for youth–
  Law and legislation
Sex instruction for youth–
  Religious aspects
Sex and law
Sex-linkage (Genetics)
Sex in literature

Sex in marriage
Sex and mass media *use*
  Mass media and sex
Sex in mass media
Sex in mass media–Law
  and legislation
Sex in motion pictures
Sex in moving-pictures
  use Sex in motion
  pictures
Sex offenders
Sex offenders' wives
Sex offenses *use* Sex
  crimes
Sex in the office *use* Sex
  in the workplace
Sex organs *use* Generative
  organs
Sex oriented businesses
Sex oriented businesses–
  Law and legislation
Sex oriented periodicals
Sex partners, Surrogate
  use Sex surrogates
Sex in the performing arts
Sex perversion *use* Sexual
  deviation
Sex predetermination *use*
  Sex preselection
Sex preselection
Sex in prisons *use*
  Prisoners–Sexual
  behavior
Sex in rabbinical literature
Sex related businesses *use*
  Sex oriented businesses
Sex research *use*
  Sexology–Research
Sex role
Sex-role inversion *use* Sex
  change
Sex role–Religious
  aspects
Sex role in advertising
Sex role in children
Sex role in literature
Sex role in mass media

Sex role in motion
  pictures
Sex role in television
Sex role in the work
  environment
Sex role on television *use*
  Sex role in television
Sex selection *use* Sex
  preselection
Sex shops *use* Sex
  oriented businesses
Sex and social service *use*
  Social service and sex
Sex surrogates
Sex surveys *use* Sexual
  behavior surveys
Sex symbolism
Sex and tarot *use* Tarot
  and sex
Sex teachers *use* Sex
  educators
Sex in television
Sex in television–Law and
  legislation
Sex on television *use* Sex
  in television
Sex in the theater
Sex therapists
Sex therapy
Sex and witchcraft *use*
  Witchcraft and sex
Sex in the workplace
Sex worship *use*
  Phallicism
Sexaholics *use* Sex
  addicts
Sexaholism *use* Sex
  addiction
Sexiness *use* Sexual
  attraction
Sexism
Sexology
Sexology–Research
Sexual abstinence
Sexual abstinence,
  Postpartum

Sexual abstinence–
  Religious aspects
Sexual abuse *use* Sex
  crimes
Sexual abuse of children
  use child molesting
Sexual addiction *use* Sex
  addiction
Sexual addicts *use* Sex
  addicts
Sexual animosity
Sexual arousal *use* Sexual
  excitement
Sexual attraction
Sexual attractiveness *use*
  Sexual attraction
Sexual aversion disorders
Sexual behavior *use* Sex
Sexual behavior *use* Sex
  customs
Sexual behavior *use*
  Sexual ethics
Sexual behavior,
  Psychology *use* Sex
  (Psychology)
Sexual behavior surveys
Sexual climax *use* Orgasm
Sexual compulsiveness
  use Sex addiction
Sexual connection *use*
  Sexual intercourse
Sexual crimes *use* Sex
  crimes
Sexual cycle *use*
  Menstrual cycle
Sexual cycle of women
  use Menstrual cycle
Sexual delinquency *use*
  Sex crimes
Sexual deviation
Sexual deviation–Law and
  legislation *use* Sodomy
Sexual deviation in
  literature
Sexual diseases *use*
  Sexual disorders

Sexual diseases *use*
  Sexually transmitted
  diseases
Sexual disorders
Sexual disorders in
  children
Sexual division of labor
Sexual ethics
Sexual ethics for
  teenagers
Sexual ethics for youth
Sexual excitement
Sexual fantasies
Sexual folklore *use* Sex–
  Folklore
Sexual harassment
Sexual harassment–
  Investigation
Sexual harassment on
  campus *use* Sexual
  harassment in
  universities and
  colleges
Sexual harassment in
  universities and
  colleges
Sexual harassment of
  women
Sexual harassment of
  women–Law and
  legislation
Sexual headache
Sexual hygiene *use*
  Hygiene, Sexual
Sexual identity (Gender
  identity) *use* Gender
  identity
Sexual instinct
Sexual intercourse
Sexual lust *use* Lust
Sexual masochism *use*
  Sadomasochism
Sexual obsession *use* Sex
  addiction
Sexual offenders *use* Sex
  offenders

Sexual offenses *use* Sex
  crimes
Sexual organs *use*
  Generative organs
Sexual orientation
Sexual partners, Surrogate
  use Sex surrogates
Sexual perversion *use*
  Sexual deviation
Sexual preference *use*
  Sexual orientation
Sexual psychology *use*
  Sex (Psychology)
Sexual sterilization *use*
  Sterilization (Birth
  control)
Sexual surrogates *use* Sex
  surrogates
Sexuality *use* Sex
Sexuality in dance
Sexually abused children
Sexually abused teenagers
Sexually oriented
  businesses *use* Sex
  oriented business
Sexually oriented
  periodicals *use* Sex
  oriented periodicals
Sexually transmitted
  diseases
Sexually transmitted
  diseases–Prevention–
  Equipment and
  supplies
Sexually transmitted
  diseases–Study and
  teaching
Shakespeare, William
  1564-1616–Sexual
  behavior
Sheath contraceptives *use*
  Condoms
Sheaths, Penis *use* Penis
  sheaths
Sheehan's syndrome

Shield, Dalkon
  (Intrauterine
  contraceptive) *use*
  Dalkon Shield
  (Intrauterine
  contraceptive)
Shivaree
Short luteal phase *use*
  Luteal phase defects
Sick–Sexual behavior
Simple urethritis *use*
  Urethritis,
  Nongonococcal
Single fathers
Single men
Single mothers
Single-parent family
Single parents
Single parents–Sexual
  behavior
Single parents' children
  use Children of single
  parents
Single people
Single people–Sexual
  behavior
Single persons *use* Single
  people
Single women
Single women–Sexual
  behavior
Singles (Persons) *use*
  Single people
Smoking in pregnancy *use*
  Pregnant women–
  Tobacco use
Social hygiene *use*
  Hygiene, Sexual
Social role
Social service and sex
Social work with gays
Social work with
  homosexuals *use* Social
  work with gays
Social work with lesbians
Social work with
  prostitutes

Social work with single
parents
Social work with single
people
Society and gynecology
use Gynecology–Social
aspects
Society and obstetrics *use*
Obstetrics–Social
aspects
Society and oral
contraceptives *use* Oral
contraceptives–Social
aspects
Society and pornography
use Pornography–
Social aspects
Sodomy
Soldaderas *use* Camp
followers
Solicitation (Canon law)
Songs Erotic *use* Erotic
songs
Spacing of children *use*
Birth intervals
Speculum (Medicine)
Sperm banks
Sperm penetration *use*
Sperm-ovum
interactions
Sperm *use* Spermatozoa
Sperm-ovum interactions
Spermatocidal agents *use*
Spermicides
Spermatocides *use*
Spermicides
Spermatogenesis
Spermatorrhea
Spermatozoa
Spermicidal agents *use*
Spermicides
Spermicides
Spinsters *use* Single
women
Spiritualism and marriage
use Marriage and
spiritualism

Spontaneous abortion *use*
Miscarriage
Spousal rape *use* Rape in
marriage
Spouses
Spouses *use* Husbands
Status, Marital *use* Marital
status
Statutory rape
STD (Diseases) *use*
Sexually transmitted
diseases
STDs (Diseases) *use*
Sexually transmitted
diseases
Sterility *use* Infertility
Sterility, Female *use*
Infertility, Female
Sterility, Male *use*
Infertility, Male
Sterility in humans *use*
Infertility
Sterilization, Female *use*
Sterilization of women
Sterilization, Sexual *use*
Sterilization (Birth
control)
Sterilization, Tubal *use*
Tubal sterilization
Sterilization (Birth
control)
Sterilization (Birth
control)–Complications
Sterilization (Birth
control)–Law and
legislation
Sterilization (Birth
control)–Moral and
ethical aspects
Sterilization (Birth
control)–Religious
aspects
Sterilization (Birth
control)–Religious
aspects–Catholic
Church
Sterilization, Eugenic

Sterilization of criminals
and defectives *use*
Sterilization, Eugenic
Sterilization reversal
Sterilization reversal Male
use Vasovasostomy
Sterilization of women
Still-birth *use* Stillbirth
Stillbirth
Streetwalkers *use*
Prostitutes
Strikes and lockouts–
Abortion services
Strip-tease *use* Striptease
Strip-tease, Male *use* Male
striptease
Strip-teasers *use*
Stripteasers
Striptease
Stripteasers
Structural-strategic family
psychotherapy
Structural-strategic marital
psychotherapy
Students–Sexual behavior
Style, Life *use* Life style
Subordination of women
use Sex role
Sudden infant death
syndrome
Support (Domestic
relations)
Surgical gynecology *use*
Generative organs,
Female–Surgery
Surrogate motherhood
Surrogate mothers
Surrogate sex partners *use*
Sex surrogates
Surrogates, Sex *use* Sex
surrogates
Swinging *use* Group sex
Switch of infants at birth
use Infants switched at
birth

Switching of infants at
  birth *use* Infants
  switched at birth
Symphyseotomy
Sympto-thermal method
  of birth control *use*
  Natural family planning
Syphilis
Syphilis–Complications
Syphilis–Diagnosis
Syphilis–Homeopathic
  treatment
Syphilis–Inoculation
Syphilis–Research
Syphilis, Congenital,
  Hereditary, and
  Infantile

-T-

Taboo
Tampons
Tampons–Complications
Tariff on condoms
Tarot and sex
Teachers, Lesbian *use*
  Lesbian teachers
Teen pregnancy *use*
  Teenage pregnancy
Teen-age marriage *use*
  Teenage marriage
Teenage child molesters
Teenage fathers
Teenage marriage
Teenage mothers
Teenage parents
Teenage pregnancy
Teenage prostitution *use*
  Prostitution, Juvenile
Teenage sex offenders
Teenage sexual abuse
  victims *use* Sexually
  abused teenagers
Television in birth control
Television in family
  planning *use* Television
  in birth control

Temperature method of
  birth control *use*
  Natural family
  planning–Temperature
  method
Temporary marriage
Tenderness (Psychology)
Tension, Premenstrual *use*
  Premenstrual syndrome
Termination of pregnancy
  use Abortion
Terms of endearment *use*
  Love names
Test tube babies *use*
  Fertilization in vitro,
  Human
Testes *use* Testis
Testicle *use* Testis
Testis
Testosterone
Therapeutic abortion *use*
  Abortion, Therapeutic
Therapy, Divorce *use*
  Divorce therapy
Third trimester of
  pregnancy *use*
  Pregnancy–Trimester,
  Third
Thyroid gland diseases in
  pregnancy
Time determination of
  ovulation *use*
  Ovulation–Detection
Time of Conception *use*
  Conception–Date of
Toilet (Grooming) *use*
  Beauty, Personal
Tort, Liability of
  obstetricians *use*
  Obstetricians–
  Malpractice
Touch
Toxemia of pregnancy
Toxic shock syndrome
Trachoma
Traditional birth services
  use Midwives

Trans-national adoption
  use Intercountry
  adoption
Transexualism *use* Sex
  change
Transexuals *use*
  Transsexuals
Transsexualism *use* Sex
  change
Transsexuals
Transvestites
Transvestitism
Treponemal infections *use*
  Treponematoses
Treponemal pallidum
  infection *use* Syphilis
Treponematoses
Treponematosis *use*
  Treponematoses
Trials (Abortion)
Trials (Adultery)
Trials (Bigamy)
Trials (Child molesting)
Trials (Crime passionnel)
  use Trials (Crimes of
  passion)
Trials (Crimes of passion)
Trials (Divorce)
Trials (Infanticide)
Trials (Obscenity)
Trials (Pimps)
Trials (Rape)
Trials (Seduction)
Trials (Sex crimes)
Trials (Sodomy)
Trials (Statutory rape)
Trichomonas vaginalis
Trichosanthin
Trimester of pregnancy,
  First *use* Pregnancy–
  Trimester, First
Trimester of pregnancy,
  Second *use* Pregnancy–
  Trimester, Second
Trimester of pregnancy,
  Third *use* Pregnancy–
  Trimester, Third

Triplets
Troilism *use* Group sex
Trophoblastic tumors
TSS (Disease) *use* Toxic
  shock syndrome
Tubal ligation *use* Tubal
  sterilization
Tubal occlusion *use* Tubal
  sterilization
Tubal pregnancy
Tubal sterilization
Tubal sterilization–
  Complications
Tube-tying (Birth control)
  use Tubal sterilization
Tubectomy *use* Tubal
  sterilization
Turner's syndrome
Twins

-U-

Ultrasonics in obstetrics
Umbilical cord
Umbilical cord–Prolapse
Umbilical cord–Ligature
Umbilicus *use* Navel
Unborn child *use* fetus
Unborn children (Islamic
  law)
Underwater childbirth
United States–Armed
  Forces–Gays
Unmarried couples
Unmarried couples–Legal
  status laws etc.
Unmarried fathers
Unmarried men *use* Single
  men
Unmarried mothers
Unmarried people *use*
  Single people
Unmarried persons *use*
  Single people
Unmarried women *use*
  Single women

Unwanted pregnancy *use*
  Pregnancy, Unwanted
Unwanted pregnancy,
  Liability for *use*
  Wrongful birth
Unwed mothers *use*
  Unmarried mothers
Urethritis Nongonococcal
Urethritis, Simple *use*
  Urethritis,
  Nongonococcal
Urinary organs–Diseases
Urningism *use*
  Homosexuality, Male
Urnings *use* Gay men
Urogenital organs *use*
  Genitourinary organs
Urogynecology
Urologists
Urology
Uterine adnexa *use*
  Adnexa uteri
Uterine appendages *use*
  Adnexa uteri
Uterine cervix *use* Cervix
  uteri
Uterine hemorrhage
Uterine mothers *use*
  Surrogate mothers
Uterine muscle *use*
  Myometrium
Uterine prolapse *use*
  Uterus–Prolapse
Uteroscopy *use*
  Hysteroscopy
Uterus
Uterus, Pregnant
Uterus–Abscess
Uterus–Cancer
Uterus–Diseases
Uterus–Displacements
Uterus–Excision
Uterus–Growth
Uterus–Hemorrhage *use*
  Uterine hemorrhage
Uterus–Prolapse
Uterus–Radiography

Uterus–Rupture
Uterus–Secretions
Uterus–Surgery
Utilization of birth control
  clinics *use* Birth control
  clinics–Utilization

-V-

Vagina
Vagina–Diseases
Vagina–Inflammation *use*
  Vaginitis
Vagina–Prolapse *use*
  Uterus–Prolapse
Vaginal birth after
  cesarean
Vaginal candidiasis *use*
  Candidiasis,
  Vulvovaginal
Vaginal contraceptives
  use Contraceptives,
  Vaginal
Vaginal diaphragms *use*
  Diaphragms, Vaginal
Vaginal hysterectomy *use*
  Hysterectomy, Vaginal
Vaginal prolapse *use*
  Uterus–Prolapse
Vaginal smears
Vaginismus
Vaginitis
Valentines
Vamps *use* Femmes
  fatales
Van Buren's disease *use*
  Penile induration
Vas deferens
Vas deferens–Occlusion
  use Vas occlusion
Vas deferens–
  Reanastomosis *use*
  Vasovasostomy
Vas deferens–Surgery
Vas occlusion
Vasectomy

Vasectomy–
Complications
Vasectomy–
Immunological aspects
Vasectomy, Reversal of
use Vasovasostomy
Vasectomy camps *use*
Vasectomy clinics
Vasectomy clinics
Vasocclusion *use* Vas
occlusion
Vasovasostomy
VBAC (Obstetrics) *use*
Vaginal birth after
cesarean
VD (Disease) *use*
Sexually transmitted
diseases
Venereal disease
education *use* Sexually
transmitted diseases–
Study and teaching
Venereal diseases *use*
Sexually transmitted
diseases
Venus (Roman deity)
Venus deities
Version (Obstetrics)
Victimless crimes *use*
Crimes without victims
Victims of crimes
Virgin birth
Virgin birth (Mythology)
Virginity
Virginity–Mythology
Virginity–Religious
aspects
Virus diseases in
pregnancy
Vital records *use* Registers
of births etc.
Voice, Change of
Voluntary sterilization *use*
Sterilization (Birth
control)
Vow of chastity *use*
Chastity, Vow of

Voyeurism
Vulva
Vulva–Diseases
Vulvectomy
Vulvovaginal candidiasis
use Candidiasis,
Vulvovaginal
Vulvovaginitis

-W-

Wassermann reaction *use*
Syphilis–Diagnosis–
Wassermann reaction
Wastage, Fetal *use* Fetal
death
Wedding anniversaries
Wedding ceremony *use*
Marriage service
Wedding costume
Wedding etiquette
Wedding music
Wedding sermons
Wedding service *use*
Marriage service
Weddings
Weddings, Military
Wedlock *use* Marriage
Weight gain in pregnancy
use Pregnant women–
Weight gain
Weight gain, Maternal *use*
Pregnant women–
Weight gain
Wet-nurses
White-slave traffic *use*
Prostitution
Widowers
Widows
Wife abuse
Wife abuse victims *use*
Abused wives
Wife and husband *use*
Husband and wife
Wife rape *use* Rape in
marriage
Wild women

Witchcraft and sex
Withdrawal (Birth
control) *use* Coitus
interruptus
Wives
Woman-man relationships
use Man-woman
relationships
Woman-marriage *use*
Woman-to-woman
marriage
Woman-to-woman
marriage
Womb *use* Uterus
Women, Gay *use* Lesbians
Women, Victims of
crimes *use* Women–
Crimes against
Women–Crimes against
Women–Diseases
Women–Health and
hygiene
Women–Hygiene *use*
Women–Health and
hygiene
Women–Legal status laws
etc
Women–Physiology
Women–Psychology
Women–Sexual behavior
Women–Socialization
Women–Sterilization *use*
Sterilization of women
Women in art
Women camp followers
use Camp followers
Women-hating *use*
Misogyny
Women homosexuals *use*
Lesbians
Women-men relationships
use Man-woman
relationships
Women prisoners–Sexual
behavior
Women's health services–
Law and legislation

Women's underwear *use* Lingerie

Wooing *use* Courtship

Words Obscene

Words Obscene–English language *use* English language–Obscene words

Working class–Sexual behavior

Wounds in pregnancy *use* Pregnant women–Wounds and injuries

Writings of gays *use* Gays' writings

Writings of homosexuals *use* Gays' writings

Writings of lesbians *use* Lesbians' writings

Wrongful birth

Wrongful conception *use* Wrongful birth

Wrongful pregnancy *use* Wrongful birth

-X-

X chromosome

X chromosome– Abnormalities

-Y-

Y chromosome

Y chromosome– Abnormalities

Young adults–Sexual behavior

Youth–Sexual behavior

APPENDIX 2
LIBRARY OF CONGRESS SCHEDULES

The following information was drawn from the *Library of Congress Classification Schedules* published by Gale Research, current as of August 1993. Libraries using the Library of Congress system keep the most up-to-date schedules in their cataloging department, where they may be accessible with special arrangement. The complete schedule for "Sexual Life," is given below, as this is where most general, interdisciplinary, and social science works are classified. Following are abridged schedules for some of the more specific aspects of the topic; a comprehensive guide, *Sex and Reproduction in the Library of Congress Classification Schedules*, is available from the National Sex Information Network (see X230).

HQ Family. Marriage. Woman.

SEXUAL LIFE

HQ 12-18	History. Sex customs.
	See also: GN479.65+ Ethnology; GR462 Folklore of sex; GT2600+,
	Love, courtship, betrothal, marriage (manners and customs)
HQ 18	General works on adults.
HQ 18.3	Biography of sexologists
	Sexual behavior and attitudes. Sexuality.
HQ 19-23	General
HQ 25	Curiosa
	By sex, age, or other special groups
	See also: HV5201.S48 Sexual behavior of alcoholics; HV8836
	Sexual behavior of prisoners; UH630 Sexual behavior of
	soldiers
HQ 27	Adolescents. Young adults–General works
.3	Boys
.5	Girls
HQ 28	Men
HQ 29	Women
HQ 30	Aged
.5	Handicapped
.7	The sick
	Sex instruction. Sexual ethics
	See also: HQ728+ Treatises on marriage; RA788 Sex hygiene
HQ 31	Practical works. Popular manuals. Scientific treatises.
HQ 32	Sexual ethics
HQ 34	Textbooks for use in secondary schools
	See also: HQ53, juvenile textbooks
	Works for special groups

HQ 35	Adolescents
2	College students
HQ 36	Men
HQ 41	Boys
HQ 46	Women
	See also: RG121 Female sex hygiene
HQ 51	Girls
HQ 53	Children. Juvenile works
HQ 54	Handicapped adults
HQ 55	Aged
	Sex teaching
HQ 56	General works
HQ 57	Works for parents on teaching children
HQ 57.3-.6	Sex instruction in the schools (including curricula)
HQ 58	The medical profession and sex teaching
HQ 59	The Church and sex teaching
HQ 60	Sex research
HQ 60.5-HQ 60.7	Sex counseling
HQ 61	Love and religion. Religious emotion and eroticism
	See also: BL65.S4 Sex and religion; BL460 Sex worship; BM720.S4
	Sex (Judaism); BS680.S5 Sex in the Bible
HQ 63	Sex relations and the church
	See also: BT708 Sex (Theology); HQ1051+ The Church
	and marriage
HQ 64	Other miscellaneous aspects. Esoteric theories.
HQ 71-72	Sexual deviations.
	See also: HV6556-6593 Sex crimes; RC556-560 Psychiatric aspects
HQ 74	Bisexuality
	See also: RC560.B56 Psychiatric aspects
	Homosexuality. Lesbianism.
HQ 75	Periodicals. Societies. Serials.
.2	Biography
.3-.6	Lesbians
.7-76.2	Gay men
HQ 76.25	General works
HQ 76.3	Juvenile works
HQ 76.5-.8	Gay liberation movement. Homophile movement
HQ 77.7-.9	Transvestitism. Transsexualism
HQ 79	Sadism, masochism, fetishism, etc.
HQ 101-440	Prostitution
HQ 447	Masturbation
HQ 449	Emasculation. Eunuchs etc.
HQ 450-470	Erotica
	See also: PN6110.L6 Love; PN6233 Anacreontic literature
HQ 471	Pornography. Obscene Literature.

THE FAMILY. MARRIAGE. HOME

HQ 763-766   Family Planning. Birth Control.
              See also: GN482.4 Ethnology; HB875 Neomalthusianism; RG136+
              Gynecology
HQ 767   Abortion
              See also: HV6537+ Infanticide; RG734 Gynecology
HQ 767.7   Sterilization

BF Psychology

BF 692   Psychology of sex. Sexual behavior.
              See also: BF723.S4 Child psychosexual development; BF 720.S48
              Infant psychology; N479.65+ Ethnology; HQ1075
              Sociology

GN Anthropology

PHYSICAL ANTHROPOLOGY. SOMATOLOGY
              Human variations
GN 211   Sex organs
GN 235-236   Reproduction. Sexual functions
GN 238   Puberty
GN 241   Fertility

SOCIAL AND CULTURAL ANTHROPOLOGY.

GN 480   Family. Forms of marriage.
GN 484.3   Sexual behavior. Sex customs
     .4   Marriage

GT Manners and Customs

CUSTOMS RELATIVE TO PRIVATE LIFE

GT 2460   Birth Customs
GT 2600-2630 Love. Courtship. Marriage. Sex customs.
GT 2650   Courtship. Betrothal
GT 2660-2810 Marriage customs

HV Social pathology. Social and public welfare. Criminology

CRIMINOLOGY
HV 6556-6570 Sex Crimes

K Law (General)

COMPARATIVE LAW. INERNATIONAL UNIFORM LAW
Criminal law and prcedures
K 5194-5198   Sexual offenses

KF Federal Law

SOCIAL LEGISLATION

KF 3771   Birth control. Family planning. Population control

CRIMINAL LAW

KF 9325-9329   Sexual offenses

QM Human Anatomy

QM 416   Male organs of generation
QM 421   Female organs of generation
QM 601-695   Human embryology

QP Human Physiology

QP 251+   Reproduction. Physiology of sex
               See also: HQ31+ Sex instruction; RA788 Sex hygiene

QP 253-257   Male sex physiology
QP 259-265   Female sex physiology
QP 277   Physiology of the embryo
               See also: QM601+ Human embryology; RG610+ Human fetus

RC Internal Medicine

INFECTIOUS AND PARASITIC DISEASES

RC 200-203   Sexually transmitted diseases. Venereal diseases.
               See also: RA644.V4 Public health; RC870+ Diseases of the
                           genitourinary system

PSYCHIATRY.

RC 556-560   Sexual problems. Psychosexual disorders. Sex therapy.
               See also: HQ71+ Sociological aspects; HV42.5 Social services; RA1141
               forensic medicine; RC875+ Male functional disorders; RG159+ Female
               functional disorders

UROLOGY. DISEASES OF THE GENITOURINARY SYSTEM

RC 875-899   Diseases and functional disorders of the genital organs (General and
               male)

RG Gynecology and Obstetrics

GYNECOLOGY (RG 1-499)

RG 1-103   Reference, Background, General Works
RG 110   Handbooks, manuals, etc.
RG 121   Popular works
RG 133   Conception
               See also: QP281 Physiology; RC889 Impotence and sterility (General
                           and male); RG201 Sterility in women.

RG 133.5-135   Reproductive technology

RG 136-138   Contraception. Birth control. Contraceptives. Sterilization.
                See also: HB875 Neo-Malthusianism; HQ763 Social aspects of birth
                              control; RCC888 Male contraception; RG734 Induced abortion

RG 161-181   Menstrual disorders
                See also: QP263 Physiology

RG 186   Menopause
                See also: RC884 Climacteric disorders

RG 201-205   Infertility in women

RG 211   Abnormalities and malformations of the female genitals

RG 218   Infectious diseases of the female genital organs

RG 261-483   Diseases of the genitals and reproductive organs.

OBSTETRICS (RG 500-991)

RG 500-547   Reference, Background, General works

RG 551-591   Pregnancy (RG 551-591)

RG 600-650   The embryo and fetus. Perinatology
                See also: QM601+ Human embryology

RG 651-721   Labor. Parturition.

RG 734   Induction of abortion
                See also: HQ767 Social aspects; RA1067 Criminal abortion; RG648
                              Spontaneous abortion

RG 761   Cesarean section

RG 801-871   Puerperal states

SOURCES

The following resources were among those consulted in compiling this volume. Subject and title searches of the New York Public Library's on-line catalog CATNYP and the book and series files of RLIN were conducted in January 1993.

American Book Trade Directory 1992-1993. 38th ed. New Providence, NJ: R.R. Bowker, 1992.

American Library Directory 1992-1993. 45th ed. 2 vols. New Providence, NJ: R.R. Bowker, 1992.

American Reference Books Annuals. Englewood, CO: Libraries Unlimited, 1969-1992.

Ash, Lee, and William G. Miller. *Subject Collections: A Guide to Special Book Collections and Subject Emphasis as Reported by University, College, Public, and Special Libraries and Museums in the United States and Canada.* 6th ed. 2 vols. New York: R.R. Bowker, 1985.

Balay, Robert, ed. *Guide to Reference Books Covering Materials from 1985-1990. Supplement to the 10th ed.* Chicago: American Library Association, 1992.

Berkman, Robert I. *Find It Fast: How to Uncover Expert Information on any Subject.* New York: Harper and Row, 1990.

Blazek, Ron, and Elizabeth Aversa. *The Humanities: A Selective Guide to Information Sources.* 3d ed. Englewood, CO: Libraries Unlimited, 1988.

Books in Series in the United States 1985-1989. New Providence, NJ: R.R. Bowker, 1989.

Books in Print 1991-1992. 44th ed. 8 vols. New Providence, NJ: R.R. Bowker, 1991.

Chitty, Mary Glen. *Federal Information Sources in Health and Medicine: A Selected and Annotated Bibliography.* Bibliographies and Indexes in Medical Studies v.1. Westport, CT: Greenwood, 1988.

Clearinghouse Directory: A Guide to Information Clearinghouses and their Resources, Services, and Publications. 1991-1992. Edited by Donna Batten. Detroit: Gale Research, 1991.

Data Base Directory 1991-1992. 7th ed. White Plains, NY: Knowledge Industry in cooperation with the American Society for Information Science, 1991.

Directory of Online Data Bases. Edited by Kathleen Young Marcaccio. Santa Monica, CA: Cuadra/Gale, 1992.

Directories in Print 1992. 9th ed. 2 vols. Edited by Charles B. Montney. Detroit: Gale Research, 1992.

Directory of Special Libraries and Information Centers 1993. 16th ed. 2 vols. Edited by Debra M. Kirby. Detroit: Gale Research, 1992.

El Hi Text Books in Print. 120th ed. New York: R.R. Bowker, 1992.

Encyclopedia of Associations. 27th ed. 12 vols. Edited by Deborah Burek. Detroit: Gale Research, 1992.

Federal Staff Directory. 14th ed. Edited by Ann L. Brownson. Mt. Vernon, VA.: Staff Directories Ltd., 1992.

Fisher, Kim N. *On the Screen: A Film, Television, and Video Research Guide.* Littleton, Co.: Libraries Unlimited, 1986.

Government Research Directory 1992-1993. 7th ed. Edited by Annette Piccirelli. Detroit: Gale Research, 1992.

Guide to U.S. Government Publications. Edited by Donna Andriot. McLean, VA: Documents Index, 1990.

Haselbauer, Kathleen J. *Research Guide to the Health Sciences: Medical, Nutritional and Environmental.* Reference Sources for the Social Sciences Series. Westport, CT: Greenwood, 1987.

Huber, Jeffrey T. *How to Find Information About AIDS.* 2nd ed. Haworth Medical Information Sources. New York: Haworth Press, 1992.

Index and Abstract Directory: An International Guide to Services and Serials Coverage. 2nd ed. Edited by Ellen Rice. Birmingham, AL: EBSCO Publishing, 1990.

Katz, Bill, and Linda Sternberg. *Magazines for Libraries.* 7th ed. New Providence, NJ: R.R. Bowker, 1992.

Lesko, Matthew. *Federal Data Base Finder.* 3d ed. Kensington, MD: Information U.S.A., 1990.

_____. *Lesko's Info Power.* Kensington, MD: Information U.S.A., 1990.

Li, Tze-chung. *Social Science Reference Sources: A Practical Guide.* 2nd edition. Contributors in Librarianship and Information Science no. 68. Westport, CT: Greenwood, 1990.

McInnis, Raymond G. *Research Guide for Psychology.* Westport, CT: Greenwood, 1982.

Newsletters in Print 1993-1994. 6th ed. Edited by John Kroledit. Detroit: Gale Research, 1992.

Research Centers Directory 1993. 17th ed. 2 vols. Edited by Annette Piccirelli. Detroit: Gale Research, 1992.

Robinson, Judith Schiek. *Subject Guide to U.S. Government Reference Sources.* Englewood, CO: Libraries Unlimited, 1985.

Ryan, Joe, ed. *First Step: the Master Index of Subject Encyclopedias.* Phoenix, AZ: Oryx Press, 1987.

Robinson, Ruth E. *Buy Books Where-Sell Books Where: A Directory of Out-of-Print Booksellers and their Author-Subject Specialties 1992-1993.* 8th ed. Morgantown, VA: Ruth E. Robinson, 1992.

Schwarzkopf, Leroy C. *Government Reference Books 88/89: A Biennial Guide to U.S. Government Publications.* 11th ed. Englewood, CO: Libraries Unlimited, 1990.

Sheehy, Eugene P., ed. *Guide to Reference Books.* 10th ed. Chicago: American Library Association, 1986.

Staff of American Book Collector. *Directory of Specialized American Bookdealers.* Ossining, NY: Moretus Press, 1992.

The Serials Directory: An International Reference Book. 6th ed. Edited by Ellen Rice. Birmingham, AL: EBSCO, 1992.

The Standard Periodical Directory 1992. 15th ed. New York: Oxbridge Communications, 1992.

The Subject Guide to Books in Print 1991-1992. 35th ed. 5 vols. New Providence, NJ: R.R. Bowker.

Ulrich's International Periodicals Directory 1992-1993. 31st ed. New Providence, NJ: R.R. Bowker, 1992.

United States Government Manual 1991-1992. Office of the Federal Register, National Archives and Records Administration. Washington, DC: Superintendent of Documents, GPO, 1991.

Washington Information Directory 1992-1993. Washington: Congressional Quarterly, 1992.

Webb, William H. *Sources of Information in the Social Sciences: A Guide to the Literature.* 3d ed. Chicago: American Library Association, 1986.

Woodbury, Marda. *Youth Information Resources: An Annotated Guide for Parents, Professionals, Students, Researchers and Concerned Citizens.* Westport, CT: Greenwood, 1987.

_____. *A Guide to Sources of Educational Information.* 2nd. ed. Arlington, VA: Information Resources Press, 1982.

Indexes

TITLE INDEX

Reference numbers without letters refer to page numbers. Items are arranged alphabetically, ignoring the words "a" and "the."

NAME INDEX

This index includes names of all organizations, institutions, businesses, government agencies, specialized publishers, etc. mentioned in this volume.